ATHENS ASCENDANT

ATHENS ASCENDANT

George Dent Wilcoxon

IOWA STATE UNIVERSITY PRESS / AMES

1 9 7 9

GEORGE DENT WILCOXON is Professor of History at Kansas State University in Manhattan, Kansas. He received the A.B. (1936), M.A. (1938), and Ph.D. (1941) degrees from the University of California, Los Angeles.

Composed and printed by
The Iowa State University Press
Ames, Iowa 50010

First edition, 1979

Library of Congress Cataloging in Publication Data

Wilcoxon, George Dent, 1913-
Athens ascendant.

Bibliography: p.
Includes index.
1. Athens—History. 2. Greece—History—To 168 B.C. 3. Civilization, Greek. I. Title.
DF285.W55 938.5 78-10527
ISBN 0-8138-1935-0
ISBN 0-8138-1130-9 pbk

TO MY PARENTS

CONTENTS

PREFACE

My intent has been to trace developments in Athens during her period of steady ascendance, from the period immediately preceding the time of Solon until the climax of the Periclean Age, and to estimate their significance. Events elsewhere in Greece and beyond have been treated only insofar as these concern Athens. For instance, the battle of Thermopylae receives less attention than the accompanying naval action at Artemisium, because, to the best of my knowledge, no Athenians participated in the former. Yet Thermopylae cannot be omitted altogether, because results there were certainly meaningful for the future of Athens. Since cultural, and especially intellectual, matters are difficult to restrict, these have received a somewhat freer treatment. Throughout, the emphasis has been on how the Athenians' spirit of individualism and love of freedom led to the growth of liberal institutions.

On the technical aspects a few words will suffice. The *Oxford Classical Dictionary* has been taken as a guide in the spelling of Greek words in the Latin alphabet. The translations are mine unless otherwise indicated.

Grateful acknowledgement is made to my colleagues Robin Higham, George Kren, and James C. Carey for friendly advice and assistance; also to my sometime colleague, Kenneth S. Davis, of Princeton, Massachusetts; to Suzanne C. Lowitt, of the Iowa State University Press, who contributed greatly to the improvement, and especially to the tightening of the manuscript; and last, but surely not least, to an old friend, Christos Economou, formerly of Athens, who acquainted me with so many of the things about his city, and Greece generally, which are scarcely ever to be found in books.

Manhattan, Kansas
October, 1978

GEORGE DENT WILCOXON

ATHENS ASCENDANT

1

Antecedents: Myth and Reality

1000–600 B.C.

FROM all we can learn about his earliest activities the Greek was always an individualist. Like other humans slowly sapient, he hunted, herded, ate, slept, sought the society of his fellows, and, valuing protection along with companionship, repaired dutifully to the ancestral hearth. After that, his pattern of conduct became less regular. With shocking abruptness, the oldest and holiest texts tell of contention within the tribal circle, of bickering with open breaks and fights, then of heroes unreconciled going their separate ways. Ties became attenuated, though rarely severed. Ever on the go, thus constantly exposed, most Greeks were too shrewd to cut themselves off completely. Dissatisfied with their bleak northern homes, they had dared to forge through unfamiliar passages possessed by mountain dwellers bound to resent their passing. Ill will here might be dangerous, frequently disastrous. A Greek had to have his wits about him; no survival was possible without helping hands nearby. But just as surely, when peril had been surmounted, paths were likely to diverge. Each had his own notion how things were best done, each wanted his own grip on reality. Such persons needed a decent leeway.

Not that Greeks were withdrawn because of resentment or an overweening pride. Men warmed by the meridional sun loved to talk, which required an audience. Greeks were and are gregarious when given time to be; anxious too, to confer on one another the benefits of a wide-ranging experience. Their lithe language, whose beauty was to them a gift of the gods, gave conversation an added sparkle. But only if intensity of feeling did not erupt into violence could discourse be enjoyed. And eruption was all too probable. The brethren were impatient listeners, suspicious to a degree, and, each pushing his own prestige, eager to debate. Sons of the hard soil so certain of their convictions did not give ground easily. Some wisdom could be gained through dialogue, but they preferred the evidence of their senses.

Greeks also chose independence. When he worked, the Greek was alone even with others near. Cooperation he could and did learn—before most of mankind—but even so, his thoughts were his own, imparting a tinge of reluctance to necessary discipline.

To what extent these tribal people were aware of a shared heritage is difficult to say. In migratory times they were too diverse and refractory to be gathered under a common name, much less a common roof. The term "Hellenes" did not gain universal acceptance until about the seventh century B.C., and "Greeks" was not heard until the Romans tagged them with it centuries after that. Those of the generic group who first attracted the attention of literate people roundabout seem to have called themselves (as Homer did) *Achaioi,* usually anglicized as Achaeans. Egyptian records of the thirteenth century referred to attacks by the *Akaiwasha,*[1] and the Hittites of central Asia Minor noted raids on their property by the *Ahhiyawa*[2]—ample evidence that the Achaeans ranged free and wide while mere precocious infants, ethnically speaking, intent to explore the far edges of the Great Inner Sea. The Hellenic breed was a race of adventurers almost from birth.

But their heroic feats did not yet include written records, so exactly where they came from and what prompted them to migrate are mysteries still. Drought, winter chill, a temporary insufficiency of food, may be partial answers, though not entirely satisfying because the land they left must have been more fruitful than the frowning, craggy terrain that surrendered grudgingly to the advancing nomads. Religion was possibly a factor: some diviner pointing with prophetic finger. Enemies may have prodded from the rear, catalyzing an inbred wanderlust. A pastoral folk had to keep moving anyway, and it mattered little where they went so long as grass was plentiful. "Plentiful" is hardly a word to be applied to that perplexing offshoot of southeastern Europe called Greece, but it had enough to meet current needs. Some grains grew in that locale: barley, millet, and a little wheat, along with fruits such as the grape, fig, and quince. The climate was warmer too, yet bracing enough to act as a constant spur. Maybe the ultimate reason so many migrations came to rest there is that the peninsula made a geographic cul-de-sac. The only way out was back, which stubborn Hellenes were loath to accept. Thus a peculiarity of character hardly admirable in itself could lead, by a maze of crooked steps, to unimagined achievements.

Whether Achaeans first entered Greece by a land route from the north, or whether they came westward across the Aegean Sea from Asia is another unsettled point. Archeological remains, our only reliable evidence, locate them in many of the coastal areas of Greece, particularly the east coast, and some of the interior sections during the second millenium B.C., but do not clearly indicate an order of settlement. One fact however, is fairly certain. Near the beginning of the millenium, nomadic groups, presumably Achaean, began moving down out of the Macedonian Balkans onto lower lands where the diminishing hills of Thessaly make room for two extensive plains amidst the broken topography, the only wide level expanses in the whole country. Here the newcomers gradually established themselves, dominating older inhabitants usually referred to as Pelasgians.[3] One cluster of downs and dells was looked upon with such favor that it gained the name of *Achaea Phthiotis* (possibly meaning "land where the Achaeans settled first," from Gr. *phthano,* "to come before"), Homer's "deep-soiled Phthia" where Achilles grew to manhood before going off to Troy. This area was also the first spoken of as *Hellas,* from a city supposedly founded by Hellen, mythical ancestor of the entire Greek race. After several centuries that designation would come to cover all lands belonging to those myriads who called themselves his descendants. But there was much time and space to cross first.

In their new home the proliferating Achaeans developed their Bronze Age culture and gradually expanded south and west. In time other names appeared—Aeolians, Boeotians, Arcadians, to mention but a few—Greeks who may have been offshoots of the same stock, or later migrants, or a mixture. In a period about which so little is known, the whole subject of derivations is unclear. Boeotians spoke an Aeolic dialect, for instance, which was one among many.[4] The Aeolians may or may not have been a separate people. By one theory Aeolian was simply another word for Achaean,[5] and it may characterize groups of dissidents defending their right to differ. Significantly, Homer spoke of the Greeks generally as "Achaeans," but his *Iliad* is supposed to have been phrased originally in Aeolic.[6] The exact nature of the relationship evades us.

Inevitably, these alert and grasping invaders drove onward to occupy everything in their path which they could win. The central zone offered no particular obstacles; here Boeotians, alive to self-interest, settled and gave their name to the most fertile section.[7] For the majority of Achaeans a further advance was blocked, first, by the narrow neck of the Isthmus of Corinth, sole bridge to the more inviting southern peninsula, and secondly, by the great fortress city of Mycenae, which controlled the low saddle between the mountains and the two seas. For a thousand years more or less Mycenae had been the most important site at this end of the European continental mainland,[8] (whence the term Mycenaean Age), the stronghold from which Pelasgian chieftains had dominated this strategic belt, possibly with help from the Minoan sea kings of Crete. The decline of Minoan power must have affected the Pelasgians and others who had formerly been under the suzerainty of Crete. They gradually yielded to the intruder; Achaeans eventually mastered Mycenae, then spread over the entire Peloponnesus. Finally Crete itself was occupied—as is proved by the discovery that Late Minoan inscriptions, written in puzzling Linear B syllabary, actually embody Greek words.[9]

Then, for a period (ca. 1400–1100 B.C.), Achaeans were lords of this little world. At its outer edges Egyptians and Hittites attested to the formidable qualities of these foemen scarcely removed from the primitive, who might be guests and traders one day, absconders or pirates the next. Precepts of honor did exist among them, but these grew slowly, and had definite limits beyond which one might take advantage even of a friend unless obligations were recognized (the encounter of Diomedes and Glaucus in the sixth book of the *Iliad*, is the most famous example). But after gifts had been exchanged there could be no further enmity or deception;[10] those outside the bond might be plundered as long as pledges had not been given. Achaeans preyed upon one another as well as on the declared enemy.[11] That they were masters of the land did not mean there was enough of it to go around. In this uncertain scheme of things, each kept his own interests foremost. Prizes went to the most wakeful and resourceful.[12] During this period, only two events were of enough significance to galvanize Achaeans into anything like united action. The first occurred late in the thirteenth century when one of the sons of the exiled King Oedipus appealed to seven of the mightiest Achaean chieftains to help him expel his own brother from the throne of Thebes. The other came about a generation later, when Agamemnon, king and overlord at Mycenae, commandeered the lesser kings to support him in his famed war against Troy.[13]

The feats of Achilles and Odysseus prepare one to expect still greater accomplishments, but already the primacy of the Achaeans was fading. Later in the same century a new Hellenic people, the Dorians, entered Greece from the northwest and struck unerringly toward its core. Though speaking a dialect of the same language and holding the same gods in a general way, they recognized no friends among those who had preceded them. All were treated as foes, all were alike felled or subdued by these most warlike of the Greeks. Lightly touched by civilization in their northern homes, the Dorians of the twelfth century had not as yet developed skills comparable to the Mycenaean in pottery, masonry, or relief decoration. They did know how to smelt iron,[14] and with iron swords hacked their way to continuous victory.

These latecomers were clever enough to borrow legends that suited their purpose; learning that the sons of Heracles had been expelled from their homes, the Dorians gave out that they were merely supporting rehabilitated exiles, restoring the Heracleids to their rightful seats of authority. Whether Temenos, Cresphontes, and Procles were actually grandchildren and great-grandchildren of the superlative strongman, or upstart name-droppers out for their own good, as seems more likely, these were the tribal chiefs who led the Dorian invasion. Their first home inside Hellas was at that pivotal spot in north central Greece thereafter fittingly called Doris.[15] From this they beat a path southward to the rocky sanctuary of Delphi, overlooking the Gulf of Corinth, finally to leap across the waters, entering Peloponnesus by the westerly region of Elis. All the best parts of the peninsula were conquered sooner or later: Mycenae, Laconia, Messenia. Tisamenes, grandson of Agamemnon, was killed at Mycenae while defending his inheritance. His death extinguished the Pelopid dynasty.

Sparta put up the stubbornest resistance; there the conquest was not completed for generations. When it was, the triumphant Dorians trod their vanquished opponents underfoot, reducing most to serfdom (the Helots), the rest to an intermediate noncitizenship. Elsewhere after their victory, the Dorians intermingled to a certain extent with the other Greeks. But in the new Sparta—now officially called Lacedaemon, from the name of an early Dorian king—intermarriage was strictly prohibited. The Dorian Spartans constituted a caste of soldiers above and apart from the rest of the population. A militarized state was in the making, one which would shortly take over the leadership of Hellas for centuries.

The main losers, of course, were the Achaeans. After an unavailing resistance some submitted, while others broke toward the north and east seeking lands untouched by the Dorians. This involved them with another Greek-speaking people, the "Iavones," or Ionians, who had occupied certain eastern districts of continental Greece and the north shore of the Peloponnesus until now, without attracting unusual notice. Giving way to pressure, the Ionians were able to retain nothing but the rocky headland known as Attica on the European mainland. Scant shadow of pride for them at this stage. Driven by desperation, a large number of these fled in their turn to the islands of the Aegean and the shores of Asia beyond, a movement afterward explained as colonization.[16] Thus in a sense, the Ionians were forced to become a sea-faring people. Of their city-states on the European continent only Athens continued to uphold the Ionian tradition, for what that very doubtful association was worth.

Who these Ionians were and where they came from is anybody's guess—except of course, that they claimed to be of Hellenic stock. The Athenians of the classical period insisted that their ancestors "had always been in the land,"[17] which hardly squared with the general theory of the Greek migrations. But the insistence of the Athenians may only mean that their remembrance had become clouded, or it may signify that they had a strong Pelasgian strain in their bloodstream, something usually taken for granted. It has even been suggested that the Ionians and Pelasgians were actually the same people, descendants of an earlier wave of immigrants from the east.[18] How these Ionians fit into the overall picture is as much a mystery as ever, and their name presents a puzzle with the rest. Apparently, it was first used in Asia, and applied to those fugitives who had found a new life on the other side of the Aegean. "Ionia" became the common term for the Greek settlements along the central portion of the Asian coast from Phocaea to Miletus, settlements of which Athens boasted herself the mother city.[19] For themselves, her men preferred the style "Athenians" to "Ionians," as being more prestigious;[20] but they were also distinctly conscious of their leadership of the Ionian peoples.

Why did they favor the designation of their own city? A more special, local pride, partly, and the euphoria based on deeds of many generations. For behind all this was the dignity that an impressive antiquity confers. Athenians clung to the legend that their polis had been founded by Cecrops, far back in the bosom of time. Ironically, it was really much older than Cecrops or any progenitor of whom they had heard. Modern excavation has unearthed the remains of a Neolithic village on the Acropolis antedating 2000 B.C. Whether the site was occupied continuously from that period has not been determined, but certainly Athens was Pelasgian before it was Hellenic.[21] *Athenai* was not originally a Greek word any more than the goddess after whom it was called was Greek. The heavenly lady had probable antecedents as the guardian goddess of Mycenaean princes, and before that as a protector of the kings in Crete;[22] and by the same token Athens was most likely under Cretan influence of some sort during the second millenium. This condition must have continued into Mycenaean times, when newcomers replaced Pelasgians or mixed with them. The legend concerning an annual tribute to Crete, with a shipload of noble youths forming a part, points to such a relationship. And the emancipation from this hateful arrangement was the proudest story that primitive Athenians had to tell.

Artifacts found on the Acropolis and in the grave pits of the Ceramicus section to the northwest indicate a fairly steady human presence from these earliest days. Those of the Ceramicus do not go back so far, but provide the only unbroken record of human activity in Greece down to historic times. The vicinity of Athens must have seemed immediately advantageous to all comers then. Obviously its advantage derived from the jutting limestone crest of the Acropolis commanding the narrow central Pedion (plain) of the Cephisus river below. In other respects the situation was far from ideal. Military considerations aside, there were other parts of Attica one would rather have. Westward beyond the Cephisus and the bordering hills of Mount Aegaleos spread the fertile Thriasian plain with its slender cornstalks waving toward the Isthmus. And on the other side of the Pedion rolled the hills of the *Mesogeia* ("heartland"), full of vines and orchards that sloped down to Marathon and the sea. Both areas were preferable, economically, but the Pedion with its river united them. Directly at the site of Athens two more streams, the Eridanus and the Ilissus, flowed down past the Acropolis on either hand to meet the Cephisus curling away to the west. Understandably, this bit of ground had to be held for tactical reasons. The Ionians' conquest, if it can be called such, brought them no balm. The stubborn, stony soil of the Pedion permitted nobody an easy living. The flocks of the occupants had to scrounge far and wide merely to keep alive, offering their owners scant returns of milk and meat. Efforts at agriculture could bring forth only reluctant crops of grain. There was no danger here of a people going flabby or obese.

Over silent centuries the Athenian community was built before a single name emerges, and then it was one that is dubious at best. Tradition held that Cecrops was the first King of Athens, but regarding him there was nothing reliable. Some authorities asserted that he had come from Egypt or Crete, which seems to associate him with the older civilizations farther south. Possibly he had been the leader of a prehistoric invasion—possibly. Some modern investigators have insisted that he was not a man at all, but the derivative eponym of a tribe of primitive residents about the Acropolis, the Cecropes.[23] Others have distinguished him as a local deity metamorphosed into a legendary hero. It is hard to know what to make of one described as a lizard-man, serpent below the waist. In spite of such drollery the Athenians of afterdays took him very seriously,[24] believing that the famous contest which Athena won over Poseidon for the sponsorship of the city occurred in his reign. The goddess's gift of the olive tree, symbolizing cultural attainments and the arts of peace, was judged better than Poseidon's offering. Thus was forecast the future role of the city. Inferentially its name was given at that moment, and henceforth its citizens were all, metaphorically, at least, the "children of Athena." The modesty of the Virgin Goddess would not be compromised by a figure of speech. And the intangible tie with divinity meant much to people who believed.

After Cecrops, by the usual account, had come Erichthonius, Erechtheus, Pandion, Aegeus. (Some accounts place Pandion before Erechtheus and some likewise mention a second Cecrops as the father of Pandion.) But again suspicion is aroused. The third name sounds like a duplication of the second, and some versions placed Erichthonius even before Cecrops. It would be natural for Athenian mythographers to do so, for Erichthonius was held to be a son of the god Hephaestus begotten accidentally on Mother Earth as he yearned for the unattainable Athena. She, despite having repulsed Hephaestus, felt a special responsibility for the progeny. Hence she accepted Erichthonius as her foster son, decreeing that he and his descendants should rule over her land and people. So was founded the first dynasty of Athens.

The names of these pristine rulers are very likely those of spirits worshiped locally in Attica, humanized with the passing of time.[25] Modern science has stripped the flesh away from most such prehistoric heroes. But the spirit-heroes were quite real to the men of ancient Athens, and each was important in the lore of the community. Erechtheus had saved the settlements from northern assailants (Athenians believed), and had built the primitive palace-temple on the Acropolis, the first *Erechtheum*. Pandion had succeeded him at Athens, then acquired a second throne at Megara, thereby establishing Athens' claim over the Isthmus—and a political relationship more to the liking of Athenians than of Megarians. Aegeus, born during his father's residence at Megara, had returned to Athens and ruled quietly there, reputedly dividing the state into its four main regions. He was courteous and hospitable to all, especially to the sultry enchantress Medea of Golden Fleece fame, who after her flight from Corinth lingered with him and afforded him pleasant diversion. In due course they had a son, but Aegeus had already fathered a far mightier offspring to take up his scepter.

Theseus is incomparably the most famous of legendary Athenian heroes. He, too, was the result of Aegeus' indiscretion, though one sanctioned by the gods and even predicted by the oracle at Delphi. Brought up by his mother Aethra, princess of Troezen, the young prince set out for Athens after he had grown strong enough to possess himself of a heavy sword that his father had left beneath a huge rock.[26] No one had been able to move it before Theseus. On his way to the capital he proved himself by numerous feats of valor, killing a succession of notorious brigands who infested the roads of Attica. The most dreaded of these was a certain Procrustes, who habitually disposed of his victims by strapping them to an iron bed, then "adjusting" them to fit its length. Those too short were stretched or hammered out, those too tall had a portion lopped off. In case any seemed a close fit, the bandit had another bed of different size he could use. Fighting Procrustes and vanquishing him, Theseus tied him to his own bed and did to him as he had done to others. Continuing his journey to Athens, he was promptly recognized and welcomed by his father Aegeus, who installed him at the court as royal heir.

Theseus' renown spread rapidly to the corners of the Greek world. Each new adventure seemed greater than the last, but none was more fondly retold than the first task undertaken for his father. In token of submission to Minoan Crete, Athens had to send a regular tribute to the Cretan capital, Knossos, part of which was a yearly offering of seven choice youths and seven maidens to be slaughtered and eaten by the Minotaur, the insatiable human-headed bull who dwelt in the depths of the Labyrinth. This was Minos' great palace of many rooms and twisting corridors so confusing that no one could find his way out unaided. Theseus volunteered to be one of the seven youths, apparently after a secret understanding with his father that he would try to kill the Minotaur and deliver Athens from the baleful obligation. If successful, on the return voyage he was to replace his black sail with a white one, so Aegeus would be relieved of his anguish at the earliest moment.

Arriving in Crete, Theseus had one bit of luck. As the victims were paraded through the streets of Knossos, the king's daughter, Ariadne, took stock of his robust masculinity and fell in love with him. Glowing with the thought that such as he might conquer even the Minotaur, she sent a messenger to Theseus, guaranteeing to show him a way out of the great palace on condition he would take her home as his wife. Theseus agreeing, she gave him a ball of thread to be fastened to the outer door and unwound as he proceeded toward the interior. Provided with this, Theseus boldly entered the Labyrinth before the others, in advance of the scheduled sacrifice. The Minotaur was not yet expecting victims; the Athenian prince was fortunate again in finding the monster asleep. He was without weapons, but fell upon the beast at once, beating it to death with his bare fists. This aspect of the tale is especially hard to accept, but is perhaps no more of a strain on the imagination than the rest!

Rewinding the thread, Theseus escaped from the palace. Then taking Ariadne and collecting his Athenian friends, they regained the ship, leaving Knossos as quickly as possible. However, difficulties soon separated the betrothed pair. Ariadne became seasick during a storm, so Theseus put her ashore on the island of Naxos, then returned to his ship to make necessary repairs. But the storm increased in fury, driving him out to sea, where the vessel was buffeted about the Mediterranean for many weeks. When he came again to Naxos, Ariadne could not be found; it was presumed she had died. Another version of the story furnishes a more pleasant outcome, relating that the god Dionysus suddenly materialized before the startled Ariadne, left alone on Naxos, and claimed her for his bride.

Theseus' conduct is not greatly to his credit. In neither version does he waste much time in mourning. His journey back to Athens was marked by yet another tragedy. Somehow he had neglected to replace the black sail with a white one. King Aegeus, watching from the shore, was overcome with despair and hurled himself into the sea, which ever since has borne his name—the Aegean. If there are any glimmerings of history in this spectacular bit of myth, these may tell of a time when prehistoric Athens was connected with Minoan Crete[27] (like the other chief places in Greece during the Mycenaean Age), and finally broke the tie.

Now king in his own right, Theseus gave himself to the business with all his tremendous energy. He domineered over Athens' neighbors as well, and later tradition insisted that he conquered all of Attica, placating the subjugated by giving them Athenian citizenship *(synoecismus)*. Athens thus became the first—and so far as is known—the only Greek state to share her privileges with others, initiating a principle that Rome and modern nations would follow in their turn. It is also asserted that Theseus voluntarily gave up his absolute powers, established "constitutional" government, divided the people into social classes, and granted the vote to all.[28] A council was created to help him administer the city (one is astonished that he needed any help!), and it was believed that Athens' first town hall *(Prytaneion)* and council chamber *(Bouleuterion)* were built by his order. He was also supposed to have instituted coinage in Attica—long before coins are known to have existed anywhere in the world. Such a record of accomplishment naturally has aroused the suspicions of moderns and not a few ancients, even when doubting was blasphemous. However, the Athenians confidently declared he had performed everything needful, as epitomized in their saying, "Nothing without Theseus."

But he would not be Greek nor the ideal Athenian were he to cool his heels at home. Heracles had been his model since childhood, and he longed to emulate the deeds of this most awesome of Zeus' sons. The two met, became fast friends, and went off together on the Argonaut voyage. Another frolic took them to the land of the Amazons, from which Theseus brought back as captive one of the virago-warriors, variously called Antiope or Hippolyta. She became the mother of his eldest son, Hippolytus. The two heroes parted temporarily, and Theseus found himself a new bosom companion, Peirithous, king of the Lapiths. They in turn performed many prodigies of valor, and were among the distinguished party that gathered to track down the great Calydonian boar. During the hunt Peirithous exposed himself recklessly, and was saved from the boar's tusks by his gallant Athenian friend. At Peirithous' wedding festivities, when a band of drunken Centaurs became unruly and tried to ravish the Lapith women, it was Theseus who led in restoring order, killing those Centaurs who refused to submit.[29]

His arrangements for the well-being of those about him did not stop with personal friends. Events required him to intervene in Boeotia, setting a precedent for Athenian claims of suzerainty to the north, in the distant future. Thebes had been the scene of much turbulence earlier, because of the startlingly dramatic circumstances connected with the reign and fall of King Oedipus, and afterward because of the struggle between the sons of Oedipus for the vacated throne. One son, Polynices, had raised an army in which six of the stoutest Hellenic chieftains undertook to help him recover his heritage. But the attack on Thebes had failed, and the Thebans had denied the right of decent burial to the fallen. The grieving relatives had appealed to Theseus, who led his own army against Thebes, took the city, and forced its people to bury the dead in keeping with the requirements of religion. Yet he did not retain Thebes for himself, or allow it to be despoiled by his troops. When his mission was accomplished, Theseus returned as quietly as he had come. More, at Athens he courteously received and granted sanctuary to the aged and helpless Oedipus when no other state would receive him. In a barbaric age, Theseus set an example of civilized behavior which the cultured Athenians of the golden age loved to look back upon. Thebans, however, were not so fond of remembering; nor did the incident endear Athens to them. To the north, Thebes was to be Athens' most stubborn foe.

It was not to be expected that the progeny of Erichthonius could produce another like Theseus. Tradition listed five more kings in this first Athenian dynasty before it came to an end with Thymoetes. Nothing substantial is recorded about them; probably some of these names, like several of the foregoing, belonged to local deities. Why so little attention was given the younger representatives, and so much to Theseus is another mystery. The possibility exists of course, that Theseus was actually historical, or at least that some of the feats attributed to him are in some fashion true, such as the union of Attica and the capture of Thebes.[30] These were deeds to stir every Athenian heart. It was not without reason that the Athenians revered Theseus.

The Dorian invaders who wrought such havoc and disrupted life elsewhere in Greece at first did not trouble Athens. Attica was bypassed because of the poverty of its soil. As the Dorians swept onward into Peloponnesus many of the Greeks already there were dispossessed, some of them coming to Athens. It was from these, according to legend, that her second line of kings was obtained. In their former home the Neleids were royalty already. Once they had ruled at Pylos in Messenia, the principal city and port of southwestern Peloponnesus. One of them, Nestor, had been among the Greek chieftains in the Trojan War, honored by the rest for his wise counsel. But the generations that came after him had been unable to hold their own in Messenia against the advancing Dorians. Certain members of the family had crossed the seas to Ionia, winning distinction there, but the main stem was transplanted in Athens. A Neleid named Melanthus championed the Athenians so well in a conflict with Boeotia that he was chosen to the vacant throne. Then in the reign of his son Codrus the Dorians finally turned back to claim Attica.

The assailants had learned beforehand from the Delphi oracle that they would prevail and conquer provided they spared the king's life. But the priestly pronouncement reached Codrus' ears also. Fearing the enemy were too formidable to withstand, the king disguised himself as a peasant woodcutter, went forth to pick a quarrel with them and was slain. When the Dorians discovered the identity of their victim they were dismayed and abandoned the campaign. Attica was saved and the grateful Athenians numbered the self-sacrificing sovereign in their list of the hallowed. According to one improbable version, the citizens abolished monarchy—their primitive form of it, that is—because no one else could be as good as Codrus.[31] However, many more generations of Neleids are mentioned as reigning, along with the Medontids, who may be the same or a related family (Codrus' son was named Medon). There was still an official with the title of king *(basileus)* much later in Solon's day, and on into the fifth century.

Wherever the truth may lie, those who wielded the real power in Athens kept pecking away at the city's earliest constitution, which tradition ascribed to Theseus. As Plutarch tells it (on the basis of sources long lost),[32] Theseus had first called the Athenians together and organized them into social classes, *georgoi* ("farmers"), *demiourgoi* ("workingmen"), and *eupatridai* ("sons of noble fathers"). Actually, the first two must have existed previously, almost from the beginning; Theseus' innovation was the creation of the *eupatridai,* an aristocracy which composed his *Boulé,* or royal council (Council of the Areopagus, so called because it met on Areopagus rock, just below the Acropolis) and supplied the king's executive officers.

These Eupatrids were the ones gradually forcing changes in the constitution, naturally to gain more for themselves. In so doing, they had a built-in advantage, standing at the top and controlling a pyramidal structure still older, Athens' basic family system, organized on blood lines for the holding of land. In this system, Athens' landowning families each constituted a household *(oikos),* worshiped the same set of gods, including deified ancestors, shared the same business interests and methods, faced the same problems. In barren Attica such problems could be more perplexing than elsewhere, and solving them became an art which developed into a science, the one we know as economics (from Gr. *oikonomia*). The Athenian family had to be closely knit. Several related families with a common male ancestor made up a clan *(genos),* and several of these that were related formed a "brotherhood" *(phratria).* At both levels, these functioned as corporations, holding meetings, electing officers, passing decrees.[33] A number of phratriai together composed a tribe *(phylé),* the largest unit presumably based on community of blood. Four such tribes, called *Geleontes, Hopletes, Argadeis,* and *Aigikoreis,* made up the primitive Athenian state.

Over this organization the Eupatrids were positioned to exercise an authority nearly airtight. They held the tribal kingships, also the phratry chieftaincies. Theseus (if it was he), recognized the realities by creating them a separate class, and declaring them his royal council. The Eupatrids were thus able to overawe the remainder of the upper class, called *gennetai* because belonging to a genos. And between them the two could easily dominate the much more numerous georgoi[34] and demiourgoi of the lower classes, who were merely *demos* ("people," in other words, commoners), and who seem somehow to have been admitted to the phratries,[35] but without land, had no genos for a backbone.

In an aristocratic state, land was the key and agriculture the economic base. Those with a steady, comfortable income from it possessed the best horses, weapons, and armor, often could arm their clansmen as well; with their military might, obviously they had the means to exert pressure in the state. The Eupatrids, previously the king's assistants, thus were able to compel him to share his prerogatives with them. A major event occurred when most of the basileus' executive functions were taken away and given to a new, elected official, the *archon* ("chief"), who became for the next two centuries the most important person in Athens' government. Either shortly before or afterward, the king was also deprived of his military command, which was conferred on an elected *polemarch* ("war chief"). The basileus retained mainly religious duties, mere vestiges of his former splendor, and like his two colleagues, was elected to a one-year term. Finally, the Eupatrid aristocrats, apprehensive that they had left the archon too much power, transferred his judicial responsibilities to six *thesmothetai* ("interpreters of the law," in other words, judges). These nine elected yearly became partners and frequently rivals in a system to distribute authority widely among the nobles, preventing any one leader from an arbitrary control that might threaten their vested interests. If any should try, the aristocrats' Council of Areopagus could cut them down.

All very nice for the Eupatrids and for their gennetai retainers who might hope to climb to the top rung themselves someday. But fate was not as kind to Athens' demos, who very possibly lived closer to the level of subsistence than those in any other part of Greece. Amongst these, the demiourgoi were in the situation least uncomfortable. Many of them were town dwellers who had profited by Athens' years of comparative peace to attain considerable skills in lines such as pottery, furniture-making, carpentry, metal and leather goods, products which allowed them a fair living if the government's policies were conducive. But since the *Ekklesia* ("People's Assembly") counted for little in the eighth and seventh centuries, the demiourgoi had scant influence with the government.

The peasant georgoi had less room to maneuver. Their land ranged from mediocre to poor, by our standards, and their products were perishable. What they had to trade, above local consumption, had to be sold quickly at the prevailing price; they were at the mercy of the market and the upper class elements who maintained it. A fortunate minority might rank economically with that upper class. But most of the georgoi would run the gamut from small proprietors to those landless ones who worked for them.[36] In his struggle with the market, the proprietor tended to fall behind, having to borrow and pledge, finding it ever harder to redeem his pledges. A miserable and growing number had lost out already, the *hektemoroi* ("sixth-share men"), who having forfeited their lands to the mighty, were forced to work them for no more than one-sixth of the produce.[37] Scattered and scarcely organized as they were, the georgoi could do little about their plight. Hoes and sickles made but poor weapons. They were dissatisfied to the point of exasperation, and willing enough to make common cause with that other segment of the demos, the demiourgoi. The latter, as their markets widened, found themselves in a somewhat stronger position. Such diligent people would have to be heard sooner or later, and as they acquired the means to arm themselves it became imperative that the nobles should lend them an ear.

But nobles do not willingly share privileges. The aristocrats of Athens made no concessions, and with the weight of tradition behind them held the lid on until an explosion threatened. It came sometime in the score of years after 640 B.C., when a handsome and popular Eupatrid named Cylon seized the Acropolis with the aid of relatives and soldiers provided by his father-in-law Theagenes, tyrant of Megara. Cylon had won acclaim for himself and Athens by a double victory in the Olympic games. Probably, like his father-in-law, he had made a great show of sympathy for the demos, and had spoken in vague terms of helping them. It was the customary way tyrants attained power all over Hellas in the seventh and sixth centuries before Christ. Once in power, their own interests became paramount.[38]

But the demos did not rise to support Cylon as had been expected. Perhaps he had not wooed them sufficiently, perhaps they were cooled by the sight of Megarian troops occupying their ports and citadel. It has been shown that Cylon's coup was really a reactionary one, against the interests of the Athenian demos, since the Megarians, by occupying the island of Salamis and preventing use of the harbors of Phaleron and Munychia, were denying the masses access to cheap grain from overseas.[39]

Instead it was the nobles who acted. Their powerful Council of Areopagus was dominated at this time by the archon Megacles, head of the prestigious Alcmaeonid clan. At his urging the Acropolis was surrounded and an unceasing watch maintained. The trespassers soon ran out of food and water. At the last minute Cylon and his brother managed to escape, but the rest in their despair took refuge in the Temple of Athena Polias, suppliants at the altar of the goddess.[40] Sacred law commanded that anyone coming here had the right of sanctuary; thus the heads of the state were in a quandary.

Finally, to break the impasse, the councillors gave a solemn pledge that if the conspirators withdrew from the Acropolis promptly, their lives would be spared. The offer was accepted but as the suppliants emerged they were seized and put to death by Megacles' order. Now the citizens were horrified, not so much at the breach of faith as over the pollution of Athena's shrine. The goddess would be quick to punish them unless reparation were made instantly. Therefore not only Megacles, but the whole Alcmaeonid clan was exiled from Athens—forfeiting all its property—a sentence identical to the one pronounced against Cylon and his brother.[41] The stain was deep and lasting. For centuries people talked of the "curse of the Alcmaeonids" even when the decree against them had long been lifted. While the gods lived on Olympus, the stigma adhered.

The commons had remained quiet through the whole affair, but loyalty to the polis did not improve their condition. If anything, their lot was worse, for the immediate result of the recent violence was prolonged trouble with Megara. Cylon had fled there as a matter of course, and Theagenes took up his son-in-law's quarrel. With or without a declaration of war, normal relations were suspended, and Megara, Athens' nearest foreign market, was closed to Athenian merchants. Theagenes' bands raided far into Attica, burning fields, depriving the peasants of what little they had. The tyrant conveniently forgot his democratic sympathies. Georgoi and demiourgoi suffered alike. Desperate as the people were, it would take less than ever to provoke a general rising—which may have been the object of Theagenes' depredations. Even the Eupatrids were not a solid block to resist revolution, as Cylon and his friends had demonstrated.[42]

The foundations of the state were wobbling. Whether it was strong pressure from below or a prudent resolution of those above, a decision was made about 621 to put the laws of Athens in writing. For this pupose a citizen named Draco, who may have been one of the thesmothetae for that year, was entrusted with an extraordinary commission to draw up and inscribe the judicial customs of the land as he understood them. Whoever he was, Draco must have had a thick skin as well as a strong sense of duty. Only a person thus constituted would agree to take on so thankless a task. It was a foregone conclusion that his legal monument when finished must contain *some* sections objectionable to this person or that one, nearly everybody in fact, while the few who approved would not give incautious praise.[43]

Nevertheless Draco did his job. What his code actually specified cannot now be ascertained, because most provisions were later modified or superseded. But the basic principle was an austere justice which decreed capital punishment not only for murder but for lesser offenses such as stealing and destruction of property. Although similar features are found in most early codes of law—like that of Hammurabi or Rome's Twelve Tables—the outcry of the citizens was almost automatic. As the story goes, Draco was asked by a friend why he had set such harsh penalties. The crusty scribe replied that in his opinion any sort of wrongdoing deserved death, and that for major crimes he was sorry he had nothing more severe to inflict![44] Facing up to responsibilities was part of the Greek birthright; he permitted no concessions to evasion or weakness.

Yet though it was said afterward that the laws of Draco were written in blood, they did contain some humane elements. Strangely, these are found in the sections relating to homicide, the only portion of the code regarding which we have definite information. Draco made a distinction between premeditated and unpremeditated killing.[45] Up to this time murder had customarily been punished by the victim's relatives, who seldom stopped to consider causes or premises. It was the religious duty of the next of kin, particularly, to track down the offender. Since the origins of quarrels were hard to trace and were not seen by all parties in the same light, they frequently led to disastrous blood feuds which weakened the state. These Draco tried to forestall. If the homicide were unintentional, the person committing it had the right to appear before a special court of fifty-one judges *(ephetai)* and make his explanation. If this were accepted he was allowed to depart into exile, and the victim's relatives could not pursue. However, the offender might not return to Attica until the aggrieved granted him full pardon, if ever. To act otherwise was to invite renewed violence.

Draco also tried to protect those falsely accused. If such a one were in danger, he was entitled to take refuge on Areopagus Hill and ask a hearing before the full Council.[46] This being granted, he stood on the Stone of Hybris (Presumed Offense) and replied to the charges of his accuser standing on the Stone of Implacability. If the council found in favor of the defendant, the plaintiff had to desist. Likewise, when a man killed in self-defense, steps might not be taken against him. But with a known and fugitive slayer, avengers had the same rights as before. In these days the state did not itself intervene to punish murder unless there were none who had an obligation to avenge—or if those having such an obligation should fail. The basic idea was that pollution should be cleansed away and the gods appeased. Also, the social order should not be unduly disturbed; the government acted only when necessary.

The code was sparing in this instance, but such niceties brought scant thanks. Beyond the faint comfort of a settled and known law, it did nothing to alleviate the distress of the demos. Yet it also placed some restraints on the power of the nobles, which these lords of the land did not especially appreciate. As he probably expected, Draco found himself in general disfavor and for his own safety withdrew to the island of Aegina, where he remained until his death.

If, a little more than a hundred years later, Athens was pressing Sparta for the hegemony of Greece, the contribution of Draco must be taken into account. At the beginning of the fifth century B.C. her people stood on the threshold of greatness, infinitely more advanced than their forebears. And it is significant that in spite of emendations and deletions, they still referred to Draco's writings as "the laws" (*thesmoi*—a word which had associations with the gods),[47] while all later promulgations bore other names. Athens had a higher regard for the old original than she was willing to admit. With that feeling went a belated and somewhat ambivalent gratitude. Tardy amends were made by Plato and Aristotle two and one-half centuries later, when each endorsed Draco's mandates as the legislative groundwork for their ideal commonwealths.[48] Better praise would be hard to find.

2

The Tempering Wind

600–590 B.C.

AS the sixth century B.C. opened, Hellas was no closer to unity or accord in government than in the days of Homer. Yet, even without accord had come the materials and groundwork of a common culture, one already comparable to those previously established in the Orient. And naturally, Hellenes valued their own attainments higher than those of distant *barbaroi* with whom they had slight, if any, acquaintance. When the Greeks adjudged themselves to be civilized, each state cited its own contribution to the general weal. In the distribution of applause, a generous measure was owed to the Athenians, certainly. Not all would agree, however. There was an impression at Sparta and Corinth, even more at Argos—proud inheritor of neighboring Mycenae—that civilization had developed within the bounds of Peloponnesus,[1] emanating gradually northward. They tended to see it as clinging to those of Dorian derivation, and to look on other tribes as lesser breeds. Although not themselves of one mind about it, all could point out that Zeus was secured to them through his sanctuary at Olympia, where they had the Games and the reckoning of the years; that Heracles had labored, loved, and sired in the peninsula, making them a race of heroes; and that Agamemnon was lord of all the Greeks against Troy. Argos had long since appropriated Agamemnon, and everything Mycenaean that she found of value. Sparta in turn claimed him too. Both preferred to ignore the Achaean blood of the Homeric warriors. The Dorian ancestors of sixth century Spartans and Argives had not come into the land until another two or three generations after the exploits so often retold.

Though there were strong objections to Athens' claims to increased

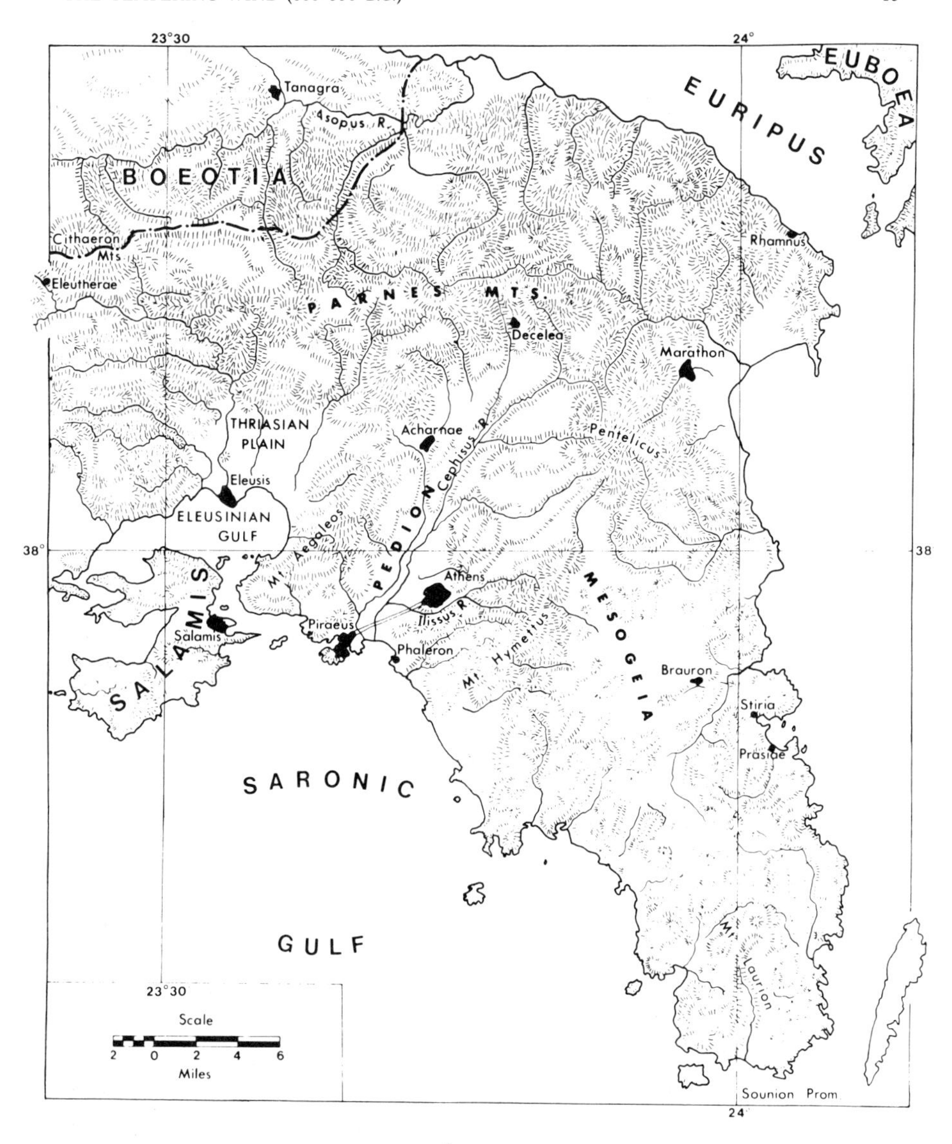

ATTICA

significance, the Peloponnesian point of view was hardly more acceptable. If Agamemnon was southern, then Achilles was northern; Heracles had performed his prodigies all over Hellas; and Father Zeus granted his favors wherever beauty was meritorious. The perceptive traveler going north would not find brilliance diminishing. He could pass Attica with its swarming

Athens if he chose. Just beyond was fertile Boeotia, centered upon "seven-gated" Thebes—Athens' nearest rival—where Cadmus had given the Greeks their letters, and Oedipus had freed them from the all-devouring Sphinx. Toward Boeotia's western border lay Mount Helicon, home of the Muses, who imparted knowledge and eloquence to those worthy of such inspiration, each one presiding over a branch of the arts. There was no dearth of enlightenment here.

Capping the mountains to the west was misty Parnassus, beneath which the town of Delphi pitched precariously—Delphi, with its noble shrine of the Pythian Apollo (so called because in pre-Greek days the cult at Delphi was devoted to a sacred "python," which Apollo, on his arrival, was said to have strangled). This shrine was venerated throughout the Greek world. Even the Spartans came there occasionally to consult the oracle, possibly when they felt that Zeus might be absent from their own Olympia, following the impulses of his charitable heart. The Father was filled with such an abundance of goodwill toward certain deserving mortals that it was hard for him to withhold it. But whether at Olympia or on the equally hallowed ground of Dodona in Epirus his intentions for the regular run of mankind often remained obscure.[2] The utterances of the Pythian priestess at Delphi might be even more so, as she strove to interpret the thoughts of Zeus' glorious son. Fortunately the assisting priests became adept at assembling her entranced phrases into intelligible sentences, even into hexameter verse, to reassure the anxious postulant.[3] With such facilities for authoritative communication, Delphi was a magnet for all. Moreover it was a Dorian community, though established amidst the Aeolian peoples of central Greece—hence still a respectable place for the Spartans of Lacedaemon and others from their peninsula to go.

But the circuitous paths of the north must lead one back to Attica and Athens, in spite of Boeotian and Peloponnesian prejudice. It is small wonder that such a feeling arose. Athens was a city as ancient as any, but there were many doubts about the hybrid inhabitants. The Ionian people who persisted here had filled the least notable page of Hellenic prehistory, so far as origins went. Whence their ancestors had come, only the gods knew. Religious sanction and a bit of luck had preserved for them this piece of the continent, out of all their mainland stakes.

Yet the purebloods (if that is what they were) from beyond Attica's borders were forced to make concessions, however grudging. Athenians worked steadily and worried little about their dubious background, bringing quality goods to the *Agora,* the city's marketplace. Little is known about this earliest gathering place, later destroyed by the Persians, except that it nestled around the entranceway to the Acropolis, with its temples mainly on the south side. Ancient authority informs us that it contained sanctuaries devoted to *Athena Themis* ("Athena of Justice"), to *Zeus Meilichios* ("Zeus Gracious and Mild"), to *Demeter Chloe* ("Demeter of the Tender, Young Plants"),[4] as well as ones for Apollo and for the old hero, Theseus. But only the temple of *Aphrodite Pandemos* ("Aphrodite of All the People") has been verified as to its position,[5] just beyond the south slope. Apparently there was also an altar

grain, wine, or oil after harvest when prices were lowest, and were hardest pressed to buy after a long winter when prices were soaring.[11]

The other large class, the demiourgoi of the towns, had more leeway to negotiate for their wares, but they too could be caught off balance, especially those who were landless and unable to grow their own food. Obviously a few profited by the fluctuations, but those best able to survive were the ones well off already, who were becoming richer while the majority were losing ground.[12] Discontent grew to open anger, and with it a perceptible cleavage among citizens, a separation into factions mainly along geographic lines, as all groped for a remedy. The men of the Plain, occupying the "best" of Attica's rather mediocre lands, presumably her central Pedion and the Thriasian district westward toward Eleusis and the Mesogeia, thought it best to tighten aristocratic control in the hands of a stalwart, unyielding few. Men of the Shore, dwelling along both of Attica's coasts but more thickly in the south, wanted "reasonable," moderate reforms in recognition of the substance they had gained as merchant shippers, the state's newly rich. Formerly attached to this group, but now having nothing in common with this increasing wealth, the men of the Hills, relegated to the poorest lands mainly in northeast Attica, were breaking away; though confused and disorganized, with no clear notion of their objectives, they clamored for relief from their debts and a fresh start that would treat everyone alike.[13]

These geographic units were not completely discrete, of course. The Eupatrids were in general the party of the Plain,[14] but some of them such as the Alcmaeonids who had grown rich through commercial activities supplementing their agricultural income, had developed ties with the Shore crowd. The demos were even less solidified. Amongst them, the demiourgoi, depending on trade, would tend to line up with the Shore too, even those who lived away from the coasts. The most poverty-stricken of them, like their compeers among the georgoi and hektemoroi, probably drifted toward the Hill faction. The rest of the georgoi might be found in any of the groups. Being fundamentally conservative unless disturbed, individual farmers could be found with the Plain, Hill, even the Shore, depending on the nature of his purse and his temperament.[15]

Between the three a confrontation was developing, one which threatened revolution, not excluding the prospect of a tyranny. Aggravating the menace, a remnant of the Cylonians had returned, stirring people to vengeance against the Alcmaeonids. The homecoming of Cylonians called renewed attention to the supreme peril, the losing and dragging war with Megara, then at the height of her power as a commercial and colonizing state. Megara's possession of Salamis was much more than an injury to Athenian pride; it was a vital danger, since Salamis pointed a close finger at the Thriasian plain, indicating an easy route of invasion from Peloponnesus, bypassing the mountains which gave Attica its natural protection.[16] And the surveillance Megara was able to exercise over Athens' ports, curtailing importation of cheap grain, was driving the Athenian commons to desperation.

Something had to be done quickly; but what, and where was the man everyone would trust to do it? Ideally, to please all sides, the deliverer should be an exalted person, who had walked every street of life and some of the alleys, a sort of merchant prince of proven justice and benevolence, yet one who had encountered the hardships of Attica's farmers and was not unacquainted with the griefs and disappointments of the lowliest. In short, a messianic figure.

Normally expectations of such magnitude are doomed, but Athens was fortunate in this crisis to find a champion who met all the tests. Solon, the son of Execestides, had impeccable credentials although he was loath to show them. His parents were connected with the nobility of the city, while his father's ancestors claimed descent from Codrus and the old royal line of the Neleids. Yet despite its illustrious antecedents Solon's was a house already known as friendly and charitable toward the common people. In fact, goodness was almost its undoing. Solon discovered that his father's acts of generosity had impoverished them all. When disaster struck there were many friends ready to assist, but the son was ashamed to be beholden to others, so he declined, merely saying that "he was descended from a family who were accustomed to do kindnesses rather than receive them."[17] Thus although nobly born, he had gone into business with notable success, acclaimed as much for his uprightness as for efficiency at his work. In the process he traveled widely but where he went on these early journeys is not known. Since Athens' trade centered within the Aegean's rim, it is a fair guess that at least Miletus and Rhodes were included in his itinerary.[18]

With such respect as he now commanded, Solon could hardly escape being drawn into the internal politics of the city, caught in the wake of constantly recurring economic crises. He tried to stay out. The bitterness of factional quarrels distressed him, and none knew any better than he that all sides would be dissatisfied with a solution not entirely favorable to any one of them.[19] Yet, in an attempt at peacemaking, apparently it had been he, sometime between 610 and 600 B.C., who had induced the Alcmaeonids to submit the charges against them to a special court of three hundred nobles.[20] Probably there was growing public pressure for the trial, fostered by the miscarriage of the Megarian War, for which the Alcmaeonids could be held responsible.[21] Solon was the right person to persuade these lofty ones since he seems to have been on friendly terms with them and as a merchant may have belonged to the Shore group himself.[22] The Alcmaeonids were condemned and left Attica for an undetermined period.

Next, on the evidence of his poems, Solon addressed himself to the irritant of the dragging war, which by report was going so badly that the Athenians had given up the struggle and had even passed a decree forbidding anyone on pain of death to propose reopening it. The story that Solon had to feign madness to flout such a prohibition is patently false; the Assembly did not yet have the power to make such decrees. Solon must have read his stirring elegies to the Eupatrid nobles (probably in an Areopagus session) by virtue of the heralds' right inherent in his family.[23] Nothing is known as to the course of the renewed conflict but that Solon was chosen a general, and that the conquest of Salamis from the Megarians is in some sense traceable to him seems fairly established.[24] Athens was relieved of the threat of invasion and was free to use her own ports again without fear of attack.

These gains made Solon the hero of his generation, with three great bases to his strength. Foremost was his spotless reputation and the fact that he stood well with all classes, having something in common with each. In addition, he was well known to all Athenians now through his literary efforts, which, though delivered to the nobles, must have been quoted and requoted in many an Athenian household. (Among these utterances was his famous line, "When things are *even,* there is no strife," which each one interpreted in his own way—the well-to-do thinking he meant a fair proportion, the poor, absolute equality, including a redistribution of land.)[25] Finally and probably most important in the popular mind, he was credited with the victory over Megara and the acquisition of Salamis.[26] Thus it was a culmination not wholly unpredictable, when in 594 he was chosen archon with a special *autokratia,* that is, having full power to mediate disputes and legislate for the crisis without need of ratification.[27] Here was a compliment unmatched in the history of Athens and rare in the history of the world.

Nearly all would agree it was a tough assignment, but few besides Solon himself could realize how staggering it actually was. To see every side, to be fair to all, was hard enough, requiring an extraordinary amalgam of knowledge and expertise in economics, politics, jurisprudence, and human psychology. To satisfy all was, of course, impossible. From his broad base of experience he could do no more than his best, and in his balanced view he conceded that the peasant georgoi were right in one assumption. In any drastic overhaul, land reform was basic and came first, yet this was the problem most complicated by conflicting customs, media fluctuations, and contractual arrangements not always susceptible of proof. Faced with a legal maze in which not only he but his entire program might become engulfed, Solon decided on the simplest and boldest course. In a sweeping decree, he says he "pulled up the horoi" and thus canceled the debts on land, freed those who had been enslaved for debt, and even freed and brought back those Athenians who had been sold into slavery abroad.[28] It was also provided that in the future no loans could be made with persons pledged as security. The legislation was soon universally called the *seisachtheia,* or "shaking off of burdens," afterward gratefully remembered as the greatest blessing Athens' demos had ever had.[29] The extreme value that Greeks have historically placed on personal freedom, has won for Solon an increasingly high regard in the eyes of his people.

Despite its magnificence, the seisachtheia cannot have been as clear-cut as Solon would have us believe, nor do his writings, being poetry, give us a precise description either of the ailments or of his remedies.[30] Because of his omissions vital questions of interpretation remain, and the best of scholars have disagreed about them. It was all very well for Solon to say that he "pulled up the horoi," but without knowing more about the actual process, or about the exact nature of these stones, it is hard to assess the legal implications of his act. Did the horoi have any legal standing as property deeds? Or were they merely boundary stones, and if so, how "official" were they? Were they mortgage records? Or simply notices that a certain proportion of the annual crop was already obligated?

If Solon appears as a sort of messiah, he is as difficult to pinpoint as others of that ilk. On his record, some have called him a revolutionary, liberating the oppressed and restoring their lands,[31] a viewpoint which traces to antiquity.[32] However, a conservative interpretation of Solon started among the late Athenian writers too, insisting that debts were not canceled but merely the interest on them lowered.[33] And there is a valid in-between approach, since Solon is described as a mediator, and he referred to his work as essentially a compromise.[34]

Mysteries about the horoi account for many of the differences in scholarly opinion. Even the most enthusiastic admit that Solon could not have canceled all the debt transactions since the "beginnings" of Attica.[35] His legislation must have been limited to those merely on personal security which were current and unclosed; else there would have been an interminable investigation of land titles throughout Attica, with no possibility of proof in many cases. As previously seen, most Attic farmers probably fell gradually in debt, first to the status of life tenant, then to hektemoroi, as successive sixths of their crop became obligated. When the end was reached, the creditor had the choice of keeping the hektemor and his family as serfs to work the land now transferred to him (through a "sale" of "possessory" rights, allowing the debtors the option of redeeming the land if ever able to do so)[36]—or to sell them as slaves. Quite obviously from that time on, the creditor could do with the horoi pretty much as he pleased and probably could do so anyway if his debtors were illiterate.

Which leads to the question, how and by whom was Solon's uprooting of the horoi to be enforced? If by the archon himself and his personal followers, they would have to be hardy indeed if the local magnate and his retainers met them at the markers with drawn swords. This was the likeliest reaction, but Solon mentions no such confrontations in his poems, nor are these spoken of elsewhere. Leaving execution to the debtors would be even less feasible. Except rarely, when debtors happened to be nobles, they would not have the military training or means to withstand an aristocratic creditor. Athens had no regular police to help; if left alone against a magnate, debtors might find worse things than their current lot.[37]

But it would seldom come to this. Evasion of obligations was easy for both sides. Just as it has been suggested that debtors' obligations inscribed on the horoi were there to prevent the debtor from selling a part of his crop secretly before rendering his account[38] (how would this *really* prevent it?), so on the other hand, it must have been easy for the powerful creditor to control the horoi for his purpose. Solon is represented as announcing his decisions on the seisachtheia rather suddenly,[39] but with news traveling faster than official action, creditors caught would be mainly the negligent—or the honest.

To see the reform in its proper light, these intangibles must be taken into account. Many deserving demos could be and certainly were helped; but the nobles had ample opportunity to subvert. In the maze of tangles, Solon must have developed criteria of his own, unmentioned, for determining whether unfair advantage had been taken of the tenant farmer, by charging excessive interest, for instance;[40] or whether when liberated, he was also entitled to the land that he claimed. And it is difficult to see how he could be accorded title if there were no clear record of it. Judges were still aristocrats; when cases came to the courts they would have to be convinced of flagrant misconduct on the part of their fellows, or of an airtight case for the peasant, to render a decision in his favor.

After Solon's time the hektemoroi disappear from history and the credit is assuredly his. By one view, he lifted most of them to the class of free, land-owning farmers;[41] by another, they became free laborers but without land.[42] Doubtless both are partly right, depending on where and how Solon drew the line. That he did draw it shrewdly and as fairly as he could, seeking justice for both sides, is affirmed by his poems and, more significantly, by the aftermath. For if debtors received cancellation, freedom, lands, everything they claimed, how did he stand "as a mark in the midway between the two hosts"?[43] What did the creditors receive?[44] Indisputably, some of them suffered by the arrangement, but most were in a position to stand it. Had too many of them been hit, as armed nobles they had the strength for a military coup and surely would have attempted one, despite the promises and extraordinary powers given to Solon. That they remained quiet is a tribute to his moderation and good judgment. Probably Solon, as a fellow Eupatrid, was able to persuade his peers to accept cancellation of debts largely uncollectable,[45] convincing them too that they gained little from sullen serfs and slaves, embittered and left without incentive.[46] A merchant himself, he could explain that in a rising commercial economy they actually would fall behind by such intransigence. Such talk could not make the nobles happy, but for various reasons enough of them were reconciled to keep the peace. A specious story avers that at the end a great public festival, also called Seisachtheia, complete with religious sacrifices, was arranged to honor the arbiter for his wisdom and fairness. If true,[47] this would indicate eventual satisfaction of a sort by a substantial segment of the public: enthusiastic approval from the gainers, thankful relief on the part of those who may have feared to lose but had not. A whimsical banquet, with some strange couch-fellows.

Thus Solon's famous Unburdening of the People can hardly have been all that he claimed for it. If a trifle overexuberant, it was not a heedless boast; by himself he had not the means of ascertaining results of such magnitude. Emancipation of hektemoroi serfs and those others enslaved had been a great advance, though it left some without means of support, therefore worse off. Beyond that, it suffices to say that some, an incalculable number, had received a fresh start. It was something else to keep them on the right road. Solon continued to make adjustments in the economic system. Though the much acclaimed improvement of Athenian currency on the firmer standard of the Euboean drachma, can be assigned to him only doubtfully if at all,[48] there is reason to believe that he did in some way reduce the units on weights and measures currently in use at Athens, also lowering interest rates, actions that would strengthen Athens' economy by stimulating the export trade.[49] In this connection, Solon's sound economic judgment was never better displayed than in his decree confining Athens' exports to olive oil, the crop for which her soil was best suited. The same ordinance gave the destitute some protection against starvation by conserving Attica's small stocks of grain within her borders.

To check the mushrooming of large estates, Solon limited the amount of land that could be held by one person; besides tending to the creation of small peasant farms, perhaps this would catch some of those evading his legislation on the horoi. Reaching a wider range of the population was the pressure he applied to make all Athenians learn a trade, and his ruling that every father must teach one to his sons in order to have a legal claim on their support when he would be incapacitated or felled by old age. The importance of this provision, immediate and ultimate, would be hard to overemphasize. For people of his own time it furnished the best possible advice on how to make ends meet. With many, agriculture by itself was hardly sufficient as a way of life in Attica. But when they diversified their efforts, developing some handicraft skill as a sideline, the problem of subsistence began to be solved.[50] For the Athenians of generations to come, this was better than a theoretical lifting of debts and the gift of a landless freedom they might not be able to preserve. Better because it trained them in the self-reliant qualities that would make up their special genius. Men of that latter day would be distinguished from other Greeks above all by their readiness and capacity for work, by the individual's confidence in himself which only the skill of long practice gives.[51] Countless other leaders would do well by the men of Athens. But it was Solon, more than any of these, who gave them the possibility of greatness.

He was not yet finished, but from the sources it is unclear whether the rest of his tremendous achievement came during the year of his archonship[52] or whether he was called back later and given an extraordinary commission to overhaul the entire government.[53] It now appears, almost incredibly, that both his economic reforms and the following political reforms were accomplished during his term as archon.[54]

Foremost among his constitutional changes, Solon either instituted or renovated a system whereby citizens were marshaled into four classes, or income groups, with a graduated scale of obligations and rewards. The most affluent citizens, who for want of a better term were called *pentacosiomedimnoi* ("five hundred measure men")—that is, having an income of five hundred measures of grain or oil[55]—had the heaviest burdens (mainly in paying for their military equipment and perhaps some taxes), but were compensated with eligibility to the highest offices, such as those of archon, thesmothete, general, and treasurer of Athena. The *hippeis* ("knights") were next down the scale (500-300 measures), and seem to have been certified for the same positions except the treasurerships. This was obvious appeasement of less well-to-do Eupatrids, assuring them of practically the same privileges as their wealthier brethren and rich merchants.

The two remaining classes cannot be so easily summed up; statements about them are difficult to take at face value. The *zeugitai* ("yeomen," or small landowners, at 300-200 measures) were certainly admitted to the Assembly as voters, perhaps admitted also to some of the minor offices. The main problem is in regard to the *thetes* ("landless laborers," below 200 measures), at the bottom of the scale. Aristotle and Plutarch both affirm that they also became members of the Assembly, but if this is so, events later in the century become hard to explain. That those among them who had once held land — but lost it — were included, may be nearer the truth.[56] It is possible that the rest may have been allowed to attend the Assembly without voting, or had a limited power of voting on the magistrates and on measures that concerned them alone.[57] This would fit the general principle of Solon's reforms and would also be in keeping with the overall moderation of his actions.

The income classes are mute testimony to Solon's ability as a compromiser, the complete politician as well as statesman. By distinguishing especially the five hundred measure men as a group apart, alone eligible for the treasurerships, he seems to be nodding and smiling at them, saying, "You are the best, you're on top!" On the other hand, by making hippeis eligible also for the archonships — the most important offices — he appears to be winking at the Eupatrid knights and whispering, "Not really!" Of course there is also the interesting possibility that Solon, farsighted as he was, envisioned a time when, with Athens' expanding economy, the treasurership would become the supreme office, as in some modern nations. (Great Britain affords the best example, where the office of the Lord Treasurer gradually developed into that of the Prime Minister.)

It never quite happened in Athens. But by bringing the citizens together in the Ekklesia, Athens' Assembly, Solon took the first steps toward civic unity, judiciously meting out powers to classes in a way that provided an incentive for each individual's self-improvement. By working harder, increasing his income, he could also raise his political status. Everyone could feel that he had some share in the state, as appraised by his ability to serve it. Such service, in the sixth century, was chiefly military. The first two classes made up the cavalry, and bearing the expense of a horse as well as body armor and weapons made their outlay the greatest. The zeugitai became the hoplites (from *hoplon,* the large, round shield they carried) or heavy-armed infantry that constituted the defensive mainstay of the state, fighting in phalanx formation, shoulder to shoulder. Besides the shield they had to supply themselves with sword, spear, helmet, greaves, and breastplate, the standard equipment of the Greek soldier. The thetes were too poor to afford any of these; hence they did not immediately count in any era when the state failed to furnish military implements. Eventually they were used as rowers in the fleet, becoming ever more important as Athens' overseas interests expanded. In generations to come, the thetes would pull Athens' navy to many a victory and themselves to political power, but for the moment they had to relish such crumbs as Solon threw them. He was kinder to the country's poor than any yet had been; they had their place and a chance to improve it. Under Solon's "mixed constitution," Athens' developing oligarchy reached its highest form, the stage often called timocracy (government by the "worthy")—although worth had to be measured in terms of income.

Mention of the Ekklesia raises the question as to what powers it had before Solon's day, and what, if anything, he may have given it. Originally it probably elected the magistrates and acted on questions of war and peace. It may have shared in, or given its approval of, weighty matters such as the authority given to Solon and Draco.[58] That Solon increased its responsibility and gave it regular legislative power is suggested by later events but there is no hard evidence. Nor is it certain that freedom of speech existed in Solon's Ekklesia; not only the thetes, but the higher classes may have been restricted. The right to speak may have been limited to the archons, other ranking officers of state, and perhaps members of the Areopagus.[59] But the only reliable conclusion about the Ekklesia at this time is that it was increasing in importance.

Greater legislative powers for the Assembly are strongly suggested by Solon's other constitutional reforms which seem to be accompaniments. One was the creation of a new Council of Four Hundred, to be chosen one hundred each from the first three income classes in Athens' four tribes.[60] The Four Hundred were apparently intended as a counterweight to the Areopagus, since Solon is on record as saying he believed the city could ride out the storm better if it were anchored in two councils.[61] Unquestionably such a group would allay the people's suspicions of the Areopagus, and give voice to Athens' more liberal elements.[62] No specific functions are listed for the new Council in Solon's day, but it is described as being "probouleutic," that is, as having the duty of considering and passing upon all measures before allowing them to reach the Ekklesia.[63] Inferentially, henceforth the Assembly might expect to receive matters requiring legislation after these had been screened by the Four Hundred. Since the Areopagus had heretofore treated these areas as its special prerogative, the gain to popular government is obvious.

Another significant parallel to the Ekklesia established by Solon was the *Heliaea,* the great jury-court of all the citizens, which Aristotle called the most democratic of his reforms.[64] In fact the Heliaea may have been more than a parallel; very possibly it *was* the Ekklesia, sitting as a judicial body to review the decisions of the archons, defining and limiting their exercise of power, sometimes imposing stiffer penalties.[65] Obviously it was a necessary adjunct to the judicial system, to support the seisachtheia, giving the debtor his only possible appeal against his wealthy creditor's influence with the archons—if the debtor dared to invoke such aid. For, besides the dangers to himself, he would find the new and inexperienced Heliaea deferring first to its more knowledgeable aristocratic members. Practically nothing is known of Solon's new court in this period; certain types of cases may have been reserved for it from the beginning, but of this no record exists.[66] And if it designated powers to archons, these must have been the ones they possessed by long custom. However, the Heliaea seemed to have a right of review similar to that of the Four Hundred, and a right of decision like that of the Ekklesia. The intent in each case was clearly a wider distribution of power, restricting but not crippling that of the nobles.

These lordly ones might well have felt differently about Solon's establishment of new bodies to share the authority of their ancient Council. Actually there is no proof that he took anything away from the Areopagus. Creation of a second council implies he did, but Solon may have intended them to act as coordinates, passing upon the same matters. Again, failure to rebel by men having the power to do so, may be the best indication that Solon did not do much to the Areopagus. Whether he left it as "guardian of the constitution," as Aristotle asserted,[67] has been much debated;[68] however, since this is a function which it must have claimed previously, such action (or inaction) by Solon seems plausible. What is generally agreed is that he conferred membership in the Areopagus on all retiring archons, which made ownership of land rather than noble birth the basic qualification.[69] It was also strengthened by the steady addition of the most distinguished men in the community, a practice which in another age enabled the Roman Senate to remain dominant as long as Rome's republic lasted. Solon could hardly have wished to minimize the position of a set to which he himself belonged—both by birth and by virtue of his office.

At some stage of his constitutional reform, Solon gave his attention to the legal code and either abolished the laws of Draco or modified their penalties for all offenses except homicide. In keeping with the civic goodwill he wished to inculcate, amnesty was extended to nearly all political exiles, and it may have been at this time that the Alcmaeonids were allowed to return to Athens.[70]

Other laws doubtfully attributed to Solon were concerned with stabilizing the family unit, which he quite properly regarded as necessary to the strengthening of Athenian society.[71] The requirement that fathers teach their sons a trade is probably the best founded.The sanctity of marriage was affirmed with stern penalties for wives who broke their vows. Men got off easier, but there was a provision that sons born out of wedlock had no obligation to support their fathers. The marriage law was very explicit in regard to heiresses, too, bestowing them to assure the family's survival. If a man had no close heirs within a certain degree he was permitted to adopt; else he could bequeath or sell property belonging to his nearly extinct family. Ostentatious display by women, especially on public occasions, was severely punished. The authenticity of these and other related measures are questions on which there is no consensus.[72] It is generally conceded, in line with his policy of developing industrial skills, that he did invite foreign artisans to settle in Athens and promised them citizenship.

When his work was done, Solon quietly laid down his powers and returned to private life. Applause followed, but the hard decisions he had been forced to make brought denunciations too. To all charges Solon retorted he had liberated the commons and given them lands, given them "more than they had ever dreamt of having," yet had dealt equal justice to all, regardless of station, and in doing so had prevented violence and the slaughter of many. Time would prove him right, he said, and the Mother Goddess of Earth would bear him witness.[73]

Nevertheless the unrest persisted, and disturbances reached such a pitch that Solon decided to leave Athens for a period, hoping his absence would bring calm. Besides those dispossessed and disappointed who abused him, many others constantly intruded to ask his interpretation on fine points in his laws. Solon was convinced his measures could speak for themselves if given a chance.[74] After exacting oaths from the new magistrates that his code would not be altered for ten years,[75] he departed the city. His decrees, called *nomoi* ("ordinances") to distinguish them from the thesmoi of Draco, were engraved on wooden tablets and displayed in the Prytaneion, Athens' city hall, where Plutarch claimed to have seen their remnants seven centuries later.[76]

On this last round of travels Solon, based on the evidence of his poems, first visited Egypt, spent some time in the Nile delta city of Sais, then the nation's capital, and studied Egyptian history and institutions under instruction of the local priests. Afterward he put in at the Greek settlements in Cyprus, to receive the hospitality of King Philokypros, of the town of Soloi. The valedictory poem he wrote thanking the king implies a quick return home, and there are no poems attesting other stops in his itinerary. However Miletus, which he probably knew from earlier journeys, must have been one port of call on his homeward voyage, and if so, it was in the normal order of things for him to encounter Thales, a man like himself distinguished in the worlds of commerce and intellect. Despite this, the incident Plutarch relates concerning their encounter can hardly be historical, nor can the Asian side trip overland to Sardis to visit Croesus, the fabulously rich king of Lydia.[77] Before that, sea currents were bearing Solon to Athens; on landing he found his gentle winds churning into a violent storm.

3

Tyranny and Constitutionalism

590–500 B.C.

SOLON had done his brilliant best for the city, and was doubtless justified in believing his arrangements would prove out in the end. But Athens was not a Babylon of infinite riches, and disillusioned citizens whose hopes may have leapt too high were unwilling to wait for the millenium. If they considered he had not done enough, undeniably his reforms had given them the means to make their resentment felt. All citizens seem to have gained access to the Ekklesia and Heliaea, with rights in varying degree.[1] Initially this would not mean much to inexperienced and untutored people, but it brought them into contact with each other and with potential leaders who might give them political mobility.

Of these, the one best situated to provide gratuitous instruction was Megacles, chief of the Alcmaeonid clan (grandson of the Cylonian Megacles),[2] around whom the Shore element clustered. Megacles had excellent antecedents, having made a famous and lucrative marriage with Agariste, daughter of Cleisthenes, the renowned tyrant of Sicyon, whose power and fortune rested on his judicious protection of the commons in his own city.[3] Furthermore, of the three politico-geographic groups, Megacles' following, the Shore, had profited most from Solon's program, and as a middle force held the balance. But Megacles missed his opportunity, whether from discretion or embarrassment, or both. The notion of a people's leader usually meant a tyrant nowadays;[4] his family had been so involved with tyranny, on both sides of the question, as to be automatically suspect.

Yet Megacles was in an ideal position to pull the strings in the period ahead. Aristotle says there were four years of peace after Solon's departure,

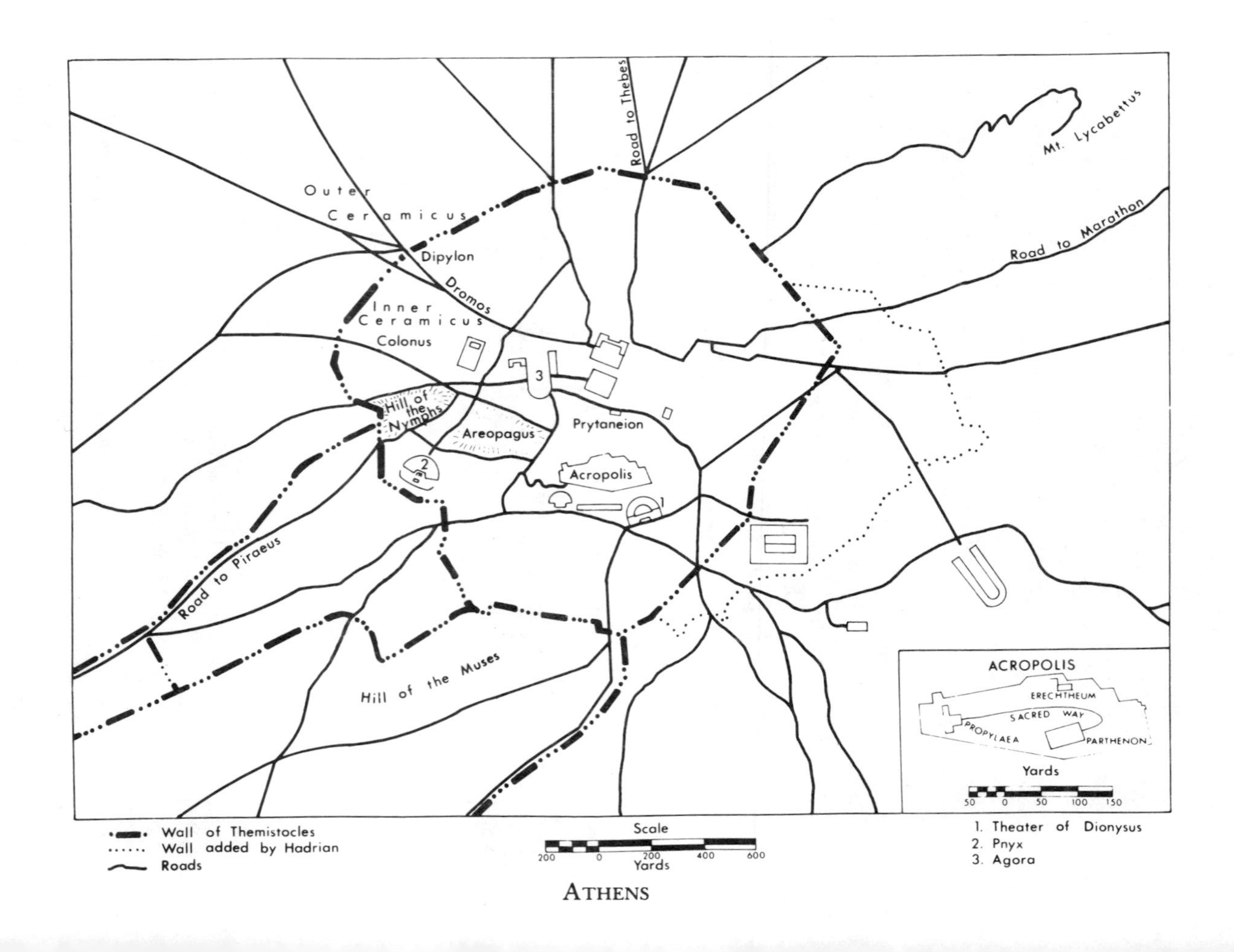
Mt. Lycabettus
Road to Thebes
Road to Marathon
Outer Ceramicus
Dipylon
Dromos
Inner Ceramicus
Colonus
3
Hill of the Nymphs
Areopagus
Prytaneion
Acropolis
2
1
Road to Piraeus
Hill of the Muses
ACROPOLIS
ERECHTHEUM
SACRED WAY
PROPYLAEA
PARTHENON
Yards
50 0 50 100 150
Wall of Themistocles
Wall added by Hadrian
Roads
Scale
200 0 200 400 600
Yards
1. Theater of Dionysus
2. Pnyx
3. Agora

ATHENS

but in the fifth, civic strife broke out so fiercely that no archon could be elected; literally, it was "anarchy."[5] The trouble was seemingly composed, but five years later it erupted again. The impasse was broken about 583, when a certain Damasias was chosen archon, and managed to have his term extended a second year. Though nothing is known of his background, as a compromise candidate he had to have Megacles' blessing and thus was probably connected with the Shore. Since Damasias refused to surrender his office after his second term, very likely he courted the demos in a way that Megacles had neglected.[6] If so, his ploy failed. One-man rule could appeal only to the have-nots. The first three of the new income classes, having a stake to defend, would be unanimous in opposing it, country squires and merchants as well as Eupatrids. With or without a fleeting cooperation between Megacles and his rival, Lycurgus, leader of the Plain, Damasias was brought down after a two months' defiance.

That such cooperation was obtained is strongly suggested by the odd administrative arrangement for the next year (581/0), in which no fewer than ten archons were chosen, after an agreement that five of these should be nobles, three of them farmers (Aristotle calles them *agroikoi* instead of georgoi) and two craftsmen (demiourgoi). The largest share to the nobles points to a transitory alliance between Megacles and Lycurgus, but perhaps a more significant weathervane was that the demos all together received equal representation with their betters. If not permanent, this was at least encouraging. Even Solon had not done so well for them politically; it irked them to remember they were his number three and four classes, restricted from the chief offices. Obviously Solon was not their man. Yet as beginners, they badly needed someone of his stature.

The unstable tripartite makeshift broke down after a year, and discord prevailed for a generation. Details are lacking, but the Shore and the Plain understood each other well enough to maintain a precarious control. Nonetheless, the fabric of the state was weakened, and worst of all, the Megarians seem to have taken advantage of the situation to win back a part of what they had lost.[7] And this meant renewed raids, renewed misery, especially for the poor peasant with a single small holding he could neither leave nor defend.

However, as it had a quarter century before, danger from without brought a transient unity about 570, as Athenians closed ranks against the enemy. According to an uncertain tradition, Solon, back in Athens, was chosen one of the generals, and performed valiantly a last service to his country. True or not, it was a young Eupatrid cousin of his named Pisistratus, either polemarch or among the generals for the year 565, who emerged as hero by capturing Nisaea, Megara's chief port. Denied this outlet, Megara's trade was stifled, and she sued for peace. Pisistratus immediately stepped into the front rank of aspiring Athenian politicians. Courteous, authoritative, and nimble-tongued, he had all the qualities to win popular approval, besides very solid abilities. His easy affability hid a high opinion of self and unbounded ambition, which posed a silent threat to the status quo in Athens—including the recent reforms. The question naturally arises as to what Solon thought of his younger relative. Unfortunately, the many stories concerning them are untrustworthy;[8] that the older man remonstrated with Pisistratus, urging him to moderate his desires into a course serviceable to the state, may hold a reasonable indication of Solon's actual attitude.[9]

And ironically, it was Solon who had paved the way for Pisistratus' continued rise. We are not told how he added to the luster of his military fame by building a reputation as champion of the downtrodden. But he could only have reached them universally through the Ekklesia and Heliaea, to which Solon had admitted the mass of the citizens. There, hesitant newcomers would be dazzled by the glib, suave Eupatrid, and easily fall under his influence. The only drawback was, not many of the lowly could afford to come to Athens to attend the Assembly. Those who did could take news of him to the far reaches of Attica, and the word would spread, however slowly. Realist that he was, Pisistratus did not rely overmuch on this. He knew he had to cultivate the country people himself.

So the supremely confident Pisistratus quietly moved among the residents of Attica, commencing with those nearest him. His principal estates lay near Brauron, twenty miles east of Athens, where the comparatively fertile ground of the Mesogeia gave way on one side to the barren inclines of Mount Pentelicus, and on the other to the equally bleak hills that led down to Sunium promontory and Mount Laurium, with its unhealthy mines. The people of this area had little to cheer them, and still less after the capture of Salamis allowed Athens freer use of the nearby port of Phaleron, to the detriment of Stiria and Prasiae on their side of the mountains.[10] All of East Attica became a depressed area, and all felt the pinch—except for a few lucky magnates like Pisistratus.

Ordinarily he would have been the envy of the hand-to-mouth hillside farmers and miners and not unnaturally hated by them too.[11] However, it was here at home that Pisistratus could best express his compassion, advertise himself as protector, implement his words with acts of charity. One who could be gracious without appearing to patronize was sure to win the hearts of his neighbors. The stricken parts of East Attica were soon won to his interest, and Pisistratus steadily extended his influence, finally splitting the Hill faction off from the Shore, molding it into a compact body to follow where he led. Yet the "Hill" combination which Pisistratus put together was neither strictly geographic nor socioeconomic. It contained a large number of disgruntled losers in Solon's debt cancellation from all over Attica, many of impure descent who hoped thereby to gain citizenship, small farmers who lived in the plains of Marathon and Mesogeia, along with landless and jobless dwellers of the metropolis, forced out of the rural districts by Solon's reforms[12]—in fact, a growing city proletariat.

Thus it was a formidable following that Pisistratus put together from the various dissatisfied elements of Attica. The city segment must have been especially valuable, since it could always be on hand to cheer whenever the Ekklesia or Heliaea met. Citizens of substance, watching silently, became apprehensive; their mounting hostility boded no good for the Eupatrid turncoat. So it stood when one day Pisistratus drove into the Agora showing wounds—or blood smears—which he declared had been inflicted by enemies seeking to take his life. The indignant demos, meeting in Assembly, voted at his request a permanent bodyguard of fifty club-bearers. Pisistratus did not allow them to remain idle. At an appropriate moment in 560, with his trusty defenders he seized the Acropolis and made himself master of the state.[13]

Still, it was not to be that easy. Pisistratus had taken advantage of a divided opposition, but it was one that quickly closed against him. Megacles and Lycurgus, once they put their hoplites and horsemen together, certainly had the strength to oust him, and at some indeterminate date not long after the start of the tyranny, they did.[14] How Pisistratus consoled himself is unrecorded. Probably he retired to his estate at Brauron and waited for the political winds to shift. What he must have suspected would happen, did happen. Quarreling broke out anew, turmoil increased, and in about a year, Megacles, recollecting that Pisistratus had at least kept good order while making no really radical moves, was ready to talk terms with the defender of the demos. What he proposed was an alliance which he hoped would recapture the Hill for the Shore, and Pisistratus along with it. He was to marry Megacles' daughter and come back to resume his position under Alcmaeonid sponsorship. Pisistratus accepted, or appeared to. According to the legend, believed by Herodotus, a tall, beautiful country girl dressed as Athena, was to ride into the city beside Pisistratus, thus invoking the deity and compelling acquiescence from the credulous citizenry.[15]

The accord didn't last long. Soon Megacles' daughter divulged that Pisistratus, who had grown sons by a previous marriage, was treating her as a wife in name only. Megacles realized that his son-in-law was aiming at a monarchy in his own line, one in which the Alcmaeonids would have no share. Hastily, he made peace with Lycurgus, called up their supporters, and probably about 557, drove Pisistratus from the city once more.[16]

This time Pisistratus left Attica, and was absent a full decade. First he proceeded to Eretria, on the neighboring island of Euboea, but seems not to have stayed long. The chief Euboean cities were busily exploiting the mineral resources of the north Aegean coast at this time. Pisistratus' friends on the island apparently let him into their schemes;[17] with his available capital and knowledge of mining gained at Brauron, he could be of material advantage to them. Soon Pisistratus was in the north himself, briefly at a settlement on the Thermaic Gulf or in the Chalcidice, then quickly moving northeast to the mouth of the river Strymon where his intelligence and charisma made him friends among the Thracian natives, from whom he must have heard of the gold and silver veins in Mount Pangaeus, farther up the river. Buying or blandishing concessions from the local chiefs,[18] he put tribesmen to work in operations that, with his administrative energy and business acumen, were mutually profitable. Numismatic evidence shows that he remained on the Strymon about nine years, accumulating enormous wealth in precious metals, which he turned into coin for easier handling.[19] While there he also began to enlist and train mercenary soldiers, possibly from among the same tribesmen he had hired as miners—for, we are told, the decision to return to Athens and recover his sovereignty by force had been taken in a family council at Eretria years before.[20]

When all was ready, difficulties melted away. Pisistratus' hoard of coins unlocked all doors.[21] After nine years on the Strymon,[22] he sailed to Eretria, which was to be used as a base of operations. More troops were hired among his Euboean friends, while others came from Argos and Thebes; from Naxos came an influential leader named Lygdamis, contributing both money and men to the enterprise. Thus strengthened, Pisistratus moved across the straits to Attica, landing on the plain of Marathon, whose hard-run farmers were sure to give him a warm welcome. His partisans flocked to him.

The lords in Athens seemed strangely unconcerned. They made no move against him until he started his overland march toward the metropolis. Only then was the Athenian army ordered out, and when it intercepted the invader at Pallene in the Mesogeia, midway in his march, it showed no disposition to fight. Incredibly, most are said to have been sleeping or gaming after the noon meal when Pisistratus suddenly attacked and scattered them to the winds. Ever a master of diplomacy, he sent his sons after the fugitives to assure them that if they returned quietly to their homes, they would not be molested. Pisistratus then entered the city unopposed (ca. 546), to commence an unbroken reign of nineteen years which ended only with his death in 527.[23]

Once more in control, the tyrant impressed everyone with his industry and goodwill, reinstituting policies he had previously employed. Miraculously, he kept his promises to the Low without hurting the High. In finding preferable farms for the needy, he confiscated only the estates of upper-class irreconcilables who left Attica rather than submit. Megacles and the Alcmaeonids were among these, though whether their estates were touched is an unsettled point; a generation later they were back in Athens, as powerful as ever. The new owners of the confiscated lands received loans on easy terms to get started, and were required to pay solely the general land tax of one-tenth on all produce, later reduced to one-twentieth. Pisistratus went among them explaining to each how he could best thrive, helping with his own funds when necessary. It was by his advice that the now ubiquitous grapevines and olive trees were first planted systematically and universally, as being most congenial to the sullen soil of Attica. Of the two, the vine was especially suitable. In fact, a given acreage of land in Attica would usually yield twice as much poundage in grapes as in grain, though most landowners produced both.[24] Ever since, Athens' agriculture has rested largely on these staples.

Vigilant and tireless, the despot covered every district of the state, studying the people and their problems, tempering justice with kindness. On one such occasion, he found a man working a plot of ground so meager that, wonderingly, he sent to ask what the fellow got out of it. Unaware, the farmer replied, "Aches and pains, and that's what Pisistratus ought to have his tenth of!"[25] Struck with the fairness of the retort, the ruler granted him complete exemption from taxes without further questioning.

An unresolved controversy still exists as to whether Pisistratus initiated the circuit of traveling judges later prevalent in Attica.[26] Aristotle asserts that he did so, to keep the farmers busy at home and out of city politics. Doubt has arisen because of the vagueness of Aristotle's evidence, but such action was clearly in Pisistratus' — and the general — interest. If hours and days had to be set aside to walk to Athens' courts, valuable time would be lost. The important idea was to keep the peasants working at what they could grow most effectively. Thus Pisistratus improved the lot of the demos, the common Athenians, in a way that even Solon had not. If the elder statesman had unshackled the hektemoroi, it was his perspicacious cousin who made it possible for them to earn a decent livelihood.[27] From this time forward, Attica became increasingly a state of individual proprietors, with clear title to the fruits of their toil. What Solon had begun to do for the artisans of the city and others nearby who could manage a trade, Pisistratus did for the rest of the rural population. Once again Athenian initiative and Athenian skills were promoted.

The country poor had needed, and received, prime consideration, but the despot's care was not for them alone. The merchants of the Shore party had no claims upon him certainly, but they discovered early he had no intention of harming them, and was more than willing to accommodate himself to their interests, if he could. His strong, steady hand at the wheel was good for business, undeniably. And significantly, it was during his "reign" that Athens' first concerted commercial expansion overseas took place. Pisistratus tightened the ties with the Aegean islands whenever events permitted. Access to the largest of the Cyclades, Naxos, was gained by helping his friend Lygdamis establish a tyranny there. Tyrants were, in their way, lonely creatures who loved company — at a safe distance. Even the benevolent ones felt more secure in having others to whom they might turn in moments of crisis.

However, it was toward the north, and particularly toward the Hellespont, that strategic neck of water connecting the Aegean with the Black Sea beyond, that Pisistratus looked with whole-souled absorption. (At some stage he seized Sigeum, close to Troy on the Hellespont's Asiatic side, for Athens to use as a base in her trade with the north.) In this direction lay unlimited possibilities for marketing Athens' wine and oil, and her highly admired black-figured red pottery, now again vying with Corinth's for top prices, wherever Greek goods were bought and sold. The success of Pisistratus' commercial policy is easily seen in the great number of Athenian black-figure vases dating to the years between 560 and 520, found on the Aegean islands, and along the Aegean and Black Sea coasts. And no wonder. This was the period of Nearchus and Execias, two of Athens' supreme ceramic artists. Both were potters, but also painters who decorated their own products. Many of Execias' ripe-curved amphora jars on which he treated with convincing realism subjects such as Achilles spearing down the Amazon Queen Penthesilea or Ajax' suicide, have been preserved. Perhaps the most exquisite example of his workmanship is a small kylix cup, now in Munich, on which he painted the god Dionysus sailing a ship of long, trim lines while a school of merry dolphins sport in the waves round about.

Fewer examples of Nearchus' work survive, but what does is of highest quality. His treatment of horses—fierce, leonine steeds champing at the bits imposed by charioteers calmly dominant—has been particularly admired. Rivaling their excellence was a potter named Amasis, who may also have done his own painting, though there is no proof. Usually the shapers of vases entrusted the decoration to other artists especially skilled with the brush. Since there is doubt as to Amasis' doubling, and he does not clearly tell us, it is safer to credit an unknown "Amasis Painter" with the bold, lively forms of gods and maenads, musicians and slaves, or Attic maidens weaving Athena's sacred peplos, that brighten so many of his objets d'art. These were the standouts in a cluster of distinguished ceramicists that included such names as Sophilos, Lydos, and the potter Ergotimos, whose painter, Kleitias, decorated the famous François Vase, with its scenes of joyous Athenian boys and girls dancing after Theseus had liberated them from the Minotaur. It is toward the end of this period that Attic red-figure begins to appear (the color scheme reversed), a type so manifestly superior in color, shading, gloss, and finish, that it drove competitors off the market.[28] Athens' virtuoso artists readily adapted to the new style and may even have devised it, though proof is lacking. To balance her economy, Athens at this time probably imported quantities of foodstuffs in exchange, the obvious items being grain and fish for her growing population—possibly also timber to build ships.

Exceeding care was taken to cultivate the natives of the coasts where Athenians traded, and permission was obtained to establish depots fortified against barbarian attack. Such depots led repeatedly to the forced emigration of colonists, which meant regular, growing settlements, and ever-closer contact with the original inhabitants. It was hardly a surprise then, when the Dolonci, a Thracian tribe from the Hellespontine peninsula (which Greeks called the Thracian Chersonesus), sent representatives to Athens in search of an experienced leader. Pisistratus allowed a prominent noble, Miltiades, of the illustrious Philaid clan, to accept the invitation.[29] The Philaids agreed, and claiming descent from Achilles' kinsman Ajax, considered it no more than their due. The aristocrat Miltiades was normally no friend to Athens' tyrant,[30] but was willing enough to become his agent in the north country, in time bringing in a colony of Athenians. The foothold thus gained was important enough that when Miltiades died, and his nephew Stesagoras succeeded him, Pisistratus' sons sent out another nephew, Miltiades the younger, whose high-handed ways with Athenians and natives alike caused him to be labeled tyrant himself.[31] This second Miltiades would return in a period of crisis, to play a major part in the city's history.

Pisistratus had done well by all classes, even the aristocrats when they were willing to cooperate. Many who had gone into exile returned, and rose to high office under the tyranny. That the government itself remained almost unchanged is astonishing. The Areopagus, Ekklesia, and archons functioned as always. While tyrants elsewhere swept aside the instruments of government, Pisistratus worked through them, reasoning with the elected officials and legislators. Usually there was no need for force, although he could call on his own guards and a special regiment of three hundred foreign archers brought from Scythia for police duty. Life continued in its orderly way, and when someone had the temerity to bring a lawsuit against Pisistratus himself, the ruler appeared quietly in court to defend himself, like any other citizen. It must be admitted also that he strictly enforced the laws of Solon, nor ever made the slightest move against the relative who had opposed him.[32]

A ruler who existed for and by the demos would naturally do his utmost for their social and spiritual life. Aside from the state religion, the deity most reverenced by the commons was Dionysus, held by myth to be inventor of wine and benefactor to man in innumerable ways.[33] The popularity of his worship is explained partly by the fact that Attica's winemaking produced enough for a very substantial export. Partly it lay in the magical properties of wine itself, with its capacity for lifting the human spirit. With the terms of life so hard thereabouts, myriads required lifting. But it was more than this. Dionysus was the son of Zeus by the Theban princess Semele (the only part of his myth that did not sit well in Attica!), therefore, half human and half divine. During a lifetime conveniently obscure and more than doubtful, he had roamed the world doing good deeds and gathering converts to his cult, in which merry revelry alternated with hymn-singing and ecstatic dancing—catalyzed occasionally by the god-given beverage. We are told that everywhere Dionysus went he was accompanied by throngs of admirers and rapturous votaries and it is easy to see why.

However, Dionysus was Zeus's son by an earthly love, and like others similarly procreated, he was eternally pursued by the anger of Zeus' wife, Hera. She arranged to have Dionysus set upon and torn to pieces by a band of titans who waylaid him when—strangely—there were none near to help. But Athena happened along in time to save his heart (was this bit invented in Athens?), which she took to Zeus on Olympus, where Father caused son to be reborn, triumphantly to sit at his right hand.[34] Many variants of this story existed, but its central significance was clear to the most unlettered Hellene. Seen in this light, Dionysus was now a resurrected god, yet still the loving friend of man, one moreover who had the ear of Father Zeus. To those who practiced his cult faithfully, a cult which was open to all, there was the implied promise of immortality, however vague, warranted by Dionysus' protective authority.

To the common people of Attica and those elsewhere in the Greek world,[35] this was considerably better than any assurance they had thus far received. The older poets had usually spoken of the human afterlife as cold, dark, and dismal, especially for the demos, who had no divine ancestors pulling for them. It is no surprise that they were taken with Dionysus, who among his other duties was also an agricultural god seeing to the fertility of the fields. Celebrations known as Dionysia had long been held in the villages of Attica. Athens herself had a festival called the Anthesteria, in which Dionysus was ceremonially called upon to bless the new wine each spring. But it remained for Pisistratus to inaugurate the Great Dionysia, to be held annually in Athens during late March or early April of our calendar, the entire observance covering six days. Its main feature was a procession in which an ancient wooden statue of the god was escorted from his preexisting temple in the Academy district, a mile or so north of the city walls, through the streets of the metropolis to a new Temple of Dionysus erected by Pisistratus on the south side of the Acropolis. While in progress trained choruses dressed as satyrs in goatskins (*tragoi,* goats) danced and sang dithyrambs, the odes sacred to Dionysus, and the leader of the chorus entertained the spectators between songs with words of his own on the god and his mythos. Then gradually, a structure that was freer yet more coherent evolved. In Athens at least, the odes lost their strict dithyrambic character; another spokesman was added for dialogue, speeches and choruses were woven into a related whole. In due course an orchestra ("dancing place") was carved out of the Acropolis slope alongside the new Temple of Dionysus, and the entire performance moved there. Thespis, a friend of Pisistratus, is said to have put together the first definite plays, soon called tragedies (*tragodoi,* goat-singers) from these materials. Thus slowly was born the great Greek tragic drama.

Having done so much for the masses and their favored deity, Pisistratus of course had comparable plans for the official state worship. Almost from the founding of the city—according to legend—there had been a regular yearly religious exercise, the Athenaea[36] to honor the divine patroness on her traditional birthday, which fell about midsummer. Very early also this had been widened into the Panathenaea, supposedly by Theseus after he unified the rest of Attica with Athens and conferred citizenship on the outlying communities. It was a clever move, whoever did it. Thereafter rustics from the remote villages could feel they too were Athenians. Each Panathenaea gave several days to athletic contests and chariot racing, interspersed with religious exercises; at its climax came another procession in which a ship was pulled on rollers from the main gate of the city down the principal avenue to the Acropolis. Hanging from the masthead was a richly embroidered *peplos,* or shawl, woven during the preceding year by girls from Athens' best families. When the Acropolis was reached, priests, magistrates, and attendant maidens mounted the steps and entered the temple of *Athena Polias* ("Athena of the City"), to fasten the sacred shawl upon the cult statue of the goddess.[37] This was their ultimate act of respect and devotion.

But Pisistratus had in mind something much more grandiose. He knew of course of the stately convocation of the Ionians in Asia Minor, the Panionium, held on the promontory of Mount Mycale, across the gulf from thriving Miletus. This met regularly for political discussions among the Ionian cities, but it had also a cultural side, the poetry contest, in which mellow-voiced rhapsodes competed in reciting sections from the *Iliad* and the *Odyssey.*[38] Motivated by brilliant accomplishments in literature, art, and philosophy—Ionia across-the-sea led the Greek world in these disciplines during much of the seventh and sixth centuries—the Ionians had even appropriated Homer, amalgamating him to their own dialect, customs, and ideas. The Panionium was dedicated to Poseidon, the sea god on whose pleasure the fate of seafaring Ionians largely depended, but it also honored Apollo, their imagined ancestor. It was extensively attended from the first, but at some stage the Ionians of the Aegean islands began to drop off, holding their own festival, the Delia, complete with games, dances, and poetic declamations. This last was so named because its locale was the gleaming white isle of Delos, Apollo's birthplace. And here, naturally, Apollo took precedence over Poseidon.

Now Pisistratus stepped in. Under the cloak of piety an expedition was sent to "purify" the island, with orders that even human graves and tombs within sight of Apollo's temple should be dug up, and the remains buried elsewhere.[39] The festival was removed to Athens. Here, with Pisistratus' help, it emerged as the Great Panathenaea,[40] to be celebrated every fourth year as an augmentation of the accustomed midsummer holidays for Athena. Athens now had her own Homeric recitation at which the contesting rhapsode had to be prepared to recite any given passage of the *Iliad* or the *Odyssey,* taking up the story where his predecessor left off. The length of the poems added more days to the festival and at the end prizes were awarded. A standard text of the epics became imperative, and it was widely believed that this was first reached and written down by a commission whom Pisistratus appointed to the task.[41] Whether true or not, Athens had the epics and her tournament became the largest in Greece, drawing visitors from every corner of the Hellenic world. Since Homer's poems stood as a Bible to all the Greeks, there was no question of their ability to draw everlastingly. To hear these monumental works recited, and recited authentically henceforth, one had to come to Athens and hear them under Athenian sponsorship. The Great Panathenaea was the most powerful magnet any Greek city could have.

This does not quite sum up Pisistratus' endeavor for the arts. He improved the architecture of the temple of Athena Polias (popularly known as the *Hecatompedon* from its hundred-foot inner chamber)[42] by giving it the classic dignity of an exterior colonnade, while its pediments were embellished with sculptures showing the mythic battle between gods and giants. In a more practical vein, he provided Athens with its first public water system, building an aqueduct that brought water from the river Ilissos to a large multiple fountain constructed in the heart of the city, which the people called *Enneakrounos* ("the Nine Spouts"). And on the banks of the same river he began rearing a vast new temple of Olympian Zeus (the *Olympeion*), on a scale so tremendous that neither he, his sons, nor any other statesman was able to carry it to a conclusion until Emperor Hadrian did so seven centuries later. It took a Roman emperor with all the resources such an autocrat would command to fulfill Pisistratus' conceptions—though in so doing, that later patron of the arts was to make changes and add ideas of his own. Paying so lavishly, he purchased the right to meddle.

By the time Pisistratus died in 527, he had somehow settled the succession between his eldest son, Hippias, and a younger one, Hipparchus, though a scant century later Athenians were uncertain about how this had been done. Some thought he left it to the elder, some to the younger, still others that he conferred it upon them jointly. Thus their notions were responsive to their political biases and reactions to vital issues of their own day—pitfalls which trapped even historians writing about the tyranny.[43] Still another possibility exists. Since Pisistratus' position seems never to have been formalized as part of the constitution, perhaps he never explicitly informed the Athenian public of the understanding he had with his sons. No vote or ratification was necessary; why bother them?

All one can safely say is that the Pisistratid tyranny continued to run smoothly for more than a decade after the founder's death. Then, about 514, Hipparchus was assassinated, either from political or personal motives, or conceivably, by a sort of accident. All accounts agree that thereafter the rule became harsher. Hippias was vengeful, became increasingly suspicious and recriminatory, turned the people against him. News of this was welcomed by exiled nobles and especially by the Alcmaeonids now led by Cleisthenes, Megacles' son—and on his mother's side grandson of that earlier Cleisthenes, the "democratic" tyrant of Sicyon. However, an Alcmaeonid attempt to invade Attica failed, showing the exiles they lacked the military strength to challenge the Pisistratids. More subtle means were soon found. The Alcmaeonids, living at Delphi during their exile, had ingratiated themselves with the oracle by organizing a drive to build a new temple, which was finished at their own expense in the purest white Parian marble. The influence thus acquired was exerted on the priestess, allegedly, to induce her to procure Sparta's help. At least that is what finally happened. After much hesitation, King Cleomenes was sent with the Spartan army to Attica, where he besieged Hippias in the Acropolis until, in 510, the despot agreed to leave Athens. The tyranny was over.

Aspirants to the vacated executive power were not long in appearing. The expatriates came back and with them Cleisthenes, who as chief of the Alcmaeonids was natural head of the Shore. His principal rival in the liberated Athens of the late sixth century was Isagoras, leader of the Plain—the old political configurations reappeared unchanged, despite a half century of Pisistratid rule. In the contest for the archonship in 508, each found himself in the same disconcerting situation—that of the purse-proud noble veering toward liberalism through the necessity of bidding for the votes of the newly important urban populace. This was a game that could become desperate, so high were the stakes. By innate impulse each of these mighty ones would prefer to bend the neck ever so slightly, if at all. But pressure of the other's competition might compel a genuflection or even utter prostration, if it came to the worst. In this match Isagoras had a natural advantage. He belonged to a family of Eupatrids who had remained in Attica throughout the tyranny, offering no opposition to the despots. Many of the poorer citizens would incline to him, if they held the Pisistratids dear, while remembering that Cleisthenes and the Alcmaeonids had been largely responsible for the expulsion of their champions. Also as nominee of the aristocrats, Isagoras was of course the candidate favored by King Cleomenes of Sparta, who may have lingered in the city long enough to influence the election. To nobody's surprise, Isagoras won.

However, Cleisthenes was not to be outdone. He had lost the enfranchised demos, temporarily at least, but by now there were a host of others still lower who did not have the vote: the metics, or immigrant Greeks from beyond Attica; those disfranchised in 510 as followers of the tyrants; slaves recently emancipated; and perhaps the landless thetes. Among these malcontents he dickered, gaining enough support eventually to outflank his rival;[44] though which of these were enfranchised as a result, and how many, is a matter still disputed.[45] For a noble, Cleisthenes' gesture was close to genuflection, but Alcmaeonids were amply practiced, and could manage it with becoming grace. Yet the outcome was far from certain when elections came the next year. Most votes lay with the other side, and without them Cleisthenes could do little, for all his promises. But fortune was kind. The accumulating pressure at last caused Isagoras to lose his head. Frantically he called for the Spartans again, and Cleomenes returned with spearmen reputed the best in Greece. Rather than provoke a struggle that might turn bloody, Cleisthenes went voluntarily into exile once more. But now he went leaving the image of a public-spirited citizen willing to sacrifice himself for the welfare of his fellows. A vast difference and a vast gain.

Those left in control of the city soon overreached themselves. Cleomenes, blunt Spartan that he was, began issuing peremptory orders to the Athenians, expelling seven hundred families and treating the rest as lackeys of Lacedaemon. However, not anticipating resistance, he had brought only a small company from Sparta. When the people turned on him in fury, even this fearless soldier had to retreat inside the Acropolis. Cleomenes and his men were subsequently allowed to evacuate, and the haste with which the king departed shows he may have been aware of exceeding instructions, perhaps incurring the anger of his home government.[46] For at Sparta real power lay with the Board of Ephors, to whom even royalty was accountable.

Cleisthenes, acclaimed on all sides, reentered the city and for the next several years after 508, was its undisputed leader. Yet what position he held, and what his actual relationship was to the government of the state, are among the many elusive mysteries about the man. So far as is known, he did not run for archon nor for any of the other offices.[47] However, the possibility does exist; records for this period are fragmentary. To go in the opposite direction and establish a tyranny would be entirely out of character for the chief of the Alcmaeonids, a clan that had fought Cylon, Pisistratus, and Hippias in turn.[48] More than that, it seems out of keeping with what we know of Cleisthenes as a person. He was ever one to avoid violence, to achieve his ends through the constitution rather than go around it. And a reformed constitution was his impressive contribution to the progress of Athens. He had initiated its reconstruction promptly, undismayed by his defeat at the polls, over the opposition of Isagoras and the Pisistratean remnant. The work was completed with the approval, in varying degrees, of all classes.

Fundamental to Cleisthenes' entire plan of reform was a political reordering of Attica, to break up hostile confrontations of Plain, Shore, and Hill. The simple truth was that these areas were and always would be unequal in economic value, causing jealousies and antipathies ruinous to the state; geography, with its economic and social concomitants, divided them. Geographic separatism would have to be annihilated. Since the beginning of Athens' history these three economic zones had been approximated to four territorial tribes. The territorial tribes were now abolished, and in their place Cleisthenes set up ten artificial ones, with each to take one-third *(trittys)* of its members from the precincts that composed the Plain, one-third from those of the Shore, and one-third from the Hill. These precincts, called demes in Attica, were the smallest political units, there being between 100 and 150 in the entire state. These were to be divided among the ten new tribes in such a way that Plain, Shore, and Hill would be represented equally in each.[49]

In this arrangement the deme became the basic political entity where citizens were registered, held their local meetings, elected officers including a *demarch* ("district head"), and had their first lessons in self-government. At this level the leaders might run the gamut from staunchly conservative to ultra-liberal, since some demes were obviously rich and others poor. But at the next level where the demes united in forming tribes, citizens from all sections were forced to collaborate in choosing tribal officers, the commander of their regiment, and their panel of candidates for the important new Council of Five Hundred, an enlargement of Solon's Four Hundred, which Cleisthenes intended for a key role in the restructuring of the state. With each tribe now containing all shades of political opinion, it became necessary to select moderate, reasonable representatives who could cooperate. And candidates would need to project a middle-of-the-road image if they wished to be elected. With such men there was a real hope that many divisive problems could be solved at the tribal level, and a real consensus reached.[50] Agreements hammered out there would take a burden off the Ekklesia and prevent unnecessary factional fighting. But before reaching the Ekklesia, every item of business had to pass the Council of Five Hundred, to which all lines of communication led.

Here the spotlight centers, but it falls on a stubborn haze. Much as is known about the Five Hundred, there are many unanswered questions. These start with the method of selection, which was strange, yet not unknown to Greek politics. At the outset, the demes elected certain candidates to be placed on the tribal list, though how many and how elected, our authorities do not say. We only know that tribal lists were long, each one well over a hundred, and that from these each tribe annually chose by lot fifty members to the Council. Eligibility was limited to two terms, which could not be consecutive. Selection by lot seems an odd way to proceed, but it was rather common among ancient Greek communities, and to them defensible on the theory that the gods operated through the lottery, making the final determination on the best candidates. Seen more prosaically, it represented a further democratization of the constitution, since lottery meant more participants, forcing more compromises.[51] The power was passed around, infinitely diffused. Yet it had the elective process at its base, combining the two principles. The Five Hundred were thus a more select body than the Ekklesia of all the citizens, whose actions they checked. And virtually all citizens of recognized ability were at some time in their lives members of the Five Hundred, thus receiving a practical education in democracy.

By and large, it appears that Cleisthenes intended the Council of Five Hundred to replace that of the Areopagus as the supervisory administrative body in the Athenian state. Its most important function was to prepare the regular legislative agenda for the Ekklesia, apart from which that body could not consider any measure. The Ekklesia could, however, by a resolution, call the attention of the Five Hundred to a particular item and require a decision. The two seem to have been intended as natural allies.[52] The idea of checks and balances was familiar long before the days of Locke and Montesquieu.

Guiding the People's Assembly was only one of the many duties of the Five Hundred. It also gave instructions to the magistrates, examining them first as to qualifications, later as to conduct, and finally, in any special charges brought against them. Trials of a political nature stemming from these, also the graver charges of treason, conspiracy, or incitement to riot, were investigated by the Council and certified to the Ekklesia. Councillors also had the care of all day-to-day business of the city; upkeep of public buildings and temples, renting of state property, collection of rentals and fees, maintenance of naval ordnance and ships, even reception of embassies from abroad.[53]

It is clear that Cleisthenes intended the People's Assembly to play a greater part than ever before, and he may have widened its powers.[54] Possibly, at this time, the thetes received full voting and speaking rights. Since Cleisthenes rearranged the tribes, it seems reasonable to credit him with creating the *Strategion,* or Staff of (Ten) Generals, one elected by each tribe to command its regiment. Generals had existed previously of course, subordinate to the polemarch. Gradually they would sap his strength, and in the fifth century they were to displace the archons as the most important officers in the state.[55]

Also controversial is Cleisthenes' authorship of the law of ostracism, although it is usually attributed to him. According to this, the Athenians might decide each year whether to hold an ostracism session, by which any designated citizen might be banished from Attica for a period of ten years. The question was settled by majority vote, originally in the Council of Five Hundred, with at least two hundred votes required for an ostracism contest. If the decision was affirmative, then at a later Council session, each member picked up a potsherd (*ostrakon,* hence ostracism) from among the myriad scattered over the ground, and wrote on it the name of the person he wished to see banished. Anyone receiving a majority of the votes went into exile, providing again that a total of two hundred was reached. The sentence was not a dishonorable one. The citizenship of the person designated was not revoked, nor his property confiscated. Both were resumed upon the exile's return. At some later date, the right of ostracism was transferred to the Assembly, where the number of required votes was placed at six thousand.

That this is a genuine part of Cleisthenes' legislation, seems now to be established.[56] Aristotle says that its original purpose was legal expulsion of the Pisistratids, prominent friends and relatives who might wish to bring them back, and any others in the future who aimed at tyranny. This would naturally relate to the period of Cleisthenes, also to his policies. It was in line with his attitude of nonviolence that he should find so humane a solution, and events proved it adequate. The mere threat of ostracism was enough to discourage would-be tyrants. For similar reasons there exists an excellent case for assigning to him the creation of the Strategion. The ten generals were placed in a position to limit the authority of the polemarch. This was the position that Pisistratus had possibly used as a springboard to tyranny. Cleisthenes would see that it should not happen again. These two final measures set the protective seal on his constitution, guaranteeing the liberties of Athens.

This is as good a vantage point as any to attempt to understand Cleisthenes and to determine his position in Athens' history. Such an appraisal is difficult, because no words of his own, no intimate portrait, no humanizing biography survive to help us glimpse the living man behind the politician. He must be viewed entirely through his actions. Such analysis has yielded surprising results. In his geometric charting of the new tribal system, for example, his wide intellectual interests are revealed, as is his familiarity with the new Ionian science of Anaximander, particularly the influence of Pythagorean philosophy.[57] Thus studied, he seems much more than the blue-blood lord of land and wealth, the station to which he was born.

However, he had to be conscious of the heritage it was his to maintain. The lesson of Pisistratus' rise was not ignored; his ostracism law, and fracturing of the old tribal system would make it hard to upset the establishment again. Modern research has disclosed that in setting up the trittyes, which composed his new tribes, he was careful to dissociate from one another any contiguous areas of Pisistratid strength.[58] Nor on the other hand, did he neglect to gerrymander the trittyes of Alcmaeonid strength so that their voting potential would be maximized.[59] The new champion of the people had the interests of all at heart, but apparently some were "more equal than others."

And an overall view of the new tribal structure supports the same conclusion. The home precincts *(demes)* of the Alcmaeonids were in the city itself. Their friends the merchants and artisans, despite the "Shore" appellative, would many of them be city dwellers. With their help, Cleisthenes certainly aimed to recapture the city proletariat from the tyrannists, and the success of his legislation would indicate that he did. Herein is seen a reason for his move to enfranchise recent immigrants to Attica, most of whom probably lived in or near the city.[60] Their gratitude helped him control the metropolis, and in the new tribal system there were metropolitan and suburban demes in each of the tribes, giving Cleisthenes a strong voice everywhere, especially in the tribal assemblies that would send members to the Council of Five Hundred.[61] Both

Plain and Hill would be firmly checked. Clearly Cleisthenes had learned from the mistakes of his father Megacles, who had avoided open involvement.

Just as clearly, he must often have reflected on the policies of his maternal grandfather and namesake, the famous tyrant of Sicyon, who had made a tribal reorganization in his own state with a purpose not entirely dissimilar. Like that progenitor he preferred the active role and courted the people to achieve his ends. Undoubtedly Herodotus voiced a belief widespread in the Athens of his day, that Cleisthenes had simply imitated his Sicyonian ancestor.[62] How much truth lay in it, if any?

With his background he could not play tyrant, nor even wish to; his every action bespoke an avoidance of coercion. On the other hand, by his day tyranny had gained a bad reputation in the Hellenic world, especially at Athens. No matter what his ambitions, the discreet statesman would shy away. He may have wished for something of the sort, but on his actions we cannot convict him. The demes, the Five Hundred, the strengthened Ekklesia, all widened the people's participation in their government, a government that rested at its base on a strong middle class.[63]

Aristotle's reference to Cleisthenes as *prostates tou demou* ("leader of the people")—a term that would henceforth be applied to the person generally regarded as unofficial head in Athens, which had no single chief executive—raises a question as to his true place in Athenian history, and what he must have considered his position to be. Besides his role as constitution-maker, it used to be said that he was the founder of Athens' democracy and her democratic party. However, recent research has shown that the word *demokratia* was not even in use until the middle of the next century, and that the political contests of this period were basically personal power struggles between the great noble families.[64]

Still, the same research demonstrates that *isonomia* ("equal laws") was a term already in popular use, and the investigation traces at least the origins of democracy to the Cleisthenic period. *Demotikos* (of, or "pertaining to the people") is also known to have been in use before *demokratikos,* and it corresponds as well to the unofficial designation cited by Aristotle. It would seem, then, that Cleisthenes was considered, and considered himself, leader of a government of and for the people, but not by the people.

At the start, those whom he led were mostly personal followers and ones with similar interests, the Shore crowd. However, he had seen Pisistratus build the Hill into a structure which endured ten years to support him when he returned from exile. For his own protection, could Cleisthenes fail to take similar steps? Without the necessity of a formal organization, one can see developing around him not a democratic, but a "people's party," a permanent if undefined body, to preserve the benefits recently gained. Their only "officer" was their prostates, but he was all they needed.

His private thoughts are beyond reach. A common impression in fifth century Athens held that he had not always been on the side of the demos, had approached them only when he found himself losing the struggle with Isagoras.[65] It may have been so. But at some stage he would have to justify his actions to the world, and what is more important, to himself. We are what we do, as the saying goes, or, we become what we do. Cleisthenes may have thrown up an elaborate camouflage, that his was a "return to the ancestral constitution," which was actually later claimed for his legislation.[66] Or he may have told himself and others he had always been the people's friend at heart, speaking piously of the intelligent noble's burden of "responsible leadership." Not inconceivably, he could have done both. In any case, he would hardly have been the first patrician to cry *Vive la Révolution!*

4

The First Blast from Asia

500–490 B.C.

THE Athens of 500 B.C. was not identical with the ancestral town of a century before. The old Agora at the Acropolis' entrance was still the principal marketplace, and probably remained so until the Persian devastation a score of years later.[1] But already another was springing up, north and slightly west of the citadel. This later one has traditionally been called the "Agora of Solon," though there is little to show that the lawgiver had anything to do with it. No architecture is attributed to him. Still he did establish the Heliaea, the people's jury-court, which from the beginning held its meetings in this vicinity. The continuous presence of so many citizens in a particular spot would naturally cause market stalls to be built nearby. Men did the shopping for their families and the easiest course would be to buy their supplies on the way home from the courts. Such was probably the origin of "Solon's Agora." Recent excavations show that the foundations of some public buildings may go back to the early sixth century,[2] particularly the lowest wall layers of the *Metroön* (Shrine to the Mother of the Gods), though beyond this nothing is definite.

However, the new Agora received a vigorous boost from the next generation. On its west side, at the foot of Kolonos hill, Pisistratus erected a temple of *Apollo Patroös* ("Apollo, Father of All Ionians"), where in his day officials were sworn in and citizens registered. In line with this, a few dozen paces to the south, the tyrant ordered a new administrative home with its own dining hall and kitchen, the Prytaneion, where those elected actually did their work and were on duty day and night. Between the two, Cleisthenes in his turn raised the Bouleuterion to house the Council (Boulé) of Five Hundred which he had created.

Thus by the century's end the city government had moved to this more spacious area north of the Acropolis, and a large part of the city's commercial business must have moved too. Not much is known about this agglomeration since it was shortly to be destroyed by the Persians and afterward to be built anew.[3] But the groundwork had been laid. A little distance to the northeast Pisistratus' sons with pious impartiality reared an altar to the Twelve Olympian Gods, the Pantheon of its day. Between it and the group of three ran the Panathenaic Way, which connected the Acropolis with Athens' main gate, and linked farther out with the Sacred Way to Eleusis, also with the long road that reached Athens from northern Greece. Hence it was a natural hub for foot and wheel traffic,[4] where a market square would predictably arise. Sooner or later, Athens' principal Agora must be here. Probably this was the ground on which the Ekklesia met also, until moved (by Cleisthenes?) to the less crowded precinct of Pnyx Hill. It offered more room than the original Agora, but not enough, finally, to accommodate all of Athens' fast-increasing electorate. It is practically certain that Athens' Ekklesia met first in the old Agora near the Acropolis' entrance, then in the new one on the north side, and finally on Pnyx Hill off to the southwest. The date of this final move is not known, but the most informed opinion places it in the time of Cleisthenes.

Even after the Ekklesia's removal, Solon's Agora was sure to remain a busy place, the real center of politics. Besides the ever-present juries, one could find Cleisthenes' Council of Five Hundred sitting in senatorial dignity at the Bouleuterion, and its revolving presidential committee, the Prytaneis, next door. Citizens tramped in by the score to make their complaints, or to see whether court service might befall them. Even in the days before paid juries, a frank unblushing curiosity about their countrymen's weals and woes would draw them thither. If not needed, a great many stayed anyway to look for friends or excitement. The Hellene was and is a convivial person. With the rest of mankind he is also a political animal, as Aristotle avers. In the Agora he encountered a host of others equally concerned about the state's problems and willing to debate every detail. Not unnaturally, it was in this familiar locale that opinion slowly shaped itself as the multifarious issues were untangled on their way to the legislature.

Here too one met the avowed, unshrinking candidate, eager to serve country and self. All who voted could gain an introduction to the prospective magistrate, put the most direct questions, scrutinize the aspirant closely as he replied—something that was not easy to do in the distance and formality of Pnyx Hill. Men have always been as important as measures, sometimes more so, and the electors swarming around wanted to know above all that this particular man meant to deal honestly with them. When Greek met Greek it was more vital than ever, and often harder to ascertain. They wanted to satisfy themselves about other things too; such as aptitude, piety, patriotism, not excluding what he might be willing to do for them. "Did you not tell us that if elected you could get us rich farms in Euboea?" "Oh, I did not say that. I said

I could lead you to Euboea where farms are rich. Getting them is yet another matter, to be taken up later, if I am elected!"

When soundings had been taken in every corner the listeners circulated like purposeful bees, combining impressions, trying to strike a balance. This of course was to determine what was best for the state as a whole. They also hoped it would not be bad for them as individuals. "L'état c'est moi" is much older than the French king who made it famous. Indeed it lurks unspoken in every human heart. Athenians of the dawning golden age were not unlike the later representatives of homo sapiens. Although disposed to ignore or excuse faults of their own, they did not take these lightly in others, and wanted none at all in their public officers unless somehow the situation could be turned to advantage. In my scantily endowed country, each told himself, I can afford to overlook nothing.

Yet they would not be Hellenes if not drawn to the ideal. In sum and substance what they looked for was *areté,* that same manly goodness or excellence that excited their poets.[5] Possession of this one hundred years before had brought Solon to the forefront almost without effort on his part. Pisistratus and Cleisthenes must also have owned a proper share, although neither elegies nor biographies about those notables have survived to attest the fact. In the opening years of the fifth century the Athenian who was acknowledged to have it in the highest degree was Aristides, son of Lysimachus. Respect for him was general, yet curiously, position had little to do with it and bearing, even less. So unobtrusive that even the earliest authors were at odds as to his background, he apparently came of a good family in the district of Alopeke, one well enough off to qualify him for the chief offices, though falling short of affluence. In his youth, we are told, he was the close friend and confidant of Cleisthenes,[6] presumably tutored by the master in the principles of the reformed constitution. How much this boosted Aristides' stock with the people, it is difficult to judge. With such sponsorship he was sure to be a focus of attention.

A century later Plato was to remark that Themistocles, Pericles, and Cimon had filled Athens with stoas and various buildings, in fact all sorts of trumpery, but that Aristides had adorned her with good deeds.[7] However, an abundance of virtue often awakens resentment as well as admiration. Perhaps an awareness of this kept him from staking his claim — also a realization of the perils that an office brings. Goodness was not then any more than now without its penalties.

To find the proper man when the people themselves were so generally agreed, seems simple enough. But such simplicity is often deceptive. Cleisthenes, after strenuous services, had passed from the scene at about the beginning of the new century,[8] his passing obscured by our lack of information concerning those few years. Yet perhaps the best indication that he really intended a permanent "party of the demos" is that arrangement for a hereditary succession of sorts seems to have been made. This was more important than at first appears, since having marshaled the demos behind him, whoever he selected as prostates tou demou[9] would also normally be controller of the state—the demos being a vast majority.[10]

Since Cleisthenes (to our knowledge) had no children, the chieftaincy of the Alcmaeonid clan descended to his nephew, Megacles of Alopeke. Party leadership should have gone with it—in the struggle between the great houses, the Alcmaeonids were not about to let slip such a prize—but for whatever reason, the third Megacles chose not to hold it directly. Or maybe Cleisthenes chose for him. Instead, Megacles allowed the post of prostates to go to his brother-in-law, Xanthippus, son of Ariphron,[11] who had married his sister Agariste. With a gathering as amorphous as the party of the demos, the prostates needed to have an extraordinary facility in handling the Ekklesia, the councils, and the courts, those bodies which Solon and Cleisthenes had made so important. Perhaps Megacles of Alopeke recognized the lack of such qualities in himself, but saw them, or thought he did, in Xanthippus. Actually the conduct of affairs at Athens in the first decade of the fifth century hardly justified such confidence. The uneasy tandem of Xanthippus and Megacles made, or permitted, distinct blunders unworthy of the heirs of Cleisthenes. A case to disprove the saying that two heads are better than one.

Manifestly, the people would have preferred the young Aristides, but Cleisthenes must have determined otherwise. Aristides' youth counted against him, also his independent line,[12] always following the dictates of conscience. Additionally, though a noble, he was not from one of the outstanding families, toward whom the demos turned deferential if slightly resentful eyes, and from whom they automatically expected guidance. Besides, he was Megacles' neighbor in the Alopeke district northeast of the city, and probably had ties of friendship with the older man. The day was coming when he would have greatness thrust upon him, but that time was not yet.

For the moment, the very nature of Athenian politics ruled him out. Thus far none except those belonging to the great houses had been able to gain enough support from all of Athens' socioeconomic groups to control the state. These were actually three in number, whether seen in the Pisistratean light of Plain, Shore, and Hill—names not accurately descriptive of them—or from the standpoint of Solon's classification, which is just as misleading. For Solon's four classes are really three, probably based on a preexisting tripartite division.[13] His first two are practically indistinguishable as to civic responsibilities, both eligible for virtually the same offices, both rating as cavalry and thus qualifying as nobles, so that any not born in that state could become so by adoption, marriage, or other means. The old distinction between blood and wealth might still be visible, but lines were becoming blurred among the *agathoi* ("the good") as they liked to call themselves.[14] Significantly, the landed aristocrats most prominently mentioned are those who had also enriched themselves through trade. With Solon, all were hippeis or above, though the term hardly describes their activities—if a single word can.

Nor does the term zeugitai exactly characterize the next class below. Certainly a large number were farmers well enough off to own a pair of oxen *(zeugos),* but the zeugite income class would also contain a great many shopkeepers and craftsmen living in Athens and the smaller towns, probably as many demiourgoi as georgoi. Similarly, the bottom class, the thetes, would include hired laborers of both town and country, besides some free farmers on the worst lands. In ancient Attica the situation was complicated by even city people farming to supplement their income, and conversely, many farmers developed handicrafts as a sideline. Each of the three citizen classes was a mixture of many elements that had a good deal in common despite their diversity. Instead of using the Solonic names, it might be more convenient simply to call them High, Middle, and Low.

Moreover, the nature of their relations was ever changing. Acts of the recent past had enfranchised the Low, given them political clout, shifted the balance of power toward the Ekklesia. Xanthippus' task was to keep welded the combination of Middle and Low, with enough support from the High to divide it against itself and safeguard the state for Megacles, his Alcmaeonid kinsmen, and their political allies of Athens' commercial wing. Cleisthenes' reorganization of Attica had given his successors a natural advantage that they could not afford to neglect. Experience had taught them that the moment they relaxed their hold, prospective tyrants loomed. And there were some in Attica who required watching, besides the ever-menacing figure of Hippias across the seas in Asia, still moving heaven and earth for his restoration.

Recently Hippias had settled at Sardis, under protection of Artaphrenes, the Persian satrap of Lydia, who received the exiled tyrant on behalf of his royal master, the mighty Darius, King of Kings, "King of the All," latest and last augmenter of the enormous Persian Empire. From this dread source came a peremptory order that the Athenians should immediately recall Hippias as their ruler; it was clear that if he came, he would come as a blind covering Persian dominance. The Athenians reacted with anger, and their wrath was all too easily translated into sympathy for others under the Great King's shadow. When the kindred cities of Ionia flamed up and appealed for help, Athens' demos reacted with more emotion than reason, and Xanthippus seems not to have restrained them. Granting it was his party's policy to resist tyranny, he could still have met the situation with tact and caution. A tangle with Darius was something they would all regret.

Yet there was no crying eagerness for blood on anyone's part. Certainly none of the Hellenes had any intention of affronting the King. Those in Europe were glad of the intervening sea, and those of the islands also based agonized hopes upon it. But the Greeks of the Asian shore had no such comfort, and it was a case of infection spreading. A latent danger was recognized from the beginning. When the kingdom of Lydia expanded westward in the sixth century, it had absorbed successively the Ionian cities which dotted the broken coastline for nearly two hundred miles. There had been no frantic struggle or anguished outcry at the time. The Lydians were not Greeks, but their monarchs were admirers of Hellenic culture who spoke Greek, made lavish gifts to the temples and oracles, petting and spoiling the Hellenes who lived among them. The Ionians under Lydia had been so well pleased that formerly, when Cyrus of Persia had urged them to rise against the Lydian king Croesus, he had evoked no response. As a result, when Lydia fell the Greeks found themselves in an embarrassing situation with the conqueror. They asked him for the same status they had enjoyed under Lydia, but Cyrus, having no obligation toward them, refused. The cities then determined on a desperate stand for independence and even sought Spartan aid, without success. Left to their own devices, they were reduced one by one. Only Miletus was fortunate enough to secure a treaty affirming her previous rights. A restless quiet settled over Ionia.

Yet the Grecian fringe did not fare badly. Cyrus was on the whole an indulgent despot and the Persian system remarkably benign. The King often chose native leaders to govern, and he continued the donations to their temples. It was not as pleasant to be ruled from Susa as from nearby Sardis, but that could not be helped. If they were no longer especially favored, the Hellenes were compensated in the larger area of trade opened to them. Darius, when he came, was as reasonable as Cyrus. Clearly, there was no broad ground for complaint.

Still, the Asian Greeks were not entirely happy. Like those on the European side they cherished their own assemblies, having the common Hellenic love of freedom. Like them, they tended to look down on foreigners as barbarians. The stigma was sometimes conscious, sometimes not. All shared a mutual pride that "the arts had grown up among the Ionians,"[15] whose "climate and atmosphere were the most beautiful in the world,"[16] forgetting or ignoring the long march of civilization in the older Orient. Almost congenital was the feeling that their kind should be masters rather than subjects. Obviously a small spark would set them off; it is strange that the conflagration was delayed a generation.

When it came, the agent in the affair was Aristagoras, governor—some called him tyrant—of Miletus, one of those accommodating Greeks somehow able to reconcile the autocratic intentions of the King with his fellow countrymen's aspirations to liberty and self-determination. A man of glib assurances and promises, his good connections together with the ability to get along had raised him above the local residents. Under the prevailing tolerance he ruled the greatest of Ionian cities, deferring only to the satrapal authority of Artaphrenes and beyond him, the Lord of All. There is an unsolved mystery in this situation. Miletus was supposed to be free, or nearly so, by the terms of her treaty with Cyrus. Yet her preceding governor, Aristagoras' father-in-law, Histiaeus, had been removed by Darius and was being held virtually a prisoner at Susa on the pretext that the King "needed his advice." Perhaps Darius had revised Miletus' treaty to his own advantage.

Aristagoras was indeed a person set apart. However, people in his position are seldom content. When exiled Greek oligarchs from the large rich island of Naxos came to solicit his assistance against their homeland, he was quick to see in it a chance to extend his authority westward into the Aegean. The venturesome governor applied to Artaphrenes for permission to intervene and together they obtained the final sanction of Darius. After their expedition had left port Aristagoras fell into a quarrel with his colleague, the satrap's deputy in charge of the ships. The latter in a vengeful mood alerted the Naxian democrats, who surprised their assailants with a stout, carefully organized defense that endured for four months with no sign of crumbling. For the intriguers there was nothing to do but return to Asia.[17]

Back in Miletus, Aristagoras found that his failure had changed everything. He no longer enjoyed the confidence of his superiors. Fearing that he was about to be removed, the crestfallen tyrant forestalled disgrace by resigning, and simultaneously, by restoring elective government in the city. This was all that was needed. Aristagoras was immediately elected general by the joy-crazed Milesians. The "liberation" of Miletus launched a wave of popular risings in Mytilene, Cyme, Ephesus, then the others. In a surprisingly short time (499 B.C.) all of Ionia had cast off the Persian yoke, and rejoiced in the benefits of "freedom."

It was not to be expected that Darius would allow such defiance to go unpunished. Aristagoras knew this only too well, and for the safety of his skin made sail for European Greece toward the end of the year, seeking allies. Naturally his quest took him first to Sparta, the acknowledged hegemon. Here he unfolded attractive schemes of conquest, dazzling King Cleomenes with a burnished bronze tablet on which was inscribed a "map of the world," undoubtedly the first thing of its kind that that wide-eyed monarch had ever seen. A marvel unknown in Europe, it was a bright vision of the treasures of the East. The wily advocate was making tolerable headway with his bluntly nonintellectual royal host when Cleomenes, studying the map in baffled wonderment, asked him how far it was from the shores of Ionia to the promised riches of Susa. Aristagoras, for once unwary, replied that "it was three months' marching,"[18] whereupon the alarmed Cleomenes ordered him to be gone from Lacedaemon before sunset. It would never do for Spartans to leave their helots lightly guarded for such a period.

Athens was his next stop and here Aristagoras had better luck. Traditionally, Athens was reputed to be the mother city of all Ionians; it followed that Miletus and the other refractory sisters had a sentimental claim upon her generosity. This, coinciding with the agitation over Hippias' prospective restoration, was bound to have an effect. And Aristagoras, till lately an insider at the satrap's court, must have been fully aware of the advantage that such knowledge placed in his hands. For him this was enough. The squirming Ionian had lost none of his audacity. The more desperate he became, the more breathtaking were his lies. Subtly flattering his listeners, he magnified the abundance of Asia, which might be theirs for the taking. Why, the Persians fought without either spear or shield, he said, hence could put up but a feeble defense at best. Doubtless he flashed before them the shining bronze map, which under the sunny sky of Athens' roofless Assembly could perform unlimited wonders. In conclusion, Aristagoras reminded his listeners of Athens' obligation to captive offspring across the sea.

Athenians listening were bound to be interested. They knew Asia was far wealthier than their own pebble-strewn peninsula. If its natives were less virile, then the prospects were positively glowing. But was this actually so? If Persians came with neither spear nor shield, how had they won so large an empire, subduing Greeks as well as Asiatics? Aristagoras' clarifications have not been preserved; obviously, his tack was to avoid quizzing if he could. The wiser sort must have looked long and suspiciously at their overplausive "cousin." The upshot reveals a troubled audience and a divided house, one over which Xanthippus either neglected or failed to exert a statesmanlike influence. The Ekklesia finally voted aid, but only a small expedition of twenty ships under command of the general Melanthios.[19] Later, the Euboean city of Eretria added five of her own ships to the Athenian twenty. Miletus had helped her previously, and Eretria was repaying the debt. A more dangerous way of showing gratitude could hardly have been chosen.

The die was cast, but the allies made their throw without the finesse of Caesar. Granted that a Caesar does not appear every day, they could yet have managed the game with more skill. Hardly a chance of success existed, but what little there was lay in controlling the sea-lanes while supplying and defending the coastal cities. A faint hope glimmered that they could hold out long enough to make Darius prefer a negotiated peace in which a greater measure of autonomy might be conceded. If simultaneously the King should have urgent problems elsewhere, something of this sort might be achieved. This was the most they could expect, and only with unprecedented luck. Independence for Ionia at this stage was the wildest of dreams.

However, luck was not with them, or—much worse—only long enough to goad them to greater follies. The volunteers that rallied around Aristagoras acted more like mad roisterers than defenders of their homes and traditions. Crossing to Miletus, they hailed the great port's deliverance, then sailed north to Ephesus, Ionia's second city. Next came the craziest action of the campaign. At Aristagoras' urging the "liberators," abandoning their base on the Aegean, marched inland nearly seventy miles to attack the satrap at his court. Swaggering up the Cayster valley, they lurched across Mount Tmolus, and tumbling down upon Sardis, stormed the poorly guarded walls. What they thought to gain, apart from booty, cannot be imagined. Again, various suggestions have been made, but none is convincing.[20] An impulse so idiotic could have but one merit: it achieved a surprise so complete there was no resistance till the very end. Artaphrenes and his household troops managed to hold the citadel, but the lower town was quickly carried by the exulting Greeks. If plunder was an object, they were to be disappointed. Fires were set by the rampaging soldiers, and since Sardis' houses were mostly made of reeds, flames consumed all but the lofty stronghold. Below, nothing could be salvaged. Even the Temple of Cybele (Lydians originally called her Kybebe, the same goddess who reached Rome centuries later as *Magna Mater,* the "Great Mother"), Anatolia's dearest goddess, was destroyed. Terror-stricken, the townspeople gathered in the marketplace or along the banks of the river Pactolus. At last a dense throng stampeded toward the lines of their tormentors, and the Greeks withdrew over the hills in sudden alarm.

This was the ludicrous climax of the Ionian "crusade," with a recession that would lead swiftly to catastrophe. Nothing good had been effected, rather the reverse. Until then, Lydians had been either pro-Greek or neutral, considering the quarrel none of their affair. Now, in a fury of anger, they called for revenge. As news of the outrage spread, the Persian garrisons of Anatolia converged in pursuit of the marauders. The latter, while marching back to the Aegean coast, were overtaken near their journey's end and a pitched battle was fought in the outskirts of Ephesus—one in which the Greeks got the worst of it. A large number were killed, including the commander of the Eretrians. The allied host rapidly dissolved, each Ionian contingent hurrying to its own city. The Athenians sought safety on their ships, then refused to take any further part despite impassioned pleading from Aristagoras. Soon afterward they returned home, considerably deflated by their experience.

For the Ionian rebels, retribution was swift and grim. Abandoned by their European comrades, they persevered in a resolute stand for freedom and succeeded in raising the vast majority of Greeks on their side of the Aegean, from the Hellespont to Halicarnassus. Even the cities of Cyprus and Caria were imprudent enough to send components. However, all Asia was at the disposal of the King, and he soon had several divisions bearing down upon the insurgents. Everywhere the levies defending Ionia were beaten, the cities recaptured one after another. Miletus alone held out.

On the sea it was not so one-sided, the Ionian fleet gaining a victory or two over Persian squadrons mainly of Phoenician sail. But the King had only to call up new masses of warships from the anchorages of his never-ending realm. Gradually the Ionian navy found itself forced back upon Miletus, where it took up a position based on the island of Lade, covering the approaches to the great city's harbor. Here under a broiling sun the oarsmen practiced hard at maneuvers for the imminent combat—too hard, maybe.[21] Before long they were tired and carping at each other in the frank, free manner of sailors. Morale slowly ebbed. The Aegean islanders hassled with the crews from Greek Anatolia, and when the final battle with the Persians came, first the ships of Samos, then those of Lesbos took off for their homes. The rest fought to the bitter end—there was no other course—but were overwhelmed by an enemy more than twice as strong. The naval battle of Lade was the death knell of the Ionian Revolt. After this Miletus was invested by land and sea, the walls were mined, and the city finally stormed in 494, exactly six years after the proclamation of liberty. After this, the Milesians might expect the worst and their fears were well founded. Most men were killed straightway; the women and children disappeared into Oriental slave marts. The law of the Medes and Persians extended again to the shores of the Aegean.

All this the King of Kings took for granted. He had never doubted the Ionians would be flattened. But His Majesty had been astonished to learn from the earliest reports, that some others from beyond his kingdom had ventured to provoke him. Darius did not deign to admit he had ever heard of the Athenians when first told of their participation, declares Herodotus.[22] Scornfully, he asked who they were. To find that the people of a single city on the edge of the civilized world had dared so much could only increase his sense of outrage. Shooting an arrow into the air to release his volcanic emotions, he asked his god Ormazd for vengeance.[23] The Lord of All was so deeply stirred that it vexed him to think the matter might possibly slip his mind. A servant was appointed to jog his memory three times a day, before each meal with the words, "Master, remember the Athenians!" Put in this way, the business was sure to be settled, and without delay. Royalty requires that its repasts be festive and a king could not long endure having his food salted with such unpleasantness. The invasion of Attica was as certain as the morning sun.

So says Herodotus. There is nothing impossible about his colorful tale, but it does not tell the whole story. Darius had made at least one, possibly two expeditions into Europe previously: once, when he swallowed Thrace and Macedonia; then again, or maybe on the same occasion, when he fruitlessly pursued the Scythians north of the Danube to places unknown (ca. 516-512).[24] These and all his actions stamp him as a monarch of unbounded ambitions. Greece lay just beyond Macedonia, so of course Darius was well posted on it, and had placed Hellas-beyond-the-Aegean on the Persian timetable of conquest long since. If Macedonia were worth having, the Greek states were more so. Absolutely then, Darius had heard of the Athenians, the Spartans, the Corinthians. He was shortly to communicate his demands for their allegiance, as his deputy at Sardis had already done.

On grounds of policy as well, he must much earlier have resolved on the acquisition of European Greece.[25] The Ionians of Asia had been restless for decades before the Revolt, and with his sources of information, the King was perfectly aware of this. He had been suspicious of Aristagoras' predecessor as governor of Miletus, removing him to an "honorable captivity" at the royal court—hence Aristagoras' elevation. Darius knew too that his Ionian subjects would appeal to their European relatives whenever hostilities broke out. It required no extraordinary prescience to see that. To hold Ionia he had to try for the rest of Hellas and the prize would be well worth the effort. The commerce of one shore of the Aegean was his; he must therefore try for the other, so closely connected were they. A party of Persian nobles eager to make capital out of the Greeks already existed at the King's court headed by Mardonius, son of Darius' brother-in-law Gobryas. They were working to convince him—if he needed convincing. Darius' anger over Athenian intervention was genuine, but it served as a pretext rather than as the real cause of the Persian invasion of Greece.

Proof was forthcoming when, in 491, the King sent heralds to the principal Greek cities requiring the tokens of earth and water as symbols of submission. Not just to the Athenians and Eretrians, but to many others who had had no part in the Ionian Revolt. Some bowed to the ultimatum, some did not. In most cases the latter returned no answer, maintaining a discreet silence. Only Athens and Sparta flared into open defiance. The bluff Spartans threw the Persian messengers down a deep well, saying they would find plenty of both earth and water there, and might take what they liked. Though woefully inadequate by any standard of diplomatic practice, the response was at least in keeping with the Spartan character.

But the Athenians went even further. They flung Darius' envoys into the "pit of punishment,"[26] a treatment accorded common criminals. For inhabitants of a city which had already offended this was utter madness, conduct truly shocking when one considers Athens' guilt in Ionia. Accumulated exacerbation because of the asylum to Hippias, the satrap's haughty meddling, the fate of Miletus, must account for it, but this was no excuse. Xanthippus and Megacles had blundered again. Now Athens could expect the worst.

For the Athenians there was no way out and no turning back. It was a brutal, senseless deed to which they had stooped, giving mortal insult to the King of Persia, King of the All, on very slight provocation. Miletus had not dared as much, yet had suffered an Assyrian kind of devastation. How Athens muddled itself into such a fix might only be explained by one acquainted with the vagaries of its amply talented but equally perverse Ekklesia. The clamorers who had decreed the assistance to Ionia must have been substantially the same that a few seasons hence would labor strenuously to save Greece. On the former occasion they behaved like lunatics; later, they were to acquit themselves as heroes. Thus do circumstances mold men.

It was unfortunate that the problem should present itself at a period when Athens' party system was still embryonic, thus without firm policies or discipline of the constituents. Although Xanthippus had functioned for several years as leader of the demos, also occasionally called *hoi polloi* ("the Many"), or *to Pléthos* ("the Mass")[27]—so wide was its range—his control was far from steady. Lack of organization left him no means of compulsion. By and large, prosperity was the best binder. When trade was lively the zeugite farmer could find buyers for his wine and olive oil, which gave him his cash surplus. But when the market slackened, as it did at this time because of Athens' disputes with Aegina, the farmer was first to suffer. Oil and wine normally had a high demand, but were not as important as bread. Usually the Greek dipped his roll in one or the other, but when necessary he could gnaw a dry loaf. Then the peasant grumbled and cursed the tradesman. Given any unusual stress, the combination of "the Many" was in danger of falling apart.

What "the Many" needed to guide them was a humble, but outstandingly successful man of wealth and impeccable reputation, or one born to elegance who had not hesitated to toil with the rest. But Xanthippus was no Solon. He was a noble of moderately distinguished lineage, elevated still higher by an Alcmaeonid marriage.[28] An heiress from this family was a fine catch, and Xanthippus could not be blamed for making the most of his opportunities. Still, a glamorous wedding did little to endear him to the demos. It was hard to see Xanthippus as a man of the people. Cleisthenes had not been either, but Cleisthenes had furnished the Many with ample evidence of his more or less sincere devotion, which his nephew-in-law had not. He might be the standard-bearer of the demos, the Many, but it was absurd to identify him with hoi polloi.

Undeniably, this weakened him vis-à-vis the poverty-stricken in his own party. The Low had not yet got the habit of asking steady alms from the state, and in passable times would remain quiet, suffering their highbrow leader. But if it came to a real pinch, and the thetes found the Middle could not take care of them, there was the ever-present threat that they might drop back nearer their own class to look for more suitable representation.

In such a case, the discontented would not have far to seek. Themistocles, son of Neocles, one not so well placed as the relative of Megacles and Cleisthenes, but just as persevering, was already making moves that would gain their favor. His position in the society of his day is difficult to affix. The ancient writers stigmatized his origin, and there is no convincing explanation why they did so. Plutarch says of him that "his family was too obscure to further his reputation,"[29] and Herodotus, that he had but "lately made his way into the first rank of citizens."[30] It is also alleged that he was poor. Yet his family, the Lycomids, belonged to the nobility, and his income was obviously large enough to qualify him for the archonship, which he had held in 493/2. One wonders if the legend of lowliness was a contrived propaganda device. Whether or not this helped his election, during his term as archon Themistocles began the building and fortification of the harbor of Piraeus, which Athens greatly needed for defense as well as commerce. Significantly, it also provided immediate jobs for men of the thete class, with prospects of permanent employment as the business of the new harbor increased. How much of this was deliberate planning by the keen-witted Themistocles cannot be proven,[31] but as early as 493, the Low had developed a good opinion of him. If others questioned his areté, they would give him the benefit of the doubt. A star was rising which the most abject could see.

Xanthippus' worries did not end here. For a prolonged period, since the days of Isagoras, the aristocrats had lacked a mutually acceptable head. Suddenly, from beyond the horizon, one appeared. Miltiades, son of Cimon, was the most renowned member of the ne plus ultra Philaid clan, but after early honors which presumably included the archonship,[32] he had long been absent in the north. Two generations before, his uncle of the same name had founded the family fortunes there when Thracian tribesmen of Chersonese—the Dardanelles region—had invited him to rule as a king, giving access to their forests, fields, mines. The Philaids were indeed despots in this lucrative northern barony, but no complaints were heard in Athens until the younger Miltiades arrested and imprisoned some of the chief men, incidentally treating Athenian colonists in the same arbitrary manner as the Thracian natives. Thus the label of tyrant was attached to him, and word reached Athens that he had married a Thracian princess, and went about accompanied by five hundred mercenaries who forced his will on the free and unfree alike. That Miltiades had a veritable lust for money and power could hardly be denied. Here too areté might be somewhat tarnished, but there was grandeur suitable to an Athenian. Countrymen who felt his sting cursed and envied—perhaps secretly admired. Why could not they have been as lucky as he?

Whatever his status in the north, it was eclipsed when the real King, the King of Kings, entered. In due course, the mighty Darius had crossed into Europe. Miltiades and his fellow princelings had no choice but to become vassals of Persia. He must have been an obedient one for many years, in spite of later vociferous denials. In 513, he had been one of those entrusted with guarding Darius' bridge of boats at the Danube crossing while the King went off hunting the Scythians. For a dozen more years "the tyrant of the Chersonese" made no trouble. But on hearing of the Ionian Revolt he had taken advantage of the King's preoccupation with Miletus to seize the grain-rich islands of Lemnos and Imbros,[33] which had previously given their allegiance to Persia.

It was a foolish thing to do. When the revolt collapsed Miltiades returned to Athens in a hurry, pursued by Darius' navy. Back home after decades of truancy, the crafty manipulator now maintained he had taken the islands merely to present them to his native city. Soon he was telling how he had opposed Darius on the Scythian expedition, inciting his fellow guardsmen to cut the bridge of boats so as to leave the King stranded north of the Danube. It was not very likely. Had the story been true, Miltiades would have paid with his head years ago—some of the guards were unfriendly to him.[34] But a desperate man does not hesitate to twist or fabricate. Athens was an uncomfortable place for him too, and it was necessary to capitalize on the rising anti-Persian sentiment quickly before vengeful colonists from the north caught up with him. Obviously, his best line was to beat a chauvinistic drum and cry danger. Much better to loose a stampede than be caught in one.

Of course Miltiades immediately took his place in the Ekklesia as one of the most prominent aristocrats. Able, audacious, and outgoing, with an already substantial reputation augmented by his own facile inventions, he was the ideal spokesman for the blueblood Eupatrids that had once comprised the party of the Plain. They were there in undiminished supply, more prudent perhaps but just as proud, and still sighing for the days before Solon. Without prospect of controlling the Assembly themselves, they needed a person of compelling magnetism to fire the hearts of the majority and win them votes. Miltiades seemed just the man. Or was he? The Eupatrids were a curiously inconsistent group, not easy to please. Though identified with the High and thus vaguely internationalist in foreign policy,[35] most of them were fundamentally Attica-oriented, stubbornly growing barley and some wheat while diversifying with grapes and olives. But the Philaids, outwardly staunch and pious, had, like the Alcmaeonids, recognized larger possibilities. Rumors reaching the stay-at-home nobles of their hero's movements in the north were enough to make them rub their chins and wonder. Not that they minded his bullying a few low-born colonists. Hobnobbing with kings and marrying princesses was another matter, however. After early support to their neighbor Pisistratus, the Philaids had been solid in their opposition to tyranny at home, never swaying from the aristocratic-oligarchic line.[36] Yet first the elder and afterward this younger Miltiades had accepted commissions from the Pisistratids, then when safely away in the north had hastened to imitate them.

All of this was disquieting, to say the least. Still, the "Viceroy of the Chersonese" could claim that in his distant possession he had simply tempered his methods to the occasion. Actually, he had good reason to hate the Pisistratids, who had killed his father. As for pretensions to royalty, had he not dared the King of Persia himself and lost his extensive properties for their sakes? Whatever the truth, it was obvious that once on his native soil in Athens, Miltiades became a strong advocate of preparedness and his cosmopolitan views were trimmed to an ardent nationalism. Under these circumstances, Attica's High, veering in the same direction,[37] could line up behind him with a show of enthusiasm.

It was lucky for him that they did. The demos shortly had its case in hand against the malefactor, and in 493 Miltiades was formally accused. Not improbably it was Xanthippus who preferred the charges,[38] anxious to head off a challenge to his authority. But of this nothing is said. Neither do we know in which court the prosecution was entered, nor what the exact nature of the accusation was, save that it involved tyranny. After much ado the trial broke down and Miltiades had the satisfaction of an acquittal. Possibly he gained by the publicity and the botched attempt to besmirch his name. A man as clever as he would be able to counterattack, even create divisions among his accusers, parading himself meanwhile as the upholder of liberty.

Something of the sort is suggested by the sequence of events. We are told that the chief archon for the year was Themistocles. If he was indeed the judge who pronounced the acquittal, it was probably because he recognized in Miltiades a valuable ally against Hippias and Persia;[39] also it afforded him a once-in-a-lifetime chance to strike at Xanthippus' primacy among the demos. Themistocles was prying at the gate.

Not long after his release Miltiades was elected one of the ten generals, who since Cleisthenes' reform were entrusted with the defense of the state. The aristocrats had brought their candidate through successfully, and for the first time in a generation were a significant force in politics. Conversely, Xanthippus had stumbled a third time. Clearly, his directorship had been shaken. On the right as well as on the left, competitors had emerged who would bear watching. Belatedly, the Athenians were finding others who could lead—and were more than willing to do so.

It was high time. Darius was already preparing Persia for war against Athens. In late summer of the year 490, the Persian armament commanded by the Median general Datis, moved up the line of the Cyclades and at last reached the island of Euboea, adjacent to the European mainland. In a spacious bay near Euboea's southern tip lay the port of Carystus, treading the foot of Mount Ocha. This community had never given offense to the King, yet Datis demanded hostages and military support, just as in the Cyclades. But from Carystus came the first absolute refusal. Oddly, the people made no attempt to flee up the nearby mountain upon the Persians' approach. However, they would not give hostages nor agree to bear arms against their neighbors. Datis had to put the town under siege. Only when he had cut them off from any hope of relief and had thoroughly devastated their fields did he obtain compliance.

The treatment of Carystus was heavy-handed, but militarily justified. Its wide roadstead offered an excellent shelter for the Persian fleet and, roughly equidistant from Eretria and Athens, might be used as a forward base of operations against each. With his headquarters at Carystus, Datis could watch both cities closely, arousing their inhabitants to fever pitch as they tried to guess his plans. It was well suited to psychological warfare and basic strategy, and in the memory of a later generation the ploy achieved its purpose.[40] The Greeks were badly frightened. As a result they formed a grossly exaggerated notion of the Persian strength. Herodotus had heard that Datis commanded 600 fighting ships, without counting transports for men and horses. He gives no numbers as to troops, but other ancient writers made estimates running as high as 600,000, based on only the wildest hearsay. A cautious modern scholar calculates that there were possibly 25,000 foot soldiers and 1,000 cavalry in the expedition anchored at Carystus.[41] Even so, it was far larger than any venture undertaken in the Aegean world up to this time.

No military campaign involving the ancient Greeks has been subjected to so much able scholarly analysis, with so little agreement about conclusions, as the one that climaxed at Marathon. Because of Herodotus' omissions and insufficiencies and the paucity of other sources, it could hardly be otherwise.[42] Each study of the subject settles, or seems to settle basic questions, only to create new ones. Then the old interpretations unexpectedly recur. To a certain extent, the issue lies between the strict classicists and scientists who take their stand upon Herodotus and archaeology, and the military experts who insist that the traditional account is not tactically plausible. But even this is an oversimplification; many positions between the two extremes have been taken. And remembering that war itself is not very reasonable and that even the best commanders make mistakes and thus are not absolutely predictable, one doubts whether the absolute truth about Marathon will ever be known.

In brief, Herodotus tells us that from Carystus, the Persian armament traveled up the Euboean coast to besiege Eretria, and on the seventh day of the siege, the city fell. Thus the Eretrians appealed for aid to the Athenians, who instead of sending it, directed 4,000 of their "cleruch" colonists on Euboea to give assistance. But the cleruchs were advised by an Eretrian that their help would be useless, so they fled across to Attica instead. Meanwhile the Persians burned Eretria, enslaved the inhabitants, and in a few days sailed for Attica themselves. They landed on the plain of Marathon by the advice of the Pisistratid Hippias, because it gave them sufficient room to maneuver their cavalry. Then the Athenians ordered their army to Marathon—an army of which Callimachus was the polemarch, and one of whose ten generals was Miltiades. A runner was sent to ask aid of the Spartans; he returned with news that they could not come for several days because of a religious festival currently in progress.

Among the many questions Herodotus leaves unanswered are several of prime importance. Did the whole Persian army go to Eretria from Carystus, or only a part of it? The doubtful story of the cleruchs aside, did the Athenians make any real effort to help the Eretrians? When the Persians landed at Marathon, where did they make camp, and where did they draw their battle line? Where was their cavalry, which Herodotus does not mention at all, after the landing? Similarly, what of the Greek camp and battle position? We are told simply that the Athenians drew up their line in "a precinct sacred to Heracles" where they were joined by their allies from Plataea. But nothing presently exists to show where the Heracleion stood, nor is there any general agreement among authorities on this point. Also, what of the numbers involved on both sides? Later writers have estimated 9,000 to 10,000 Athenians (based on the ten tribal regiments), plus 1,000 Plataeans, as against the total Persian potential of at least 26,000. But as to this, Herodotus is silent.

Commentators sharing the militarist view have maintained there was much more to the campaign than the bare outlines given us. By their thinking, the Persian commander Datis, a capable general deserving of Darius' trust, could have taken the smaller town of Eretria with about half of his total force, hence initially he would have committed no more than half his armament to this project. They suggest that he delegated the Eretrian matter to his junior colleague Artaphrenes, remaining himself at Carystus. Now the Athenians had to decide what to do. Again, Herodotus gives us little information, but apparently it was Miltiades' resolution to put the troops in motion which passed the Assembly, and there is indirect evidence that his proposal was to go to the relief of Eretria.[43] This would obviate the story about the cleruchs, which has been challenged as a later apologetic invention, because no Athenians appeared to assist the Eretrians. By the militarists' view, as the Attic hoplites were marching northeastward under their polemarch Callimachus, they heard something which altered their plans. The astute Datis, watching

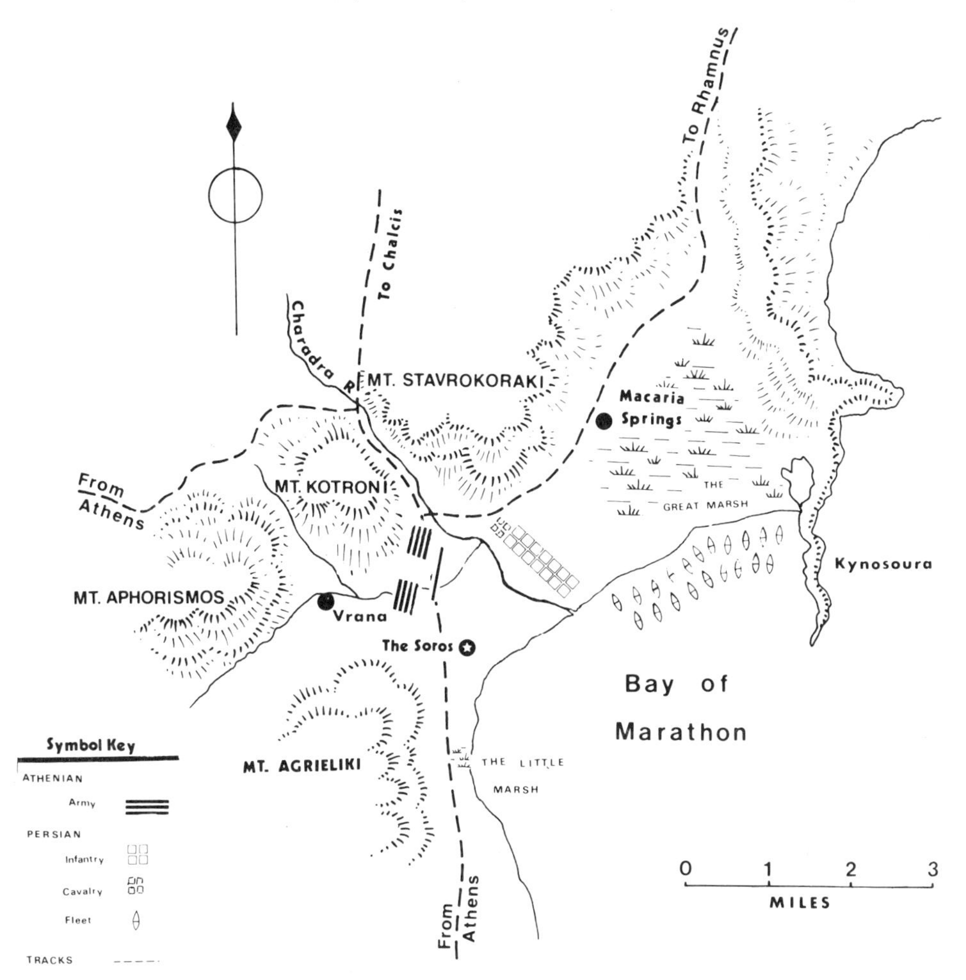

THE BATTLE OF MARATHON
ORIGINAL POSITION

from Carystus on Euboea, had anticipated them by bringing over his reserve division, landing on Attica's east coast at the plain of Marathon where he would have a free road to Athens, behind the advancing Athenians. Thus Callimachus had to give up the march to Oropus, first stage in the projected crossing to the island of Euboea, and hastily double back to the right around Mount Pentelicus, then down the small valley of Avlona to the coastal plain of Marathon, in order to protect the roads to Athens. Eretria had to be left to its fate.[44]

Virtually all students of the campaign agree that Datis must have moored his ships and landed his men close to the northern extremity of the

Marathon plain, to gain the protection of Cape Kynosoura's jutting spine. He made his camp north of the little stream Charadra, which bisects the plain, where he would have the stream's protection with that of Mount Stavrokoraki immediately to the west. Behind his camp to the north lay the Great Marsh, fed by the spring of Makaria, which assured an abundant water supply.

After this, the views of scholars diverge. Some, mindful of military science, hold that Datis must have stayed in this position even for the eventual battle, on the defensive until his other division arrived from Eretria. They argue that to give up these advantages by moving on to the open plain south of the Charadra, moreover, to select a new position with the sea at his back (as Herodotus implies), would reveal incredible stupidity in an experienced commander such as Datis. By the same token, it was news of the fall of Eretria, after several days of silent waiting at Marathon, that steeled the Athenians to a desperate attack on the Persians before the enemy forces could be doubled.[45]

The chief obstacle to this thesis, besides Herodotus' noncorroboration, is the site of the Athenian burial mound (normally located close to the center of battle) nearly a mile south of the Charadra. Assertions that the Athenians could have carried their dead such a distance, since so few were killed, have not found general acceptance. Classicists opposed to the foregoing thesis have stressed the importance of the mound (*soros*)[46] and have upheld Herodotus' narrative on most points, seeing little need to supplement it. The incongruity of Datis' position is usually attributed to overconfidence on his part (following the hint in Herodotus), or to his desire to cover the Athens road.

A major difficulty in this theory is Herodotus' glaring omission of the Persian cavalry, so necessary to Datis if he were to take a position anywhere on the open plain. To meet this problem, exponents have relied on a story found in a late scholium, or annotation on the text, stating that friendly Ionians in the enemy force had crept toward the Athenian lines and signaled the defenders that "the cavalry are away."[47] Supposedly, this emboldened the Greeks to commence their attack. However, if one accepts the scholium as true, which cannot be done easily, too many questions remain unanswered. Why was the cavalry absent? Had it ever landed? Was it still at Eretria? Or if, as one distinguished authority has proposed, the cavalry had just embarked for the dash around to Phaleron,[48] then why did not Datis quickly withdraw his infantry to a safer place north of the Charadra? To such questions and speculations, no end.

Now it becomes necessary to backtrack to consider the plight of the Athenian Assembly. An appeal for help had been received from Eretria, one which was answered sympathetically. But how? Herodotus' story about the cleruchs has already been noted, and is not very convincing. It is unlikely that Athens had 4,000 *cleruchs* (colonists of a special type, who retained their citizenship in the mother city and were governed from the mother city) in the area so early,[49] nor could this number make much difference in the outcome. If

Athens intended to send effective relief to Eretria, it would require an all-out effort involving nearly all her manpower. There were considerable risks. It was a march of thirty-odd miles to the Boeotian coast where a crossing to Euboea might be made over the neck of wild water known as the Euripus. Since this was less than seven hundred yards wide at the southern extremity, and not more than fifty at Chalcis,[50] it has been assumed that the Athenian navy could control and protect the crossing. Yet we know little about Athens' navy at this time; a year or two before, Athens had had to borrow ships from Corinth to fight Aegina. Whether her miniscule fleet of 490 B.C. could hold even so small a passageway as the Euripus against a Persian armada of several hundred is at least problematical. If the attempt failed, her main fighting force might be trapped on Euboea, and everyone knew what that meant. Nor could much be expected of the weakened remnant at Athens.

On the other hand, to deny assistance meant that in due course Athens herself must endure the full weight of the Persian thrust. It was a grim prospect either way. The debate in the Ekklesia must have been long and anxious. Naturally, the support of the Peloponnesian League would be needed, so the state runner, Pheidippides, was despatched to Lacedaemon in all haste. Meanwhile the Athenians continued to ponder how best to commit their own forces, or whether to commit them at all.

The party of the demos, its various elements loosely glued in a nationalistic fervor steadily more hostile to Persia,[51] would normally favor the more belligerent course as the best means of preserving their independence, hard won under the constitution of Cleisthenes. But in this instance the usual majority would not hold. Once again, there was disagreement between the classes, even within the classes. The Middle was concerned with commercial interests that required peace with Persia, and there were those, especially among the Low, who still felt affection for the returning Pisistratids.[52] Partly because of the recently ineffective leadership of Xanthippus and Megacles of Alopeke, party and faction tended to dissolve over the entire issue. Much more important was each individual's assessment of the situation: his temperament, his courage, his fundamental instincts.

Here was Miltiades' chance. For once the aristocrats could tip the balance, and it was his business to see that they lined up beside the hawkish wing of the demos under Themistocles,[53] strengthening the will to resist. Pro-Persian or neutral in the past, the mounting pressure of events had been driving these former men of the Plain steadily uphill. Miltiades was determined to swing them over the hump, and by playing upon their fears he swung a sufficient number. Thus he formed a combination which, if held, might make him the foremost man in the state.

Cleverly, he brought them to his point of view. Staying at home they would be too vulnerable. How he developed the theme is unknown, but from the arguments Herodotus attributes to him at Marathon, the main line is obvious. If the Persians were allowed to reach Athens and parade their impressive numbers on Attica's central plain, the people's will to resist would melt away.[54] Their only hope was to forestall the Persians by prompt resolute action at a better place. Miltiades' decree passed the Ekklesia—this is attested by three later writers—but whether his proposal was to go to the relief of Eretria (as Aristotle quotes another statesman as saying)[55] or to go directly to Marathon (as Herodotus has them do)[56] remains unsettled. In Eretria's favor were the defensive capabilities of its walls; if the Persians could be checked here, on Euboea, Athens and the European mainland might be spared altogether. If it were to be Marathon, they would at least have the advantage of the higher ground covering both roads to Athens.

So a decision was taken to confront the Persians, and a runner was sent to summon Athens' Plataean allies. The next morning the Athenian army of ten tribal regiments, spears clenched, marched out of the city northeastward, under command of the polemarch Callimachus. Miltiades, Xanthippus, and Aristides, as generals for the year 490, were among the commanders of the ten tribal regiments. Themistocles apparently went as a common soldier, as did the poet Aeschylus. Whatever their original destination, the course of events brought them eventually to Marathon. If one hews to the time-honored account, the Athenians, hearing of the Persian landing, marched there directly. However close Herodotus may have come as to this, his explanation of the Athenian command structure and its decision-making misses the mark. By his telling, the ten generals had complete control of the forces in war, took a majority vote on whether to fight, and each commanded the entire army by a daily rotation; the polemarch's post was largely honorary and he voted only in case of a tie. Having been chosen by lot rather than election, he was a military nonentity.

Such was indeed the situation when Herodotus was writing, two generations later, but it began only with the reforms of 487 B.C., three years after Marathon.[57] The contradiction between Athens' constitution as he knew it, and the Marathon story as he had heard it, resulted necessarily in a jumbled narrative. If Callimachus had little more than a figurehead's role, then why did he play such an important part in the battle?

Herodotus explains it as neatly as he can. The Persian host, known to them as the select warriors of the mighty Darius, were viewed by the anxious Athenian generals who divided five against five on whether to fight. The most insistent of the hawks, we know, was Miltiades—and with good reason. His head would certainly fall if he were caught by the King. Finding he could not prevail, that sentiment was veering the other way, the burning patriot went to Callimachus to persuade him to vote and break the tie. In the interest of the greater good, Miltiades did not hesitate to mix shrewd wisdom with abject flattery. The present was not only their best chance, but the critical moment, he said. Morale among the citizens in the metropolis was not firm; it would suffer irreparably if the army hesitated to fight where it had an advantage, allowing the Persians to appear in force before the city itself. On the other hand, if Callimachus gave them his vote and acted boldly, Athens could become the first city in Greece, and his name would be honored there as greater than those of the revered tyrannicides, Harmodius and Aristogeiton.[58] Callimachus was duly impressed and gave his approval.

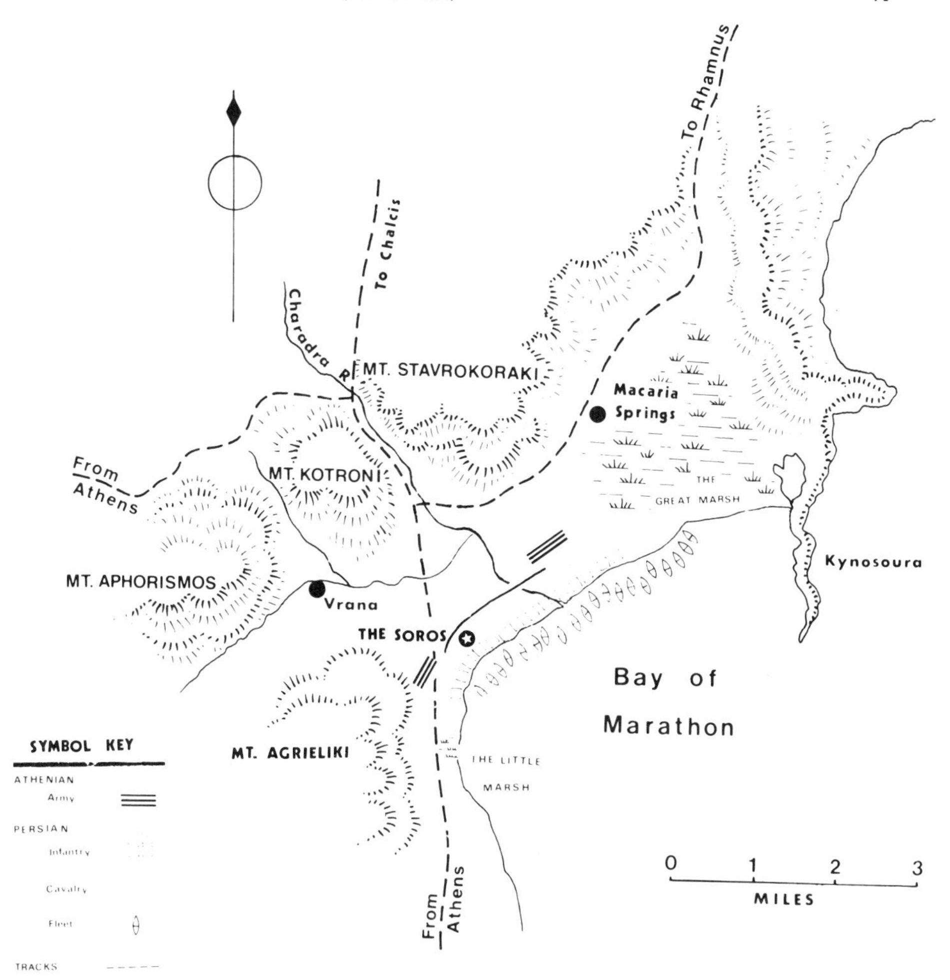

THE BATTLE OF MARATHON
FINAL POSITION

Next Herodotus relates another oddity. The decision to attack had been taken. All four generals in favor, he says, gave up their turn in the rotation to Miltiades, to give him a free hand. Yet he chose not to grasp the opportunity, but waited for his own day to arrive. Why? He who had told Callimachus that time was of the essence, now was delaying the issue. This may be Herodotus' way of telling us that several days elapsed between the confrontation and the battle, but it does not explain the contradictory behavior. A basic flaw is seen below the surface.

This becomes more apparent as the action begins. What provided the final impetus to attack, we are not told, except that it was "Miltiades' day."

Herodotus implies, without saying so directly, that it was Miltiades who determined the strategy, extending the Greeks into a long line with strong wings so as not to be outflanked by the larger Persian forces—a formation which left the center dangerously thin. However, it was Callimachus and his tribal regiment who held the traditional post of honor on the right wing, with the other tribes following "as they were numbered, in an unbroken line," and last of all, the Plataeans on the left wing.[59]

By one surmise it was news of the fall of Eretria, by another it was information that the Persian cavalry had embarked, by still another, a suspicion that the Persians themselves were about to move that precipitated the action. The explanation coming closest to conviction is an ingenious combining of the last two. By this theory, the Persian general, Datis, found the Greek position on the hills too strong to be quickly forced, and the Marathon plain not as well adapted to the use of cavalry as he had expected. Hence the impasse of several days. However, Datis could not afford to wait long, so he decided to reembark his army under cover of night, to try a more favorable landing elsewhere, probably at Phaleron. But this was a difficult and complicated operation in which the horses would have to be embarked first; its execution required more time than was available, so that at the night's end the Persian cavalry were safely on board, but a large part of the infantry were still awaiting their turn. Thus at daybreak, when discovered by the Greeks, a substantial portion of the Persian army minus its cavalry was lined up in a fatally exposed position along the seashore, where it had never intended to fight.[60]

For the Athenians, the opportunity was too good to miss. They opened the attack, charging on the run, probably for about 300 yards rather than the mile that Herodotus cites.[61] In an exposed mile run they would have tired considerably, allowing the Persian archers to cut them to ribbons. As the two lines locked in combat, the Persians appeared to have the initial advantage, breaking the weak Athenian center and pursuing its shattered remnants "toward the interior." Uncertainty as to the position of the two lines makes it impossible to locate the point of breakthrough and pursuit, except that it must have been somewhere not too far from the aforementioned burial mound.[62]

On the wings, where the Greek strength was in better proportion to the Persian, the outcome remained longer in doubt. But gradually the momentum of the attackers prevailed. The hard pressed Persian wings found themselves exposed and cut off from one another, their line broken by the impulsive forward surge of their center. Finally the embattled wings disintegrated, some men fleeing toward the shore, others northward into the Great Marsh, where large numbers were trapped and slaughtered.

Meanwhile the reserve regiments of the Greeks had filled in the vacated middle, separating the rampaging Persians of the center from the others. These were hemmed in, crushed together, and they too were struck down in their disorganized condition. The shattered remnants of the invaders were beaten back to the shore, where the triumphant Greeks chased them into the water and even tried to lay hold of and burn the ships. Here Callimachus at last fell, after carrying everything before him on the right wing. Stesilaus, one of the generals, was also slain, and Cynegeirus—a brother of Aeschylus—had a hand cut off as he tried to seize the stern of a Persian boat. Altogether the Athenians lost only 192 killed, while the Persian dead was placed, perhaps too optimistically, at 6,400.

It had been a stunning victory, as overwhelming as it was unexpected, hence one to shock and thrill all the Greeks. But Persian overconfidence and miscalculation had had as much to do with it as Athenian valor and planning.[63] In the allotment of kudos, assuredly a major share should go to Callimachus. Undoubtedly he was still commander in chief in the year 490, and the ultimate decisions had to be his. He had deployed the regiments wisely, taken the post of honor, and led the charge that routed the enemy. To what degree his powers were hedged by those of the generals, before the reform of 487, cannot be determined. Cleisthenes had made the generals important, but not yet supreme. Hence it is difficult to evaluate the part played by Miltiades. It was his decree that had brought them to Marathon, he had urged the bold course throughout, very possibly he had much to do with planning the strategy that Callimachus used. It has even been suggested, since Miltiades had acknowledged political prestige and Callimachus was relatively unknown before the battle, that the polemarch may have been Miltiades' protégé, accepting his judgments without question.[64] Subsequent developments lend credence to this, but Miltiades may have had something to do with those happenings. The polemarch's death in battle made it easy for the survivor to claim the palm, and he was in an excellent situation to do so.

But that could wait. The danger was not over. Datis had managed to reembark more than half of his men and, still a potent threat, he sailed around Cape Sunium and into Phaleron, hoping to take the metropolis by surprise. However, he made no attempt to land. Apparently, information reached him that the grand opportunity had passed. Waves of excitement about a mysterious shield signal seen flashing from a nearby mountaintop were later to rock Athens. But whether this was a warning to the Persians that they had insufficient sympathizers in the city to justify a landing,[65] or whether it was a message to the Greeks themselves about the disposition of the Persian forces, as some have claimed,[66] no one has ever been able to determine. The Alcmaeonids, not without some justification, were suspected of playing a double game, of ingratiating themselves with the Persians while simultaneously posing as the stoutest of patriots—a charge Herodotus denies.[67]

Other explanations of Datis' withdrawal are equally plausible. Rumor may have heralded the approach of the Spartans who, according to Plato, did actually arrive the next day.[68] Knowledge of this and of the outcome of the battle, would prevent any rising in the city by the partisans of Hippias. We are told also that the victorious Athenians took no rest at Marathon, but marched back to Athens before nightfall,[69] leaving Aristides and his regiment to guard the Persian dead. Datis' bold move was foiled. Giving up, he weighed anchor, then steered for Asia and home. The Eretrian prisoners were herded off with him. They were fearful of receiving the full brunt of Darius' rage, but the King treated them amazingly well. By royal decree the entire group was settled at a place called Arderica, only twenty-six miles from the Persian capital, Susa, where they long survived, a Greek island in a sea of Orientals.

One infers that in Athens the initial reaction was one of immense relief, gradually giving way to unbounded jubilation. Seven of the invaders' ships had been taken as prizes of war. When the Spartans appeared, 2,000 strong, nothing remained to be done. Nevertheless they insisted on going to Marathon to behold with their own eyes the memorable field with so many fallen Persians. Few, if any, had ever seen the awesome "Mede." Having looked their fill, they departed for Lacedaemon after many compliments to the Athenians. It was a delicious moment. Spartans did not give praise lightly.

In the bubbling metropolis, there was no question that Miltiades was the hero of the hour. Much credit was due him, all were agreed: he made the most of the situation. With his insinuating Philaid relatives and their many aristocratic friends to help, a legend was created that had grown enormously by the time Herodotus heard it. But his fame was great enough even without this. Themistocles was reported to have said that he could not sleep nights, from thinking of the trophy won by Miltiades.[70] The envy of such a rival was regal tribute, the more so because reluctantly given. The onetime tyrant of the Chersonese seemed to have picked up his scepter again, curiously, in republican Athens.

Inevitably, he was tempted to display his power. Before long he pressured the Ekklesia to vote him a fleet of 70 triremes—which must have meant nearly the whole Athenian navy at that period—and a body of troops for a purpose which he disdained, absolutely refused, to disclose. For sheer presumption there have been few like him. He would only say that his project was against a luxuriant land which could afford to pay whatever they chose to lay upon it. He hinted broadly that all who cared to accompany him would make their fortunes. Resolving not to be outdone in magnificent conceptions, the Ekklesia agreed to everything Miltiades asked. The expedition turned out to be against the island of Paros, seventy miles southeast in the Aegean. Paros had offended by contributing a single ship to the Persian armament—though it had done so under compulsion. Renowned as the home of the poet Archilochus, whose impassioned lyrics first brought the iambic into prominence, Paros was a spot singularly beloved by all Greeks for its literary associations as well as its translucent white marble, cut for the choicest of their statues and temples. Not many could join with enthusiasm in a campaign undertaken here.

Morale was not elevated by whispers that Miltiades was motivated at bottom by a private grudge against individuals on the island. His real object was most likely private gain, as in the Imbros affair years earlier. He landed on the coast and quickly drove the Parians within the walls of their city. While preparing to lay siege he sent a herald to demand an indemnity of 100 talents, threatening harsh punishment if the money were not handed over instantly. To his surprise the Parians had the courage to refuse, then began working incessantly to double the height of their walls. The bullying general tried for twenty-six days to batter down the reinforced ramparts, then had to withdraw with nothing to show for his efforts.[71] During the siege he suffered an injury to his thigh—nobody was quite sure how—which incapacitated him and grew steadily worse.

What followed constitutes an interesting lesson in Athenian politics. Athenian voters did not forgive faulty conduct, and their own gullibility increased their fury. The Man of Marathon was no longer eulogized. Sensing the opportunity for a recoup, Xanthippus filed an accusation against him for having deceived the state. The case was listed for trial before the full Assembly rather than the ordinary courts, and grimly, Xanthippus asked for the death penalty. He could now eliminate his most dangerous challenger. Save for a single appearance when he was carried in on a stretcher, Miltiades was too ill to attend the trial. The Philaids and their noble relatives girded themselves for a last-ditch defense of their hero, pointing out his many services to the state, at home and abroad. They could not secure an acquittal, but in the end managed to bring the sentence down to a fine of fifty talents. Ironically, the fallen champion was ordered to dip into his own purse for one-half of what he had intended to exact from the Parians. He died before it could be collected.[72] In due course the fine was paid for him by his son Cimon, who thus made his first public appearance an act of filial piety.

When passions had cooled, Miltiades' compatriots were able to see him in a kinder light. Indubitably, he had saved Athens and many another community. Hellas would have a longer time to prepare now for the climactic Persian onslaught. The fact that he acted from egoistic motives does not lessen his countrymen's debt to him. Were not most of them moved in the same way? His value to the cause lay in his personal contact with the King of Persia, his insights into the working of the King's mind, hence his grasp of the realities of the situation. Miltiades knew that for Athens, as for himself, there could be no forgiveness, no compromise. He stiffened the nation's backbone in an irresolute hour, and saw the Athenian polis through its first international crisis.

Whether he deserves more praise is a moot point. Larger concepts of policy seem to have escaped him. An attempt has been made to justify his attack on Paros on the ground that it was the first step in creating a line of buffer islands to absorb and soften the next Persian blow.[73] It is difficult to agree. Miltiades made no such profession before the Ekklesia when unveiling the barest details of his dubious proposition. An effective buffer policy would have called for permanent installations on the island and conciliation of the natives. Such a scheme could not hold anyway, should Persia in her power choose to come this way again. Nor do Miltiades' actions indicate that he had any such thoughts. His implied intention was to withdraw from Paros once he had his money, not to stay and fortify it against a new threat from the East. Like the earlier attack on Lemnos, it smacks of a ruse to swell his private fortune. If there were more to it, he gave no recognizable sign. One is left with the impression that Miltiades was very astute where his own aggrandizement was concerned, and if this coincided with the welfare of his country, everyone could be happy. In a moment very important to all, his self-love was Athens' salvation.

5

The Main Storm Approaches

490–480 B.C.

MARATHON was incomparably the most important, also the most dramatic, single event that had yet happened in the history of Athens. It was bound to create a deep impact on the course of events in the city, and to advance the men who had won distinction there. Of these, the two most admired, Miltiades and the polemarch Callimachus, had been quickly removed from the scene. Of the other surviving generals, Aristides seems to have been the one who gained most in the public eye. His tribal regiment had been in the very center of the battle, where it bore the brunt of the initial Persian surge.[1] And though giving ground, it had apparently held the line, because Aristides and his men prior to the victory march back to Athens, were given the honor of remaining to guard the field with its captives and booty, an assignment they faithfully performed.

Aristides' rising popularity is attested by his election as chief archon, archon eponymos, for the year 489/8, a little more than a year later.[2] The archonship, officially still the highest executive and judicial post in the Athenian government, was fitting recognition of his services, though it is difficult to know what value to assign to it at this stage. With annual elections, the office was held in turn by many, and there was a restriction, either written or unwritten, that the same person should not have it twice. Besides the famous, many comparative unknowns filled it; still, it was an honor to sit in the seat that had held Solon, Cleisthenes, Miltiades, and until recently, Themistocles. At last Aristides had reached the front rank of statesmen.

Plutarch says that it was he who introduced the measure which became the constitutional reform of 487/6; as archon he may easily have done so—

though it must have been a law passed by the Assembly rather than an executive decree—and ironically, it was one which would deprive the archon's office of real executive power in the future. Plutarch's explanation is that the citizens were asking for a greater voice in the government, and that Aristides agreed they deserved it, especially after the able defense they had made of their country.[3] The famed biographer seems to have had the right idea without the correct facts. Actually, by Aristotle's information, the real basis of the reform was the principle of sortition, the decision that nearly all the offices, including those of archon, polemarch, basileus, and thesmothetai should henceforth be filled by lot, among the two highest classes,[4] with no second terms. The concept was not new. To some degree the same principle was used in most of the Greek states, and had a sort of divine sanction, theoretically, in that the gods worked through the lottery and made the choice. Since the posts in question had usually been won by wealthy aristocrats under the old process, sortition meant a spreading and a further gain for the demos at the expense of monopolizing nobles.[5] Also, tyrants and would-be tyrants had used these vantage points as springboards to absolute power.

The threat of tyranny had been diminished, but not permanently removed. By providing a random selection for the chief offices such compulsive vote seekers, attractive but dangerous, would be frustrated. However, it also meant that the officeholders would now be men of average ability and little experience. To prevent chaos in the government, Aristides—if it was he—thoughtfully decreased the scope of these positions, distributing many of their functions elsewhere. The archons no longer acted as judges nor presided over the Ekklesia. Hereafter they served mainly as a grand jury, certifying cases to the proper courts. Similarly, the polemarch ceased to be commander in chief over the generals, retaining only a tie breaking vote on the military staff. By the day of Herodotus, a generation or two later, this was so firmly established that the historian mistakenly assumed that Miltiades rather than Callimachus had been in command at Marathon.

The other traditional offices were scaled down accordingly. One office was too vital to the security of Athens to be left to sortition however—that of strategos. For the maximum safety of the state, its best brains must be available here at all times. Therefore, the ten generals were still to be chosen by election, and now by the citizens as a whole rather than individually by the ten tribes, with no limit on the number of terms. Hereafter the important men were the generals, and the important names were those on the lists of the strategia, whereas the archonships were filled by less significant people.[6] Gradually the strategoi acquired other administrative functions that were nonmilitary, in recognition of their greater role. But even without this, under the arrangement of 487 the generals would have domineered over the archons through their ability and experience. The generalship was subsequently the position to which a superior man aspired. The archonship was not.

Aristides' asserted sponsorship of the reform raises the question of his relationship with Xanthippus, the supposed leader. As prostates tou demou, it would have been most natural for demos to come to him for changes in the laws. Perhaps they did and found him unresponsive. But that they should then go to Aristides without his permission—which would follow from these premises—this Xanthippus would have every right to regard as a slight and a challenge to his leadership, which had not always been satisfactory in the past. That Aristides was archon, or had just been, was at best a partial excuse.[7]

The readiest explanation is that Aristides, with his irreproachable character, was really above partisan political alignments. The fact that Aristotle lists him on both sides, and that modern interpretations have placed him in every part of the spectrum,[8] shows that he was actually committed to none. Aristides would do what he thought was right in any situation. Such an attitude commands respect, so Xanthippus cannot have been overly resentful. The prostates had little to fear from this quarter and may have even perceived advantages in having Aristides introduce a measure so patently aimed at his opponents of the old aristocracy. A man such as Aristides, insistent upon his independence to decide, was not intending to build a personal following or to mount a challenge.

However, Xanthippus might look with greater apprehension elsewhere. In the view of some,[9] the real motivating force behind the constitutional changes of 487/6 was Themistocles, who saw in the device of successive generalships the possibility of greater and continuing power for himself. If so, he masked his moves admirably; none of the ancient sources question his motives here. But he was already a luminary in Athens, having earned the gratitude of the thetes during his archonship in 492.[10] He had enhanced his reputation by fighting bravely at Marathon,[11] though he was not mentioned as one of the generals. How he managed in 487 must remain conjectural, but to appear simply as a backer of Aristides' proposals gave the perfect screen for his ambitions, while further ingratiating him with the demos. Actually, no one on his side of the Assembly could object; Xanthippus would want to be a general every year too, now that these men were becoming the chief officers in the state—and all others might aspire. Only the minority of staunch aristocrats were sure to disapprove. What is clear is that the mainstream of the demos wanted the reform, and stood to benefit by it, and Themistocles stood to profit with them.

Similarly, it cannot be positively affirmed, nor yet denied, that he was an instigator in the notable political event which occurred almost concurrently. For it was in 487 that the ostracism law was applied for the first time, against Hipparchus, son of Charmus. Since the fall of the tyranny Hipparchus had been the leader of the remaining Pisistratid faction in Athens, and he was prominent enough that Cleisthenes had wanted him exiled even before the start of the century, when the ostracism law was first passed.[12] The initiative failed at that time, but taking the cue, Hipparchus had conducted himself prudently and quietly for more than a decade. Then the episode of the shield signal had brought him under suspicion, although there was no hard evidence to connect him or anyone else with it. Who introduced the issue in the Ekklesia now is also a mystery, but ostraca cast in 487/6 bearing Themistocles' name do at least implicate him.[13] However, it was an issue on which he could obtain strong support against a mutually acceptable victim, since the Alcmaeonids were also suspect and anxious to divert public scrutiny from themselves. Thus Hipparchus, son of Charmus, fell under the ban and promptly left Attica never to return.

His expulsion was only the beginning. An ostracism contest was moved in the following year, and this time it was Megacles himself, Megacles of Alopeke, who was exiled. If he had been a prime mover in the earlier expulsion, he now became the victim of this law. His family had long been notorious for its shifty political manipulations, and with public furor at fever heat over the shield signal, they would be peculiarly vulnerable.[14] Now the Alcmaeonids, in their turn, must pay.

Themistocles' involvement in these and other actions that followed can only be guessed, partly because of the scarcity of our information on the period, partly because he covered his tracks so well. However, most modern authorities have held him responsible, and the unearthing of ostraca bearing his name far more than any other Athenian politician's[15] tends to support the conclusion. In many contests, over a number of years, it would seem that the Athenian citizens were aware that it was he who had launched the attack either directly or indirectly, and friends of intended victims voted against him, both out of resentment and in an effort to save their man.

The ostracism law was the ideal instrument to carry Themistocles to the top and he must have recognized its usefulness very early. The possibility exists of course, that it was Megacles who first forced action on Hipparchus, but if so, Themistocles backed him with enthusiasm. No regular trial or charges needed even be filed in an ostracism contest. A whispering campaign would do it and Themistocles was a master of innuendo, trained in sophistic reasoning.[16] Failing an issue, an allegation or merely a slur would serve him. And nothing could stop it.

Such tactics are indicated by ostracisms in the years immediately following; each time, a man was banished simply on the charge of being "a friend of the tyrants."[17] It might be more to the point that they were banished because they were friends of the Alcmaeonids, though the claim that one of these unnamed was Alcibiades, son of Kleinias, assertedly an Alcmaeonid ally who had helped Cleisthenes with his legislation, seems not to have been substantiated.[18]

Then, in 484, it was the turn of the exalted Xanthippus, the prostates himself, whom Aristotle described as the first exile "unconnected with the tyranny."[19] The statement arouses speculation that years before, the Alcmaeonids may have chosen him as their "front man" because, unlike themselves, he could not be accused of playing a double game.[20] Clearly, too, in this instance Themistocles needed a better case than one based on the dubious shield signal.

At some stage during the decade, Themistocles began to push strongly the naval policy with which his name was associated. Certainly this seems the most logical moment and he must have based his appeal mainly on the lingering, unsatisfactory war with Aegina, rather than the threat of a new Persian invasion, which (surprisingly) the Athenians did not at first take very seriously.[21] Earlier, Aeginetan raids on Phaleron caused Themistocles to start work on the new protected harbor at Piraeus. The raids had not ceased, and with sporadic fighting in this undeclared war proceeding to Athens' disadvantage, Themistocles was justified in asking not only for completion of the Piraeus, but for more ships to match Aegina's navy.[22]

Politically, it was also expedient for him. The Low and a large part of the Middle could be expected from economic motives to support such a measure, and Xanthippus would be caught between these and his Alcmaeonid backers, who, with their diverse interests, would be in a quandary themselves. Certainly Xanthippus recognized the challenge to his leadership but there was little he could do about it. Viewing it from his personal perspective, as a factional attempt to upset the Alcmaeonid combination (and rightly so!), he had to resist. There were other considerations of course: the implied threat to the Solonic-Cleisthenic constitution and to the hoplite army. In any case, resistance or hesitation would be fatal, giving Themistocles enough ammunition to link him with the enemies of Athens: Aegina, Persia, the Pisistratids. Some such combination of factors was necessary to bring down one as highly placed as Xanthippus.

The coveted position of prostates had thus been vacated, but there was still another who stood in the way before Themistocles could consider himself safely ensconced. However, that person was the one hardest to attack, the man virtually sanctified by the approval of the great Cleisthenes—Aristides, son of Lysimachus, far-famed as the Just, whose actions were so honest and open that he was all but invulnerable. However, as Plutarch tells it, Themistocles could contrive so that even purity could be made to look like deceit. Citizens, so the biographer says, had long had the habit of unofficially asking Aristides to settle their disputes to avoid the delay and cost of judicial proceedings. Themistocles set the rumor going that this was a subtle attempt to undermine the public courts, that by judging everything in private Aristides had already made himself a monarch, not even needing a bodyguard.

What issue brought them face-to-face in the Assembly remains in doubt. Many believe it was the naval question—with his rural background, Aristides is likely to have agreed with Xanthippus about this—culminating in opposition to the naval bill of 482.[23] Previously, a rich vein of silver had been discovered in the mines at Mount Laurium. Instead of the usual money distribution, Themistocles proposed using the proceeds to build 200 triremes for their war with Aegina. In their duel over the use of the monies, Aristides' immense residue of goodwill gave him a victory or two, but Themistocles at last secured the passage of his bill. Yet it may finally have won by default, because during the same year the inevitable ostracism contest was moved, and when the people had weighed rumor along with the issues, Aristides became the latest victim.

Finally, Themistocles could clearly call himself Athens' prostates. He pressed ahead with his program of fleet construction so that Athens might settle the score with her irritating neighbor on the Saronic Gulf. But suddenly the war with Aegina was all but forgotten in the rush of more startling developments. News had come from across the Aegean that a new Persian armament, far mightier than the Marathon expedition, was assembling at Sardis preparing to invade Greece. A seemingly spontaneous and universal feeling arose that the Greek states must consult for their self-preservation, and Sparta, the acknowledged leader, invited the others to attend a congress which she hosted in the spring of 481.[24] It is a foregone conclusion that Themistocles went as Athens' representative.

However, little could be done until they knew more about the invader's plans. Therefore, at this first session only perfunctory steps were taken. The supreme command was given to Sparta as a matter of course. It was also decided they should send spies to Asia to ascertain details of the King's plans. Also, ambassadors were despatched to doubtful or distant Greek states, notably, Argos, Corcyra, Syracuse, and Crete, to implore their aid. Then the Congress adjourned, agreeing to meet again at Corinth, later in the year.

Providentially, happenings in Persia had given Athens a longer breathing spell than could have been expected. After Marathon, Darius had begun the new buildup without resting. However, quite soon his preparations had been interrupted by a revolt in Egypt, and before this could be put down the Great King died in November, 486, in the thirty-sixth year of his reign. For the Greeks there was one worry the less, and a tremendous relief despite the continuing graveness of their situation.

Xerxes, Darius' designated successor among his many sons, was not nearly as talented a man. The strength of his claim lay in the fact that he was also the son of the immensely prestigious Queen Atossa, daughter of the revered Cyrus, founder of the Persian Empire. However, he had several full brothers with the same advantage, and numerous half-brothers able to assert themselves. Some did, and these had to be dealt with by force or diplomacy before Xerxes emerged triumphant.

Not for months and possibly years, was the new King's scepter safe. Finally, when his attention was called to the unsettled score with Athens, he replied that Egypt must come first.[25] Xerxes is represented by Herodotus as lukewarm to the whole idea of European invasion and reluctant to move. It is true that he did not have the strong personal motive of his father, nor the same insatiable ambition. Yet many considerations would prevent his dropping it, not the least of which were pride and filial piety. Moreover, the war party at Susa was undiminished, and its chief, Mardonius, still longing to be satrap of Hellas, was even more influential with Xerxes than with Darius.[26] In addition a number of Greek expatriates, such as the Pisistratids and the exiled King Demaratus of Sparta, were working ceaselessly for intervention. Under the combination of pressures Xerxes gradually yielded. He conceded that after the Egyptian rectification Athens' subjection should have the next priority. Accordingly, when the disturbance on the Nile was quieted in 484, the new King irrevocably committed himself to the invasion of Greece.

After such a lengthy interval, the planning and preparing had to start afresh. Herodotus declares that this covered four full years, and that when assembled it was "by far the greatest armament that had ever been seen or heard of."[27] Long before the Oriental juggernaut was ready, Hellas had word of the enormous arrangements. Bridges were readied for the Hellespont crossing, with others to span the rivers of Thrace. A canal was cut through the easternmost prong of the Chalcidic peninsula, on whose shores in 492 the first fleet of the Persians had been wrecked through exposure to the fierce northeast gales. Ships were commandeered from the ports of Egypt, Phoenicia, Caria, Cilicia, Ionia. Supplies were slowly hauled west and stations established to store them the entire length of the route.

Xerxes himself came down to Sardis in the autumn of 481, where the military levies from all the provinces were to meet, poised to advance as soon as winter was over. Despite Herodotus' assertion, it is doubtful that the majority arrived until the spring of 480. To provision so gigantic an army lying idle over the winter merely multiplied problems.

As soon as the warmth of spring permitted, the armament departed Sardis for the Hellespont, the baggage going first, then the fighting men marching in nations. Far down the line Xerxes rode in the royal chariot, preceded by one thousand select Persian cavalry and the same number of infantrymen, carrying lances with knob-ends of gold. Behind the King's chariot and that of the sun-god Ormazd came the 10,000 Immortals with lances of gold or silver tip. In their wake marched other provincial regiments, stringing out over tens of miles.

Hardly had the host been set in motion, however, when an accident deranged the plans. A sudden storm broke the two bridges across the Hellespont, which had been painstakingly constructed by Phoenician and Egyptian engineers. In a blaze of anger, Xerxes is said to have ordered the engineers killed, then decreed that the Hellespont waters should receive three hundred lashes and a set of chains cast in them as punishment. The tale is scarcely credible, though it does reflect the worst traits in the King's nature. And it gives Herodotus one of many chances to assail Persian unreasonableness and lack of self-control—uncivilized conduct. Finally other engineers arrived—Greeks this time!—and two new bridges were built, with more than six-hundred ships anchored in two lines to reinforce them.[28] And of course this time the structures held, so by the end of April, 480, the army had crossed into Europe.

Herodotus estimated its basic strength at 1,700,000, and declared that the crossing took seven days and seven nights. But this "basic" calculation did not include cavalry, free allies, ships' crews, technicians, or the contingents that joined them on the European side. By a fanciful projection of Herodotus' estimates, a modern writer has come up with a grand total of more than 5,000,000, not including camp followers![29] But he is quick to add that the traditional figures are untrustworthy and out of all reason. Probably there were about 200,000 troops in the invading army.[30] If they took seven days to cross the Hellespont, it was not so much the numbers, but rather that the problem of supply necessitated a wide spacing. The small Balkan streams on the European side could provide water for only one Persian division at a time.[31] At Doriscus in Thrace, Xerxes was joined by his fleet of assertedly 1,207 warships,[32] which after a brief union had to depart to circumnavigate the Chalcidice while he marched westward. It rejoined Xerxes at Therma, the modern Thessalonica. Here a brief halt was called for a final checkup, then the whole expedition turned the Macedonian corner and swung south into Greece. Earlier, Xerxes had sent envoys to the Greek states demanding the usual tokens of earth and water. To all but Athens and Sparta, that is. On them, the King had an obligation to visit utter destruction.

If the astronomical figures cited by Herodotus serve no other purpose, they convey some sense of the terror felt by the Greeks at the approach of such a wehrmacht. Yet most Greek states were minded to resist, if the chances were at all reasonable, and the majority seem to have sent representatives to the first Greek Congress at Sparta.[33] Substantially the same numbers must have originally attended the follow-up Congress at Corinth, where the Hellenic League was established. There were some abstainers, such as Argos, never willing to be a party to any scheme that included Sparta. But numerous defections by Greeks in the exposed north did not take place until Xerxes had crossed into Europe, and nearly reached Greece.[34]

By the time of the meeting at Corinth, probably in the autumn of 481, the Congress States had obtained the information they wanted. The Persians were coming by both land and sea, and their expedition, geared to the long northern land route, gave the League a little more time to prepare. On the other hand, all efforts to enlist the western Greeks had failed. Corcyra promised the aid of her substantial navy, but invented excuses to keep it at a distance. The Corcyrans never appeared. And in remote Syracuse, the tyrant Gelon bluntly told the ambassadors that not one of their countries had given him assistance in his war against Carthage, and they should expect none from him.[35]

Thus the Hellenic League was thrown back on its own resources. Almost immediately it received envoys from loyal Thessalians of the north asking for assistance in defending their borders against the advancing foe. The situation in Thessaly was critical, since its most influential clan, the Aleuadae, had already submitted to the King, and others would be strongly influenced to follow their example. Hastily, an expeditionary force of 10,000 was mustered and sent off under the joint authority of Themistocles and the Spartan general Euaenetus, with orders to occupy the pass of Olympus, beneath the hallowed habitation of the gods. The League's army started with good intentions, but never reached its destination. Instead, for reasons undisclosed the commanders halted twenty miles south, in the beautiful Vale of Tempe. From here, however, it was still possible to protect Thessaly and most of northern Greece. But they were not to stay even in this spot for long. Soon secret emissaries arrived from King Alexander of Macedon (thought to be friendly, though he had hastened to the camp of Xerxes), warning them that they would be easily swept from their position if they stayed there. Simultaneously, inquiries made by the Greeks revealed that there was another pass into Thessaly which could be used to circumvent them.[36] Thereupon, Themistocles and his colleague scrapped their plans and returned to the Isthmus. Probably the generals took the only prudent course, but it was a severe setback just the same. The cities of Thessaly now opened their gates to the invaders and the entire north fell into line.

In truth, the rush of events had caught the Greeks ill-prepared. Those at the Congress were agreed on resistance, but much uncertainty existed among them, and every step they took betrayed their confusion. King Leonidas of Sparta, half-brother and successor of the fugitive Cleomenes, had been voted commander in chief, yet a less eminent Spartan unconnected with the royal family had led the troops to Tempe. Imperfect knowledge of the terrain had forced his hasty retreat.[37] The officers in charge did not know the north as they did their native Peloponnesus. Even now with the enemy pressing on into central Greece they remained uninformed and undecided. Many southerners in their hearts preferred to hold at the Isthmus, yet they realized they could not afford to antagonize Athens and the states lying on the other side. The next defensible spot below Tempe was the pass of Thermopylae, adjoining the narrow gulf between Malis and Locris. A stand would have to be made here, or much of central Greece, including Athens, would also be lost to the League. There is no solid evidence to show that the Peloponnesian members were reluctant to make a strenuous effort north of the Isthmus,[38] but they were obviously relieved that Thermopylae could be held by a small force, eliminating a great risk, and the need to commit their main body.

Much modern speculation has centered on the undisclosed strategy devised by the Congress which led to the amazing Greek victory. All such explanations are after-the-fact rationalizations based on what actually did occur. The favorite theory is that Thermopylae was intended as a holding operation to delay the enormous Persian army long enough so that the Persian navy would have to supply it through dangerous waters where the Greek fleet might pounce at the right time. The forces being more nearly equal by sea than by land, the Greeks had a better chance this way. If they could destroy or cripple the Persian fleet with its services of supply from Asia, the King's army would have to withdraw, regardless.[39]

It is possible that Themistocles had some such notion; he was a bold man with original ideas, and a strikingly broad grasp of the overall situation. But the vast majority of Greeks at the Congress were men of more limited outlook, and as products of a particular parochialism, were not likely to agree on any but the most cautious and obvious measures. Herodotus has often been blamed for lack of insight in saying that the Greek strategy at Thermopylae was simply to maintain the pass, and that the fleet was sent to the northern tip of Euboea merely to keep touch with the army, and protect the equally narrow pass of the Euripus[40] — both purely defensive actions. Recently it has been suggested that this was really all that the militarily nonprofessional, Greek politicians at the Congress had in mind; they felt that if the Persians were held up at the pass, with supplies running low, these troublesome invaders would simply go away[41]—an observation which seems to square with the facts Herodotus relates. A fatal flaw in this ingenuous plan was that the presiding Spartans at the Congress knew little about the area of Mount Oeta, to which Thermopylae was the key, or of the existence of a mountain path that circumvented "the Gates." And the Phocian and Locrian delegates, who wanted an army sent to protect them, were not about to mention the fact.[42]

The decision taken, the Congress despatched an army of only 7,000 men northward, which the dominant Lacedaemonians deemed sufficient to hold the mountain line. Probably to reassure the agitated residents of central Greece, Leonidas, king of Sparta, was placed in command with 300 Spartan hoplites accompanying him. For their halfhearted gesture the Lacedaemonians gave the usual lame excuse to the indignant peoples thus exposed: the Olympic Games as well as their own Carnean festival were then in progress. Extensive reinforcements were promised when the celebrations would be over. Those who remembered the similar occurrence at Marathon would find this but scant consolation.

Themistocles would have preferred more aggressive action from the Congress, but he did not have the same power over the obstinate Spartans as with his own government. Back in Athens, as prostates, he was now in firm control, strong enough that he allowed the Ekklesia to pass a decree recalling ostracized citizens in the interest of national unity. This of course meant the return of his rivals, Xanthippus and Aristides. Having put both down, Themistocles assumed their unquestioning subordination to him in resisting the common enemy. In any case, he would not be there to greet them. Already Leonidas and his 7,000 were marching north to take up their position at Thermopylae. Themistocles, as strategos for the year 480, was called upon to lead the ships of Athens toward the corresponding area offshore. Artemisium, so-called because a Temple of Artemis was located on this beach at Euboea's north end,[43] was where the Greek contingents would assemble to watch the sea path which paralleled the land route. The League concentrated 271 triremes there, with Athens contributing more than half. Because of this the Athenian captains thought their leader ought to have overall authority, but Themistocles wisely deferred to the Lacedaemonian admiral, Eurybiades, when convinced that the other Greek units, especially the Aeginetans, would follow a Spartan, but not an Athenian.[44] In return, it seems to have been understood that Themistocles would have a major voice in battle planning.[45]

The time for action came in August of 480, when the Persians arrived in the contested area first by land and shortly afterward by sea. However, events did not develop as anticipated. Any hope Themistocles may have had of bringing about a conflict in favorable waters faded when his comrades caught their first glimpse of the massive Persian fleet. The mere sight of the great number of ships riding at anchor on the opposite shore, at Aphetai, nearly unnerved them. Then when two of the three scout ships sent to reconnoiter the enemy were sunk, dismay overtook the Greek seamen. Despite their commitment to cover Leonidas' flank, a clamor arose to abandon Artemisium and head south. A storm which disordered the Persian fleet, destroying perhaps a third of it,[46] did not allay their fears. Eurybiades and many of the captains agreed with the rank and file.

Themistocles, still hoping for a Greek offensive, used all his wiles to hold both admiral and men in line.[47] Typically, he managed—with more than a little luck. Herodotus relates that the Euboean residents were suddenly frightened into "volunteering" a gift of thirty talents if the Greek would stay and venture a battle to defend them. They entrusted the sum to the devious Themistocles, who assertedly gave five talents to Eurybiades, another three to Adeimantus, the Corinthian leader, and kept the remainder himself.[48] The incident has often been doubted, but Themistocles' lavish display of wealth in after-years suggests that the story, though much exaggerated, has some foundation in truth. The astonished sailors obeyed orders to row out for a tentative thrust at the foe in late afternoon, so dusk would cover a quick withdrawal. They surprised themselves by sinking thirty ships. Concurrently they heard that a Persian squadron of two hundred, sent around Euboea to take them in the rear, had been dissipated by another storm. Fifty-three Athenian ships detailed to watch the back approach now joined the main group at Artemisium.

Days later the Persian grand fleet counterattacked, trying an enveloping movement which would provide scope for their greater numbers. The Greeks went out to meet them, and though losing seventy triremes in a savage all-afternoon battle, held their own and fought off the encirclement. This was far short of what had been hoped, but was really the utmost that could be expected.[49] Their opponents wisely maneuvered the fighting close to the inlet's mouth, refusing to be lured into the narrow waters, where the Greeks might have an advantage—their only advantage. So while failing to destroy the enemy, the Hellenic mariners had attained considerably better spirits—up to the moment when the news from Thermopylae struck like a death knell.

The accompanying resistance on land faced much greater odds from the start. Given the Peloponnesians' less than enthusiastic attitude toward the Thermopylae venture, Leonidas and any others who chose to stay in the pass had but a very poor chance.[50] They could only have been saved by the unlikely event of a quick naval victory decisive enough to discourage Xerxes completely, or solid reenforcements promptly sent by the Congress. Neither possibility materialized. For two days Leonidas' small force held off the Persian myriads, with the Spartans doing most of the fighting and having considerably the better of it. Then Xerxes heard of the mountain trail (from a "Greek traitor") and sent over this trail his best troops, the so-called Immortals, to take the Greeks in the rear. Of course Xerxes' scouts would have discovered the path before long, even without local assistance. Leonidas did not know of it until his arrival at the pass; he has sometimes been blamed for detaching only 1,000 Phocians, who proved inadequate to guard the trail.

They fell back in confusion, allowing the Immortals to circle behind the pass. Most of the Greeks, receiving advance notice of this, escaped southward before the net closed. Whether the king dismissed them out of mercy or was using them in some desperate strategem that failed, or whether they simply broke and fled, is not known. Leonidas' few hundreds of Spartans and Thespians who remained in the pass at Thermopylae were slaughtered to the last man.

Report of the final tragedy at Thermopylae was said to have been brought to the Greeks at Artemisium by a native who rowed across to Euboea that very afternoon. The climactic sea battle was just over, and the council of naval captains was debating whether to resume the fighting the next day despite their severe losses. Themistocles was avid in urging such a course, pointing out that the Persian losses had been even greater.[51] In addition, he hinted that the Ionian and Carian squadrons of the imperial fleet might desert to them, bolstering their strength considerably. But hints were not enough; he had nothing tangible.

The tidings from Thermopylae tipped the balance against him. The Spartan admiral and the Peloponnesian units had little confidence now, and in all probability had regarded this campaign as another holding operation, anyway.[52] Now men could think of nothing but home and family, exposed to the invader. Under the cover of night they broke camp and by the morning were gone, with the Corinthians leading the way down the coast of Euboea toward the Saronic Gulf, the Athenians under the reluctant Themistocles bringing up the rear.

In this, his second of many quarrels with the captains, Themistocles may well have been right. He had drawn the Persians out of open water, not as far as he had hoped, but far enough for the Greek ships to have an edge. On the last day at Artemisium, momentum seemed to be swinging toward the Hellenes, so much so that by the next dawn the Persians could hardly believe they had departed. Another twenty-four hours at the inlet's mouth, and the imperial navy might have been seriously crippled, compelling Xerxes to withdraw even before he got to the heart of Greece. From that standpoint, the doomed Leonidas had been successful. He had held up the advance on land, however briefly, and given the Greek sailors an advantage which they had not quite been able to capitalize upon. Leonidas was dead; but Themistocles yet lived, to scheme, squirm, push, while breath was in him. He had missed thus far, but the real strength of his design was its elasticity, its alternatives. He knew of other stretches of water as well or better suited to his purpose than Artemisium. No need to despair; the Persians might still be caught.

6

Cloudburst over Hellas

480–479 B.C.

FOR Themistocles, in doomed Attica, the problems were multiplying. Shepherding his agitated and despairing people, he met the tests with an adroit blending of energy and suasion which characterized him at his best.[1] No doubt about it, Athens would have to be evacuated. If the much-debated Themistocles Decree be true,[2] or has any substantial foundation, he had foreseen this as a likely necessity even before the Artemisium campaign, and had laid plans accordingly.[3] If so, it was a wise move on his part. Conducting an effective evacuation requires time. Meanwhile the Persians covered the intervening ground in only nine days.

Convincing an entire people to abandon their homes and all property except the few items that can be carried is surely the most difficult task to confront any statesman. Calling on Delphi to help was a masterly way to go about it. The reply of the priestess, advising quick flight before ruin descended upon them,[4] was just what Themistocles needed to get them moving. But he also had the problem of morale; the oracle had been too grim in holding out virtually no hope. So his messengers were directed to approach the Pythia again. And this time they must have divulged something of the prostates' intentions,[5] for her reply that "a wooden wall would remain unshattered," and that "divine Salamis" would "destroy the sons of women" was less pessimistic than her first pronouncement. But the reference to Salamis was entirely equivocal, noncommittal;[6] the "sons of women" were not identified. But Themistocles could claim that "a wooden wall" signified that their wooden ships would save them, and that Salamis would not have been called divine unless this referred to a Greek victory.

Thus backed by the holiest authority in Greece, Themistocles could bring his proposals to the Athenian public. All must leave the endangered mainland, embarking for Salamis, Aegina, or Troezen. The only unresolved question is whether he introduced these in the Ekklesia, as the challenged Decree would indicate, or through the Board of Generals.[7] Since Themistocles had recently received an added, new distinction as *strategos autocrator,* placing him above his colleagues, with the right to take action on his own authority, he could have issued the Decree however he chose. The possibility also exists that shortly afterward he induced the old Areopagus Council to sweeten his measure by offering a bounty of eight drachmas to every man who would volunteer for sea duty. As a former archon, he was also a member of that body, and was, for the moment, all-powerful in Athens. It was he who had persuaded the Greek fleet to put in at Salamis long enough to cover the evacuation of Attica; the lives of all Athenians depended on his ability to hold the fleet at Salamis.

Complete unanimity on the departure was not to be expected, of course. According to Herodotus, some refused to leave the city out of piety, others because they were too poor to do so. And some, he says, taking the prophecy about wooden walls in a completely different way, threw up plank barricades around the Acropolis, preparing to defend their citadel to the bitter end.[8] Yet this too may actually have been dictated by Themistocles or the Greek High Command, to fit in with overall strategy.[9]

The defenders did not have long to wait for action. In a matter of days Xerxes and the Persians were at the gates of Athens, entered, and promptly fired the city. At their leisure they established a base on Areopagus rock, then laid siege to the hardy handful on the Acropolis above. The Median archers poured flaming arrows into the makeshift boards and planks, soon destroying the barricade. But when Persian infantry charged up the western slope, the defenders beat them off mainly by rolling stones down upon them. Amazingly, the patriots held their position for perhaps two weeks;[10] then the Persians found a secret path up the north rim, stormed the heights and slew the cornered men. The old original temples, the sanctuaries of Athena and Poseidon, were reduced to ashes.

Meanwhile Themistocles was finding no relief from troubles, only a greater variety. His naval colleagues were becoming unmanageable again. If his new position had been conferred partly with the idea of impressing them, or of giving him greater weight among them, there is no sign that it had this effect. The evacuation completed, the captains became more restless as their ships continued to lie in the harbor at Salamis. Themistocles was grimly resolved to hold them there for the all-important battle, but was having an increasingly hard time. Their inclination to retreat to the Isthmus reasserted itself as soon as they heard that the Spartan regent Cleombrotus and the Peloponnesian army were at the Isthmus but would come no farther. News that the Persians had entered Attica added to their agitation.

Sensing their attitude, the admiral Eurybiades called a conference of the officers, and from its beginning he assumed that Attica was lost. There could be no question of staying; they must go elsewhere. Where would be the best chance for a showdown battle? The replies revealed how dispirited they were. Most opted for the Isthmus, saying that if defeated there the open water would afford them a safe retreat to their homes. Here at Salamis they were cooped in, none could get away. No talk of victory was heard despite the good showing at Artemisium. "Thermopylae consciousness" hung heavily over the meeting.

Still, no immediate decision was taken. Probably Themistocles prevented one by refusing to commit the Athenian ships. Mounting tensions reached the explosive point two weeks later when word came that the Acropolis had fallen. Many of the captains ran straightway to their ships and raised the sails. When the council of captains convened, it confirmed the general impulse. Unwaveringly, the majority voted to abandon Salamis, ignoring protests from Athens, Aegina, and Megara. The remainder of the captains dispersed to prepare for departure, treating the issue as settled.

The losers must have been both dejected and frightened, but it is to Themistocles' credit that he never faltered or despaired. Allowing only a breathing spell to clear the air, he kept after Eurybiades with argument and artifice, exerting all his powers to move the admiral to overrule the council of captains.[11] If permitted to depart for Peloponnesus, each would seek his separate home and the fleet would disintegrate, Themistocles declared. There would be no battle at all. Eurybiades would see his authority vanish in the breeze. The guileful strategos was dipping into his legerdemain, trying every sophistic trick he knew, and what he suggested by inference was more telling than his actual words. How many would go "home" to Peloponnesus? Not the Athenians, Aeginetans, or Megarians. Their considerable squadrons must be canceled out at once.[12] The commander should weigh all aspects before taking any irrevocable step. He was a Peloponnesian, the southern peninsula was dear to him. But if he sailed off now without the Athenians and those others who felt cheated, would he have enough left to protect Peloponnesus' shores?

Such words could not miss their mark. Finally Eurybiades agreed to call the captains again. All knew who was responsible and Adeimantus the Corinthian accused his Attic colleague of taking unfair advantage. "Themistocles, those who start too soon at the games are whipped." "True," came the quick reply, "but those who wait too long are not crowned."[13]

In his speech to the captains, Themistocles assumed yet another stance. Nothing was said about the damage to the admiral's authority or dispersing to their homes. Instead he pointed out that removing to Peloponnesus would bring Xerxes' navy as well as his army there, in overwhelming concentration against them. In the broad waters of the Isthmus the Persians would be vastly superior, having more ships and more room to maneuver lighter craft. Their own fortune, their sole opportunity lay here in the narrow straits between Salamis and Attica, where the heavier Greek vessels could confine the enemy and bear down upon them. Here they could fight a preventive battle to keep the war from reaching Peloponnesus.

It was measured rhetoric by a master of the process, but it could not convert minds already made up. Adeimantus broke in angrily, saying that Themistocles should have no voice; since Athens was no more, he was a delegate without a state. Themistocles retorted that he had two hundred ships manned and equipped for war, and if Adeimantus thought the Athenians needed territory before speaking in council they could take it anytime, anywhere—from Greeks themselves if necessary, he added significantly. Then turning once more to Eurybiades, he said, "If you stay here and behave like a brave man, all will be well—if not, Greece will be destroyed. For the entire outcome of the war hangs on our ships. Listen, and be guided by my words. If not, we Athenians will embark our whole people and leaving what cannot be moved, go to Siris in Italy which has belonged to us till memory fades, and which we are destined to colonize. Then, too late, you will wish for such faithful allies, and remember my admonishing."[14] Yet the most telling argument was that in the Greek fleet, Athens' ships were at the least a plurality despite recent additions from elsewhere. Deprived of them, the Hellenes would fall easy prey to the Persians, wall or no wall. With the well-known expediency of the Spartan, Eurybiades ruled that they must stand and accept battle at Salamis.

From Athens' center down to the sparkling, blue Saronic at Piraeus—where the magnificent new harbor was already taking shape—is six English miles. To the open beach at Phaleron, where Xerxes preferred to plant his standard, it is barely five. From both, Salamis is easily visible beyond the intervening waters. And from Mount Aegaleos, on the coast five miles west of Piraeus, it is only a thousand yards away across the narrowest part of the inlet. Here, according to the gossip heard by Herodotus, Xerxes ordered his throne placed on the spot where he could best witness the final destruction of the Greeks.[15] Whether or not this is so, the view afforded is breathtaking. Below in one direction is the deep-hued Saronic, widening on an unobstructed skyline; in the other, stretching toward the sunset, lies the half-moon Bay of Eleusis, nearly stopped at both ends by the long island of Salamis with its purple-tipped hills. A convenient refuge, the bay might also become a death trap for the unwary.

In the period of crisis that led into Salamis, Themistocles' actions eloquently bespoke the typical, yet inimitable Hellene that he was. The subtle plan he was gradually unveiling had such an admixture of deception and surprise that even now it is impossible to be sure of all the ramifications. Aeschylus in his play tells the story in one way; Herodotus, in a manner somewhat different. That given by the poet is properly literature rather than history, but it has a peculiar distinction. In all probability Aeschylus was himself an eye-witness, also a participant in the momentous combat, and he composed his famous tragedy within the next eight years. He would not be apt to distort or overly embroider events well known to his audience. But some of the events were not well known, and Aeschylus had a propagandistic motive for writing his drama. So, if closer to the situation than Herodotus, the poet is not on all points more trustworthy. Where they differ, the two accounts must be weighed against each other.[16]

At least there is no dispute as to topography.[17] The long eastern channel leading from the Saronic to the Bay of Eleusis is bisected almost equally at its entrance by the islet of Psyttaleia (now called Lipsokutali). The Persians had been watching both passages for many days, without stirring from Phaleron. The reason is self-evident, the same that had dominated the earlier maneuvers off Euboea. If the Persian navy sailed on to the Isthmus, it might be that the Greeks would follow, fight, lose, and/or scatter to their homes. But it was just as possible that they would cut behind and strike at the Persian supply lines, and choke off the vital flow from Asia. If the united fleet refused, the Athenians alone could do it and probably would.[18] When his dispositions were completed, suddenly, in the dark of night King Xerxes sent the Phoenician and Ionian divisions of his fleet to block the eastern channel, the one occupying the opening between the Attic coast and Psyttaleia, the other between Psyttaleia and the Salamis shore. A picked company was landed on the islet itself to slay any Greeks who might be there. His third squadron, the Egyptian, he sent around Salamis to seal off the western channel running past Megara.

Why had the King done this, himself precipitating the all-important conflict? Herodotus accounts for it by an incredible story: that Themistocles had secretly sent his faithful slave Sicinnus to the Persians to say that the Athenian commander wished Xerxes well, wished also to inform him that a great fear had seized upon the Greeks, that they were dispirited and quarreling, and minded to flee without fighting. The King had only to block the escape route to catch them all.[19] The story could at once be dismissed as fantastic, were it not that the poet Aeschylus tells the same story in simpler form, with differing details in his drama, *Persae* ("The Persians"),[20] produced only eight years after the event. Since the intent of the play was to honor Themistocles, who was present at the performance, this can only mean that Aeschylus' informant was Themistocles himself. Not that this establishes the story—its truth is past knowing. But manifestly, Themistocles was telling Aeschylus and the Athenian public what he wanted them to know, and in the form he wanted it known—merely that he had informed Xerxes that the Greeks were considering flight.

However, Themistocles' admission forces a re-examination. If he did communicate with the King, his messenger could hardly stop with a few words; Xerxes would need convincing, and along the lines that Herodotus suggests. Moreover, under the existing circumstances, was this not what the "prudent," self-interested Greek of the fifth century would do?[21] The Persian tide was then at its maximum, the Thermopylae strategy had ended in deep disappointment; most of the northern and many of the central Greeks had already gone over, even the very reluctant. Of course Themistocles still hoped and would strive for a Greek victory, but realistically the chances were slim.[22] Had he not better insure himself against the probabilities? The fact that a generation later he convinced Xerxes' successor that he had been ready to betray the Greek cause, and ended his life as governor of a Persian province, is very significant. So although Herodotus' account contains imaginative flights perhaps tinted with Alcmaeonid spite against Themistocles, ironically, there is a chance that he may have hit nearer the truth than Aeschylus.

Whatever had happened, Xerxes was closing in. But the captains at Salamis still did not know, nor were they willing to believe. The night before the battle they were still divided, still quarreling, still bitterly blaming Themistocles. Herodotus' story that it was Aristides somehow penetrating through the Persian lines from Aegina who brought the first positive news of the encirclement is open to doubt.[23] More likely, it was a Greek trireme of Tenos, deserting Persian service, which brought the information that hushed every protesting voice. Then, some cheerfully, others with sullen reluctance, the Greeks began to prepare themselves for the struggle of their lives.

They had but a short time to do it. At dawn, all who bore arms were assembled to hear the hortatory speeches of their leaders. It was generally agreed that Themistocles distinguished himself above his colleagues. Wishing beyond everything to heal the dissension among them, he reminded his listeners that in every man there are two natures, the noble and the base. Good or ill fortune for humans is largely determined by the opportune prevalence of the one spirit over the other. He did not need to impress upon them that now, if ever, was the moment for noble deeds. Each must be his bravest and best, with so much depending on them. Freedom or slavery for all the Greeks will ride on their oars. As Themistocles was the last speaker, the men were then ordered to their ships. Shortly afterward, when every rower and marine was in his place, the paean was raised by thousands of voices and in a long line the Greek ships, about 300 in number,[24] moved out from the protection of Cape Kynosoura into the open channel.

Leading the way was the admiral Eurybiades, with his sixteen Lacedaemonian triremes. Coming from the beach behind Cynosoura, with their bows pointed north toward the open water, these and the other Peloponnesians would constitute the right wing in the final battle line, the post of honor in any Greek array because the commander in chief was with them. The center was occupied principally by the Aeginetans and Megarians. Coming out to complete the center, also to make up the left, were the Athenians, whose triremes were the newest and fastest. The Corinthians were not a part of the battle formation, having already been sent off to oppose the Egyptians at the western (rear) outlet. Counting them, the Greeks possessed 366 ships of war.[25] Remaining behind on the Cape to be called upon whenever needed was the Athenian hoplite army, assertedly under Aristides' command. And crowding the shores of Salamis were the townspeople of Athens, watching the action upon which their destiny depended.

Eurybiades seems to have allowed Themistocles a free hand in developing his strategy. The Athenian commander had arranged for the Greek ships initially to turn toward the Persians as though intending to fight, then to waver and start backing toward the inner channel. It would look as if the

Greeks had resolved in desperation to break through the blockade, but on seeing the tremendous strength of the enemy they lost their nerve, taking flight. Was Themistocles really prepared to charge that battery of warships, doubly formidable in open waters, if the Persians did not snatch at his bait? An alternative is hard to imagine, but the truth will never be known.

Fortunately, it was a decision he did not have to make. Ariabignes,[26] the Persian admiral, leapt at what appeared to him a golden opportunity. Without pause he ordered his fleet forward into the channel with his best sailors, the Phoenicians, leading the way through the right inlet between Psyttaleia and the mainland. The Ionians followed a trifle more slowly on the left, using the aperture between Psyttaleia and Salamis. Ariabignes' purpose was to cut the Greeks in two, reducing their confusion to utter chaos as quickly as possible.[27] Boldness was called for; with the King, his half-brother,[28] watching from the shore, he wanted a spectacular triumph.

Nevertheless, to sail into the midst of the Greeks was beyond the bounds of reasonable daring. The ships of the Orient tended to be taller,[29] and those of Phoenicia were reputed swifter than the opponents',[30] but in general they were less stoutly built. Consequently, Asiatic men-of-war did little infighting, and even though they were equipped with rams, these were not much used. Oriental naval captains preferred to stand off at a short distance, overcoming an adversary by raining down arrows and javelins. Conversely, the long, low Greek galleys endeavored to make the most of their projecting prows, and their rowers were especially trained to wheel about quickly, so as to crash an antagonist broadside. They did their best work at close quarters.

The Persians must have known this, but since the Greeks were ostensibly in full retreat, there was no apparent danger. The speedy Phoenician vessels bore down on their prospective victims, trying by sheer momentum to drive them apart. But the Greeks, while continuing to back away, managed to retain contact with each other. Their line widened to a tremendous semicircle, reaching ever farther back into the channel, and into this bulge poured Phoenician and Ionian ships by the hundreds, intent on breaking through. It never quite happened. But as the vast floating arc began to drift backward away from Cape Kynosoura, the agonized throngs of Athenians on the shore loosed an exasperated cry, "Madmen, how much farther are you going back?"

The reproach was unnecessary. Under Themistocles' plan the circle could stretch until it nearly reached both shores of the channel, to pack the greatest number of enemy inside. But his strategy depended on cooperation with the hoplites on Salamis, and he had no intention of losing touch with his people. The Phoenician warships pressing ahead had by now dangerously exposed themselves to the Athenian galleys on the outer edge of the circle. Suddenly an Athenian ship, that of Ameinias of Pallene, reversed its stroke and charged the attackers. In quick succession others along the line did the same, so that gradually the Phoenician advance ground to a halt.[31]

On the opposite flank a similar movement was taking place at almost the same instant. There the Aeginetans had gone forward to help the Lacedaemonians—the Aeginetans were later to claim that one of their vessels had charged the enemy first—in their case, the Ionians. At this point the deadly Greek prows came into play. The Persians, who could not bring their numbers to bear, found that they had neither room nor time to maneuver defensively. As a result all were crushed back toward the center where they had still less space, being soon reduced to a haphazard mass. The Greeks, having preserved their lines of organization, proceeded to the work of destruction with inspired efficiency. The Persians, having lost theirs, were powerless to prevent it.

Still they fought on as best they might, laboring to make their weapons count as the conflict developed at close quarters. Ariabignes, the admiral, kept hurling javelins and shooting arrows incessantly as he strove to drive his ship against that of Themistocles. Ameinias intercepted and locked with him before he could do so. Nothing daunted, Ariabignes rushed forward at the head of a boarding party to overrun Ameinias' trireme. He was struck down by a spear, and the boarders were repulsed. So perished the Persian leader at Salamis, "the bravest and strongest of the King's brothers."[32]

After hours of exhausting but fruitless struggle, the spirit of the Persians began to evaporate. Thoughts of safety and escape replaced those of victory, as they commenced to give way before the advancing foe. As the Greeks surged back toward the channel's entrance, the Athenians and Aeginetans, in their respective areas, led the attack. At last, by expert ramming and slicing so as to snap the oars of the Persians, the Athenians were able to sweep their half of the entrance clear of the enemy.[33] Then a body of warriors, either hoplites from the Cape or men of the fleet, possibly led by Aristides, landed on the islet of Psyttaleia, where they made short work of the stranded Persian soldiers.[34] But if the Athenians distinguished themselves in the early and middle parts of the battle, it was the Aeginetan contingent that dominated the last phase. For it was their squadron which made the first breakthrough, and pressing the enemy relentlessly over to the Attic shore, then swung around to deliver the flank attack which was the final coup de grace. And as the retreating Persians naturally fled toward their original base at Phaleron, they unavoidably ran straight into the toils of the Aeginetans, to be cut down.

How many of the King's "thousand ships" were destroyed, it is impossible to say. No figures are anywhere given. Many must have eluded the Greeks' encircling net; probably many more had not even been able to enter the channel. Besides these the Egyptian squadron was still unscathed, and the Pontic flotilla was being held in reserve. Persian naval strength remained adequately high; nevertheless, the scales of sea power tilted at a different angle. What Themistocles had hoped to accomplish at Artemisium, he had done at Salamis. If Greece was not yet saved, its people could now see a light in the sky.[35]

For Xerxes, too, the outlook was altered. Seated upon his throne, the King had watched the affair with growing astonishment changing to impotent rage. His Universal Majesty ordered a search for those responsible, finally venting his fury on the surviving Phoenician sea captains, whose heads he ordered struck off.[36] Later he told himself that the subject races had lost the battle,[37] and briefly contemplated building a mole from the mainland to Salamis, to give his undefeated Medes and Persians of the land army a chance to clean out this infernal nest.[38] However, he now became aware that the campaign was to be longer and more arduous than he had first surmised, and he wearied of the Greek project. Subordinates could finish this uninteresting business. The Sovereign of the All had more important things to do. What good could these half-starved people do him, with their tiny, poverty-stricken land?

The King of Kings had had his fill of Hellas. Boredom was a part of it, but obviously there were deeper currents. To continue longer on the scene of disaster was more than his imperious spirit could endure. Xerxes was not a man schooled in self-control, much less self-mortification. Another consideration weighed with him. Unless he were supremely resourceful, much of his vast military would now of practical necessity have to be withdrawn. Such a body could hardly be provisioned in Greece unless the shipping routes to Asia were open and secure. If the grand army had to go, there were good grounds for his going with it. Still, the King could not appear to be running away. If he retired from Greece, he had to do so with dignity.

Mardonius, ever the unctious courtier, was ready with words perfumed to soothe as well as to facilitate a prompt departure. He spoke artfully in his own interest, apprehensive that the King would blame him as instigator of the Greek war. "Do not sorrow, master, nor let your mind dwell on the recent mishap. Our success does not depend on a few wooden boards hammered into ships, but on our peerless cavalry and archers. With them we may storm Peloponnesus whenever you say. Or if you would rather wait and leave that to others, it may be done when you will." The Greeks in their ships would not dare to come ashore and face the land army, he asserted. If Xerxes considered that his presence was required in Asia, of course he should go. Mardonius besought the King only to leave enough troops that he himself might complete the task so nearly done. More than half of Greece was already in their hands. All that remained was to force the Isthmus and overwhelm the last, defiant peninsula.

His conscience eased, Xerxes lost no time in commencing the evacuation. Remnants of his fleet may have left Phaleron even before he did, though probably they did not flee eastward on the night after the battle, as Herodotus implied.[39] Nor is there anything to support the Greek notion that Xerxes himself fled in terror. He was in no present danger. His army was unbeaten, and the chances for a final victory were from a Persian standpoint still good. Few of the Greeks desired to molest him as he led his forces back over the Cithaeron range into Boeotia. Leonidas' brother, Cleombrotus, now commanding the Panhellenic army at the Isthmus, proved adept at finding religious reasons for not doing so. The immediate reaction was to let well enough alone.

But among the dissenting few were Themistocles and the Athenians. On the sea they wanted to pursue and destroy the remainder of the King's navy, then go on to the Hellespont and demolish the bridge of boats, cutting off the King's retreat. They did for awhile pursue the Persian ships, but could not overtake them. Then the admiral Eurybiades, supported by the other captains, called an absolute halt. They wanted Xerxes out of Europe, and when Themistocles could not sway them, he astounded his Athenian comrades by switching sides to agree with the majority. He did so because he perceived a way to ingratiate himself with the Persians, says Herodotus, who adds that Themistocles sent the long-suffering Sicinnus to Xerxes (still in Attica) a second time to say that all the other captains had wanted to destroy the bridge, but that he, Themistocles, had dissuaded them.[40] True enough, the Athenians obeyed him, this time. But they could not have been happy—and they must have wondered.

For most of the Greek allies, the waning months of the year were spent in rejoicing and thanksgiving. But before everything, the spoils from Salamis were collected and the first fruits sent to the shrine of Apollo at Delphi. Afterward the chiefs removed to the Isthmus for celebrations and new deliberations. There, in the Temple of Poseidon, another portion of booty was dedicated to the sea-god who had granted them their victory. The rest was divided among the leaders. Inquiry was made as to which of the Hellenes had distinguished themselves most at Salamis, and it was decided by ballot that the first prize should go to the Aeginetans, the second to the Athenians. In jubilation the Aeginetans sent off their trophy, three gold stars studding the top of a bronze mast, to Delphi. In the sanctuary it received a place of honor where all might see, next to the glittering bowl contributed by Croesus. But the contest for individual awards resulted in a blowup peculiarly Greek. Each captain was asked to write down two names, that of the person most deserving, and the name of him who came closest thereafter. As Herodotus tells it, each man wrote his own name at the top, with "Themistocles" underneath.[41] Because of this no first prize was given, and it was decided there could not be a second without a first.

Nevertheless Themistocles was the man of the hour.[42] During the winter of 480–479 he visited several of the Greek cities, receiving universal acclaim, especially at Sparta. Lacedaemon bestowed its highest mark of esteem, the crown of wild olive, on its own naval commander, the admiral Eurybiades. But on his arrival a similar crown was presented to Themistocles, also the most splendid chariot that could be found. During his stay praises were heaped upon him, conduct unheard of among undemonstrative Spartans, and when at last he departed a select guard of three hundred aristocratic youths was ordered to accompany him to the border. Never before nor after did Sparta accord such signal recognition to anyone.

For a season the applause of each nation greeted Themistocles wherever he went. And by his own admission, he loved it.[43] At the next Olympic Games, the spectators turned their heads away from the contests to watch him as he entered. While present he drew more attention than the athletes, and that being so, he remained long. People craned their necks to see him, and those who knew where he sat pointed him out to admiring newcomers. It was all balm to Themistocles' soul, and he confessed to friends that at last "he was reaping in full measure the harvest of his toils in behalf of Hellas."[44]

The people of Athens as a whole were not as cheerful as that one Athenian currently traveling about the countryside acknowledging the plaudits of the Greek world. At some stage, as the Persian army retreated, the Athenians began recrossing the bay to their homes on the continent. What number found it practicable to do so, we are not told. Their city had been destroyed, their fields burned; Attica was a poor land anyway. Furthermore, winter was approaching, and such shelter as they could throw together would do little to keep out the cold. A good many must have considered it wiser to remain on Salamis, which had not been ravaged. Even if they should go back, what protection had they, what assurance the Persians would not come again? On the contrary, the overwhelming probability was that the invaders *would* return. That being the case, "going home" seemed an exercise in futility.

Contributing to the Athenians' unrest was a conviction that their allies had failed them. The naval victory was all very well, but they thought they had a commitment from the Congress that its army would seal off Attica and adjacent parts of central Greece. The Peloponnesians could not remember anything so explicit. Their portion of the Congress' army was stuck at the Isthmus, where Cleombrotus was still building his wall. Even when it was finished he kept piling superfluous stones on stones. Once, and once only, did he put his troops in readiness to venture out. But as the cautious Spartan was offering sacrifices to ascertain the will of the gods, suddenly there came a partial eclipse of the sun (October 2, 480 B.C.), generally regarded as a sign of divine disapproval. The prudent Cleombrotus called off the march, and subsequently led his hoplites back to Peloponnesus. With the wall completed and the naval threat removed, why take unnecessary chances?

The effect of this on the waiting Athenians is not hard to imagine. Although normally a pious folk, they were not inclined now to wait upon the deities. Their impatience may have been reflected in the elections held during the winter. Aristides and Xanthippus were chosen again to the Board of Generals, but apparently Themistocles was not.[45] For the hero of Salamis to fail at the polls in 479 was shocking; the reasons can only be conjectured. Were the citizens dissatisfied with his sudden, bewildering shift of opinion about the conduct of the war after Salamis? Many must have disagreed with his idea of a sustained naval push across the Aegean, which would drain manpower away from the defense of Attica. Might their now illustrious champion have compelled Cleombrotus to move, had he wanted to? One thing they must surely have resented: his continued absence in other Greek cities, where he was being wined and dined while they shivered in makeshift housing on bare earth.[46] Even so, the end was not in sight.

The residents of Attica were understandably peeved, but from another Greek's standpoint, that of one born farther south, unrelenting warfare was hardly realistic. Mardonius and his army were in Thessaly, presently at a safe distance. If a pledge had been given the Athenians (something that was rather hazy in Peloponnesian minds), no date had been set. Anyway, Salamis had given adequate security to those superior Hellenes of beyond-the-Isthmus; the heart of Hellas would survive. Until they knew the Persian viceroy's intentions, it seemed inadvisable to stir. Those living in the exposed regions saw it differently, of course, and as the months passed without action Athenian discontent boiled into futile indignation. Their bitterness toward Cleombrotus and Sparta almost matched the wrath they nursed for Persia. At Salamis, Attic triremes had forestalled danger to Peloponnesus; now Peloponnesus was ignoring Attica.

The Spartans had recently sent their surviving king, Leotychides, out to replace Eurybiades in charge of the allied fleet, which had moved to an advanced position off Aegina. He found he had only 110 ships and could not take the offensive; the Athenians spitefully kept theirs in the Bay of Eleusis on the plea that this was necessary to protect their citizens, scattered and ill-defended. The rift among the Greeks persisted and continued to grow, in a topsy-turvy situation. Manifestly, Athens had the greatest seapower, yet most Athenians were for the moment united in wanting a land victory to guarantee them their country, with no dissipation of strength to other ventures. Hence their reluctance to cooperate with Leotychides. Lacedaemon was looking out for its interests. Athens must do the same.

Mardonius, wintering in Thessaly, watched with keen interest the course of events while getting ready to turn them to account. If not the first Persian to take note of Greek disunity, he was the first to form a plan for using it. The very audacity of his project was astounding, so much so that one questions his sincerity, and if that be granted, whether he had gotten a full and explicit clearance from the King. It seems impossible that he should not have done so, but it is equally incredible that Xerxes should have given his consent. For it involved nothing less than a complete reversal of the policy laid down by Darius. His expedition in 490, and the present one had both been undertaken with the aim of chastising Athens. Now Mardonius offered the Athenians full pardon, the return of all territory, and a guarantee of continued self-rule together with a Persian alliance on terms of complete equality. The proposals were made through King Alexander of Macedon (a fifth generation ancestor of Alexander the Great), who played at being friendly with both sides and was an acceptable intermediary. The Persians would go farther, said Alexander; they would give Athens even more land and also help rebuild her temples. The Athenians must have been dumbfounded. Alexander urged them to accept without hesitation while their luck held.

The intent of the plan could hardly be disguised. It was instantly apparent to all the Hellenes as soon as the word spread. With the Athenian fleet crossing to the other side, Persia's naval superiority would be staggering;[47] she could land her regiments anywhere on Peloponnesus, nullifying Cleombrotus' precious wall. The peninsula would be engulfed by an Oriental wave. To a Greek mind it was so ingenuous as to be almost insulting, but Athenians might well ask themselves, why not? Xerxes willing, Athens would come off scot-free, probably to be placed over the others as Persia's deputy. What had Peloponnesus done for Athens, that Athens should stand with her now? Here was a chance to get out of the war on better terms than they had a right to expect.[48]

It was a clever scheme with definite prospects for success, if all conditions were right. Peloponnesus was promptly alive to the danger. An embassy from Lacedaemon arrived so quickly that it found Alexander still dawdling in the city. The envoys were profuse with compliments, consolations, and choice morsels of sentiment. Spartans could find plenty of words when the stimulus was strong. Could Athens abandon the rest of Greece to the barbarians, they asked—she, to whom so many owed their freedom? Could she bear to think of the rest of them as slaves? Peloponneisans had all felt deeply the miseries endured by Athenians, the loss of their harvests and homes. Out of compassion they had come with a counterproposal. Let Athens send her women and children, her aged and crippled to Lacedaemon, and the Spartans would take care of them for the duration. Do not believe the blandishments of the Persians, they warned, for in them is neither truth nor faith.

An implication was intended to linger that Hellenes alone were worthy of trust, and always supported each other. The Athenians must have listened with scepticism. It was hard to generate enthusiasm over the Spartan bid after all they had heard. Probably more than a few were inclined to play both sides and drive them up—Themistocles, for one, if indeed he were back from his triumphal tour. No hint is given as to how the factions lined up, but in the end it was Aristides who rallied the people, and his motions that passed the Ekklesia. Alexander was informed that the Athenians valued freedom more than their own safety or self-interest, and that "So long as the sun keeps his present course, we will never join an alliance with Xerxes."[49] With the aid of the gods they would resist him as long as his troops remained in their land.

The reply to the Spartans is even more eloquent of Aristides' personality, and it began with a reproach as gentle as it was proud. No doubt the Lacedaemonians had feared that we might make terms with Persia, he said, though it is strange that they could, knowing as well as they do our temper and spirit. But since they needed to be reminded, "Not for all the gold ever mined or that which is still in the earth, would we side with the Medes in shackling our countrymen."[50] They have burned our temples and desecrated our holy images, and it is our duty to oppose them "while a single Athenian is alive to breathe." But also, "We remember well our fraternal tie with the Greeks, the mother tongue, the shrines, the sacrifices which we share, yes, even our conduct and way of life—if the Athenians betrayed all these it would be unforgivable." The Spartans were thanked for their kindness and their offers of sustenance, "but as for us, we will stick it out as best we may, and not be a burden to you."[51] Aristides' motion concluded simply by requesting the Peloponnesian army to come to their aid as soon as possible, since now they must expect the worst from the Persians. But suddenly, the envoys were taciturn Spartans again. Having gotten what they wanted, they left for home saying as little as possible.

Nobody doubted that Aristides was a good judge of the intentions of the invaders. In the late spring or early summer of 479, Mardonius broke up camp in Thessaly and marched south. On hearing of this threat, the Athenians sent messengers reminding Lacedaemon to hurry its troops. The Ephors replied coolly that nothing could be done at present. As usual it was a religious festival, the ever-convenient Hyacinthia, and of course it would be unconscionable to offend the gods. Behind the screen of excuses, the reasoning of the Ephors is hardly a mystery. Athens, having turned down the Persian proposal, had lost her bargaining power. Besides, battlements had recently been added to the Isthmus wall, and the Peloponnesians felt doubly secure. Athens was left to face the enemy unaided. Wearily her residents scrambled out of jerry-built hovels and once more sought transportation across the bay to Salamis. Another chill-to-the-bone winter was in prospect.

Mardonius was advancing, yet he did not lay waste to the country as he came. Locris, Phocis, Boeotia, all were spared, and amazingly, even Attica. Not without reason. Alternative schemes were shaping in the viceroy's agile mind. Other sizable states might be persuaded to defect, nor did he despair of Athens' eventual acceptance despite Aristides' vigorous rejection. Thebes was already on his side, to be used as the main base of operations. From there he boldly made overtures to Sparta's enemies inside Peloponnesus, especially to Argos. If the Argives were sturdy enough to divert the Spartans, holding them in the heart of the peninsula, he might be able to storm the Isthmus wall. The Argives seem to have encouraged the idea briefly, finally confessing that at the moment they were not strong enough to detain the Lacedaemonians. That hope was gone.

Thereupon, with Attica already in his grasp, Mardonius renewed his negotiations with the Athenians. A second ambassador was sent, on this occasion to Salamis, to tell them that the original offer was still open. On arrival he was taken first before the Council of Five Hundred, where feeling ran so high that they stoned the only one of their number who wanted to submit the proposal to the Ekklesia.[52] It was a bad mistake. Even though violence to the ambassador had been avoided, the incident was sure to reach the ears of Mardonius, who would no longer have any cause to stay his hand.

In their extremity it was Aristides to whom they turned again—whose influence was as firm now as before his ostracism. It was he, Plutarch asserts, who moved the appointment of three commissioners to Lacedaemon charged to make urgent representations on the necessity of Peloponnesian aid. Those he nominated were among the foremost in the state: Xanthippus, the general Myronides, and the young Cimon, Miltiades' son, who had won popular attention at Salamis. But though a formidable trio, nothing they could devise, nor any pressure attempted, got a commitment out of the Ephors. Even the veiled threat that Athens, if unsupported, would have to reconsider making terms with Persia elicited no response. If the only Athenian to declare for such a course had been put to death, Spartans need not worry overmuch. The commissioners had an impossible task, and deep down must have sensed it. Probably they cooled their heels at Lacedaemon considerably longer than the ten days stated by Herodotus.[53] Finally Aristides made the journey himself to add his voice but seemingly he too failed to budge the Ephors. Naturally, one wonders why Themistocles was not chosen one of the commissioners, since he was the man of the hour, and particularly, since he was so influential with the Spartans at this time. The mystery remains. His omission seems to indicate that he was not one of the generals for this year, also that he was temporarily out of favor with the Athenians for various reasons mentioned previously.

Then came the last day, the final interview. The commissioners agreed there was no hope, no point in further appeal. They came merely to take their leave, but could not refrain from a bitter observation that Sparta had left Athens no choice but to deal with Mardonius and fight at his side against their fellow Greeks. But the Ephors cut them short, and with unaccustomed Laconian laughter called them "sleepyheads." "While you have been sound asleep, our men have been mustering and by now must be at Oresteum in their march against the foreigners."[54]

Various attempts have been made to explain the Ephors' odd reversal; none are completely satisfactory. Was it really a change of mind? One authority contends they had meant to support Athens all along, and were only waiting until the harvest was in.[55] If that was the case, it is strange they did not say so. Other writers have maintained that Sparta could take no action while she was apprehensive about Argos' intervention. Another thinks there was an undetected but fair-sized war party at Lacedaemon, that surprisingly gained the upper hand.[56] Herodotus' explanation is simplest of all. He says the Ephors were cautioned by a prominent Peloponnesian neighbor, Chileos of Tegea, against pushing the Athenians too far; if the Athenians switched sides, Persia would have too much.[57]

Of course, the Ephors didn't need Chileos to tell them that. Even if not the brainiest men in Lacedaemon, they had plenty of advisers, besides the *proxenos* or official "friend" resident in each of the chief Hellenic cities, to give intelligence reports on current developments over the Greek world. Doubtless they knew what was going on in Athens, and were able to gauge tolerably well any shifts of sentiment there. In fact, these could be read in the faces of the commissioners, who typified all hues of Athens' political spectrum. Athens' vulnerability and the changing complexion of affairs forced the Ephors to reconsider their position.

When at last they did decide, it was for an all-out effort. An army of some 50,000 was called up, perhaps the largest in Spartan history. Only 5,000 were heavy-armed Spartiates, but this included more than half of the adult males who were full citizens. Another 5,000 were *perioikoi,* and the rest were light-armed helots. The perplexing question concerned who should lead. One of the two kings, Leotychides, was away acting as admiral of the fleet. The other, Leonidas' son Pleistarchus, was a mere child. His uncle Cleombrotus had been named regent after Thermopylae, but had distinguished himself mainly by his inactivity. Then he died unexpectedly during the winter.

Fortunately, Cleombrotus had left a grown son, Pausanias, and it was he whom the Ephors now placed in supreme command. Though young and unseasoned (his name is not previously mentioned),[58] this Spartan prince was to direct the largest force yet assembled in Hellas. While moving up the Isthmus he was joined by the levies of the allied Peloponnesian states, also by volunteers from beyond the peninsula. Fatefully, the host passed the protective wall built the previous year, and as it marched up the neck of the Isthmus the men of Megara fell in. Waiting at Eleusis were the hoplites of Athens, 8,000 strong under Aristides, recently elevated to the extraordinary post of strategos autocrator, which Themistocles had held the preceding year. Here Pausanias picked them up, and a brief halt was called while all swore to the so-called "Oath of Plataea," to fight together until victory was achieved and the barbarians driven from their land. With an army which by now approached 80,000,[59] he headed northward for the defiles of the Cithaeron which would conduct him into Boeotia. By Herodotus' estimate they were still fewer than the enemy, but Greece had never seen anything on such a scale where her own sons were concerned.

In the meantime Mardonius burned Athens a second time, and cut back over the mountains well ahead of the Greeks. Attica was off to one side, but Boeotia was on the main line from Peloponnesus through the heart of Greece up to Thessaly, and with his military position hinged on Thebes, the Persian viceroy could not leave this area undefended. Lying parallel to the Cithaeron range a few miles to the north, and running directly across the southern part of Boeotia, was the river Asopus. Here Mardonius distributed his divisions and waited. He might have occupied the heights himself, but chose not to. If he could trap his adversaries between the mountains and the river, the war might be ended at once, especially if the Greeks began to quarrel among themselves, as they so often did. Mardonius was in no hurry to precipitate the conflict. As he saw it, time was on his side. Besides, he was still waiting for the considerable reinforcements that Xerxes had sent him under Artabazus, satrap of Lydia. These had stopped enroute to besiege Potidaea, but were now drawing near.

It was in mid-August of 479 that the Greek army tramped out of Eleusis on the road winding northwest through the Attic frontier town of Eleutherai toward Boeotia.[60] This well-beaten path would take them over the Cithaeron by way of Gyphtokastro Pass and eventually to Thebes—but long before Thebes they would meet the Persians. A mile beyond the Pass on the Boeotian side was the village of Erythrae, and on descending the northern slope, they began to fan out into battle formation. It was none too soon. Not far ahead the road was blocked by the vanguard of the enemy. Hastily, the Hellenes completed the extension of their line, the Megarians taking the extreme left with the Athenians next to them; then came the Tegeans of Arcadia, while the Lacedaemonians and allied Peloponnesians held the right.

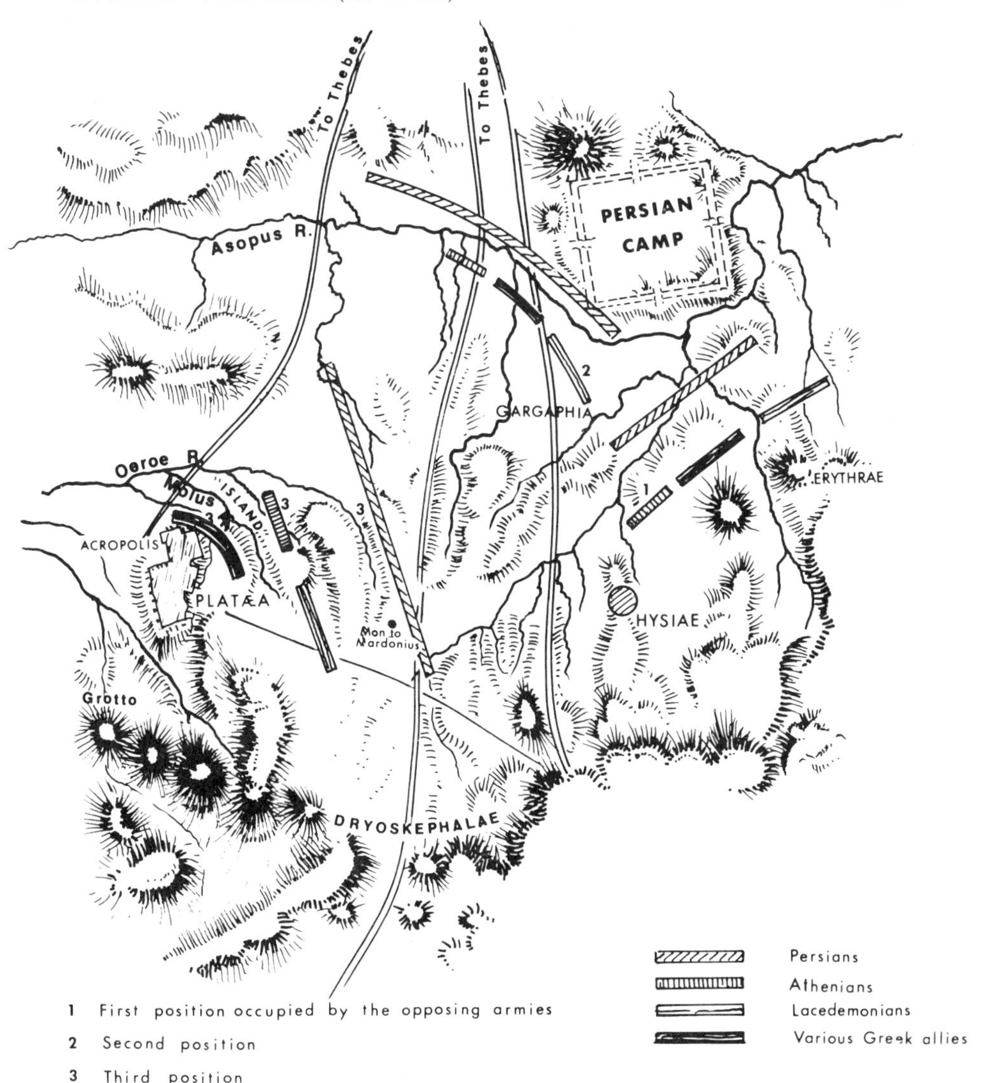

BATTLE OF PLATAEA

The high ground helped, and only the Megarians were seriously exposed. But the Persians were quick to recognize an opportunity and sent a body of horsemen under their chief of cavalry, Masistius, plunging at the unprotected men. The Megarians were hard pressed, and after stubborn resistance had to give way. Then Aristides' Athenians moved in to stiffen their ranks, effectively stemming the tide. Although probably intended only as a probe by the attackers, their feint became more than that. They were loath to give up a sector so hard won, and the struggle intensified as they continued to strike at the strengthened lines. Their leader Masistius was clad in impenetrable mail, but his wounded horse threw him, and unable to move in heavy armor, he was killed by a spear thrust in his eye as he lay prostrate. The cavalry fought furiously to recover his body, but were repulsed with more losses.

A valuable lesson was learned by the invaders in this day's combat: an indiscriminate old-style cavalry charge could not make headway at close quarters against massed, organized heavy infantry in a carefully chosen position that had natural flank protection.[61] The Athenians held the field, finally carrying off Masistius' exquisite gilt armor as a trophy to be placed later in the temple of Athena Polias on the Acropolis. After rejoining the main army behind the river Asopus, the Persians grieved for their fallen general and held a ritual of mourning for him.

No longer challenged, the Greeks proceeded downhill to improve their situation, then stopped as Pausanias decided to shift the entire line a mile or two farther west, so that his left wing covered the town of Plataea, near the foot of Cithaeron's slope. His reason for doing so is not clear. Herodotus says it was to obtain a more plentiful supply of water,[62] but this may be questioned in view of later events. In Herodotus' account a hazy period follows in which it is hard to get the true picture. For more than a week neither army took any significant steps, and we are told simply that the omens were inauspicious on each side. Both generals were slaughtering animals sacred to their gods, but apparently the gods were not touched. Neither commander was getting the response he wanted. Yet the Greeks seem to have been active to a degree. There is some reason to believe that on the left wing the Athenians tried an offensive, perhaps crossing the Asopus, and that they had no success. There was more trouble down the line. Mardonius was clearly outmaneuvering the Greeks despite his initial setback. By their move to the left, the Greeks had given up Gyphtokastro, the Pass through which they had entered Boeotia. Persian scouts promptly seized the spot, intercepting the supply trains coming from Peloponnesus. Meanwhile mounted Mede archers covered the fountain of Gargaphia, Pausanias' main source of water, shooting anyone who attempted to relieve his thirst. Soon the spring was choked with Greek dead and dying. Gargaphia had to be abandoned.

After holding this advanced position for ten days Pausanias deemed it necessary to call a council of war. Hunger and thirst were telling on his forces; unless access to water and the supply trains were quickly reestablished, the fighting qualities of his men might deteriorate. It was decided that during the night they should backtrack up the slopes of Cithaeron to a spot known as "the island" because its soil was nearly enclosed by two branches of the mountain stream Oeroe.[63] Here was the water so direly needed.[64] Removal was imperfectly managed in the gathering gloom, but once again literary obscurity makes it difficult to know what really happened. Herodotus blames the obstinate pride of a Spartan captain who long refused to give up his stand when the others did.[65] Yet this officer appears to have reached the new location in good time. More probably, trouble was caused by the Athenians crossing the position of the lesser allies, going from the left to the right wing, so as to occupy the place of honor alongside the Spartans.[66] To Mardonius, watching behind the Asopus, this confusion was too inviting to resist. In his own mind, he thought the Greeks already a beaten, disorganized mob.[67] Against the advice of the newly arrived Artabazus, against even his own original resolution, he crossed the river and opened the battle.

As usual with the Persians the first assault was made by cavalry, at the earliest possible moment—shortly after dawn. The Spartans and Tegeans had to bear the brunt of it, having reached the new locale ahead of the others. The situation steadily worsened. The Persian infantry too was soon on the scene, to mount the major offensive. Planting their wicker shields before them as a protective barrier, they poured "clouds of arrows" into the Lacedaemonians crouching behind their own bronze bucklers. Fiercely beset, Pausanias sent a messenger requesting the Athenians to come with all speed, or at least to detach their archers to neutralize those of the assailants. But the Athenians were by now engaged with the hostile Greeks in Mardonius' army, particularly their old adversaries, the Boeotians. The Lacedaemonians continued to endure, not daring to counterattack because of the religious sacrifices, uniformly unfavorable since their arrival.

It was an intensely agonizing moment, and the gods were thus far refusing to cooperate. At last the Tegeans could contain themselves no longer and rushed their tormentors. The better disciplined Spartans remained kneeling stoically in their places, despite losses, straining their ears for the signal of release. But the official diviner kept sacrificing animal after animal to no avail. At length Pausanias, tears crowding his eyes, turned toward the Temple of Hera with hands uplifted to supplicate its goddess and the other Olympians not to let his men be slaughtered by denying permission to fight. At that instant, so say the chroniclers, good omens were received. The command to advance was given, and the Spartans too charged on the run. The Persians put down their bows and prepared to receive them in close combat. However, they were at a disadvantage here. Their wicker shields were not much comfort against iron-pointed weapons, and their own spears were shorter than those of the Greeks.[68] Nevertheless, they fought with splendid bravery, and when nothing else availed, desperately seized the Greek spear-shafts to break them. Singly or in groups they dashed against the firm Spartan wall only to perish.

The battle was hottest where Mardonius on a white horse, surrounded by 1,000 picked troops, set the example by his courage and skill. Here many fell on both sides as the bodyguard tenaciously defended its general. But when Mardonius was finally struck down, the Persian will to resist collapsed altogether. It was obvious to them by now that their losses were catastrophic. The survivors turned and fled along the road to Thebes. Nor did they tarry there for more than a breathing spell. Eventually, most were gathered in by Artabazus with his reserves posted well to the rear. Artabazus had never been enthusiastic about the Greek venture, had sought until the last minute to dissuade Mardonius from the fatal commitment.[69] Collecting the fugitives, he marched rapidly back through Phocis, Locris, and Thessaly, his only goal being to reach the Hellespont and the safety of Asia as soon as possible.

The battle of Plataea had given the Greeks ashore a victory on land to match Salamis, one which in the end confirmed Salamis in every respect. For the action had not seemed a success until that final charge. The Athenians' gain on the first day had been erased later, and the whole army forced back from its advanced station. The second line was stubbornly held under heavy attack. Ultimately, it was the rigorous training of the Spartans that prevailed, as their sturdy phalanx plowed a wide path through Mardonius' best troops. The other Hellenes fought well, especially the Athenians who with particular relish felled three hundred of the Thebans opposite, but their efforts did little to decide the issue. The credit unmistakably belonged to the Lacedaemonians and Tegeans. On the field of battle all the Greeks gave thanks to the gods, and after burying their dead "in nations" (in other words, those of each state together), statues of Zeus and Poseidon were erected.[70]

But Apollo was honored beyond the rest. A full tenth of the spoil was set aside for his house of worship at Delphi, and close to the altar was placed a gold tripod resting upon a bronze column composed of three entwined serpents. (Much later this column was transferred by the Byzantine emperors to medieval Constantinople,[71] to be placed in the center of the Hippodrome, where it may still be seen.) Finally, it was Aristides who suggested that the town of Plataea be ever afterward considered sacred and inviolable, also that the anniversary of the victory should be observed there by a festival every fourth year, called the "Eleutheria" commemorating the "freedom" of the Greeks. It was a fitting gesture. Hellas was at last free of the invaders.

By contrast, the final action of the fleets was never in doubt. The Persian navy, badly damaged at Salamis, had as soon as possible recrossed the Aegean to relative safety. Broken in spirit as well, and indignant over Xerxes' treatment of the Phoenician captains, the Asiatic seamen no longer had the will to fight, but remained listless in the harbor at Samos.

Characteristic disagreements among the Greeks kept the victors from pursuing very far. The main Greek fleet under King Leotychides of Sparta could not leave its base at Aegina until the Athenian government permitted its navy, now commanded by Xanthippus, to rejoin. Eventually, in the spring of 479, the reunited fleet advanced to the island of Delos, and later, on the invitation of Samian sympathizers, they set sail for Samos to seek out their adversaries.

The Persians did not wait to be trapped, but fled across the narrow channel to the Asiatic mainland. Here they had so little confidence that, under the brow of Mount Mycale, they beached their ships, drove protective stakes around them, then entrenched themselves on the shore. Leotychides sailed by, assessed the situation, then disembarked his own men a few miles up the coast to march back for an attack by land. In the assault that followed, during which Xanthippus' Athenians distinguished themselves, the Persian barricades were stormed after a desperate resistance, most of the defenders were slain, and the ships burned.[72] The victory at Mycale was won, assertedly, at nearly the same time as the one at Plataea.[73] For the Greeks of Ionia, henceforth, the prospect of liberty loomed once more.

7

The Leadership of Themistocles

479–473 B.C.

IT had been generally assumed that after Mycale, the business of the Hellenic League would be ended. Before any of the voyagers were back, however, the delegates began to reconsider. There was a growing feeling that those among the European Greeks who had sided with the Persians ought to be punished. Even the Spartan commissioners were sympathetic to this viewpoint in cases that involved their own interests. Consequently, King Leotychides had barely brought his squadron into Aegina when he was sent off again, this time to expel the Aleuadae as rulers of Thessaly. The policymakers at Sparta had apparently been struck by another idea. If Lacedaemon could create a counterpart of its own Peloponnesian League in this distant northern region, and make it dependent on herself, she could with a minimum of effort well nigh control Greece. It was an attractive hypothesis, certainly. But Leotychides, though he spent the winter of 477–76 marching hither and yon over the broad Thessalian plain, had little to show for his energy—or lack of it. The Aleuadae evaded him; they managed to retain the loyalty of their people, and their chief stronghold, Larissa, did not fall. Leotychides continued to report victories that had no substance. It looked very suspicious. By spring he was recalled to Sparta to face charges that the Thessalians had bribed him. Eventually, to escape prosecution, he retired to an obscure existence at Tegea.[1]

This created another problem. By the spring of 478, the Hellenic Congress had come so far along the road to panhellenism that it decided to launch a second naval expedition to secure the outer fringes of the Greek world. Leotychides would have been its logical leader; but since he was in exile, so to speak, the Ephors had no choice but to prolong the authority of the regent

Pausanias. They had qualms about this too. The youthful regent had commemorated his Plataea victory with a tripod at Delphi containing a swaggering inscription in which he took all the credit.[2] But no other royal Spartan was available. Pausanias it had to be. He was given twenty Lacedaemonian ships, to which Athens added thirty under Aristides, and the islanders still another thirty. Their immediate destination was the island of Cyprus, which had a large Greek population known to be sympathetic to the common cause. Once there Pausanias had no trouble driving the Persian garrisons out of the Greek cities. Most of Cyprus was recovered. Afterward the Spartan regent steered for Byzantium, which he was fortunate enough to capture before the end of the summer. This was a most valuable acquisition, anchoring the northern end of the straits as Sestos did the southern. Once more the Hellenes had possession of their important trade route to the Black Sea.

But it was here that trouble began anew. Though still a young man, Pausanias already had experienced successes enough to turn an older, wiser head: Plataea, Cyprus, now Byzantium. He had led the largest Greek army ever assembled to a resounding victory over the greatest nation in the world. Yet he was not king even in his native state, nor could ever hope to be in the normal order of things. He was merely filling in for his child cousin, Leonidas' son, Pleistarchus. Doubtless he felt there was something unfair in this, and doubtless too he boiled at the restrictions that watchful Spartan Ephors always placed on their field commanders.

In the very responsible position that he held, mistakes by Pausanias were inevitable; however, the sketchy information about him makes these hard to evaluate. He is said to have grown arrogant in his command, to have insisted on an exaggerated discipline, punishing violaters with floggings and irons.[3] There were stories also of his wearing rich Persian robes, forming friendships with titled Persians, even creating a bodyguard for himself from the Persians and Egyptians captured at the straits. If the panoramic sweep at Byzantium, with the all-enveloping Bosporus bending below him like the Stream of Ocean, imparted notions of grandeur, it was not unnatural. What little is known of Pausanias' character, from the Plataea inscription, makes this seem probable. Yet he appears to have been in good repute at Byzantium for a year or two.[4] And the Ionian captains who complained about his overbearing ways had a deeper grievance in Sparta's refusal to extend the war of liberation across the Aegean.[5] Pausanias was subsequently recalled to Sparta and deprived of his command, probably because he was no longer acceptable to the allies.[6] The charges of Medism (treasonable relations with the Persians) would come later.

The Ionians preferred Athenian leadership, for they realized that it was more congenial to their cause. And Athens was quick to recognize the opportunity, quick to fill the void, fortunate as well in having the right man to do it. Aristides now commanded her naval contingent at Byzantium; in the crisis, his conduct was officially circumspect. Reportedly, he had rebuked Pausanias' arrogance in his mild way, but made no move against him that could be considered disloyal. When the other captains asked him to assume supreme command, he had replied that such action could be justified only by some flagrant overt act of Pausanias which the whole fleet would agree in condemning.[7] All very proper, but the door had been opened at least by a crack. Glimpsing the light, the Ionian captains moved to create such an incident, goading Pausanias to curse them for nearly running afoul of his vessel, after which they loudly renounced their allegiance to him. Whatever the truth of the matter, Aristides seems not to have dissuaded them.[8] When the Spartans sent out another admiral, Dorcis, to replace Pausanias, Aristides was firmly in control. Athens was on her way.

The historian Thucydides, an Athenian himself, assures us that the Spartans were now thoroughly disillusioned with their commanders, and having no further interest in the war, were quite willing to turn the leadership over to their friends, the Athenians.[9] Actually, the return home of the repudiated Dorcis seems to have left the Spartans distraught.[10] Aristotle admits that the prevailing mood was one of resentment against Athens,[11] and another account reports an excited debate pro and con.[12] It was obviously a jolt to Lacedaemonian leadership, and a cause for grave concern rather than placid acquiescence. But Sparta was caught flat-footed; bewildered, disunited, and with no heritage of experience in dealing with unforeseeable contingencies that involved human relations, she had no choice but to accept the accomplished fact.

Conversely, Athens was willing and ready. In tacit recognition a number of Greeks turned simultaneously to her for direction. It is true, of course, that in Aristides the captains had chosen an extraordinary Athenian; that he was on the scene at the right time was of immense advantage to his city. But the Athenian system was geared to the individual, encouraging the fullest development of extraordinary potentialities. Intellectual jousting, competition between minds in Ekklesia and Agora, even the physical testing of one another at the palaestra, or wrestling school, saw to that. Although these individuals did not often measure up to Aristides, still it is significant that such leaders could be found on occasions. In Sparta, where rigid conformity was the rule, an Aristides could hardly have emerged. Taking a longer look at Lacedaemon, such a leader as Aristides coming from Sparta can scarcely be imagined.

During these crucial months the residents of Athens were rebuilding their city. When the reconstruction started, mixed emotions about the war had placed definite restraints on their ardor. The Persian navy had been defeated, but not the grand army, which was after all the more fearsome of the two. A land victory was imperative, without which they could never be safe. Mardonius, whom Xerxes had left to finish the task of conquest, was still in the north; any day he might order the advance that would threaten their reconstruction and send them scurrying back to Salamis. Which was just what did happen. Work launched under such a shadow could not be carried out very enthusiastically or efficiently.

The citizens' dissatisfaction was probably reflected in their election of Xanthippus and Aristides to the generalship, both long associated with the policy of land defense, and in the temporary shelving of the naval-minded Themistocles. While the crisis at home existed they wanted no sailings to Ionia, no dissipation of energy elsewhere. That could wait.

After Plataea it was different, of course. Now there was room for optimism, at home and abroad. But the Athenians' upsurge had actually started before Plataea, even before Mardonius evacuated their country to position himself for the climactic battle. And the one who had rallied them was none other than Aristides—who persuaded them to turn down the Persian offer; who pressured the Peloponnesians to come to their rescue; Aristides again, who authored the high-minded statement that the Athenians would not betray Hellas nor be a burden to her either, but would bear their own ills as best they might.[13] Small wonder then, that when his idealism vindicated itself in practice, gaining Athens a universal goodwill, his grateful countrymen made him strategos autocrator in charge of their land army at Plataea, sending him afterward to command their naval contingent bound for Cyprus and the straits. How much of Athens' later success was fostered by Aristides' initiatives cannot be calculated, but his part in the final total must be regarded as an ample one.

The effect of his buoyant spirit is reflected in the gusto that the Athenians evinced in the process of rebuilding. Reason enough to be thankful. A bad storm had spent its fury, the winds were blowing them fair. The citizens could give themselves wholeheartedly to the task of reconstruction. The new Athens would be bigger and better, a monument to victory. With few major differences. The older Agora at the Acropolis' entrance could be allowed to dwindle. There was little need to restore it, since the newer one on the north could now be enlarged to meet all present and foreseeable needs. Just as obviously, the Acropolis temples would have to await a more prosperous generation who would find the money to build anew. But the residential district began to rise rapidly, as all contributed their labor in a mighty communal effort. Women and even children joined in, and finally, with surging optimism, they commenced to erect new walls out beyond the ancient bulwarks. Stones were dragged from the former foundations, and everything capable of being used, even sculptures and grave markers, were boosted onto the rising lines.[14]

In the thick of things and spurring the workers to ever greater activity was Themistocles, now in Athens and once more in control despite his recent slight setbacks. Presently such events were but bare ripples on the tide of his fortune. As the man who had saved the day at Salamis was he not, even without office, the first man of Athens—and more, the first in Greece? For him the trappings of officialdom had become unnecessary. Though never to hold the post of general again, so far as is known, he dominated affairs at Athens over the next few years from his place in the Assembly. The archons and the generals bowed respectfully, all manner of men paid court, conceding they knew where the real power lay.[15] His role and power as prostates was simply made more evident. All must understand that his was the voice that settled issues and framed policies in the city.

For the moment none disputed it. His fame redounded to the edges of Hellas and beyond. Lacedaemon acclaimed him with the rest. So when the Spartans heard with disapproval of the latest activities in Attica, they hesitated to express themselves in their usual forthright manner. A few years earlier they might have peremptorily ordered the wall building stopped. But Lacedaemon's hold over Athens had been weakened by her dilatory conduct between Salamis and Plataea. Nor could her Ephors talk to the savior of Hellas as though he were an underling. It was doubly impossible when they had to contend with as bold a spirit as Themistocles.

Instead of a stern imperative, the Spartan ambassadors came with a mild counterproposal intended to bolster their own faltering League. Let Athens and the other cities north of the Isthmus abandon fortifications, they urged; Sparta herself had no walls, deeming her valiant men the best possible barrier to attack. Now they would extend this protection to everyone. Lacedaemon was prepared to undertake the defense of all Greece. Themistocles must have had sardonic thoughts of the days immediately before and after Salamis. In any case, he had no intention of seeing Athens reduced to dependence on Sparta again. It was less sensible than ever now that fortune was beckoning. There were other considerations. As leader of the demos he saw clearly, possibly before anyone else, that the welfare of the Athenian masses demanded an imperialistic foreign policy.[16] The corn and fruits of Attica could not take care of their increasing population. More than any of her sister states, Athens must either expand or face inevitable decline.[17]

But Themistocles was not one to show his hand prematurely. Rather, in the Ekklesia he appeared to reflect on the matter, then proposed that three commissioners be sent to Sparta to hammer out an agreement. He offered to be one himself, and was elected on the spot. Displaying a genuine concern, the prostates left for Lacedaemon as soon as he could make arrangements. Before departing, however, he urged the citizens in private to build the walls with utmost speed, and told his two colleagues not to come until these had reached a safe height. All inhabitants of the city were to work unceasingly until a proper level was attained.

Once in Sparta, Themistocles played the game as only he could. For several days the devious commissioner did not even present himself to the Ephors, saying he had no authority to act alone, but must wait for the others to join him. While he marked time, Spartans arriving home from the north informed the Ephors that the Athenians were still raising their walls. The angry magistrates sent for Themistocles. Without a trace of embarrassment, the great man denied everything. With becoming mildness he reproached them for listening to rumors, suggesting that they send reliable investigators to discover the truth. At the same time the absent prostates smuggled out secret instructions to Athens that the Lacedaemonian visitors should be kept under guard until Themistocles returned. In a few days his two colleagues arrived and together they paid an official call on their hosts. With no apologies for his past conduct, Themistocles suddenly changed his tune. Athens now had walls, he announced, and was well able to protect herself. Nor had she thought it necessary to ask anyone's consent. In the dark days before Salamis, when her residents had resolved to leave their city and seek a new home in the west, "they did not first seek the advice of the Lacedaemonians." And in subsequent deliberations between the two states, "they had found their own counsel as sound as anyone's."[18] The Athenians knew as well as Spartans what was for the common good, and what was best for the individual. They would always be willing to discuss these matters, but a defenseless city would not have its proper voice in talks between them. It would be a fine thing for all of them to have walls, he concluded drily.

The speech of Themistocles was as momentous as it was daring. Athens considered herself the equal of Lacedaemon; this he had as much as said. What could Lacedaemon do about it? The Peloponnesian League was no help in this instance. Themistocles had consistently ignored it, and he did not trouble to define Athens' relation to it now. Listening, the Spartans tried not to show their annoyance. There was still some residue of goodwill toward the northern neighbor for her gallant behavior in the recent war.[19] So they replied that their proposal had only been a suggestion which Athens might take however she wished. It was Sparta's only possible answer. Her own observers were being held as hostages in Attica until the Athenian commissioners were safely away. This trickster from the north—once honored by them as a hero—seemed to have thought of everything.

Once back home, Themistocles did not rest. Athens had made her choice. At his behest the citizens had flung up the new walls so hastily that anything within reach, even household furniture, was thrown into them. Since there was no time to bring stone from a distance, items ready at hand were sacrificed no matter how valuable. But surrounding the city with walls was no longer enough. Piraeus must be fortified too. If Athens were cut off from the sea, walls would not be of much use. This step was as important as the other, maybe more so. Since Athens' newfound strength lay in her navy and merchant marine, a logical move would have been to rebuild the entire state around Piraeus after the Persian devastation.[20] Its harbors were sheltered, and its hills, though not as high as the Acropolis, afforded some protection on the land side. As for the Acropolis, its heights had not availed against the Persians. Nor would they against any major enemy in the future.

But so sweeping a shift was barred by sentiment. All the city's traditions were centered on the Acropolis, and the reverent might question whether their goddess could be comfortable anywhere else. Here Apollo had begotten Ion, and Athena had adopted Hephaestus' son, Erichthonius, their second king. To Athenians the mere sight of the Acropolis and its proud temples, even when in ruins, was proof to them of their divine descent. Pious enthusiasm distorted their rationality.

Still, on the other matter there was no argument. After Athens, Piraeus would have to be walled too, with effort and expense almost as great. Immediately Themistocles ordered ramparts to be constructed all around the seaward peninsula — it was a favorite project he had started years before when he was archon — with moles to protect the naval stations of Zea and Munychia, on the south side. The larger harbor of Kantharos, to the north, was strengthened with two walls, one running the length of each side. Themistocles' arrangements were obviously a service to the whole population, but a very particular one to his thete supporters, most of whom lived in the districts nearest the docks. He was ever adept at aligning the interests of his fellows with his own. Long afterward Aristophanes remarked in *The Knights* that "Themistocles had kneaded Piraeus onto the city,"[21] but Plutarch thought it more truthful to say that "he had fastened the city to Piraeus."[22] It may have caused him some concern that the two fortified rings were several miles apart, but that might be rectified later. A convalescent nation rising from a bed of ashes could not attempt too much at once. Reviving health and unremitting toil would eventually make secure her path to the sea, if not to the stars.

None could doubt that Themistocles was feeling his dominance. When he declined for Athens an assumed second place under Sparta, he rejected a similar status for himself. Proudly conscious of the distinction that Salamis had conferred, he looked forward to the meeting of the Amphictionic Council in 476, as an opportunity to parade his prestige before all of Greece. Established originally as guardians of Demeter's temple at Anthela, and Apollo's at Delphi, the *Amphictionies* were in the normal order the closest thing Greece had to a continuing national Congress. Even so the resemblance is distant, since the Amphictionic Council dealt mainly with questions of religion and the finances involved, being concerned with politics only to a lesser degree. Nevertheless Sparta came to the meeting with a proposal to expel from the Council those states which had refused to fight the Persians. It was not an entirely disinterested motion on her part, as the members chiefly affected would be, besides Thebes, the Thessalian cities, which had recently defied Spartan intervention, and in the Peloponnesus, her old enemy Argos.

Themistocles was immediately in the forefront, objecting. Only thirty-one states had been involved in the war, he said, and since many of these were small and without influence, the Council would be run by two or three of the largest participants. He thought it better to let bygones be bygones. All of Hellas should be represented.[23] Nothing so democratic and urbane to equal Themistocles' magnanimity was heard at the meeting. The gain to Athens in public relations had to be enormous.

Furthermore, Lacedaemon's latest attempt to bend the Thessalians and other dissidents to its will was exposed. But if the Spartan delegate was not guileless, neither was Themistocles. Shamelessly, he was bidding for support from members Sparta had tried to oust, seeking to mold them into an Athenian power bloc. The ploy achieved a certain success, and needless to say, the Lacedaemonians never forgave him. Before their eyes he was charting an independent and audacious foreign policy that threatened Lacedaemon's leadership of Greece. No wonder they bristled. Forgotten already was the fervent reception of three years before. Their object henceforth was to bring the tireless intriguer down.

They would have to wait awhile. For the moment there was no stopping him. The wave that had started at Salamis must roll out its course. Nevertheless Spartans had noticed the little eddies of riptide too, the great man's occasional reverses, for example, and it brought them a mite of satisfaction that these occurred abroad as well as at home. So he plumed himself as a diplomat? Soon after Salamis, Themistocles had tried to levy an exorbitant tax on the Aegean islanders, to be transformed into wages for his thete followers who made up Athens' ship crews.[24] Sailing boldly into their ports, he had said that he came representing two mighty gods, Persuasion and Necessity.[25] Some of the islanders paid forthwith, notably those of Paros and Carystus. However, the people of Andros replied that they had two gods, Poverty and Helplessness, who would not allow them to pay. For their courageous defiance the Andrians had to stand siege, but in the end it appears they escaped punishment. Actually, Andros was an island not ill-favored by nature. Though mainly mountain, its range contained several fertile valleys; its wine was famous throughout antiquity. The inhabitants were plucky enough to hold out against injustice, and the example they set was not lost on their Aegean neighbors. Themistocles quickly found that he had cast away whatever influence or goodwill he possessed with them, and soon desisted from his operations. In this area, at least, he had outlived his usefulness. That may be one reason why the Athenian people replaced him with Xanthippus as naval commander, and after Xanthippus, sent out Aristides. Well aware of his own deficiencies, the tolerant Athenian of the streets could grin at peccadilloes in private, but he could not overlook them on the world stage. Nothing damaged national prestige as much as the ridicule of his peers, not did he like the laughter of the other Greeks. In this he was human too.

For Themistocles' many antagonists on both sides of the seas the best course was to give him latitude. But time was required for the desired effect. At present they had to bear his superior smile. There was ample cause for this. The news he had from the north was all good. To the democratic chief[26] and his entourage at Athens it must have been a subject for joking that the benefits he enjoyed were brought about by his onetime rival, Aristides. It would be jesting with a sting, considering the prostates' failure with the Andrians, but after all was he not the final winner? The old adversary was a subordinate now, ever since his offer of cooperation before Salamis. His one-year stint as autocrator, his little triumphs garnered since, had simply strengthened the popular front, ultimately to serve his chief's purpose. And why worry about one so self-effacing?

It was true that at Byzantium Aristides had become surfeited with success. All the mistakes of Pausanias had turned to his advantage, or rather, Athens'. The captains at the straits could not help contrasting his modestly reasonable demeanor with that of the haughty Spartan regent. While Pausanias had made himself resented, Aristides had gone among them cheerfully, discussing mutual problems in a familiar way, through open conferences seeking adjustments satisfactory to all. Thus when Sparta withdrew from the war, and even before, a new orientation was already discernible. The democratic political practice of Athens' Agora had been instituted at Byzantium and was already functional there. Aristides was moving among the captains, mediating their disputes, harmonizing them, as he had once done in the marketplace at home. If, in this vital moment of transition, Athens had searched for somebody to sell her system and managerial skill to the outland Greeks, she could have picked no better salesman.[27]

That the Athenians were at last delivered from the Mede, most felt assured. But this was true only in a finite sense. If Persia learned to make proper use of her tremendous potential, then no one was safe. Common anxiety about an enemy, who though defeated, still possessed the resources to overpower and enslave them, made some sort of lasting association imperative. It was a foregone conclusion, of course, that such a combination must be based on Athens' leadership. This sine qua non had been tacitly admitted when the captains transferred their allegiance from Pausanias to Aristides. The members who did not resign persevered in this decision and in the next couple of years made moves to fasten themselves more tightly to Athens' protection.

Whether this arrangement amounted to an extension of the former compact, or whether it should be regarded as something new, is not easily determined. The Hellenic League had never had a written constitution, nor official articles defining it as an entity, so far as is known. Nor had the older Peloponnesian League, so-called, — a body which ancient writers referred to simply as "the Lacedaemonians and their allies." Even the term "allies" conveys a meaning too hard and fast, in a modern sense. The actual Greek word was *symmachia,* or "fighting together." Meetings were held but agreements reached were apt to be more fluid, not so strongly binding as in present-day counterparts with their precise legalities. There was a delightful elasticity to the thought, expression, and understanding of the Greeks that made them hard to pin down — and sometimes got them into trouble.

Thus it is difficult to say whether they regarded the enterprise formed at the straits as an instrument freshly designed or an old one renovated. So much of it was circumstantial, offhand. It was in Athens' interest to keep it that way to a certain point, to exploit the existing flexibility and cut corners. The aspect of continuity she could be expected to stress at least for awhile, to retain as many adherents of the Hellenic confederacy as possible, even those who had been leary of Attic leadership on the eve of Artemisium. Against Persia the optimum was needed.[28]

However, at Artemisium Athens had been represented by the slippery Themistocles. The protest may have had reference to him. It is important that when at last every ally conceded the initial association to be completely altered, reoriented toward Athens, the Athenian they had to deal with was Aristides. When passing from defense to offense, to a scheme whose aim was not only to free Persia's Greeks, but more dubiously, to undermine Persia and make her pay,[29] Aristides' presence—whether he understood it that way or not—gave a sort of psychic reassurance, almost a guarantee of justice, insinuating also that Athens would be a trustworthy guardian and guide.

At the same time the discriminating Athenian was careful not to claim too much for Athens. It was Aristides, we are told, who suggested that the headquarters of the new body be situated at "holy Delos," reputed birthplace of Apollo, therefore revered by Ionians and all Greeks.[30] He thought this was the best spot for the treasury, safeguarded in Apollo's temple under the eyes of the god, since a common fund would be necessary for the war that must go on. It was an excellent choice, for more than religious reasons. The island was centrally located in the southern Aegean, with a fine harbor to house the combined fleet. Delos' rugged beauty, with its intimations of deity, might well have an inspiring effect on the allies' delegates when they came to meetings of the Synod, intended as the governing council of what would henceforth be known as the Confederacy of Delos.

The contribution of Aristides to its inception was so significant that when the hour came round for the oath meant to bind them, he was the person chosen to take it, symbolically, for the entire assemblage.[31] The rite was one used by Greeks on rare occasions, evidence now of the good feeling engendered by the recent open, democratic procedures. After the oath, ingots of iron were cast into the sea, the implication being that the vows should hold until the iron rose to the surface again, that is, forever. And it was Aristides, at the end, who heaved the ingots overboard.[32] Without him, how many of the members would have been willing to make a commitment so astonishing, so unreserved?

His reward was plenty of work in the foreseeable future. Treasury assessments on the individual states had to be made, and no one else was so universally trusted. The habit of consultation which had made him so many friends was resumed and Aristides spent most of the years 478 and 477 traveling through the islands and cities of the Confederacy taking stock of the assets of each. Thucydides asserts that his total assessment was placed at 460 talents,[33] but this figure has often been questioned.[34] The actual cash collection for the first year, 477 B.C., seems to have been only about 230 talents.[35] However, before judgment can be passed on Thucydides' statement, other problems emerge. Since originally many members contributed ships and men, did Aristides' estimate include the value of ship contributions as well as money? If so, on what basis did he equate them, and what allowances were made for upkeep, repairs, services, sailors' pay, including extras for overlong campaigns?[36] Staggering problems, all, with few obvious solutions which can be agreed upon today, but Aristides met them somehow, fairly and squarely, winning unanimous approval.

Athenians watching at home could not but be grateful to their representative at the straits, even if their altruism was not quite on a level with his. It was all very well to make concessions to keep the confederates happy. On these matters it was best to say nothing at present. But every Athenian knew that in their city all power was centered in the Ekklesia, which would have to ratify the Delian arrangements, and might also change them, the oaths notwithstanding. And in the Ekklesia it was Themistocles, not Aristides, who was paramount.[37] So Aristides was getting a favorable reception for his quotas. That was fine. He had been authorized to take the oaths which committed Athens equally with the others—or was it really equal? When disagreements came, and the representatives flocked to Delos to iron them out, strong Athens would have a natural advantage over the rest, if she could keep them apart; if she could find an excuse to draw them to Attica and Pnyx Hill, where Themistocles and his necessitous allies of the thetic class could have at them, the gain would be still greater.

For it was plain that the Confederates needed Athens even more than she needed them. One as shrewd as Themistocles was sure to make the most of *that* situation. He was always a man to profit by observation, and it was clear that Sparta had far fewer problems, far better control in her own peninsular alliance where her voice equaled all the rest, than in the Hellenic League where she had one vote among many. The explanation was that the Peloponnesian League rested on a series of treaties between Lacedaemon and each of the other members, Lacedaemon being always one-half of the contracting parties. Whereas, in the Hellenic all had been equal participants through attendance at the Congress of Corinth.

There was a world of difference. To satisfy his needy followers, it behooved Themistocles to avoid the pitfalls of the latter organization, which had been so costly to Sparta, and this time at least, so lucky for Athens. It might not always be so, and if not, Athens' discharged ship crews could swell the ranks of the unemployed. Manifestly, their political spokesmen in the home government—beginning with the prostates himself—could not allow this to happen.

Exactly how they managed, the records do not reveal. Apparently not much was settled in the meeting at the straits except that Athens should be the leader in the continuing struggle against Persia, with Aristides to make the assessments; the allies should be autonomous; and the Synod and treasury should be located at Delos. This left many details to be worked out (or left hanging), and a considerable leeway for Themistocles and those like-minded back home. The loophole they intended to enlarge was buried deep in the character of all Greeks and their institutions. No matter how many ingots were sunk, how many promises made, how much power pledged to the Delian Synod, no Greek could conceive of these taking precedence over the decisions of his own town assembly. No doubt the ingots meant that the Confederacy should be eternal—unless, by a paradox peculiarly Greek, his town assembly should decide otherwise. The revolts occurring later would bear this out.

But the silent unspoken exception that all members allowed themselves was far more advantageous to Athens than to any of the rest. For she had the most power, and in her capactiy as manager for the others, she was in a position to give her Ekklesia a de facto authority over the Delian Synod. Because of this, some have considered the Delian organization bicameral,[38] a view not generally accepted,[39] and for which proof is lacking. But in practice it would tend to work out that way, to the satisfaction of Themistocles and the embryonic imperialists at Athens. If the Athenian Assembly decided otherwise, what could the Delian Synod do, whether or not Athens had a member on it?[40] Athens controlled the armed forces and her treasurers controlled the money, even while it remained at Delos. As the years passed Athens made individual treaties with the various members when she could, to reinforce and tighten her control. So the last laugh was Themistocles', though he and his friends must have understood the advisability of treading lightly for the moment. Aristides had appeared to be thinking in terms of an egalitarian Synod of unchallenged authority. Obviously, for the realistic politicans at Athens, this would not do.[41]

As for Aristides' arrangements, these might be modified at leisure. The total he had arrived at had been divided among the confederates, to everyone's satisfaction. But there had been no settlement as to how the payments should be made, whether in cash or in service. Seemingly, Aristides was leaving this to each member's inclination, assuming each would continue to do what had previously been done. But the realists at Athens could not concur.

Heretofore the service principle had been the normal order, and undoubtedly the larger states such as Samos, Chios, and Mytilene would prefer to continue their donations in ships and men, even insisting upon it. The unpleasant alternative for them was a sizable money payment. When dealing with these weighty ones it was best to give way. They were powerful enough to defend themselves in all but the gravest of crises. But the monsters were not numerous. The great majority were smaller, many of whom might choose to pay, or be persuaded to do so. These were the ones for Themistocles to belabor, since their money could be turned into jobs for Athens' poor—her demos, the Low. Athens would build the ships, provide the crews for the confederates who found service inconvenient or pinching. Even if they did not, it might come to the same. Themistocles could be gracious or sinister; he could coax or threaten. And for small states, if immediately exposed to Persia, it was a serious affair to brave his wrath. So Athens' strength grew visibly, under their gaze. They furnished the means, but the units created were Athens' and they were unquestionably loyal to her. Even in this early period of camaraderie Themistocles' design must have been transparent, its latent menace recognized. But comfort and inertia stifled any misgivings.

Any who were disenchanted could do little, except to their own disadvantage. Themistocles was so canny at the game of getting without giving, it is still not clear whether Athens belonged to the Confederacy, making a contribution of her own, or whether she stood outside, beyond and above, administering for the rest through a series of contracts. Ships, crews, and marines she did provide, on an enlarging scale that finally dwarfed the other contingents. But did she pay for any part of these? Or, as one modern authority asserts, did all the money come from the nonservice members?[42] Themistocles managed well enough to keep us from knowing, and very possibly the system of separate treaties enabled him to hoodwink the members as well. Significantly, it was arranged that all the *Hellenotamiai,* the Delian treasurers, should be Athenians,[43] and Athenians they continued to be as long as the Confederacy existed.

It is easy to blame Themistocles for his presumed part in shaping the Confederacy and to trace its eventual decline to actions he originally instigated. Yet it should be remembered that the negotiations were as "free" as historical forces permitted, with none of the bargaining states dissatisfied to the point of breaking off and going it alone. Utter realist that he was, Themistocles knew the confederates would use Athens as long as it suited, and would desert without the slightest compunction when their purpose was served. Athens must be just as hardheaded, get what she could out of it. Sentiment and gratitude do not count in politics. On the other hand, there was a benevolent Athenian statesman overseas who could almost prove the contrary. Without Aristides, the Confederacy might never have been born. Without Themistocles, it would not have endured the span that it did.

The new organization was soon to have its mettle tested. The almost forgotten Pausanias, recalled to Sparta to answer for his conduct, had wormed his way out of the charges and was at large again. Evidence against him was inconclusive and he received only a stern reprimand. Angry and vengeful, the ousted commander suddenly reappeared at the straits with hired ships and a private army, probably before the end of 477. How he was able to raise them remains a mystery, but his connections with Persia suggest an explanation.[44]

Sailing into Byzantium, Pausanias easily made himself master of the city, probably while Aristides was away making the assessments. That the royal Spartan had recently domineered over the area may have weakened the garrison's will to resist. Titillated by the fast coup, he next struck at Sestos, and equally fortunate, found himself in possession of both ends of the vital water road to the Black Sea.[45] Though his grasp on Hellas was not quite a stranglehold, still, if unchallenged, he could make her writhe in agony from hunger. Athens and other Greek states drew badly needed cereals from many of the Mediterranean lands, but few fields were more fertile than those surrounding the Pontus and Propontis, regions that today would include the coasts of Bulgaria, Rumania, Russia (the Ukraine), the northern shores of Turkey. From their faraway ports came minerals and timber as well as quantities of grain, but all shipments had to first pass the Bosporus, then the Hellespont. Pausanias was now in a position to intercept these. If Persia were backing him, Greek independence might still be endangered.

It all happened too quickly for the Confederacy to react in time. Aristides was busy with his sensitive task. The fleet was probably centered on Delos, or dispersed among the islands aiding him with his assessments. Athens could not afford to wait. Her economy was jeopardized and her pride hurt by the loss of two posts so recently acquired, so strategically placed. Without waiting for the wheels of the Confederacy to grind, she sent out an expedition of her own under Cimon, son of Miltiades, a young man as yet undistinguished except for his Philaid ancestry. Was this permissible under the new agreements, without sanction from the Synod? Maybe, but if so the action is more likely to have originated in the Strategion, the Board of Generals, than in the Ekklesia where Themistocles held sway. Themistocles was not inclined to tap a Philaid or anyone from the High, let alone a son of Miltiades.[46] He was once reported as remarking that the laurels won by the father at Marathon would not allow him to sleep. He wanted no more sleepless nights.

Cimon soon discharged his duties in a manner sure to add a tinge of personal worry to the prostates' public gratification. Although a fledgling general, he chased Pausanias out of both his strongholds, so quickly that the renegade did not have time to extricate all his forces. At both Sestos and Byzantium a goodly number of highborn Persians fell into Cimon's hands. The officers were able to ransom themselves at such a price that Cimon gained four months' wages for his men, and had enough left over to make a handsome gift of gold to Athens' treasury.[47] Naturally, Athens' demos found it hard to dislike him; he had no trouble over reelections. Pausanias sought safety on the Asian side of the Hellespont, where the Persians would be less genial hosts after failures that had been so costly to their kinsmen. To their relief, the meddling Spartan was shortly called home to answer for his latest follies. He was never to return.

Cimon remained on guard at the Hellespont with an armament partly Athenian, partly confederate. Through him Athens was again in control of the Pontic lifeline. Aristides apparently joined him at the straits within a year, to begin that close friendship so significant for them and their nation. The elder statesman's arrival was timely; Cimon was first noted for his Philaid air of authority, youthful inconsiderateness, and brusque manners. Thus there was danger that he would offend the allies as Pausanias and Themistocles had. Aristides at once took him in charge, leading him to see how much might be gained through tact and courtesy; triumphs in diplomacy were as valuable as those won in the field.[48] The metamorphosis was gradual, but in a few years so complete that it baffled later biographers like Plutarch, who found it difficult to form a coherent estimate of Cimon's character. The youth who seemed so unattractive, at whom many continued to cavil, was, thanks to Aristides, finally accounted the wisest, bravest—and most benevolent—of his generation, superior to his own father, and at last equal to Themistocles as a statesman![49]

Together the two men set the Confederacy in order. Aristides was at first commander of its fleets, but rather soon he seems to have turned the actual campaigning over to Cimon, content with an administrative role for himself. Events showed it a wise decision. For in spite of scant years and experience, Miltiades' offspring proved an inspiring leader and resourceful contriver of every type of military operation. He was probably Athens' finest general,[50] and ever eager to learn, steadily improved upon past conduct. Yet he did not press for opportunities to display his military skill. After the first flush of exuberance had passed peace was always dearer to him than war. In one or the other, friends and foes received the same polite, kindly treatment.

With the Hellespont once more secure Cimon's next move was a logical follow-up. The Persians had been swept from the straits, but they still held Doriscus in eastern Thrace, and a hundred miles west of it heavily fortified Eion, at the mouth of the Strymon river. The former was of no particular importance to Athens, but Eion was. Although now outflanked the Persians would not give it up, for the Strymon valley was the heart of Thrace and had gold and silver mines plus extensive stands of timber. From here also they had a check on the rulers of Macedonia and a listening post against the Greeks farther south. While Eion was maintained, Persian designs upon Europe were not without significance.

For the same reasons Athens and her confederates could not ignore the place. Disembarking near the Strymon's mouth late in 476, Cimon speedily defeated the local troops on the open plain and drove them within the city. But he found Eion's walls too stout to be stormed. Applying the precepts of Aristides, he offered to let the defenders depart with the honors of war. However, Boges, one of the most courageous Persian officers, refused either to evacuate or surrender. There was nothing for Cimon to do but settle down to a long siege and to cut off the supplies coming from friendly natives farther up the Strymon.

All during the bitter Thracian winter the blockade continued. When food and hope were gone Boges built a huge funeral pyre, unhesitatingly threw into it his children, his wives, all the household slaves. Then, standing on the walls, he flung his treasure-hoard into the Strymon, and last of all leaped into the flames himself.[51] In Persia Xerxes accorded special honors to his memory, afterward bestowing favors upon his living kindred. For the Confederacy Eion was a needed link with the Balkan peninsula; for Athens it was the portal to a region rich in the resources she most lacked: besides the minerals, timber for her ships, and food grains for the fast-growing population of Attica.

The gods had been good to Cimon, but what transpired shortly afterward seemed almost a special mark of divine approval. Certainly his friends took it as evidence of the blessings that could descend from Olympus, though the affair generated in a definitely less rarified atmosphere. The island of Skyros was (and is) a desolate piece of ground occupying a lonely part of the central Aegean, closer to Europe than to Asia. It had recently drawn the notice of Athenians when Delphi disclosed to suppliants from Athens that their legendary hero Theseus was buried in this unlikely spot. Obviously, a person so exalted ought to be removed instantly to a proper resting-place in Attica.[52] Coincidentally, Skyros attracted attention in another way. One group of its inhabitants, the Dolopians, were so poor that allegedly they supplemented their farming income with occasional acts of piracy. Made more reckless by unpunished lawbreaking, they not only robbed but made captive some Thessalian merchants traveling through their territory. This called down upon them the wrath of their betters.

When the Dolopians were condemned by the Amphictionic Council, which had a wide but vague jurisdiction in the north of Hellas, the other Skyrians repudiated the privateers and ordered them to make restitution. The Dolopians, tardily alarmed if not repentant, appealed to Cimon to protect them — whether they actually offered him their city, as Athenians insisted,[53] is a matter of conjecture. At any rate, he came only to execute the judgment of the Amphictions, and after compensation had been made, expelled the Dolopians as outlaws, securing their land for the Delian Confederacy. Probably he did not take it without a struggle, but Attic tradition preferred to neglect unpleasant details. It made no difference anyway. Apollo had spoken, in shrine and council chamber, working in mysterious ways to bring Cimon to the island.

Sitting alone in mid-Aegean as it did, Skyros was a convenient stopover on the route to Thrace and the Hellespont. Though this thought can never have been absent from the Delian commander's mind, it did not cause him to forget the quest for Theseus. Approaching the problem with the zeal of a modern archaeologist, Cimon made up in enthusiasm what he lacked in scientific understanding. After a fury of digging, a giant skeleton was duly uncovered in a grave of the Chalcolithic period,[54] and devout Athenians gathered round knew without having to be told that this could be none other than the fabled unifier of Attica. As the greatest of classical biographers reverently tells it:

> Straightway . . . Cimon pitched in with exceeding warmth, came after much searching to the sacred spot, had the relics carefully wrapped and placed in his own trireme, and with fitting ceremony brought them back to Athens after a span of about four centuries. It was principally because of this that the Athenian people had such a fondness for Cimon.[55]

A general, returning to his people flushed with virtuous conquest and bearing the remains of a demigod as well, *their* demigod, could be sure of a hysterical welcome. Climax was piled on climax. All ancient authors agree that above all else the bringing back of Theseus fixed Cimon firmly in the hearts of his countrymen, and his reputation was further enhanced by the psychological juxtaposition, the association of the two names in the people's minds. But the effect came to more than the cause. The infinitely venerated Theseus was out of this world, perhaps had never been in it; Cimon was definitely warm flesh, with a lifetime ahead to reap the benefits of the ghostly relationship. In all of this he had but carried out the mandate of the Amphictions and his own Assembly, doing no less than his sacred duty. Still, all prejudices and imperatives aside, there was purpose in his piety. And why not? A son of Miltiades would surely not be the last to realize that with enough ingenuity man's aspirations can identify with heaven's providence.

It would be asking too much of human nature that everyone should rejoice in the good fortune of Cimon. A great deal had been wrought by his own hand and brain, admittedly. But he had also been lucky, and coolheaded observers might say that his luck had not been unmixed with deceit. He had been invited by the Dolopians as a friend, then had stolen their land. The Dolopians had been thieves, it was true, but was he any better? And as for that heap of bones he had brought back. . . .

Not surprisingly, among those to be numbered with the unadmiring was Themistocles. He was hardly the man to praise another's merit anyway, and though his own brilliance had shadows with its light, he enjoyed deflating and exposing errant mankind—unless it genuflected. Following Cimon's dutiful return to Athens there was the customary round of entertainment, feasting the young lion. After one dinner party, as the wine went around, Cimon was persuaded to spark the muses by singing and playing on the lyre. Though without special distinction in these arts, the prevailing opinion held that he performed very creditably. But Themistocles' reaction to all such activity was vented in a sour comment. Himself, he had scorned tinkering with flute and lyre, the prostates said, but "he knew how to take a city that was small and insignificant, and make it glorious and great."[56] He had good reason to be apprehensive of the amiable junior, who made no bones about his aristocratic background and views while rubbing elbows with one and all. Then came more cause for worry. The Spartans, sensing a shift in Athens, began to cultivate Cimon and make their communications to the Athenian Assembly through him. Cimon understood them better than Themistocles, they intimated. Relations between the two powers might be improved if this promising scion of the Philaids had more say in inter-Greek affairs. At last Sparta was striking back at Themistocles for the raising of the walls. For the prostates this was a matter for reflection, and rather disturbing at that.

It is difficult to understand or evaluate Themistocles' position in the Athenian government during these years.[57] One doubts if even he were entirely clear on the situation. It is strange to find no allusion to him as one of the generals in 479, and we can only guess at the reasons. He may have considered it humiliating to give way to Aristides, on whom his prized post as strategos autocrator had been conferred. Hence Themistocles may have resigned office, or avoided it. The possibility exists too that he was not even a candidate in 479, being absent from Athens at the period of election, traveling from state to state while gathering the plaudits of Hellas. However, the generalship was an extremely important office, and one feels that Themistocles would have arranged his own selection somehow if he really so desired. And as first man in Greece, at the moment, there was little he could not have had for the asking—unless the Athenian voters were already offended by his jarring megalomania. A strange pass indeed, if he could dominate the Ekklesia for years more, by voice, logic, and craft—as seems to have been the case—yet could not win an election; repeatedly, could not even place among the top ten candidates for the generalships. Here was a striking and stinging humiliation, a clear indication too that Athenian citizens did not like him as a person—also, that some of the many stories about him were not merely believable, but in some sense true.

Egotism, with its many ramifications, may be the key.[58] Because it is not one year, but many that must be accounted for. The astonishing fact is that Themistocles is not recorded as holding the strategia in any of the next several years either, nor ever again. In view of his prominence this admits of but two explanations besides that just mentioned. Either he was retiring from political officeholding, declining to be presented to the voters so as to escape the humiliation of repeated rejections, or he believed that he had risen so high that office was no longer necessary to him.[59] Like many great ones to come, he was probably convinced that his name alone had acquired an all-sufficing grandeur. "I am not king, but Caesar." We may have a fair indication in that, like the majestic Roman, he placed his statue among the gods.[60]

As important as the generalship was, it would hardly be enough for him now, so mighty had he grown. To demean himself by sharing his authority year after year with nine other men of smaller worth and fame! Possibly the title of autocrator would have satisfied his towering ambition, if given permanently, with testimonials of unceasing adulation. But Athens' Ekklesia, ever unpredictable, had not done this. Rather, it had plucked the rare, unprecedented honor from him and thrust it upon Aristides, the man it considered completely trustworthy. For Themistocles, after a brief period of delirious happiness came the dash of cold water. Even more frustrating, he could not quarrel with Aristides, who had offered to follow his lead, even support his war policies. But with Salamis fresh in their minds, how could the citizens take anything away from him, or fail to load *him* with every magnificance? Secretly, he must have regarded the Assembly's action as an indelible affront. From this, his reluctance ever to hold office again may easily be inferred.[61]

Nevertheless he was still prostates until somebody should upset him,[62] and his policies persisted. Subordination of the islands had been his idea, but he had been so brash about it, the undertaking nearly died at birth. Without doubt he pushed the Delian project wholeheartedly, but events compelled him to recognize Aristides as a better man than he was to make it go. Very well. Aristides, after his single stint as autocrator, might stay on as general years on end, sailing about the Aegean, keeping the Ionians happy. Plutarch quotes Themistocles as remarking contemptuously that this island-hopping, this fixing and collecting of quotas was "not fitting work for a man, but merely for a purse."[63]

Yet gentle as he was, Aristides was not dangerous. With him gone, Themistocles should have no trouble with the Ekklesia. Except for young Cimon, when he came on his occasional visits. From a Themistoclean viewpoint, his homecoming in 474 fresh from the Skyros triumph, had been something of a nightmare. It gave him such an easy access to popularity, the demos joining the nobles in cheers for the young hero as the remains of the ancient one were laid to rest. A publicity stunt of course, yet it was hard to accuse the perpetrator of partisan intent. He got on well with *some* who were on the other side. Odd that Cimon was so respectful to Aristides, the number two man, yet bent neither knee nor neck to the prostates himself. And though no polished orator, the young man had a bluff, openhanded manner of speaking that made the Ekklesia think every phrase came from his heart.

Eloquence was not needed. His military record spoke for him, and military conquests counted heavily with the Athenian public. Odd again, how quickly Eion and Skyros had dimmed Salamis in their thinking. Best wait for him to err. Cimon was repeatedly a general now, taking more daring risks on the widening battleground overseas. Themistocles' risks these days were all on Pnyx Hill, in the milieu to which he was long accustomed.

As Athens' helmsman, Themistocles' accomplishments since the Persian invasion had been impressive, commencing with the circumvallation of the city. These were double walls actually, with an interval wide enough to drive supply wagons between them,[64] ramparts which in their entire length came to nearly eight miles. The walls of Piraeus were made later, and the harbor facilities completed. He shored up the Acropolis' revetments and laid the foundations of a new Temple of Athena to replace the ruined Hecatompedon. Other credits were his ingratiation of the Amphictionies toward Athens, strengthening her connections in Thessaly and the north, the Delian follow-up. He could pardonably "point with pride"—like many a modern politician. In spite of checks and challenges, his stock remained high.

8

An Era of Good Feeling

473–467 B.C.

IF Themistocles had accomplished nothing else, he would still be memorable in the development of Athens for his breaking of the hereditary hold of the dominant families in leading the citizen body and for giving the Athenian voters a greater freedom of choice in their search for democracy. As has been seen, Cleisthenes had created a sort of "People's Party" (especially through his gerrymandering of the trittyes) as an auxiliary to his reformed constitution, a party that he led as the first prostates tou demou.[1] Undoubtedly, he and the Alcmaeonids had intended that this post—the most prudent retreat down from tyranny, now generally detested—should remain in their family. For positions of power and honor, the hereditary principle was universally accepted in the ancient world; unless the designated heir were utterly inept, anything else was virtually unthinkable.

However, there was an awkward problem in the situation of the prostates. The office did not carry a monolithic power or an invincible army behind it, a fact that much later would enable the comparable "First Citizen" in Rome to turn his "unofficial" status into an official, absolute mastery passed to the lineal heir, regardless.

In Athens, the prostates had to be not only admirable, but had to have the qualities necessary to prevail with the people in their Ekklesia; hence, when the Alcmaeonids came up short, they turned to a relative by marriage, Xanthippus, to maintain *their* dominance—somewhat dubiously, in the interest of the People.[2] But Xanthippus was less than an ideal choice. His fumbling gave others a chance, and Themistocles was bold enough to challenge for the prize, utilizing popular support to defeat the prestigious

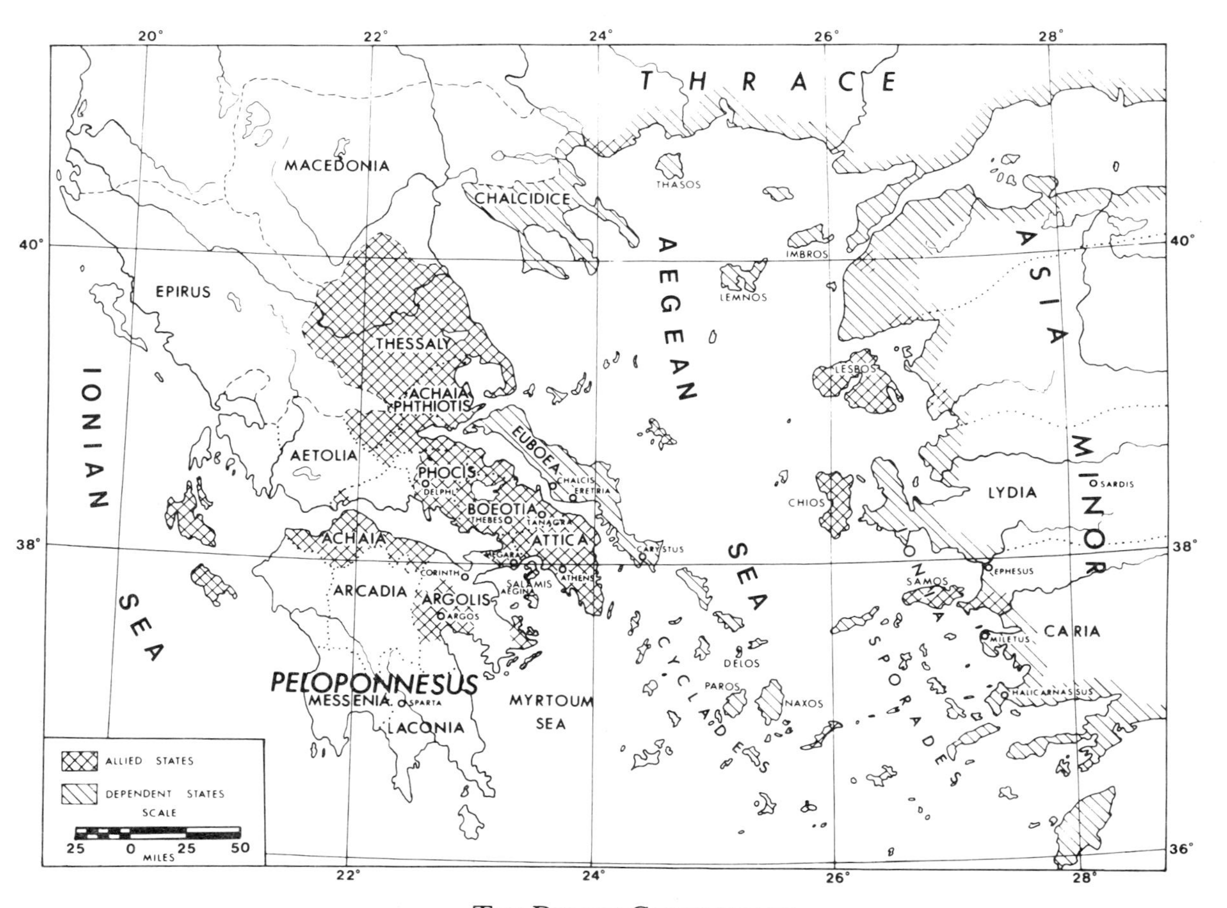

THE DELIAN CONFEDERACY

families, oust all of his rivals including Xanthippus, and establish himself as prostates. For the first time in Athenian history, the People may be said to have chosen their own leader. The word "democratic" had not yet been coined, but with essential power centered in the People's Assembly, and with apparent consecutive voting blocs holding together to secure the leadership they wanted, something that can be called a democratic party is at last visible.[3] Obviously Themistocles was a noble, and probably wealthier than he cared to admit, but he had defied the nobility and possibly even his own family.[4] Down the ages, such persons have been leaders of democracies as often as not.

Yet Themistocles' few known policies cannot be identified as democratic.[5] He must have professed some democratic intentions, dependent as he was on support by the demos, but it sufficed that his early policies as prostates—the naval building, the resolute defense against the invader, then the raising of the walls—were what the People wanted at the time—in that sense democratic. But it was simply a coincidence of agreement, or a clever stint of persuasion on his part, not a concession to popular will.

This is important, because in the postwar years a divergence of opinion between prostates and demos developed which made all the difference. At a time when the Athenian People were eager to push the offensive against Persia, Themistocles curiously cooled toward the project, suddenly diverted his shafts toward Sparta.[6] Modern admirers have lauded him as farsighted, ahead of his day in perceiving that Lacedaemon was the ultimate obstacle to Athenian leadership of Greece,[7] but in reality he was out of step with public sentiment in Athens on this vital issue, thus exposing himself dangerously. This did not result in any real trouble for years because, although at home in Athens, he was obviously supervising the Delian enterprise, thus appearing to be in line with national aspirations. Nonetheless the people were gradually undeceived.

As he separated himself from their most ardent desires, they saw him in a clearer, colder light. His character flaws were no news to them, the pride, the greed, the ruthlessness, but once they had been disposed to forgive if not forget. Now, with increasing irritation, the unforgotten was actively remembered.

It was peculiar how the Athenians did feel about Themistocles, peculiar but not incomprehensible. They appreciated his abilities to the full and had agreed he should be general—when peril necessitated. But when crises were past they could afford the luxury of a prejudice veering steadily against the man and his hauteur. Fatefully, he had done little to counteract this, failing even to bind the thetes to him by a positive program, mistakenly relying on the magic of his name—only to discover that he received few votes and was not elected strategos. Themistocles, well aware of the general feeling, once remarked bitterly that the Athenians treated him like a plane-tree, running for the shelter of his branches during storms, then stripping him when the weather became fair.[8]

It sometimes roused him to fury, yet in his position as prostates he was unshaken. For many years he mastered the Ekklesia by the force of his will, wit and prestige, so what citizens would not give him voluntarily at the polls they were constrained to do when feeling the power of his presence on Pnyx Hill. Themistocles could put them down with a sneer, a laugh, a whiplash retort—often more telling than fact or reason. There was nobody in the Ekklesia to stand up to him, provided those two other notables stayed out of town.

However, the appearance of submission was deceptive, falsely reassuring. The great man had been growing careless, exposing his pettinesses to the public gaze. The magic spell was breaking. In his megalomania he failed to recognize and correct mistakes as he once had. At the Pnyx, when he cast his pearls, too often these were wrapped in self-praise. Listeners might be pleasurably excited by references to Salamis, but did not like to have it recalled continually, and particularly not if their own efforts did not receive proportionate attention. There was altogether too much of Themistocles in Athens these days, both of the man declaiming from Pnyx's bema, and of his carved likenesses set up in public places.[9] It is strange he did not realize this. If the prostates thought he could do exactly as he pleased, he was foolishly letting his guard down.

By an undeviating law of politics that works against the "ins," Themistocles' foes were increasing and they were closing in. With or without collusion they scrutinized his activities, happy in their intuition that this man's activities would not bear close scrutiny. Stories of his double-dealing began to circulate early, and they multiplied. And again, it was an outlander who did the most damage. The poet Timocreon was a disillusioned former friend, living in Athens because his native city of Ialysus on the island of Rhodes had exiled him for cooperating with the Persians. He had cultivated the prostates, entertained him lavishly, in the expectation that the great man would use his influence to remove the sentence of banishment. But Themistocles lifted not a finger to help.

The angry Timocreon knew how to take his revenge. His poems had won him a considerable reputation throughout Hellas; he now took up his pen possibly as early as 478[10] to tell the whole sordid story. Themistocles, he declared, had promised for a fee to get the sentence canceled, and had actually taken the money; then others had paid him more not to proceed. The poet was out of pocket. It was inferred that the affair had started somewhere out in the islands, when Themistocles was still active in Delian matters. He had accepted three talents of silver—enough to make a poor man rich—then sailed for home without performing.

So Timocreon had come to Athens too. He kept on composing, and his effusions had a highly political flavor. As a bard from the "provinces," he served as Athens' self-appointed expert on popular opinion within the Confederacy. "Some may like Pausanias, or Xanthippus, or Leotychides," he sang, "but I shall praise Aristides as the best man ever sent from Athens. However, everybody hates Themistocles, the villain, the liar, the traitor . . ."[11] Timocreon poured out more rhymes and songs, and since he was a well-known lyricist publicizing a person even better known, his creations were widely circulated. These might deal with anything, from dishonest tricks by which the prostates amassed his wealth, to ostentatious banquets at which he played the tightwad by serving stale meat to suffering guests. In one poem he congratulated the Athenians on having the wisdom *not* to elect Themistocles a general that year! The bard grew ever bolder and at last cast his heaviest spear. He had been exiled for secret dealings with the Persians, he admitted, disgraced while a mighty one who was also guilty sat silently at the meeting and concurred in the condemnation.

> Timocreon, 'twas not he only
> With the Medes his country fobbed.
> There are other foxes lurking,
> Bushy-tails that should be bobbed.[12]

Even with no names mentioned, and certainly without any proof, such shafts were bound to find their target—and barbed with ridicule were doubly effective. Themistocles' penny-pinching was common knowledge. And doubtless many thought they could now understand why he had grown lukewarm to the Persian project. Slowly the climate of opinion darkened; his thete followers especially would be displeased, since they looked forward to war with Persia as a source of pay and booty. The prostates, sensing the change, found it increasingly difficult to keep his temper. The once obedient Ekklesia was restless now, its members heckled with mounting insolence till Themistocles shouted at them, "Why are you angry with those who have done the most for you?"

Unfortunately for Themistocles, it was about this time that he confirmed the citizens' suspicions by making a monumental display of both his ego and wealth. Close to his house in the Melite district of Athens he began to erect a temple for Artemis, the tutelary goddess of his family, and named it the Temple of *Artemis Aristoboulé* ("Best in Counsel"). Since this was not a traditional designation for Apollo's sister, citizens were not slow in asking why he had chosen it. Themistocles answered it was because Hellas had been saved and Athens had grown great through *his* counseling. Clearly, the shrine was not so much a memorial to Artemis as to himself. His own statue within the sanctuary erased all doubts. Now the swelling murmur became an uproar of disapproval. Finally, in or about 472, the inevitable occurred. Someone rose in the Assembly to propose an ostracism meeting.

Even with no information on the sponsor, the source is easily guessed. The Alcmaeonids had never forgiven Themistocles his audacity in wresting the leadership from them. Whenever feasible, they would certainly try to get it back. Over the past decade they had watched him closely, and of course had noted his steady decline in popularity. They could be counted upon to serve him as he had served them, and it is strange only in that they waited so long. Fraternal disharmony, or disputes with other nobles may provide an answer, as well as their lack of a suitable family candidate to advance as prostates.

What may have broken the impasse was the return of Aristides from his tour of foreign duty at Delos and Byzantium. Although not an Alcmaeonid himself, he had been steadily on good terms with them, and with the other nobles too.[13] With such honor as he possessed after the Delian arrangements, there was no question that automatically, without effort on his part, he would be regarded as prostates once Themistocles were out of the way. And this too would be a step toward democracy. To beat Themistocles, the Alcmaeonids would have to use his own action as a precedent and go outside their family and its immediate connections for a viable candidate. Since Aristides could not be expected to sanction the scheme, the preliminaries to the ostracism contest of 472 most likely took the form of a whispering campaign at which Themistocles himself was so adept: Alcmaeonid agents moving among the citizens saying, Wouldn't you rather have Aristides than Themistocles as your prostates? If Aristides was really the one responsible for the reforms of 487/6 (as Plutarch asserts), they had a good case to take to the people.[14] If Aristides had also initiated the practice of finding jobs for them through the Delian organization,[15] the case would be even better.

The Themistoclean faction was soon alive to the danger, and fought back as well as it might. How large it was and whom it included are not known, though circumstantial evidence indicates they may have been the group now regularly identified as the radical democrats.[16] The chief bastion in their defense of Themistocles was Aeschylus' drama, *Persae,*[17] presented at the Great Dionysia of 472, in which the young Pericles, son of Xanthippus, acted as chorus trainer—the earliest notice on record of the famous statesman. The drama detailed exultantly the events leading up to Salamis, then the battle itself; and though Themistocles is not named, his strategy and wiles receive full attention. Here was a reminder to the people of Athens that their prostates was the greatest of heroes; it was also an open rebuke to them for ever doubting him.

This defense would hardly be enough. Fresher in Athenians' minds was the fact that Themistocles had been soft on Persia recently.[18] A large segment particularly of the Low, where his only real support lay, would be disaffected. The High had always been against him. The Middle abided him while triumphs and profits rolled in, but could not be expected to after ill will toward him in the Delian community threatened business. His prospects were grim indeed.

Intensifying the prostates' difficulties was the nature of the ostracism process itself. Citizens were simply asked to write the name of the person they considered most objectionable or most dangerous to the state. At this stage the qualifications seemed to describe Themistocles. His supporters realized they were going to have a steep uphill struggle if they hoped to build some other prominent Athenian to a level of public disapproval so as to draw more namewriters than their man. In this they were badly frustrated; they faced a classic dilemma. Aristides was their real adversary, but his record was so positive, and the man himself so loyal, cooperative, and harmless that they could not touch him. Others of equal prominence, like Xanthippus, had faded from the scene. Only one was left of comparable stature, he who freely displayed his differences, or at least his independence. By his bold and unbending attitude, he seemed almost to invite the contest.

So it had to be Cimon. And there were *some* grounds against him. Cimon, who had stolen Skyros; Cimon, who had brought back that weird skeleton, who by inference appeared to be associating himself with the hallowed Theseus. However, these charges would not weigh heavily with most Athenians, and might conceivably boomerang. The risk would have to be taken. By the time they picked up their potsherds all informed citizens must have understood that the race lay between Themistocles and Cimon. And the hearts of all those supporting Themistocles sank at the prospect of a tussle with Cimon, as popular with the thetes of their party as he was with his own set.

Who was to vote against the winner of battles, who had provided pay and booty for soldiers and sailors, crew jobs for the unemployed, victories for the whole nation? The verdict was foreshadowed in the several successive generalships gained by the younger man,[19] while the elder was failing at the polls every time. When the sherds had fallen, Themistocles was sentenced to exile.[20] The victor of Salamis, hailed as savior of Greece only seven years back, was compelled to leave the land of his birth. The jubilant Timocreon composed a special ode for the occasion, which began

> Goddess, make this song of mine
> Ring throughout our land of Greece,
> Praise to thee for justice done.[21]

Seldom has anyone prepared a more enthusiastic valedictory.

From Athens the rejected statesman went to live in Argos, but even there he could not resign himself to ordinary life. Events elsewhere in Peloponnesus enveloped him, and soon he was visiting the other cities of the peninsula on mysterious missions that the authorities at Lacedaemon looked upon with suspicion.[22] Then the bubble burst. Shortly afterward the Spartans seemed to have their long-sought proof against Pausanias. By Thucydides' improbable account, Pausanias was trapped into an unwitting confession by the Ephors, then fled to a nearby temple where he met his death by starvation.[23] The Ephors claimed the evidence of Pausanias' Medism also implicated Themistocles, and they asked Athens to take further action.[24] Unluckily for Themistocles, the charges against him coincided with information of a new Persian armament forming in the heart of Asia, which was gradually moving up to renew the struggle. This new excitement was all the Athenians needed to convince them of Themistocles' guilt.[25] The Alcmaeonids, especially, were glad of the opportunity, and one of them named Leobotes introduced a charge of high treason against the illustrious exile.[26] Officers were sent to Argos to apprehend him, but Themistocles escaped to the island of Corcyra off the west coast of Greece, proceeding to Epirus where he was granted refuge. He was condemned to death in absentia, either by the Ekklesia or the Areopagus,[27] and his property was confiscated.

After many adventures the fugitive crossed into Asia and at last, about 465, arrived at Susa, where Xerxes had just been succeeded by his son Artaxerxes.[28] Here Themistocles needed all his audacity, and it did not desert him. Confidently addressing the new King, the exile allegedly stated that no one had opposed the Persians more fiercely than he while it had been his duty to resist, but that nobody had done them a greater service afterward in allowing them to depart from Hellas unharmed. Still fearing the King's anger however, he asked as a boon that Artaxerxes should delay his reply till a full year had passed.[29] Thus he averted the royal ire, and ever resourceful, ultimately secured an appointment as governor of Magnesia in Asia Minor.[30] Here, several years later, Themistocles died.

As already noted, it was in the year 472 that Athens' reigning dramatic poet Aeschylus produced for the Dionysia festival a trilogy of plays which included his famous *Persae*. The other two works have been lost, and the three seem not to have formed an organic whole in subject, as trilogies usually did. Possibly though, it was the all-important subject matter that preserved *Persae* in preference to the others, for this one told the story of Athens' glorious triumph only seven seasons gone by—or rather, retold the thrilling episodes that had so exalted the Athenian spirit,[31] to listeners who had actually lived through them and would never tire of their recall. Probably the teller had himself been one of the participants (though in his epitaph he mentioned only Marathon, dispensing with his subsequent military record). Here is a rare case when the author of a drama might have been able to include himself in the cast of characters. At any rate, he was in a splendid position to know what really happened—and he had to be extraordinarily careful in detailing the events to an audience that had also witnessed them. For all of these reasons, *Persae* is a piece of great literature which can also claim to be veritable history, in spots a genuine source. With certain reservations, to be sure. Aeschylus was daringly infringing Greek literary tradition by making living history instead of remote mythology the theme of his production. And to meet literary objectives he had to rearrange history—a bit.

In conformance with the classic unities, the drama has a single setting: not Salamis, but the Persian capital Susa, where the action must be narrated by messengers arriving with weighty news. Indeed, Aeschylus tells the story much as Herodotus was to tell it later, with a few minor differences. The major surprise and a bold departure from historical truth for poetic purposes is that the author lays the entire blame on Xerxes' uncontrolled ambition, against which even the spirit of the dead Darius warns. Instead of a laggard son reluctantly obeying the last wishes of his imperious father, Xerxes is depicted as an unrelenting master whose insatiable lust for land and power brought eventual ruin to the noble and previously invincible Persians. In his treatment of the Persians as a people, at least, Aeschylus was judicious, even generous.[32]

One wonders how the Athenian audience took it. So soon, were they capable of anything approaching objectivity? At the time, they had lost their entire substance. The whole business had been perilous and but for a few key decisions, the Hellenes might now all be slaves. But theirs had been a struggle for freedom, a successful effort over the best that Asia could send against them. If Persians could be cast in the heroic mold, what did it make of their opponents? With that thought, Athenians could file out of the theater in a contented frame of mind.

Beyond question, *Persae* made Aeschylus the literary lion of his generation in Athens. But his position was already strong, with social rank to supplement his own merit. Scion of an old, respected family originally from Eleusis, he had been born in Athens about 525, was an established poet by the beginning of the century,[33] and gained fame of a different kind at Marathon. He won his first dramatic triumph a dozen years before *Persae,* at the Panathenaic competition of 484, though we don't know which of his plays were presented in that year.

By 472, Aeschylus stood unchallenged. He would write plays that critics would judge greater, but none that could strike the Athenian public with more force than *Persae,* the epic struggle in which all had participated and he with them. An interminable round of feasting must have followed the Panathenaic presentations of 472, banquets at which Aeschylus would deserve a central seat of honor, beside the surviving generals of Salamis, where he might recite his sonorous verses to wild applause. Not impossibly, he had been one of the ten generals himself—in that year or another conveniently close. Whether with sword or pen, he carried his honors easily.

Our picture of events at Athens in the decades following the Persian Wars is obscured somewhat by a paucity of sources. Herodotus' narrative ends with the capture of Sestos. Thucydides is basically interested in developments of a much later time. Both historians were living in Athens during much of the mid-fifth century, yet Herodotus makes only casual references to the intervening period, while Thucydides uses it merely as background to his proper subject. One must fall back on commentators who, if hardly less eminent, are at a greater distance from the facts. Problems of chronology and interpretation likewise interpose.

Surveying this indistinct panorama, the most startling feature is the incredible comeback reportedly made by the Council of Areopagus. Incredible, because that ancient and august body had been repeatedly brushed aside in the previous century; moreover, the current march toward democracy gave it little if any hope for the future—rather the reverse. Yet we are told, for the space of a generation, it became once again the dominant organ in the state. And this without receiving any augmentation of its powers.

According to the treatise *On the Constitution of Athens* (attributed to Aristotle), the Areopagus Council was able to recover its old position sheerly because, at the hour of Athens' greatest danger, when elected officials despaired to the point of not performing their duties, it was the Areopagus that assumed responsibility, directed the people over to Salamis and even offered bounties to those who would volunteer as crewmen. Subsequently it guided Athens' efforts toward victory. During the remainder of the war and afterward, the Areopagites continued to function and did the job so well that nobody objected. "The people bowed to their prestige."[34] The treatise is vague about what this council of nobles did precisely, or what rights it claimed. Since its position was analogous to that of the Senate in republican Rome, presumably it revived old precedents and like the Roman Senate, handled many matters which had been delegated to other agencies and not specifically denied to the Areopagus.

One advantage would accrue at least for a time. Athens' Areopagus also resembled its Roman counterpart in that its ranks were constantly recruited from ex-magistrates, who became members for life. Hence until 487, when archons began to be chosen by lot, the Areopagus Council would contain men of higher ability and deeper experience than the average which prevailed in Athens' other governmental organs; even after 487, this superiority would decline but slowly, not to disappear till a full generation had passed. Such persons would not hesitate to express themselves, would automatically undertake tasks, assert authority, move to action while greener, less confident public servants were wondering what to do. Something on this order may have happened in the Salamis crisis, although Aristotle probably overstated the renewed importance of the Areopagus.[35]

Any increment of authority must have come at the expense of Cleisthenes' pet creation, the Council of Five Hundred. The latter's awkward, unwieldy arrangement by which one group of fifty had to give up their own occupations for one-tenth of the year to administer the state, succeeding the group before it, indicates a lack of continuity, a probable disinterest and inefficiency which invited intrusion by a more cohesive unit. In such a case the Areopagus could simply forestall the Five Hundred's rotating prytaneis in quick, diligent attention to the usual prytanic business: preparing of legislation, supervision of magistrates, examination of foreign affairs. Lack of a written constitution, hence the absence of clear distinctions between the powers of particular bodies, would readily permit this.

The indifference of the prytaneis themselves, ordinary citizens who begrudged the time spent away from farm and shop, would do the rest. Likelihood of their unconcern may be inferred from the scarcity of inscriptions and literary references either to the Five Hundred or the prytaneis in this era. Fragments exist of a play by Teleclides, a contemporary comic author, in which he represents the prytaneis as meeting only to eat cheese and drink wine instead of attending to business.[36] Why bother their heads or pass weary hours when their work had already been done better than they could do it?

Sudden resurgence of the Areopagus may go far in explaining the shifting political winds of the postwar period, and especially the difficulties encountered by Themistocles. The Areopagus could of course cooperate with him on the war and all measures for the defense of the city, but a council mainly of conservative nobles would tend to resist an aggressive imperialistic follow-up that deranged the normal order of inter-Greek relations. Nor were these elders, as guardians of Athens' morals, likely to approve of a politician whose conduct bespoke repeated lapses from virtue. Probably Themistocles lost the Areopagus years before losing the Ekklesia. The Assembly by a majority vote could always compel the councils to act, which must be the reason he was able to retain his control until 472. But the constant and increasing pressure from above had to be an important factor in his overthrow.

For the same reasons the Areopagites must have been very favorably inclined toward Aristides, who slipped effortlessly into the post of prostates after the mighty one's fall.[37] Aristides' Delian arrangements angered nobody, endangered nobody. Besides, he was known as a moderate democrat, sincere in his concern for the downtrodden, but without any crusading zeal for the decapitation of nobles. There was no tension, no distrust here, on either side. As Cleisthenes' pupil, Aristides was naturally committed to upholding the Five Hundred, but if these had a tendency to relinquish their duties to the older council—why, he could only agree that Solon's co-opting of former magistrates to the Areopagus had made it the ablest group of men in the state and no longer an exclusively aristocratic clique. What cause to interfere with them, while things were going so well?

And if the Areopagus was satisfied with the elevation of Aristides, it was delighted with the corresponding rise of Cimon. It would be hard to imagine a statesman who met their specifications as well as he did. A peerless aristocrat of proven military prowess, yet with no inordinate ambitions that would raise fears of tyranny, he was popular with all classes, though fairly conservative in his views, a "safe" person. Finally Cimon was on the best of terms with their Spartan friends and gave Athens a good reputation abroad, generally.

The fine relationship between Cimon and Aristides was another source of gratification. Party chiefs so unchallengeable were well able to keep their partisans in line. This absence of rancor and factional strife was just what the Areopagus needed to maintain its proficient if high-handed direction of affairs. So its members could give enthusiastic allegiance to the distinguished duo at the top, pave new roads for them. However contented they might be with the latest prostates, there can be little doubt that their favorite was the handsome young friend, the idol of the generation now taking over. His unbroken sway in Athens, over nearly a score of years, can be attributed at least in part to steady support from the Areopagus.

Cimon, son of Miltiades by his second wife — a Thracian princess — was utterly different in temperament from his father, and altogether more likeable. The once presumptuous Philaid youth had become simple and unassuming in maturity, cheerfully mixing with High and Low alike, scarcely conscious of riches and lineage — or so it seemed. In the Salamis campaign he enlisted and fought as a common marine, and though commended for heroism had asked nothing in offices or rewards. It was the people who pushed him forward, says Plutarch, tired as they were of the posturing of Themistocles.[38] Aristides had reckoned his potentialities and taken him up, in an act of spontaneous generosity. All gates opened without a call or knock.

In appearance Cimon was tall and well formed, with a mass of curly hair. His bearing, the biographer tells us, was one of quiet dignity which could melt to a warm friendliness or compose itself with calm fortitude.[39] He was governed by a sense of propriety and self-possession that lifted him above his fellows. Yet he never lost the common touch. In a life that was so much given, necessarily, to the rough business of campaigning, he never failed to be gentle in manner, careful and considerate of the men in his charge, above all setting them an example of humanity, temperance, and frugality in his own conduct.

This was the more remarkable in that it had not always been so. In youth Cimon's behavior had been unruly and extravagant, like that of other young aristocrats. He possessed all the proverbial addictions: garish clothing, gay parties, wine, and women — though there is some doubt about his singing. According to his near contemporary, Stesimbrotus, he had never been trained in music, which for a well-bred Athenian was something of a disgrace. Miltiades had been too busy with his own problems to attend to his son's instruction, apparently. If his education was defective, as some assert, it was not from want of money. But the point has not been settled beyond question. And whatever the truth about his early life, responsibility soon wore out Cimon's recklessness. The transformation, when it came, was as amazing as in Shakespeare's Prince Hal. He broke with the other life completely, once and for all.

In this, the tutelage of Aristides must have been significant. Cimon could not fail to be impressed by the transparent goodness of the man who befriended him.[40] Consciously or unconsciously, the disciple began to walk the same path. He attired himself modestly and took only plain food, eating and drinking sparingly. Yet there was plenty on the table and, says Plutarch, it became common knowledge in Athens that any might come to dinner who wished, if they would be content with his humble fare. None was turned away hungry.[41]

Later he went a step further and ordered the fences taken down from his property, letting it be known that passersby could help themselves to fruits, olives, or whatever they found. If he heard of deserving citizens in desperate need, or saw "poor people of the finer sort" in distress, he would send a friend with an anonymous cash gift to ease their difficulties. One may ask how "anonymous" such gifts really were and how well the secret was kept. Writers of antiquity had no trouble finding out about it. But contemporary opinion saw nothing wrong and scarcely impugned his motives.[42] Quite the contrary, considering the attendant circumstances. His donations, like his dinners, were managed quietly, notwithstanding the publicity they received.

An ironic twist of fate had brought Cimon to the forefront in Athens. There were many things in his favor, of course: wealth; character of the sort generally admired in aristocrats, even possessed in his gay youth; absolute loyalty joined to a military record that began at Salamis; his Philaid birth. As if this were not enough, he married an Alcmaeonid heiress, Isodike, daughter of Euryptolemos and granddaughter of Megacles of Alopeke. It was never a handicap to be connected with great families—then or twenty-five centuries later—and it is a rueful reflection on the state of affairs to discover how closely related the men at the top usually were. The leaders of each rising generation tended to be the children of those in the foregoing.

Still, Cimon's father had departed under a cloud, and the son's first recorded act was the payment of a fine assessed against the parent.[43] But time dims the memory of defeat; Marathon would loom larger in the public imagination than the Parian disaster. Beyond question the paternal tie had a host of advantages, despite the many unpleasant reminiscences concerning Miltiades. Cimon probably received his first command against Pausanias at the straits because he knew the area well, having grown up there on his father's northern barony.

Back in Athens after his first round of victories, he naturally took his place at the head of the aristocratic echelon, and in him the Eupatrids had a far more effective helmsman than in Miltiades. Even his deficiencies worked in his behalf. In the Assembly he was said to be a hesitant, even awkward speaker, not given to airing his views with fluency or frequency. Phrases that have survived cause us to doubt this judgment, but it contributed to his image as the disinterested public servant, direct, honest, and unambitious for himself, the "man of few words" whose every word was golden.

The enigma in Cimon's case lies in his position as a clear, if judicious conservative at a time when the tide was running strongly in the other direction. True, it would have been hard for a Philaid to be anything else, but such a background did not restrain other patricians in politics. Noble after noble renounced his political heritage, kicking over the traces to emerge on the side of the demos. People loved them the more for it. Cimon did not do so, nor did he ever court the commons in this guise. He resisted firmly all attempts to level the classes; rather, he sought to harmonize them on the basis of the status quo. It could hardly be done, but Cimon tried.

In the Assembly he never hesitated to condemn motions which seemed to him discriminatory or self-seeking.[44] The constitution of Cleisthenes he appeared to regard as ideal and all-sufficing—Cimon's conservatism could bend that far, at least—so we are not surprised to find him taking little interest in further reforms.[45] Athenians applauded his frugal habits, even imitated him to a degree. And their ardor was not noticeably dampened by the perception that what he did proceeded from an admiration of things Spartan, from trying to live the austere Laconian life. It was an attitude extremely popular among certain Athenian nobles, those who were able to discipline themselves to the high, severe style. A sentimental reverence for Lacedaemon was the ultimate shibboleth of the old order in Athens.

For other public figures in Attica this might have been a fatal blunder. In Cimon's case it seemed not to matter. The people adored him anyway. They accepted unquestioningly from him what they would reject from a lesser person, and far more than most men in Athenian history he could speak his mind freely without harm. Perhaps the meals and money so carelessly given (were they really?) had their effect after all. Even the lowliest could assume he was not indifferent to them. His friendship with Aristides gave added comfort and Aristides stood unopposed at the head of the democratic majority. The two notables continued to get along perfectly, making the next several years an era of good feeling in Athenian government, when for a term friction disappeared entirely. The decade beginning about 472 may have been Athens' happiest.

Prosperity and expansion were the basic causes, and Cimon contributed immeasurably to both, solidifying himself in the process. The general who could bring victories by land and sea was certain to be admired by the zeugitai who formed the army regiments, and by the thetes who were the backbone of the navy. Here was the standard-bearer the Eupatrids had been looking for, one who could attract all classes effortlessly, honorably. When Cimon was present in Athens with his service men at his side, he controlled most situations with ease. It was well nigh impossible for him to lose at home, in Ekklesia or Strategion, as long as he kept winning abroad.

And the victories continued to come. While the now aging Aristides confined his autumnal energies to Athens, Cimon gave undiminished attention to foreign affairs. Personally both men were noted for the mildness of their rule, though circumstances might have forced their hands. About 470, Athens was faced with a novel occurrence in her Aegean community, one calling for positive action. In that year Naxos, "the jewel of the Cyclades," calmly renounced her obligations and tried to resign from the Confederacy, for reasons unknown. On the surface her decision defied logic, for the Persians had coveted Naxos first of all, for her lush vineyards, heavily bearing fruit trees, the minerals of her mountains. Geographically she lay exposed in mid-Aegean, a prey to any strong power. Nor did she have any cause to complain of the financial burden. Her assessment, equated at nine talents,[46] was comparatively small for an island her size—attesting the fairness and moderation of Aristides' calculations in 478. Hence her sudden announcment must have jolted the Delian confederates and mystified them too.

However, it is only just to admit that there was another side. As the Naxians saw it, the Persian threat had receded. Though their quota was not disproportionate, the islanders were not enthusiastic about paying for protection they did not need. There were no enemies near enough to scare them. Why could not Naxos take care of herself, at less expense? Another factor may have been present, though proof is lacking. Possibly, even probably, Naxos' change of front was occasioned by oligarchs returning to power. This had been the group who had invited the Persians in 501. Oligarchs were plentiful on an island as rich as this. Finding their voices after thirty years of suppression, they would not care to support an association like the Delian, dominated by democrats.

The move was clearly illegal, contrary to the oaths taken in 478. Athens was entirely correct in insisting now and ever after that none could secede from the Confederacy until it was dissolved by the consent of all.[47] An allied fleet and expeditionary force was sent from the metropolis under an unnamed commander who by all odds must have been Cimon.[48] A blockade was set up and in time the secessionists had no choice but to surrender. No details are given by Thucydides (our only informant), but it is a fair guess that the Naxian democrats had never favored separation, and that they helped bring about its collapse.

Naxos lost her autonomy and in future had to pay a money tribute. Hers was the first instance of the Confederacy coercing one of its original members, and whether it was done by the Delian Synod or the metropolitan Ekklesia, Athens must have guided the resolution.

Assuming the Synod at Delos did give some sort of sanction to Naxos' punishment, the same session of 470 B.C. produced a determination to renew the offensive against Persia, and with more audacity than discretion, to carry the war to Asia. The decision was not without some justification. The King had never deigned to make peace, had never accepted the verdict of Salamis and Plataea. He still possessed a foothold on the Aegean, and word had recently been received that behind its southeastern corner, on the sands of Caria and Lycia, he was preparing a last grand armament against the Hellenes. Not much was known about Xerxes' plans, but whatever they were, the Delian members were agreed on a single point: it was best to nip them in the bud if possible.

Other reasons for intervention could be cited. Not all of the Greek cities in Anatolia had been rescued. Those north of Miletus on the Asian coast had profited by the battle of Mycale, but those to the south remained shackled. The Delian confederates had committed themselves to the cause of total liberation and the job was unfinished. Also, it had been assumed from the start that one of the Confederacy's objectives was revenge. In this last was much heat with but little light, and that flame a lurid one coming from visions of plunder and a meretricious glory.[49] Prompted by the subtle mixing of reason and emotion, Athens and her allies acted as one to forestall a new invasion.

With such incentives, results might be expected in due course. Possibly in 469, possibly not until the next year, Cimon sailed toward the Carian coast below Miletus with two hundred triremes.[50] Off the island of Cnidos, the Ionians of Asia joined him with another hundred. Their combined strength was impressive. Cimon had recently broadened the lines of the Athenian ships and placed bridges on their decks so that the hoplites serving as marines could carry their assaults into the enemy's ships.[51] Here was a surprise element added to the usual naval strategy, by which vessels maneuvered to strike their opponents broadside.

Reinforced by the Ionians, Cimon coasted southward freeing the Greek cities of Asia one by one, then the Carians living beyond them were invited or persuaded to enter the Confederacy. Another not-so-subtle change was in the making. The venture was no longer a purely Hellenic crusade and the voluntary principle was conveniently forgotten. The defenders of "freedom" were discovering how hard it was to draw a line between their own liberties and those of others.

With more than the Greeks emancipated,the dauntless Cimon rounded the southern tip of Asia Minor and leaving the Aegean behind, pressed eastward along the Mediterranean coast in search of the Persians. The Persians were not eager to find him. The King's general, Ariomandes, was slowly concentrating his forces near the mouth of the Eurymedon river in the province of Pamphylia, and was not yet ready for action. The army units were completely assembled, but Ariomandes was waiting for a squadron of eighty Phoenician vessels on its way from Cyprus. Even so, his naval components already outnumbered the oncoming Athenians; he was reported to have an imperial fleet of between 350 and 600 warships massed in the roadstead of the Eurymedon. With such power Ariomandes might feel reasonably safe.

But his Athenian challenger paused not a moment. Entering the vast Pamphylian Gulf, Cimon made first for the city of Phaselis, which having been colonized by Greeks, was presumed to be friendly. Surprisingly, the place held out, compelling the use of force. Indignant at such a reception from Hellenes, Cimon laid waste the land round about and assailed the city walls. Fearfully, the natives prepared for a desperate resistance. However, in the allied fleet were men from Chios, whose island state had a long tradition of friendship with Phaselis. They went to work to soften the commander's wrath, and succeeding, shot arrows over the walls wrapped with messages reassuring to the besieged. A parley was arranged and Cimon forgave them on the condition that they pay ten talents and contribute ships to the expedition. The Phaselians agreed quickly and got off easier than expected.

From them Cimon must have also learned the position and numbers of the Persians. Without an instant's delay he struck out across the Gulf toward his adversaries. The King's still-gathering fleet lay at anchor near the Eurymedon's mouth, but at the approach of the Athenians, it started to retreat up the channel of the river to avoid engaging before the awaited reinforcements arrived. Cimon followed boldly, even though the banks of this stream two hundred miles into the heart of Asia were lined with Persian infantry.

It was extremely hazardous, but the strategos' dash and foresight served him in good stead. At about this stage the Persian commander Ariomandes must have become aware of those recently installed bridges on the Greek triremes, also of the hoplites crowding around, preparing to use them. To him this dictated a thorough change of plans. To proceed up the narrowing river would be to coop his own ships where they could not maneuver (as had happened at Salamis), thus exposing them simultaneously to the prows of the Greeks and to the bridges waiting to be lowered. Indeed, since the Hellenic vessels were heavier and less mobile with the new paraphernalia, the Persians' best chance would be back in the open waters of the roadstead they had just left.[52]

Ariomandes appears to have recognized this, and to have ordered a reversal of the rowers' stroke, but his recognition came too late. The Greeks were bearing down closely, and from the first fierce onset Cimon and his men maintained the advantage their momentum had given them. The Persians, after a vain attempt to hold their line, lost courage and headed for shore, beaching their ships, and running to obtain protection from the troops on land. No mention is made of the part played by Cimon's bridges, but in a naval battle developing at close quarters these must have been used with devastating effect. Two hundred of the imperial vessels were captured, not counting those that fled or were destroyed.

It was a magnificent victory, yet Cimon was not ready to rest. Part of his project was to prevent another invasion of Greece by slaying the Persian dragon in its lair. Yet here, on these very banks, the King's army remained defiantly intact. It seemed almost foolhardy that Cimon should take his myrmidons ashore for a hand-to-hand combat in the interior of Asia, nevertheless the general gave the order. Plutarch tells the story with characteristic gusto. When the Persian infantry regiments marched down to menace him at the river's brink, Cimon was seized with the idea of disembarking his already hardworked Hellenes, to carry the fight to the enemy's ground forces, fresh though these were and greatly outnumbering his own. Seeing his men were enraptured by the victory just won and impatient to have at the remainder of the barbarians on land, he gave the signal to plunge ashore and his hoplites advanced upon the foe with joyous shouts. The Persians received them without giving ground and there developed a violent and bloody battle, long undecided, with much slaughter on both sides, including many Athenians who were most distinguished in public office. But after hours of desperate fighting the Athenians at last broke the ranks of their opponents, drove them from the field, and captured their tents piled with immense riches.[53]

If the first achievement was extraordinary, the second was almost incredible. To have splashed out of the water helter-skelter, hastily forming up in impromptu fashion, then to force their way through a numerically superior foe already on land, a foe knowing that land and holding the better, higher position, was an accomplishment to defy logic. One surmises some of the same factors prevailed here that had been important at Plataea and Mycale: the probably greater length of the Greek spear; bronze shields and body armor over protection mostly of wicker and leather; a more cohesive spirit; and of course, the élan in soldiers already winning. Even so, it was an action to make everyone marvel. The Persians should never have let the Greeks reach terra firma.

Nor was this all, according to Plutarch. After the battle Cimon got word that the Phoenician squadron expected from Cyprus had reached the Anatolian coast and lay anchored at the port of Hydrus. Hoping to fall upon it before the news of Eurymedon spread, he set out with all speed. His energy was repaid. The relaxing Phoenicians were caught completely off guard. Guessing the truth from the sudden appearance of the Athenians, they were too dismayed to put up a vigorous defense. If the main fleet had already been destroyed, what were the possibilities for a mere eighty against the invaders' three hundred? Demoralized as they were, all of their vessels were taken or sunk, and most of the sailors killed.[54]

Persia's last armament against Greece had been obliterated. The cities of Caria and Pamphylia still holding off thereupon hastened to join the Confederacy, which now extended one hundred and fifty miles east of the Aegean along the southern coast of Asia Minor, pointing like a warning finger at the core of the Persian Empire. To Xerxes it was the last straw. The King of Kings had slackened considerably in his declining years, giving himself more and more to the pleasures of the senses. The Greeks might thank heaven that Xerxes was no Darius. Henceforth he did not stir even to protect his western provinces. An automatic truce prevailed for the two or three years left in his reign. In or about 465, he was murdered in a palace plot concocted by one of his own officials.

For Cimon it was a glorious homecoming. He was to win other great victories, but the multiple triumph of the Eurymedon in 468 crowned them all, and set a mark hard to surpass even in imagination. The Athenians, wild with joy, declared that he had put Salamis and Plataea in the shade. Those had been towering successes, but single ones. Nor on either of those memorable occasions was the total result so clearly the consequence of the perceptions of a sole commander. One can conjure up the ringing acclaim as Cimon towed the battered hulks of the vanquished into Piraeus and dedicated his trophies in the Acropolis temples. He had made his city mistress of the Aegean and something more. Just the booty of the campaign had enriched her beyond expectation. If Athens was not yet a sovereign capital, she soon would be.

In tacit recognition of such dignity the Ekklesia voted to use part of the Eurymedon spoils to rebuild the south wall of the Acropolis, pulled down thirteen years before by Mardonius. Ever afterward it was to be known as Cimon's Wall. From his own funds the conqueror provided for the planting of sycamore trees in Athens' Agora, which would give wayfarers and lingerers some relief from the searing heat of Greek summers, incidentally softening a rather austere landscape. In addition, he placed sycamores in many parts of the metropolis, while olive trees were planted in the Academy district west of the city walls, hitherto a waterless waste. So in a very special sense, Cimon was the creator of Plato's—and Milton's—"groves of Academe."

Everybody in Athens had reason to think well of Cimon, even if some were unconvinced. For the nobles he had shored up a declining prestige, preserving the shreds of their power from new assaults by the demos. His presence gave living proof to the commonalty that Eupatrid leadership might still be the best, in military matters at least. To the middle classes he had opened a wider area of commercial transit in the expanding Delian organization and his expeditions meant huge contracts to shipbuilders, armorers, weavers, and vintners, amongst others.

But the lower classes may have gotten the most through him in the long run. To them he was the deliverer of victory with its rewards, hence the answer to the ever-pressing problems of employment and security. He needed rowers for the fleet, laborers on the docks, workmen for his projects in the city. He could even gain them new homes with farms overseas, where as cleruchs they would have a fresh start toward a more opulent life, yet retain their rights as Athenian citizens. This had been done at Eion and again at Skyros. The natives among whom they settled were generally jealous and resentful, which tends to show that the cleruchs had a pretty good life.

One smiles to think that Cimon the conservative was in the end able to do more for the thetes than their friend Themistocles. Unwittingly, he had given them the strength to raise their voices to a loud, insistent chorus in the next generation. And as sharers of his conquests they would demand to be heard. Finally, no one had done more to advance the cause of imperialism, so dear to the democratic interest, than this aristocratic advocate of conciliation with all Hellenes and deferential friendship toward Sparta.

His was a comprehensively healthy influence, not only for Athens but for all of Greece. With Aristides and himself setting a notable example of friendly cooperation, those staunchest of individualists, the Athenians, might be persuaded to pull together for the common good—a pattern of conduct which could serve other Greeks as well.

9

Drift and Rift

467–460 B.C.

AMONG the Athenians' military exploits, none can rank higher than the Eurymedon campaign. Cimon's homecoming to Piraeus trailing in his wake the symbols of Oriental despotism, possibly in the late summer of 468, was a sight to thrill all citizens present to watch. Elated, they joined in the roaring welcome for the man who more than any other had made Athens a world power. Worries were dissolved, problems were for the moment forgotten.

In the metropolis this sense of well-being lingered beyond the waning autumn. Then, in the following spring, Aeschylus voiced the feelings of all Athens in one of his greatest plays, produced for the Dionysia of 467. His *Seven against Thebes*, with its famed story of fratricidal strife between the sons of Oedipus, seems hardly the medium for the prevailing mood. Yet Athenian drama was a vital part of the life of the city, and rarely did it fail to reflect the contemporary scene. Much speculation has centered on the character of Amphiaraus, acclaimed the noblest of the seven attacking chiefs—one who would never have been a party to such an offense except for an oath given to his relatives—as with the rest, he is described to King Eteocles of Thebes:

> Not merely to *seem* best, but truly so *to be*,
> Plowing his mind with deep and solemn ponderings
> Which bring forth fruitful judgments righteously.[1]

Plutarch discovered a version, with the word "best" changed to "just," which asserted that the audience in the theater turned instinctively, one after another, toward the spot where Aristides sat, so well did the description fit him.[2] The story has often been doubted, and rightly so, but one must remember that in its original form it probably had a special meaning to his fellow Athenians. For the designation *aristos* ("best") was not only a play on his name, which listeners would be sure to catch if lovingly rolled on the tongue, but one associated with him by his contemporaries probably before the term *dikaios* ("just").[3] Also, there existed a situation unmentioned in the drama itself, of which mythologically minded Greeks would be perfectly aware without a reminder. Amphiaraus had a son named Alcmaeon, one who was sworn to avenge him if he met with a tragic death, and who actually did avenge him later by visiting devastation on Thebes. Though the name was a coincidence, it would instantly call to mind the connection between the Alcmaeonids and Aristides, now directing Athens' policies with the great family's blessing. Obviously, this was better left unspoken, since the Alcmaeonids, with the lesson of their ostracisms before them, had no desire for prominence and injudicious publicity.

So much coincidence seems to bespeak a definite intent of the poet, and there is even more. That Aeschylus goes out of his way to enlarge on Amphiaraus' good qualities, perhaps giving him an undue emphasis, has been noticed.[4] Beyond that, he has the scout report to King Eteocles that Amphiaraus has reproached Polynices for joining with the foes of his city, becoming in fact a traitor to his fatherland. At this point one recalls that five years before, in his *Persae,* Aeschylus had defended Themistocles against the Alcmaeonids' onslaught. But Themistocles had been ostracized, later convicted of treason in absentia, and he had then offered his services to Persia,[5] still regarded by most Athenians as their great enemy. Aeschylus must have been astonished, mortified, and finally disgusted. Was he now loyally offering arm and pen to the new leadership? It was something he could conscientiously do. And if the spectators turned to look at Aristides at the right moment, it may have been deliberate planning by the poet: advance information leaked that certain lines were intended as a compliment to the reigning prostates, or instructions to the actors particularly to project the proper words—or both.

Such gleanings are of course subsidiary to the main subject, a grim comment on needless war. But there was much that was currently meaningful and coincided with the overall theme. Thebes was the most conspicuous Greek state to have medized during the Persian invasion; in a sense she was still guilty in the sight of free Greece. Aristides-Amphiaraus seems to be offering peace, on behalf of magnanimous Athens to all Greeks, while specifically telling the Thebans he would rather not punish them unless the other Greeks (the Delian Confederacy) insist, but if they made trouble, he and the Alcmaeonids (specifically, Athens) would have to move against them. To apprehensive Thebans, watching the build-up of Athenian acquisitions and alliances all around them, in Euboea, in Thessaly, in Thrace, the message was clear: Do not come between Athens and her destiny.

Thus seen, Aeschylus had done well by Aristides, according fitting recognition of an illustrious career nearing its close. Were there other words for Cimon, repeatedly victorious even before Eurymedon, to match those for his mentor? Elsewhere in the play, the messenger speaks again in commendation of his state and its leaders, words which sound strange when one remembers that it is landlocked Thebes to which he refers.

> Courage, every mother's child! Our country lives,
> Freed from the threat of bondage. And the boasts
> Of haughty men are stifled. Fair weather gives
> Our ship of state good sailing. Now she coasts
> Evenly, undamaged by the waves. Our walls firm stand
> With gates made fast, and swords to guard this land.[6]

The beleaguered Boeotian city had withstood Polynices' attack, it is true, but the references to ships and waves seem to imply naval engagements, and the remark about walls could be an allusion to the one Cimon built on the Acropolis' south side, as well as to the Theban Cadmeia. He who had carried the Athenian standard into Asia manifestly deserved such acknowledgement.

There was yet more. The chorus' concluding song expressed perfectly the vein of exultation charged with destiny which pervaded the whole of Attica, a theme much more appropriate to burgeoning Athens of the fifth century than to legendary, doubtfully victorious Thebes.

> Zeus who watches from the height,
> Enthroned 'midst his Olympian kin,
> Has saved us through his boundless might
> Over foreign foes to win.
> With Zeus' help, the savage tide
> Was broken, stopped, and dashed aside![7]

Exuberance and adulation were natural responses, and for a splendid season the city lavished its love. That the enchantment should last longer would be asking too much. Complete accord in the body politic, when benevolent conservatives clasp hands with broadminded liberals, is a condition seldom attained, more rarely known to endure. Athens came closer to the ideal than other Hellenic communities, but even there such satisfactions were fleeting. Over the last several years a remarkable cohesion was apparent in the state, instilled by the almost effortless harmonization of Aristides, once again at the helm. Themistocles' departure in 472 must have instantly conferred upon Aristides the high responsibilities of the prostates by a double elimination, since Cimon, the only other possible candidate, was his close friend and pupil. Certainly his benign influence had been felt during a much wider span, extending, one suspects, even over the self-centered victor of Salamis, who knew Aristides would be trusted when he himself might not.

But all good things have their term. Sometime in the three years from 467 to 465 Aristides passed from the scene. Despite his distinction, we are told he died a poor man,[8] his hands unstained by the lucre that had tempted so many. Having been part of the life of Athens for nearly half a century, his removal disturbed it as nothing else could. He had led the democratic majority from a position essentially central and independent. There was nobody left who could do the same.

Or was there? Not inconceivably, someone might fit the description without too much adjustment. With Aristides' death, the thoughts of most Athenians would naturally gravitate toward his famous pupil and collaborator. At the moment, Cimon was the only person of comparable stature left.[9] A few years before it would have been hard to think of him as a democrat, but why could he not be one now? He had declared his devotion to the constitution of Cleisthenes, that fundamental testament of Athenian democracy, and tacit approval of the subsequent reforms of 487-86 was a logical inference from his close association with their presumed author. These measures were mainly political. But in economic terms, who had done more for the demos, and especially the thetes, than Cimon, in naval employment, the founding of cleruchies, and the distribution of rich booty after many a victory?

Cimon's right wing Eupatrid relatives might frown; people had not forgotten that adventurer, Miltiades. But the son was more open and affable than the father and had used his vast inherited wealth for the public good. If the Alcmaeonids could be democrats, as they now were considered to be, then why not a Philaid? The fluidity of Athenian politics was such that differences were easily dissolved. Desirable conversions were readily managed. To his contemporaries and to those who came after, Cimon's credibility was such that at least one twentieth-century authority has evaluated him as basically a moderate democrat,[10] the inheritor of Aristides' mantle, and, like him, in the midstream of the party. An Alcmaeonid marriage had widened his appeal, if that were possible, conferring a sort of official approval, pointing as well to a reconciliation between the two greatest families. A simple and happy solution, then, to line up behind the established favorite.

Satisfactory as this might be to prospering commoners, there was a large leftward segment far from satisfied, who deemed further reforms necessary, and to whom Cimon therefore was not acceptable. In this radical wing the foremost person was the uncompromising Ephialtes, son of Sophonides, an enigmatic figure about whose background nothing is known except his father's name. As a consequence, the usual claims have been made that Ephialtes was a man risen from the masses, but having already been once elected strategos, he must have been at least a landowner and fairly well-to-do. By all accounts he was a statesman of unquestioned virtue, absolutely incorruptible.[11] But though a colleague of Cimon's in the Eurymedon campaign, Ephialtes had no warm feeling for the conqueror or for any of his class. The possessors of pelf and status were suspect on general principles.

Given such an antagonistic attitude, a clash was unavoidable. From his seat in the Assembly, Ephialtes assailed the nobles of the Areopagus Council one after another with instances of their misbehavior, probably after auditing their accounts as officeholders.[12] Apparently the initial charges related to the personal conduct of the accused, in responsibilities other than as Areopagites,[13] but there could be no mistake as to the underlying intent, that is, to subvert public confidence in the old, august Council. Politically, this was a ploy to be expected of extreme democrats. Their ilk was bound to resent the recent extra-constitutional encroachments of the Areopagus on the powers of the Five Hundred and the Assembly. But there was also a private animosity in the attacks of Ephialtes. Lacking all the evidence today, it is impossible to decide how just was his blasting of the "Good and True," or how much was spite. But any observer could predict a felling of the aristocracy if ever Ephialtes came to power. What little is known of his character does not justify doubts of his sincerity. At the same time, it was sound political strategy for him to attack the Areopagus. If Ephialtes could gain credence for his charges against the peerless body, of which Cimon was a member, the latter would suffer through the familiar process of guilt by association. And if Cimon, whom most Athenians must now have regarded as prostates, could be lured into defending his fellow councillors, so much the better. His leadership might thereby be shaken.

According to Aristotle, Ephialtes' well-known antipathy preceded Themistocles' forced departure from Athens, and it was actually the latter's doing.[14] Seeking to escape prosecution for his own treasonable dealings with Persia, he had secretly told some Areopagites of rumors reaching him which involved Ephialtes instead. Having previously warned his younger "friend" that the Areopagus was about to seize him, Themistocles conducted some of the members to Ephialtes' house, making it appear that he did so under compulsion. The ruse had worked so well that Ephialtes fled to the nearest altar.

Whatever the truth of the story, it seems plausible that Themistocles and Ephialtes were both suspect by the Areopagus, and were sometime allies in opposing the majority in it, also that the elder had something to do with the younger man's hostility toward the body. This disaffection must have festered for years before reaching a head. The authority of Aristides would be sufficient to keep it down while he lived to control the situation. After him, Cimon's prestige sheltered his fellow councillors yet a few years. Meanwhile Ephialtes sniped away, becoming ever more aggressive, manifestly as determined to demolish the Areopagites as the other was to uphold them.[15] Between the two, it is difficult to see where the path of equity lay. One can only conclude that both men believed themselves to be right. From the Skyros episode onward till the lustre of Eurymedon had paled, Cimon's popularity was steadily on the rise, and while this lasted Ephialtes failed to make headway against him. When the great general was present in the city, a few words from him were enough to stampede the opposition. He had a natural advantage over civilian challengers and others with no comparable military record to show. Prospects for the radicals began to look brighter in 465 when the punisher of the Persians was sent off on a new assignment against the rebellious island of Thasos. No doubt Ephialtes speeded him on his way.

The Thasos campaign had its origin in events reaching back to Cimon's earlier conquest of Eion, the key port at the mouth of the river Strymon. The northernmost of the Aegean islands, Thasos juts out from the sea only a half dozen miles from the coast of mainland Thrace, where precious metals, lumber, and corn abound. Thasos was close enough to this natural storehouse for her men of enterprise to have a proprietary interest in its revenues. The Strymon valley was the gateway to western Thrace, and Cimon had of course left a garrison to occupy Eion when he captured it from the Persians. But already the Athenians were aware that a more strategic spot existed several miles north called the "Nine Ways," where all roads converged on the only place at which the uncertain and treacherous Strymon could safely be crossed. Here were the paths that led to fabled Mount Pangaeus with its mines—the source of Pisistratus' fortune and many another since. So advantageous a locale had not escaped the notice of contemporary Athenians. At their instance, Athens had decided to reserve the area for her own colonists rather than allow neighboring members of the Confederacy to occupy it. The Strymon valley, from Eion up to the Nine Ways, thus became Athens' exclusive possession, to the great indignation of the Confederates on Thasos who had looked on it as rightfully theirs. Imperialism was affecting the Thasians, too, inexorably.

Athens was prepared to ignore such objections from allies actually under her thumb. However, there were others in the district whom she had not counted upon. Athens' first tentative settlement had been massacred by Thracian natives shortly after it was founded. Then in 465, a more strenuous effort was made. A mission of ten thousand colonists gathered from many friendly Hellenic communities was sent out, one strong enough to secure the Nine Ways and the entire valley below it from native interference. But occupation of the Strymon crossing only led to another tragedy. When the main body of settlers advanced farther north toward the mining district, they were unexpectedly thwarted by the combined action of all the Thracian tribes thereabouts. Caught on broken terrain, deep in the interior, they too were annihilated.[16] Now Athens' cherished project would have to be abandoned.

The colonists had proceeded incautiously, over ground not previously known to them. Still, for such a large number to be slaughtered by natives furnished with fine weapons and armor obviously gave Athens' Board of Generals something to think about. The more these worthies pondered, the greater their suspicions, and these gradually came to rest on Thrace's western neighbor, King Alexander of Macedonia. For decades Alexander had advertised himself as a warm friend of Athens, an outspoken admirer of her culture. Why suspect him, then? The trouble was, he was everybody's friend. When the Persians came in 480 he had hastened to the King's camp to fawn on Xerxes, meanwhile sending encouraging messages to the Greeks. Then, all of a sudden, he had insisted that the Greeks' original footing at Tempe could not be held, and by urging immediate retreat, had exposed them to disaster at Thermopylae. Later, on Salamis, he had visited the Athenians in person to assure those assembled that all was lost unless they accepted the King's offer, deserted their allies, and became Persia's watchdog over the rest of Hellas. Such a friend as this would require close observation. For who would be Persia's watchdog over Athens next? No great perspicacity was needed to answer that question.

In these dealings Alexander may have been sincere, after a fashion, but succeeding events did not make him appear so. Persian failure was for him a blackened reputation. Yet Macedon's king could afford to be philosophical. The withdrawal of the Medes had left a political vacuum on his eastern frontier, and he was not one to ignore such an opportunity. The Thracian chieftains who had been frightened into acknowledging Xerxes would give their allegiance more easily a second time. Those nearest Alexander had already been cajoled into doing so, and a short march would now bring him to the all-important Strymon. To expand farther he needed to command the Nine Ways; news of an Athenian colony there would be repugnant to Alexander, whatever his smiles and blandishments. There could be no question about his willingness to lend arms and men in an all-out effort against the intruders, and he might even turn out to be the principal instigator.[17] At least, so reasoned the Athenian generals, and the royal suspect's eloquent silence seemed to confirm their judgment. Gradually opinion mounted. A score had to be settled with King Alexander.

While in this dark mood, news of the rebellion of Thasos reached them. It should not have been a surprise. Matters that had irked Macedon's king were positively infuriating to the Thasians, but their involvement was economic rather than political. Since the preceding century they had extracted gold from their island mines, reportedly bringing them about eighty talents a year.[18] A nice dividend, but the real bonanza lay ahead. In due course the men of Thasos crossed the narrow waters to mainland Thrace, where they developed mines that yielded an annual income of two hundred talents, and in good seasons approached three hundred.[19] This had been the case even before the Persian invasion. By the 460s the Thasians' holdings stretched up to Pangaeus itself, the magnet which also drew the Athenians. Probably by this time other products of the region were capitalized: the timber, amber, and grain. Disputes had already arisen in the Confederacy's Synod over the mines and markets of Thrace, contests in which Athens had a decided advantage.

Failing repeatedly to obtain satisfaction, Thasos at last renounced the Delian bond as more hindrance than help. Minerals aside, the island's resources were small; for the anxious inhabitants, commerce with the adjacent mainland was its mainstay. Without it their economy would dwindle, once those first insular lodes were cleaned out.

By the same token, Thasos' chances in a revolt were also slight. Nevertheless there were grounds for hope. Possessing a formidable navy, she was stronger than Naxos, posing the most serious challenge yet to the Confederacy's survival. Then, at some stage the insurgents opened secret negotiations with Sparta, and seemingly were promised that an army would come up from Peloponnesus to pressure Attica.[20] Definitely, sympathizers could be found in Hellas. Thasos' defiance loomed as a grand test of the Delian organization. If there were any sign of weakness, a number of other defections might be expected.

The enlarging threat was averted by a miracle. Before Sparta could redeem her pledge a terrible earthquake struck which, assertedly, killed thousands in the city and touched off a rising of the helots throughout Laconia and Messenia. All of Lacedaemon's forces were required at home; she had no troops to spare for several years.[21] Even had it been otherwise, a Peloponnesian invasion of Attica would do Thasos little good unless a general war absorbed Athens' entire energy.

Happily for their peace of mind, the Athenians had no intimations of the secret dealings. Without hesitation they ordered up the Delian armament and placed Cimon in command. The situation in the north was dangerous enough, however one took it, and presented endless complexities. Had the Thasians been in any way involved in the massacre beyond the Nine Ways? Did they have any sort of tie-in with King Alexander? Did the conspirators have an understanding with other parties still unknown in a wider project to stop Athens' expansion in the north? Because of the ensuing controversy, one wishes for a record of the deliberations in the Athenian Strategion and especially of the instructions given to Cimon before he embarked. But nothing exists, and perhaps never was made public.

On the basis of available facts, Cimon performed in his usual faultless style. As his fleet neared its destination the Thasians rowed out to attack, and were beaten heavily in the ensuing sea fight, with a loss of thirty-three ships captured. Cimon then brought his hoplites ashore, and defeating the natives' land army,[22] drove it inside the city of Thasos, on the island's north side. At this point operations became more difficult. The city was invested, but its walls could not be carried. The Thasians were prepared for a long siege, in a habitat favoring those inured to it over any invader. Thasos was a forbidding bit of earth whose granite cliffs bristled with tall fir trees right down to the beach. Centuries before, the poet Archilochos had called it "an ass's back-bone crowned with wild wood," where nothing soft or attractive was to be found. Such a place would breed a hardy race of men, ready to defend what (except for the mines) was scarcely worth defending.

Here the Athenians discovered there was more to war than fighting. Thasos did not grow enough food for its own inhabitants, much less a visiting army. What stocks it had must have been taken inside the city, compelling the foreigners to get their provisions by sea. As the summer of 465 wore away into winter, it became obvious that the Thasians were hoping for relief from the weather as well as from the Lacedaemonians. The Athenians and their allies were not used to the storms and ice of the north Aegean in that season; they would want to go home. Military action normally ceased during the cold months, anyway. With any luck Thasos ought to pull through.

But if the defenders were persistent, so was Cimon. Never one to give up an advantage won, he kept his men at their posts despite problems of temperature and supply. The siege persisted on into the next year, with the Thasians stubbornly, desperately holding out, expecting momentarily to hear of a Spartan invasion of Attica. Finally another winter passed, then another spring, another summer. Not until the autumn of 463 did starvation compel Thasos to capitulate. Athens' exasperation was revealed in the severity of the terms she imposed. The Thasians were required to destroy the walls of their city, also to give up what remained of their fleet, and all claims to the mainland mines.[23] As a matter of course, Thasos lost her standing as an equal member of the Confederacy, contributing merely ships. She had to pay an immediate money indemnity, and henceforth to render whatever tribute Athens imposed. No doubt lingered now about who controlled the Confederacy, or the direction in which it was headed.

Once again Cimon had served his country with distinction, and upon his return home after the Thasos campaign he deserved a full measure of applause. A cordial welcome is assumed. But he was not allowed to relax. During his absence Ephialtes had continued to attack the Areopagus; its worried members were in dire need of their benefactor. And as before, Cimon was ready to take up their cause. Preferring conciliation when possible, he backed off from political battles no more than from military ones. If the radicals wanted a fight to the finish, they could have it.

Apparently the radicals did, but not at the moment. The time was not quite right. Still, they had had months to draw their plans, and were prepared with a limited counteroffensive designed to brush back the popular hero. Their scheme was ingenious. Hard as it was to find fault with a general who had nothing but victories in his record, Ephialtes and his friends made out a case. A formal accusation was lodged that Cimon had juggled his financial accounts of the Thasos campaign, and an investigation was ordered. The air was heavy with portents of misdeeds to be revealed which never quite materialized.[24] Anything unsavory would be useful, whether true or not, to change the splendid image Cimon presented to the Athenian public.

The propaganda value may have been the sole objective, at this stage.[25] For the radicals, it was a matter of supreme importance to keep the mass of citizens from thinking of Cimon as a fellow democrat. Otherwise, the rank and file would assume Aristides' stamp of approval and accept him as Aristides' successor. He and he alone might bar the leftist element from controlling the Party of the Many. Hence it became necessary to make him appear like his father: selfish, insincere, money-mad, a conniver with aristocracy and royalty against the people.

On the other hand, there was danger that the radicals might lose by the accusations. Against Cimon, a charge of stealing was bound to look ridiculous. Such an indictment against one who had inherited great wealth and given much of it to charity would ordinarily be laughed out of court. Any jury impaneled was likely to include a good number of Cimon's beneficiaries and other admirers. Probably then, Ephialtes intended the action as no more than a test of sides for the present, and an insinuation for future effect. Whatever the outcome, suspicions were bound to arise.

One phase of the trial, especially, suggests such a motive. It was alleged that Cimon had accepted a bribe from King Alexander, by which he agreed not to invade Macedonia. After the Thasos success, his prosecutors insisted, he ought instantly to have crossed to the mainland and chastised the two-faced king. The charge of bribery was as preposterous as the more general one, but an interesting question hung thereby. Did Cimon have secret instructions to proceed against Macedonia after Thasos? The conqueror denied anything of the sort. Outwitting his accusers, he retorted that certain rich Ionians and Thessalians had indeed wanted him to do this, to promote their own schemes of exploitation in Macedonia.[26] Seemingly, they were not without influence in this court. Since he had seen nothing to be gained for Athens, but only a waste of money, he had not yielded to pressure.[27] In the end, the general silenced his tormentors, making good his own insinuation that they were not above serving the interests of plutocratic outlanders, however much they shouted democracy at home.

It was a shrewd riposte, giving Cimon the upper hand. And he was undoubtedly right. To have undertaken so costly and dangerous a campaign on mere hypothesis, into the middle of a relatively unknown country, close to where they had recently suffered a disastrous defeat, was nonsensical. The idea was not to be taken seriously. The investigation soon dwindled away. In retrospect, it achieves a certain odd interest from the presence of the young Pericles, son of Xanthippus, who had his baptism in statecraft here as a member of the prosecution, having recently entered politics under Ephialtes' banner.

In fact, the choice of Pericles as a prosecutor may have been a clever attempt by Ephialtes to head off Cimon from the post of prostates tou demou. To most Athenians, Cimon would seem to stand now in the "hereditary" succession, with the blessing of his immediate predecessor, Aristides. Moreover he was married to an Alcmaeonid heiress as had been another predecessor, Xanthippus. So Ephialtes would throw a son of Xanthippus at him and show Athens that the great family was not solidly behind their acquired relative. For Pericles it must have been an awkward moment, revealing to the world that, as Ephialtes' junior associate, he was not in complete harmony with his Alcmaeonid kindred,[28] but decidedly to the left of most of them. Neither he nor any of the other prosecutors pressed the charges with much vigor. Cimon was easily acquitted. When on the scene in person the victor of Eurymedon still swayed the citizens, Eupatrid or not. The inquiry was an attempt to embarrass and weaken him, nothing more. Whether Ephialtes was satisfied with the results, none but he could say.

If the radical democrats had lost but little in their first encounter with Cimon, they certainly had not gained. Undeniably, the general had carried off the honors. Despite meager expectations they could not but feel thwarted, Pericles' attitude being a significant indication. The attempt to discredit a great man, if it fails, always backfires on the accusers. Ephialtes can have counted on no more than a Pyrrhic victory. He was lucky to escape a Hannibalic defeat.

Though he had failed to blacken Cimon as an enemy of democracy, or to deprive him of his democratic supporters, Ephialtes found comfort in the prospect of better days and livelier issues. Already the gods had brought him a legacy more to his liking. Despite the humane sympathy that Greeks professed for each other, few Athenian radicals could suppress a smile over the current miseries of Sparta. The violent earthquake that struck Lacedaemon about the middle of 464, had assertedly destroyed all but five houses in the city and killed 20,000 people.[29] These figures suggest exaggeration, but the damage must have been extremely heavy. As the disconsolate survivors were picking through the ruins for relatives and friends, watchful helots seized the opportunity to attack. Sparta was saved only through the alertness of the youthful King Archidamus, who summoned the citizens to their ranks by a blast of the trumpet. Under his direction they rallied sufficiently to save their homes, but little else. The rest of Laconia had to be abandoned to the rebels. Then came the news that the helots of Messenia had also risen, massacring the garrisons taken unawares. Hemmed in by multiple disaster, the Spartans were staggering under a problem too complicated for muscled arms and matching brains. In despair, they decided to call in their allies.

It was a striking indication of Lacedaemon's humiliation that they appealed to Athens. The request was not out of order. Technically, Athens was still a member of the Peloponnesian League. The Ephors sent as their representative a Spartan named Pericleidas, who after delivering his message, made a tour of the city's altars where he sat before each, "palefaced in his scarlet robe,"[30] reciting prayers. Sparta had not been so fearful when the Persians came as she was now.

The appeal rekindled the most clear-cut political struggle in the history of the Attic commonwealth. Ephialtes and his left-wingers did not hide their contentment over Sparta's distress. Vociferously, they pronounced for rejection. To them Lacedaemon was the symbol of oppression, the upholder of selfish oligarchy against the hopes of the wholesome citizen, a gigantic slave state that was the very antithesis of "freedom."

But this was not all. They felt instinctively that Sparta disapproved of the popular reforms most Athenians were bent on having; more, that her League was the largest obstacle blocking their own expansion within and without Greece. It was a curious irony that Athens' democrats, so deeply committed to self-government at home, were no less firmly tied to an imperialistic foreign policy. No matter how they pondered the issue, their position was based on remorseless, selfish logic. Attica by itself had not the means to assure the welfare of its dense and rising population.[31] They might disguise the problem, as Pericles was to do later, by a sympathetic leniency to non-Athenians in the dependencies. But at bottom, the element of aggression was still there, without any way to get rid of it. It was galling when Athenian democrats had to admit that Lacedaemon, for all its faults, was blameless in this particular respect. Reactionary as Sparta was, she rarely forced her will on the Peloponnesian allies, or interfered with their internal affairs.[32]

These facts, and the radicals' realization of them, must be remembered when explaining Athens' reaction to the Spartan request for aid. As reformers they were violently opposed; yet their virtue was qualified by a sense of guilt that left them discomfited, frustrated, ineffectual. Welcome as the news had been, the crisis in Laconia would not bring them mastery over Athens' broad democratic spectrum—not at this juncture. Except for their leaders, the radicals were mainly the city's Low—town laborers, dockhands, sailors, and such, whose way of life was antithetical to the Spartan, and who had grounds for a hearty dislike of the dominant southerners. But the moderate democrats belonged mostly to the economic Middle, a good half of whom were zeugite farmers having more in common with the Lacedaemonian lords of the soil than with the extremists of their own party. The rest of the Middle were merchants and shopkeepers more resentful of Corinthian competitors than of business-avoiding Spartans who never blocked their path. Besides, many segments of the Middle and some of the Low were under the influence of Cimon, that Laconaphile. Whether Cimon were now a true democrat might be questioned, but there was no doubt at all as to inherited sensibilities; his instincts were purely Eupatrid, providing a link with the political opposition.

Toward Sparta, which for more than a century past was regarded as the balance wheel of Greece, the attitude of Cimon and his fellow grandees was an odd combination of sentiment not unmixed with elements of reason. From a modern view, it is almost fantastic, the sentimental passion that nearly all Athenian nobles appeared to have for Lacedaemon. Sparta had done nothing for them; since the day of Cleisthenes, she had positively ignored them. However, they remained steadfast in their admiration. Three full generations after these events, no less a person than the sensitive and highly accomplished Plato nursed a continuing fondness for the coarse, doubtfully literate Spartans.

Strange as it seems, there were reasons. Sparta was the most conspicuous of the aristocracies, also the stablest. Her primacy in Hellas was still recognized by most Greeks. This passed for proof that hers was the best form of government. Elsewhere the well-born had been inept in letting their powers slip away—not the Spartans. Too, the Lacedaemonians clung to the simple, self-sufficient life of their ancestors, the standards of the Heroic Age, by which they fondly imagined Achilles and Agamemnon, Odysseus and Menelaus, had lived. In those distant days, before the leveling had set in, nobles had been something more than mere flesh and blood. Homer's adventurers had never sought their ease in pleasant corners, never given way to the enticements of civilization, nor did the Spartans do so now. There was scant doubt that they made the best soldiers, and as every aristocrat considered himself first of all a warrior, he was bound to admire the stern, unflinching Lacedaemonians. With the present trend in politics, no matter how much the most progressive Eupatrid might approve with his mind the reforms taking place in Athens, in his heart he felt he was less than he had been, and he resented his emasculation. The man in him cried resistance. Hence he could not but feel a secret thrill when contemplating the state that had never made the slightest concession.

The Eupatrids also had their cooler moments when they made as much sense as the democrats, and sometimes more. Nearly all considered themselves more able by heredity and training and thus better fitted to govern. Having land and money themselves, it seemed to them that anyone ought to be capable of making his way without aid from the state. For the same reasons they were against the empire and naval program—these were expensive, superfluous, even dangerous. On the city fortifications there was probably less unanimity, but here too deep-seated preconceptions must have carried over, that careful diplomacy based on cooperation with other responsible states made walls unnecessary. Sparta had none, and boasted that she did not need them. In any case, the traditional land army, of which they were the backbone, was the first line of defense.

A clash in the Assembly was inevitable. Cimon's counterproposal to Ephialtes' spurning of Sparta embodied perfectly the aristocratic position in Greek affairs. Support the request, he urged, and close the breach developing between Lacedaemon and Athens. The two greatest Hellenic states should supply the leadership to overcome the inherent disunity of the Greeks. "We must not leave Hellas lame; we must not allow Athens to lose her yoke fellow."[33] It was a simple figure of speech that the humblest farmer of Attica could understand, aimed precisely at these zeugitai of the Middle, whose votes would hold the balance. In his earthy way, Cimon could be eloquent when the occasion demanded. If the fight at the Eurymedon was his greatest military success, his most satisfying political triumph came at this moment when, following up the advantage of his Thasos acquittal, he carried the Ekklesia with him against the exertions of his formidable opponents and the natural instincts of most Athenians. One assumes that the Assembly still knew nothing of Sparta's dealings with Thasos.[34] The aid Lacedaemon asked was granted, and Cimon himself sent southward into Peloponnesus with 4,000 hoplites.

Others of the allies answered the call: Mantinea, Aegina, even Plataea, which sent one-third of its entire army. No details have been preserved of the campaign that followed, but with the assistance that came from many quarters the embattled Spartans gradually won back their home province of Laconia, and by the end of the next year, 463, recovered most of Messenia as well. Those who still held out were driven into the fastnesses of Mount Ithome, an imposing pile of solid rock in the middle of the extensive Messenian plain. After this, Lacedaemon concluded she could finish the job alone. The allies were thanked and given leave to depart. With new laurels, Cimon and his men returned to Athens, once more to receive the plaudits of the citizens.

In fact, the celebrated general's peak of popularity may have been attained at this moment. On his march home, officious Corinthians had tried to slow his passage of the isthmus, asserting that he had to get their permission. Cimon retorted that other states owned shares of the isthmus, but Corinthians did not ask *their* permission to pass; on the contrary, they had violated their neighbors' territory repeatedly.[35] So what right did they have to talk? He resumed the march and Corinth did not dare to stop him. A bad mistake here by the jealous rivals, giving Cimon a story that would set Athenian hearts bounding again. Where indeed had their general not won them renown? On a single mission, he had saved the first state in Peloponnesus and humiliated the second. When the total score was cast, when you threw in the Persians, Phoenicians, and the rest, what was there left for him to do?

As it turned out, there *was* something left. For Cimon, the delicious respite at Athens was brief. In the depths of Peloponnesus it soon became apparent that the Ephors had misjudged the situation. Ithome did not fall. Unsurpassed when it was a matter of simple, straightforward spear-thrusting on an open field, for all their military reputation, the Spartans were yet deficient in siege warfare. Coincidentally, the Athenians with their engines and mechanical expertise were already hailed as masters in this field.[36] Early in 462, they and certain of the allies were summoned again.

A second time Cimon persuaded the Ekklesia to agree. Arriving in Messenia, for several months he exerted his energies against the high, craggy fortress that dominated the plain. Still it held out. The steep cliffs were impossible to climb, in the teeth of the helots' defense, and to crumble them with the primitive artillery of the fifth century was out of the question. It was a military problem with no quick solution.

Whatever news reached the Athenians from home did nothing to improve morale. During Cimon's absence, Ephialtes and Pericles had renewed their attacks on the Areopagites, not merely on individual members, but on the Council as a whole.[37] Soon they were proposing that its important functions be transferred to the Ekklesia and other agencies of all the citizens. When he heard of it, the general had to recognize his mistake in leaving the city at such a critical time. Not only that, he had brought away many of the other prestigious aristocrats to officer his regiments.[38] Those left behind tended to be the aged, the enfeebled, the debauched, those physically and morally unfit, hardly a fair sampling of the old and honored nobility. What Ephialtes and the radicals alleged about them would be at least partially true, and the Areopagus lost in the public eye as the prosecutions and legislative debates continued. By his actions, however well intended, Cimon had left his friends on the Council in a deepening crisis.

For the general there were other consequences close at hand. If the officers of Cimon's task force were of gentle birth, the rest of its personnel was not. The suspicions of the Spartans were rapidly aroused. Possibly rumors were afloat that certain of the Athenian hoplites were rejoicing over current developments; both the news from home and the state of the siege. While openly sympathizing with the Messenian helot rebels, they had grown lax, even indifferent to the siege.[39] Naturally, there is no proof of the thoughts in the minds of either party. But if the assisting troops from Attica were imbued with the sentiments they were suspected of harboring, and these took root locally, revolution might come anew to Peloponnesus.

Assuming this to be the reason for the Spartans' mistrust, the Ephors were faced with a painful decision. If they took steps against Cimon, they forfeited their best friend in the Athenian camp and lost all influence there. But perhaps this had been lost already. The enemy appeared to be in control at Athens, and their mighty friend's usefulness perceptibly dwindling. The Ephors judged the danger too imminent—Cimon and his hoplites must be dismissed. Having so resolved, the message could still have been delivered with tact to minimize the jolt. But Spartans were not noted for diplomacy; nothing in their experience had trained them for it. Cimon was summoned and bluntly told his services were no longer desired; the Athenians were to leave at once.[40] He passed the word to his troops. Mortified, they filed out of camp in full sight of the Lacedaemonians and other allies. The army marched back to Athens in a smoldering rage, nor was there anything its commander could say or do to salve them.[41] Probably he was as indignant as the rest, and downcast, besides. His proposition for joint leadership of Hellas had failed.

There could be no doubt about citizens' reaction in democratic Athens. The dismissal was considered a national affront. In the mounting fury, everyone who had raised his voice in favor of the ill-starred project was castigated, and of course, all lists began with the general himself. It was now remembered that he had frequently reproved proposers of measures in the Assembly by remarking, "the Lacedaemonians don't do it that way."[42] Cimon's philo-Laconian proclivities became a focus for spiteful digs, and even his austere manner of living was criticized. Examining more closely, why had he named one of his sons Lacedaemonios? The asperities grew more numerous and more vicious. Cimon's enthusiasm for Sparta included a fondness for her women, it was said, and some intimated that he might often be found sleeping in Lacedaemon. The nadir was reached in rumors of incestuous relations with his sister, Elpinice.

It was easy to guess what was coming. As the proper season approached, joyous radicals called for the ordeal by ostracism. Everything turned out as expected. In 461 the victor of Eurymedon was added to the most exclusive roster of all, and went into exile for the prescribed period.[43] Could the citizens have glimpsed the pitfalls a short distance ahead, they might have looked at the issues more carefully.

The last dam had been broken. Freed of Cimon's restraining hand, Ephialtes was back in action, as vehement as ever. Holding Jacobin notions of republican virtue aeons before Robespierre,[44] he was bent on exterminating privilege wherever he could ferret it out. The appeal to ostracism might be interpreted as a supporting referendum. So while never desisting from his accusations against overweening nobles for individual wrongdoing, he centered his attention on the momentous bill to bring down the Areopagus Council. Once that had been accomplished, the equality Solon had spoken of should be a step nearer, and the constitution as Cleisthenes intended it.

Bills were introduced in the Ekklesia which placed strict and severe limitations on the Areopagus' capacity to act. Again, definite information is lacking, but according to Aristotle, the only areas of jurisdiction not taken away were those relating to homicide and arson, and certain religious cases concerning impiety, such as cutting down the olive trees sacred to Athena.[45] How the other powers were redistributed is not known, but the best modern scholarship holds that supervision of the administration, examination of officials both before and after incumbency, and complaints against magistrates in office were all confirmed to the Council of Five Hundred (where Cleisthenes had traditionally fixed them). A final review was reserved to the Ekklesia, which had complete control besides over instances of treason and conspiracy against the state. Most religious cases were to be settled by the *dicasteries,* as the citizens' jury-courts were now called. And these should also have uncontested jurisdiction over suits dealing with property and contracts, and all others between individuals.[46]

Looking at all of this, the proposals of the radicals do not really appear "radical," but for the most part merely a reaffirmation of the constitution of Cleisthenes. However, a word of caution is necessary. Since this was the propaganda claim made by Ephialtes and his supporters at the time, a suspicion exists that the line taken by the victors found its way into contemporary historical writing. Cimon and his set had asserted that they too were defending Cleisthenes' constitution. So where did the truth lie? If both claims were correct, it should not have been hard for the two sides to find a compromise, or for the losers to become reconciled to an expected adjustment.

Instead, what came out of it was the most bitter factional fight in Athens since the century's start.[47] Even without Cimon, the "Good and True" girded themselves for a desperate, unyielding resistance of several years' duration, which indicated that their understanding of the antecedents was entirely different from that of their opponents. The fury of the conservatives and the intensity of their commitment can best be realized when one recalls that their grandfathers put up no comparable struggle when the Cleisthenic constitution was hammered out back in 508. Obviously, they thought the present program much more revolutionary, and far from reenacting the agreements of a half-century gone by, amounted to a breach of them. Did they really have a case, one stifled by defeat, or had they become myopic through arrogance?—as their enemies must have said. We should like to know their side of the controversy—but even the best arguments will lose when followed by a paucity of ballots. The bill to shackle the Areopagus passed the Assembly before the close of 461.

The sequence of events and the prolonged nature of the struggle make it probable that two related measures not accepted until years later were first introduced in the Assembly, or at least advanced for discussion during the same period. One was Pericles' proposal to pay public jurors for daily duty, originally at the rate of one obol,[48] but apparently soon raised to two. Manifestly such an idea would be in order because of the upsurge in judicial business, stemming from the growth of the Delian Confederacy and transfers of cases from the Areopagus. It was only fair that jurors be recompensed for the days away from their own occupations. This was ever more urgent, as court sessions came to average three hundred days out of the year.[49] For some, jury duty became almost a way of life.

On learning that under the Athenian judicial system as it now stood 6,000 jurors were regularly impaneled each year, we can readily sense the conservatives' rage. A charge of wholesale vote buying would be hurled automatically, and refutation would be difficult. A lengthy political conflict, such as the one in progress, reveals that the sides were fairly even in strength. So many purchased votes assured the radicals a comfortable margin. No date is listed for the law to compensate jurors (the first of many providing wages from the public treasury), but scholarly opinion tends to place it a year or two after passage of the Areopagus bill, that is, in 460 or 459.[50] In that case, whatever its merits, it was not simply pay but a payoff.

The second measure that seems closely connected is the one admitting zeugitai to the archonship, though it did not finally pass the Ekklesia until 457-56. The same purpose was behind it, thus the bill for the zeugitai must rank as more important than the other. Jurors, most of whom came from the lowest class, were in the radicals' column anyway. On a quite different course, zeugite farmers were a part of the broad Middle, whose votes were indispensable in a hot, close contest such as the recent one. A very wide slice of that Middle they were, and naturally inclined to shy away from the democrats, especially the radicals. These "yeomen" *had* voted democratic frequently in the past, but always under moderate leaders, tried and trustworthy.

If Ephialtes worked on them,[51] it was effort well spent. What he had to offer, eligibility to the archonship, was a cheap concession in return for their support. Archons did little other than conduct preliminary investigations and certify cases to the jury-courts.[52] But after their terms they still entered the Areopagus, where grateful zeugitai might modify that body considerably. *If* they remained grateful to the radicals. Because the farmer was an ingrained conservative, and other things being equal, he had more in common politically with the High than with the Low. That being so, the aristocrats erred seriously in permitting a rapprochement of zeugites and radicals, and again later, if they drove their agricultural brethren into the democratic camp by vainly refusing to share the archonship with them. This the nobles appear to have done, since the bill did not pass for several years. Here were blunders that Cimon, if present in Athens, could have prevented. Having ousted the harmonizing general, the radicals held the field with ample room to maneuver.

Ephialtes was entitled to a smile of pride over the success of his tactics. If as an elected strategos he was more politician than soldier, with him politics became warfare. He had pounded away steadily at the enemy's front, picked it to pieces with individual forays, battered it broadside, bargained for defections which left gaping holes in the opposite lines. Simultaneously, he maintained good order in his own ranks. He gave unceasing devotion to the democratic ideal and fought for it unflinchingly, to the end.

Commendable as this was, it leaves a question whether these objectives might not have been secured quietly, peacefully, without convulsing the state. Most of them had been obtained once before, at no such cost. The same should have been possible, unless one accepts the premise that Athens' aristocrats were drunk with power from the Delian acquisitions and that the Areopagus had asserted an absolute control similar to that exercised by Rome's Senate in the generation before Caesar. This does not appear to have been the case. Athens' domination over the Confederacy had not reached a stage to permit this, and never did quite reach it. Though Aristotle tells us the Areopagus was supreme after Salamis, he also insists that its power was by now past the peak, in a slow decline.[53] Ephialtes obviously thought otherwise. He continued to hound the high and mighty as though convinced it was wrong that they should be fortune's favorites. The nobles replied with hatred and obstruction, and they knew how to make their resentment felt. As agitation over the Areopagus bill rose, Ephialtes was murdered when caught alone, struck down by the dagger of a man named Aristodicus of Tanagra,[54] reputedly a hired assassin.

Despite his spotless public image, one cannot grieve overmuch for Ephialtes. The impression that comes through is that of a dour, humorless person with no leavening of kindliness. Perhaps early misfortune had warped him, as Aristotle implies. Whatever the explanation, he saw people and events entirely in black and white, being incapable of a wider, milder view. To the extent that he did have a larger vision, it was that of ordinary Athenian citizens collaborating to gain a better world for themselves, if not for their allies. He was a man with a cause, for which he ultimately gave his life. Perhaps it is a fitting epitaph that the first state in human history to be labeled a democracy was partly his creation.

Political events so significant could not fail to find literary echoes, in a society where life and art were as inseparably entwined as in Athens. For the Dionysia of 458, Aeschylus produced his universally acclaimed masterpiece, the trilogy of dramas on the sequel to the Trojan legend, which, from its central figure has generally been called the *Oresteia*. In this tremendous work, Athens' laureate of the postwar generation aimed to reinterpret and update the traditional story so as to reconcile the revered Homeric treatment with the advanced Hellenic outlook of the fifth century's "Age of Reason." Such important matter required a fresh perspective.

In the trilogy's first play, *Agamemnon,* the Achaeans' renowned commander comes home to Argos (actually Mycenae), his success against Troy having raised him to such a pitch of pride that the gods are provoked to contrive his ruin. But the author is careful to show the causes as entirely natural instead of supernal. Agamemnon insults his wife by introducing a Trojan princess into the household as his mistress, but the king's arrogance is nothing new. Repeatedly he had neglected, flaunted, lied to her, until Clytemnestra's indignation explodes into murder. Agamemnon, it is clear, deserves his fate. Under Aeschylus' skillful pen, theological and moral justice are made to coincide perfectly.

The same theme of sin and retribution runs through the second play, *Choephoroi* ("The Libation Bearers"). Here Agamemnon's son, Orestes, makes his first appearance mourning at the grave of his father. He had been visiting an uncle in Phocis when his father died. Now he returns with a bosom companion, Pylades, to pay his respects and assume his filial obligations. As they stand at graveside, Orestes sees a chorus of slave maidens led by his sister Electra approaching to pour religious drink offerings at the tomb. In their choral song bewailing the family misfortunes, possibly we may find Aeschylus' first hidden allusions to the recent shattering occurrences in Athens.

O sacred soil beset by fears,
O land brought to a low estate,
Men shrink to go where no sun peers
On noble halls left desolate.[55]

The direct reference is to Argos and the slaying of Agamemnon, but it may apply equally to the assault on the Areopagus and the train of violence leading to Ephialtes' death.

The plot of *Choephoroi* is amazingly simple. Orestes reveals himself to Electra, and pondering on the situation, the two become convinced they have a duty of retributive vengeance. Disguised as travelers claiming guest-rights, Orestes and Pylades will knock boldly at the palace door, burst in and stab Aegisthus, the queen's lover and accomplice, then despatch Clytemnestra herself. The plan goes perfectly, without a hitch. But after the double execution Orestes is overwhelmed with remorse, and gains no comfort from friendly reassurances. He cries out that already he sees the Furies, those three horrible-visaged sister spirits sent by the gods to punish sinners. Inconsolable, he leaves Argos, while the chorus utters a last warning that Aeschylus may also have intended for Athens.

O what will be the end, the fate
Of blood that fights and lives in hate?[56]

Not until the final drama of the series, the *Eumenides,* does Aeschylus offer more direct observations on affairs in Athens, and then not immediately, The action begins at Delphi, before the famous temple, where the blood-stained Orestes has fled to escape the Furies, who in Greek mythology must have symbolized the voice of conscience. Nevertheless the sisters have found him; they are presently asleep nearby, under a spell cast by Apollo. While the startled priestess recoils from the awful sight, the god soothes and counsels Orestes. Hasten on till you come to Athens' high citadel, he advises, and clasping Athena's age-old wooden image, claim sanctuary. Her councillors shall give you hearing and judge the case, to your relief. For truly the responsibility is mine, says Apollo, and you are not to blame. Orestes departs, but his headstart is short. The ghost of Clytemnestra appears, bent on reprisal, and she rouses the Furies to prompt pursuit.

The scene shifts abruptly to a few score yards away from where Aeschylus' audience is sitting: the old Temple of Athena on Athens' Acropolis—presumably the one destroyed by the Persians only a generation before. Orestes kneels at the altar, begging clemency of the goddess. The supplicant avers he has expiated his crime through years of lonely wandering, suffering, and prayer. Is not this enough?

> Over hills and plains I've stumbled
> With none but Phoebus as my friend.
> Always, 'hind, those scourges rumbled,
> Threatening misery without end.
> Goddess, hear me, lift my cumber,
> All my guilt is paid in dole.
> Goddess, grant me peaceful slumber,
> Hear me, raise me, make me whole![57]

He is interrupted by the chorus of Furies, arriving to carry out their baleful mission. Again they cry for the fugitive's blood, declaring their purpose to torment him till his spirit goes down to Hades. As if in reply, Orestes implores once more the protection of the goddess.

Miraculously, Athena appears in her shining helmet and armor. Professing surprise, she asks the reason for this extraordinary visitation, and receives the stories of both parties. Athena is asked to render judgment. Surprisingly, the goddess replies that this decision, too weighty for any human judge, is beyond her also. She will appoint a tribunal of the men most qualified, the finest Athenians she can find, who will swear to deliberate until true judgment be reached.

> Beyond the compass of a single mind
> Are cases of this ilk. Even such as I
> Who am immortal, should not seek to bind
> You to my sole decision. We must try
> The case before a group of judges hight,
> The city's best, to see that all comes right.[58]

This, of course, is the Council of Areopagus, which the poet praises highly, both for its intrinsic merit and for its divine origin. Athena brings in the councillors, a panel of twelve, and introduces them. Seated, they proceed to hear the case, in which the Furies act as prosecutors and Apollo as defense attorney. The arguments are strong on both sides. To the charge that Orestes' matricide is not merely a human crime, but a religious offense against heaven, Apollo answers that Orestes acted at his instigation, but that he, in turn, had the authority of Zeus so to order it. The Father moves in and through everything.

Such powerful contention leaves the Areopagites perplexed. When polled for a verdict they are evenly split, six against six. Everything hinges on Athena, who has revealed that she intends to vote, too. Swayed by Apollo's reasoning and by Orestes' contrition, she opts to free the defendant, who in his joy announces that he, as the restored king of Argos, will pledge his city to an eternal friendship and alliance with Athens. (To the audience, this was timely and welcome. For a moment Aeschylus descends to the level of contemporary politics, endorsing a move already contemplated by the Athenians as an answer to their rebuff by Sparta.)[59] The Furies, the only ones not happy at the outcome, wail that the younger gods have usurped their privileges, that the proper order has been overturned. To console the sisters, Athena offers them a share in her sponsorship of the city, renaming them the *Eumenides* ("the Good-tempered Ones") by way of sublimation, and assigns them a new habitation below the Acropolis, where they will help her watch over the fortunes of Athens and ward off evil.

So ends the *Oresteia*. The opinion is unanimous that Aeschylus was vitally interested in the recent happenings in Athens and that he used this occasion to comment, but there is substantially less agreement as to what he meant. Some, pointing out that the climactic trial concerned homicide, have taken the view that Aeschylus approved of the reform, since cases of homicide were among the few left to the Areopagus.[60] Thus he has been described as a democrat,[61] on rather slender evidence which has been challenged.[62] Others have arrived at a different conclusion, calling attention to Athena's creation of the Areopagus Council, her positive prohibition against interference with it,[63] and her warning against adding bad laws to good. Still others have sought a middle ground, making Aeschylus an advocate of reconciliation, exhorting all Athenians to refrain from strife and pull together for the common good.[64]

The truth seems to lie between the two latter interpretations; rather, with both of them. Aeschylus' praise of the Areopagites as the "best men in the state" rings clear, with no jarring reverberations. Nor is there any attempt to qualify or equivocate. On the evidence of the *Oresteia* it would appear that Aeschylus did not credit the charges made against the nobles, many of whom must have been his friends. His support of the Areopagus is strong. At the same time, he had ties with the democrats, and especially with Pericles, who had been chorus-trainer for his *Persae,* fourteen years before. And as the author of the *Persae,* he had to be aware of all that unity, fellow feeling, and cooperative effort had meant to his city. Undoubtedly, he wanted to conciliate.

If Aeschylus was a loyal citizen of Athens, he was also a citizen of the world. What has raised the *Oresteia* so high among the masterworks of literature is the universality of its theme: a good man faced with agonizing, complex, and virtually insoluble problems, yet demanding a solution; a situation in which hardly gods, much less men, could be entirely right; the inevitable mistake, and the long, educative round of cleansing through suffering. For behind the action a process was developing which participants and spectators could only dimly comprehend, if at all. As one eminent classicist has put it, what was going on was the transition from a primitive family-tribe morality of blood-guilt and revenge to a constitutional city-state ethic of universal justice.[65]

There was yet more. With the *Oresteia,* Greek thought attained perhaps for the first time a level one may call monotheistic. Throughout, but particularly in the third drama, the idea prevails of a single supreme power ordaining what is right for man and the world. Many gods are mentioned, but all do the bidding of one. This becomes obvious in the spectacular trial scene, when Apollo declares that he has merely been Zeus' agent. But much earlier, at the very beginning of the *Eumenides,* the Pythian priestess had said the same while explaining her function at Delphi.

> The Delphic fane has many rulers known
> Since Mother Earth first voiced her wishes here.
> Themis, then Phoebe, spurred my sacred moan
> Ere Zeus gave us Apollo to revere.
> But whether this or that one, come who may,
> The will is Zeus', and Zeus we do obey.[66]

Aeschylus' greatest achievement in drama was perhaps also his last.[67] Shortly after the production of the *Oresteia* he received an invitation from Hieron, the munificent tyrant of Syracuse, to visit his court where Pindar and others of Hellas' literary select had been extolled and entertained. And at Gela, in faraway Sicily, he died in 456. Among the laudations that have accumulated down the centuries, no testimonial is more impressive than the decree of his own city that anyone wishing to stage a performance of a drama by Aeschylus should be granted a chorus paid from the public treasury.

10

Moving toward Empire

460–448 B.C.

THE murder of Ephialtes was bound to create yet another leadership crisis, given the free flow of Athenian politics. For years, Ephialtes had schemed to prevent that chief of aristocrats, the ever popular Cimon, from magnetizing the democrats also, thus automatically becoming prostates tou demou in succession to Aristides.

At first Ephialtes was unable to stem the tide; Cimon probably can be regarded as prostates from about 465 until his ostracism in 461, as evidenced by his successes in the Ekklesia during those years.[1] Then, when the radicals had gained control of the party and Ephialtes had finally grasped the helm, he apparently held it for less than a year. After his assassination, his partisans had to agree quickly on a replacement, to preserve the hard won gains. Aristotle tells us that Ephialtes' chief collaborator in establishing the reforms was a certain Archestratus,[2] about whom nothing more is known. Because of his anonymity, it is presumed that he, like his martyred leader, was below the nobility; yet he would seem to have been the natural choice. Elsewhere, Pericles is mentioned as an important co-worker;[3] yet he was still young, almost a political novice. However, when the smoke clears it is Pericles, the noble, who emerges as prostates tou demou[4] instead of the nevermore mentioned Archestratus.

Immediately, one suspects the Alcmaeonids—Athens' covert royalty, claiming descent from the old Neleid line of kings[5]—who must have been as intent on recovering control of the party from Ephialtes as once they did from Themistocles, and not without reason. Nevertheless, the members of that august clan must have had mixed feelings. No doubt many of them would have preferred Cimon to the young maverick in their own family. His apparent cooperation in opening the offices to zeugites must have gone down hard with a set that held government the property of those who were best in blood and training, believing perforce in a "paternalistic democracy." But Cimon was in exile. If it came to a choice between Pericles and Archestratus, a second Ephialtes, so to speak, the way was clear. They might not like their young man overmuch, but they knew and respected him, having marked his superior qualities of mind and expression from earliest youth, as had all Athenians.[6] By their own view of such matters they would have to go along, to exert their tremendous influence for Pericles, as they had previously done for Aristides. No wonder Archestratus is never heard of again. Knowing their own relative, perhaps they already had reason to think (as Thucydides later declared)[7] that he was essentially broad-minded and not really as radical as his youthful efforts made him out—also that he would learn and benefit from the mistakes of his predecessors.

If so, they judged him correctly. Contemplation of familiar examples from Athens' past history made Pericles the most cautious, consciously circumspect statesman the city had yet seen. If he was now generally recognized as the state's foremost man, one would never guess it from his demeanor. In him there was none of Themistocles' cock-of-the-walk swagger or of Ephialtes' persistent belligerence. Rather, Pericles was urbane and pleasant with all, after the fashion of the born aristocrat, though from this also proceeded a certain coolness which sometimes struck people as standoffish. Probably it was no more than an instinct for propriety, strengthened by prudence. Conscious always of the total situation, its goals and dangers, Pericles exerted himself with quiet authority and measured commitment. Risks, if unavoidable, were sure to be calculated.

This was most notably true of his conduct in the Ekklesia. Too many of Athens' politicians had worn out their welcome by going constantly to the bema, parading their views on every trivial matter. The son of Xanthippus seldom went to the platform; friends and sympathizers spoke for him,[8] while he managed from behind the scene. He took the floor only on important occasions, at wide intervals in time, and projected an image of reticence by appearing last in debates. This suggests that he may also have arranged for others to beg his opinion, so he could make an unobtrusive answer in the spirit of disinterested patriotism without seeming to force himself upon the Assembly. It gave him the advantage of being able to refute all previous arguments if unfriendly, to supplement and reinforce those on his side, to make the last and most powerful impression on the citizens before they voted.

Over the years he grew more formidable. His natural assets were enhanced through constant practice, training the mind as well as the tongue. According to Plato, his studies in natural science and philosophy had been of great benefit, and particularly those under Anaxagoras, who had taught him how to organize his ideas to best advantage.[9] The invariable result was a masterly discourse with facts and arguments marshaled as in a lawyer's presentation, each expression artfully chosen and charged with emotion when appropriate. The effect on the audience was profound, often electrifying. Aristophanes, in his *Acharnians,* compares Pericles in his flights of eloquence to Zeus "hurling down the thunder and lightning from his Olympian heights."[10] To his friends of the Platonic circle, Socrates declared that Pericles was the finest speaker he had ever heard.[11]

It was probably this rhetorical prowess combined with the majesty of his bearing that caused people to call him "the Olympian," a sobriquet that must have been current in Athens before Aristophanes created his figure of speech. Though not untinged with irony, it was a mark of deepest respect. Yet torrents from heaven could become wearisome and finally irritating, for all the awe they inspired. Pericles had to employ his magic bolt sparingly, move with the utmost deliberation.

How deeply he realized this is attested by his style of living. Contemporary opinion pronounced him frugal in food and drink, and his only affectation in dress was a helmet worn to cover an abnormally high forehead. Pericles kept regular hours, dividing his time between the Ekklesia and Agora, where the Board of Generals met, always proceeding to each by the most direct routes. Dinner invitations and all such favors were declined, to escape even the shadow of corruption. And in rare instances when the prostates could not with courtesy turn down a close relative's bid to dinner, he would leave as soon as the postprandial wine drinking began, when conviviality might lead to indiscretions. Pericles' life was to be an open book and an immaculate one, but—knowing better than any that familiarity bred contempt—he intended it to be a book that Athenians should read from a distance.

By scanning what was disclosed, we must judge his decision well taken. His fellow citizens must have seen him much as we imagine him from the existing statues (based, doubtless, on approved originals): a man with a grave, oval, bearded face showing steady eyes, a firm straight nose, and full lips, in fact quite handsome features except for the high forehead. Beyond that they knew him as a quiet family man maintaining a well-ordered household, with a genteel wife and two growing sons. If many of his friends were avant-garde philosophers and artists whose statements and activities raised eyebrows, no fault could be found with Pericles himself. It was strange how much his countrymen knew of him, yet how little they knew him.

The impenetrable facade behind which Pericles concealed his inmost thoughts denies us an explicit answer to the question ideologically most relevant to his political career; namely, what was his private concept of democracy, seen in the light of its practice at Athens? At first consideration the problem seems to dissolve in thin air. One merely looks at the record. Fair enough, but remembering that statesmen must also be politicians, records become deceptive, as hard to see through as their creators. Athens, in the Periclean Age, represented the flood tide of popular government, and before the Greeks as a whole Pericles passed as the Great Democrat. Yet his spirit tended to belie his actions, and various acquaintances remarked that his natural bent was far from democratic.[12]

One may, say, turn to the famous Funeral Oration, preserved in Thucydides' second book. There Pericles' reflections on his city are set forth in fullest detail. True again, but the Funeral Oration is a notable example of his skill at special pleading; despite its cogency it is as slick a job as any attorney ever drafted in defense of a client. It is the truth, but not the whole truth. Back of it all lies Pericles' massive reserve, the certainty of something unspoken, that never would be spoken. A distinct impression lingers of the clever advocate, who at need could make out just as strong a case for the other side.

Nevertheless, if one accepts the high estimates of Pericles' character, one has to believe in his sincerity. Then, a critical appraisal of his position becomes necessary. As a starting point, he unquestionably went along with the main democratic changes before his time: division of civic responsibilities, limits and checks placed on officers of the state, choice of most officeholders by lot, extension of the franchise to the lowest classes, centering of authority in the Ekklesia.[13] All his actions affirm his belief in equality of opportunity, that both the state and its members would gain by broadening political experience, and that administrative efficiency and honesty would be sharpened by a watchful, challenging citizenry.

The remedial measures harmonized with other actions. Most judicial cases were confirmed to the popular courts, which Pericles obviously deemed a fairer, safer avenue to justice than the Areopagus. He could point out (as he did in the Funeral Oration) that through Athens' laws the will of the people secured equity for all. By his and Ephialtes' grace, the vast majority of cases would now be decided by panels composed of common Athenians, mostly thetes and zeugites. This would mean little if they could not afford to leave their jobs for jury duty. Thus Pericles was fully justified in asking compensation for the jurors, despite charges of bribery. In no other way could the system be made to work.

Once the stipendiary principle had been introduced, extension of it to other fields was eased. At an unknown later date, Pericles or one of his followers persuaded the Ekklesia to pay wages for army and navy service, though a precedent had been set by Cimon's maintenance grants to his troops on special occasions, that is, whenever money or booty could be found. Within a dozen years Pericles would institute a comprehensive program to beautify Athens, rebuilding the temples destroyed by the Persians, necessitating the hiring of stonemasons, artists and craftsmen, carpenters, miners, quarriers, haulers, by the thousands, thus assuming the character of a huge public works project. One way or another, virtually every needy citizen could receive some kind of employment from the state. Probably Pericles also set up the Theorika Fund,[14] which doled out coins for tickets to the religious festivals, possibly adding a little extra to recompense for the day's work missed by attending. In no case did these various payments amount to more than a few obols a day to each person, and the cautious prostates introduced them gradually over a span of years, manifestly taking care to find the money before committing such sums.

Pay was likewise provided for the archons and members of the Council of Five Hundred, at least during the period when these functioned as prytaneis.[15] But at this point the prostates drew the line. None was accorded to citizens simply for attendance at the Ekklesia. Apparently Pericles regarded this a duty owed to the state. Citizens unable to leave their businesses were not required to come, but police were sent to round up idlers on the streets; if these tried to escape they were struck and their clothes stained by ropes dipped in wet vermilion paint. Athenians apprehended with the telltale red smears were fined. The Ekklesia was filled, then, by a droll reversal of the radicals' emolument principle. Pericles had already compensated his zeugite supporters in the Assembly by securing their admission to the time-honored offices. It appears that later, at another date unrecorded, the thetes were also allowed to qualify simply through a fictional declaration that they were property holders.[16] That being conceded, Athens had traveled an infinite distance down the road to democracy, much farther than any state then existing or preexistent.

Beyond this basic credo of broadened participation, equal opportunity, and checks and balances, it may be seen that Pericles, like Solon, adhered strongly to the work ethic as giving health to the body politic. He was convinced the government should take a hand in the process by providing employment and wages to the extent practicable. In that connection, metropolitan cities like Athens had a growing amount of public business that created jobs for their people. Pericles seemed now ready to defend the proposition that in anything exceptional, any public service above the normal call to assembly duty, the cost should be defrayed by the government.[17] In thus determining, he may be said to have devised the world's first welfare state. If so, he applied the principle in a gradual and guarded manner, winning for himself another singular distinction: Pericles' Athens was one of the few nations ancient or modern, to administer a welfare program from a treasury nearly always well stocked.

It required a marvel of planning justifying his designation as the Olympian. To her sister republics in Hellas, Athens of the middle fifth century must have seemed a prodigy, discovering so many ways to occupy her citizens advantageously, then getting the money to pay them. No wonder democracy flourished. Pericles had supplemented ordinary outlets with a series of extraordinary activities in the public interest, and certainly the most important was the system of jury courts, now known as dicasteries. These were evolutionary growths from Solon's single court of the people, the Heliaea,[18] though no document survives to tell us how the change came about.

It suffices to know that by Pericles' day the dicasteries had become the main reliance of Athens' proletarians, and were therefore the fountains of his power. It was here, meeting in the Agora[19] rather than on Pnyx Hill, that Athens' indigents received their judicial assignments and their financial rewards. These were sure to come, frequently if not regularly. For 6,000 were registered as jurors annually, with 5,000 impaneled into ten courts that were always busy, the rest being held in reserve. If not used, these headed the new list to be drawn up for the following year.

Not all of those impaneled were used at one time. The board of archons assessed the weight of each case in turn, and after certifying it, determined how large a jury was needed in multiples of one hundred, with an extra person added to prevent a tie vote, as 201, 301, 401, etc. One archon presided at each trial, but did not vote himself. Moreover, he was not a judge, to state the law, make rulings, or charge the jury. He simply called the court into session, acted as a chairman, and duly reported the results. The once mighty archons had indeed been shorn.

Their humbling left something to be desired. The Athenian dicasteries were curiosities by any modern standard. There were no judges, no rules of evidence, and no lawyers either. Each litigant pled his own cause before a sea of jurors, seeking to move them with reasoned arguments, eloquence, and whatever tricks he might have. In an adversary relationship personal abuse of one's opponent was expected, and far more than in our refereed courts there were appeals to sentimentality, patriotism, and profit.[20] If the case were a criminal one, at its end the jurors simply voted on guilt or innocence, with no instructions to guide them and no hedges against prejudice. In civil disputes they found in favor of one party or the other, and if the penalties were not already prescribed by law, the dicasts had to determine these too. Though the size of the juries would tend to prevent corruption as intended,[21] nothing could be done about discrimination. An Athenian of the next generation wrote that, by his observation, the jurors often ignored evidence, shamelessly to vote for those who excited their sympathies, or those whom they perceived to be "most like themselves."[22] Under these circumstances, an aristocrat would get short shrift. This may be an extreme view of the situation, one that Pericles could hardly have desired. But by various means, the dicasteries were usually willing instruments of his policy, an almost unshakeable base of control.

To this point Pericles had led the march toward liberal reform with a bold and steady step. In the main, it had been a course well chosen. Not only for the men of less than ample means who had fought loyally for Athens, but for those even less fortunate, who, doing their smaller stint, also deserved well of the state. Then, at the close of Pericles' first decade in 451, came a strange reversal, a seeming regression, that his admirers declare was forced upon him. Whatever the situation, he and no one else brought the enigmatic issue before the Ekklesia. Citizenship was henceforth limited to those who could prove Athenian parents on both sides, legally married. If enacted earlier this statute would have excluded Cleisthenes, Themistocles, even Cimon, all of them children of foreign mothers. An explanation is not easy. The measure, so undemocratic in principle, must have been demanded by the democrats themselves or at least by a sizable segment of them. Otherwise it would hardly have gotten a hearing.

Various rationalizations have been put forward. Some modern scholars have seen it as an attempt to preserve the purity of Athenian blood from alien infiltration (something which had not worried Athenians overmuch in the past!), and mention that it was a matter on which democrats could get enthusiastic support from conservatives at a time when this was essential.[23] Another calls attention to the undoubted economic benefits of citizenship under the welfare scheme, and that Attica would now be swamped with new immigrants unless restrictions were made.[24] A third points out that democracy in the ancient world did not mean the extinction of privilege, as today, but rather "the extension of its area."[25] Degrees of validity lie in all three theories, especially the last. By it, the stoop-shouldered thetes of the harborside, given a modicum of security, saw no reason why they should share their hard won gains with undeserving newcomers. A more immediate practical problem lurked in the background, that would have most weight with Pericles, careful financier that he was. Despite the Delian revenues, Athens' funds were not unlimited. She could not afford to extend payments to the stream of metics now pouring in through Piraeus, if these should apply for citizenship. He had clung to the liberal precepts of his forefathers for a decade, but of late there had been grave developments abroad, serious enough to convince farsighted Athenians that the state's resources had best be conserved.

All the same, the citizenship bill must have nearly wrenched the democratic party apart. If many recognized no obligation to share their privileges with outlanders, there must also have been a fair number who were conscience stricken, if they took the constitution of Cleisthenes at all seriously. Pericles was most likely one of this group, the idealist and practical statesman in him sorely at odds. An implication common to all three views cited above is that he was prevailed upon to sponsor the bill because only his authority could heal the threatened rift in the party. As matters stood he must have spoken from a heavy heart, compelled to action by overwhelming necessity. Aside from this, Pericles had to detest a law which drew the line against his many friends with antecedents outside of Attica, the philosophers, poets, and artists from Ionia and the islands. Some came from Delian cities which would not be pleased with the legislation. But like it or not, the law had to be. It was not only the menace of mounting costs; overriding considerations proceeding from Athens' foreign affairs would have checked civic liberality sooner or later. Assuming responsibility for other Greek states less well situated was no doubt altruistic, and might in some instances be profitable, but losses had to be calculated along with gains. At this stage the reckoning had debits that could not be ignored.

It is far from surprising that Athens should find her external relations in something of a muddle at mid-century. The radicals' rise to power a dozen years back had brought a complete reorientation in the city's diplomacy, making it a more venturesome, exciting game for much higher stakes. In part it was a natural consequence of what had gone before: the rebuff at Ithome, the insulting dismissal of the Athenian volunteers, Cimon's fall and the repudiation of his formula for collaboration with Lacedaemon. The radicals had never agreed to it; the Ithome incident furnished them a perfect excuse to follow their natural instincts and move in the opposite direction. Very quickly they persuaded the Ekklesia to take Athens out of the Peloponnesian League, where she had maintained an anachronistic membership. Further, they deliberately spited Lacedaemon by concluding an alliance with Argos, her chief enemy in Peloponnesus. As if that were not enough, ententes were negotiated with the Thessalian cities in the north, the very places where Themistocles had blunted Sparta's initiatives a generation before and nourished a strong ill will against her. Athens, under the radicals, seemed to be throwing down the gauntlet.

It was more than sheer bravado, more than resentment over an insult, or the aversion of leftists toward mossbacks at the other end of the political spectrum. Quite frankly, the radicals dominant at Athens had tasted the delights of prosperity and power accruing through the Delian organization, and they wished these to continue. Overall, things were going beautifully. Attica's underprivileged were taken care of, while they, as soldiers and sailors, took care of the Confederacy and were supported from its assessments, which provided enough to constantly replenish Athens' coffers. A splendid contrivance, but one whose very success created new problems. Naxos, and more recently Thasos, had tried to leave, seeing the old danger as diminished and perhaps anticipating a new one. Then at last the word reached Athens that Lacedaemon had promised aid to Thasos, and would have sent it had not the helot rebellion kept her occupied at home. This could be learned from friendly Thasian democrats, once the island had fallen. It confirmed the suspicions of Athenian radicals, and hardened their animosity, convincing them that Sparta was the ultimate foe, the one remaining power to whom dissidents within the Confederacy could turn, the only one which might conceivably destroy it, hence the single impediment to Athens' greatness. Sparta must be brushed back, along with the other members of her League most likely to make trouble.

For the moment, all classes at Athens gave the resolution wide approval, including many aristocrats who were alienated by the Spartan snub. Aeschylus was possibly one of these; his *Oresteia,* produced in 458, had kind words for the Argive alliance,[26] and actually took liberties with history by calling Agamemnon king of Argos instead of Mycenae, a bit of flattery whose purpose was obvious. Similarly, the rapprochement with the Thessalians was an action nobody in Athens would contest. Breeding the best horses in Greece, Thessaly could contribute strong cavalry support for Athenian land armies that might soon be put to the test. Concurrently, Athens may have opened secret negotiations with the Messenian helots at Mount Ithome, finally nearing the end of their ability to resist. No proof exists, but the record speaks for itself. When the Messenians capitulated about 458, they did so on far better terms than rebels usually received (through threats of Athenian intervention?), and were promptly conveyed out of Messenia by an Athenian naval detachment which resettled them in a new home at Naupactus, on the northern side of the Corinthian Gulf. Athens could count on their gratitude in the stormy days ahead.

The aroused generals of Athens' Strategion were alert for leaks in Lacedaemon's League, and already they had found one. Megara, the neighbor state down the Isthmus was normally no friend, being rather too close for comfort. But she was even closer to Corinth on her other side, and the two had a continuing quarrel over territory that lay between. At last they had recourse to arms, and Corinth won. Understandably, the defeat toppled Megara's oligarchic government and brought in the democrats, who immediately withdrew their city from the Peloponnesian League and sent ambassadors to Athens to ask for an alliance.

The Ekklesia was only too happy to grant one; it hardly needed the generals' automatic endorsement. Sitting astride the Isthmus, Megara was in a position to seal off central and northern Greece from the Peloponnesians, leaving Athens a free hand in both areas. Furthermore, Megara had twin harbors east and west at a few miles' distance, Nisaea on the Saronic Gulf, and Pagai on the Corinthian. Use of the latter would give Athens her first entry to the trade of the west: Italy, Sicily, possibly even Spain. The opportunity was eagerly grasped. In 459, shortly before the resettlement of the helots, Pericles sent troops to "assist" the Megarian democrats to keep order in their city and masons to build a double wall linking Megara with her main harbor, Nisaea, on the Saronic. In the other direction, access to Pagai was protected by the ridge of Mount Geraneia jutting nearly to the Corinthian Gulf. By manning Geraneia's passes and the newly constructed wall, Athenian hoplites might coop the Lacedaemonians within their own peninsula, to Athens' obvious benefit. Pericles could allow himself a discreet smile, remembering that militarily the Spartans were at their worst when faced with geographic obstacles, natural or man-made. Directly afterward he commenced building the famed Long Walls to connect Athens with Piraeus, for more basic insurance. In the defense strategy, the only real danger was that the Athenians stationed in Megara might be so overbearing as to offend the residents, giving the impression that they were a garrison of occupation—which was not far from the truth. Knowing Pericles, one assumes the departing men were given explicit instructions on how to behave.

Having come to the aid of Megara, Athens had to expect trouble with Corinth. Athens' home fleet (smaller than the main one stationed at Samos) anxiously patrolled the Saronic, and the Corinthians, reinforced by ships from Epidaurus, promptly came out to offer battle. The Athenians had the better of a clash off the island of Cecryphalea, but this merely led to greater trials. Aegina, with Hellas' third largest navy, now entered the fray on the side of Corinth, motivated by a growing fear of Athens. The anticipated sea fight off Aegina's shores, resulted in an even more overwhelming Athenian victory. Landing on the island, the Athenian commander Leocrates proceeded to lay siege to the city of Aegina itself.[27] A major city like Aegina would not fall quickly, might never fall, but it was a rare satisfaction to see her so closely confined, virtually eliminated as Athens' closest maritime rival.

There was more yet to come. Corinth had been temporarily crippled on the sea, but was still able to exert herself on land. Shrewdly, her leaders concluded that to push the siege of Aegina, Athens must draw some men away from the Isthmus barrier, thus thin out the line. Suddenly the Corinthians burst through the lightly guarded passes of Mount Geraneia and advanced upon Megara. By so doing they hoped to ease at once the pressure on Aegina and to help themselves to another slice of the Megarian plain.[28] But Pericles met the thrust without having to divert hoplites away from the island. Scraping together a reserve brigade of under-age youths and superannuated men, he sent it to the relief of Megara under the general Myronides, another veteran of the Plataea campaign. The hastily assembled Athenians did not hesitate to challenge the invaders, and in a heated conflict outside the city held their position so doggedly that at last the Corinthians lost their zest, left the ground and returned home.

Myronides' men claimed the victory, erected a trophy on the field, and gathered around to celebrate. But another act was still to be played. The retreating Corinthians were jeered so unmercifully by relatives and friends for abandoning the fight to an army of misfits, that they returned several days later and set up their own trophy. In response to this, the Athenians poured out of Megara and assaulted their opponents with such fury that the latter fled back whence they had come. To make matters worse, several companies of fugitives took the wrong road, then were hemmed in by surrounding ditches, to be slaughtered by the pursuing Athenians. For Myronides it was a splendid double triumph, tightening Athens' hold on the Isthmus.[29] It must have been shortly after this that the Messenian helots from Ithome were brought to Naupactus, a strategic harbor on the north side of the Corinthian Gulf in its narrowest section, recently seized by the Athenians for use as a naval station. The rehabilitated helots could be relied upon to defend the spot fiercely against all intruders from the hated Peloponnesian League, and to join their Athenian hosts in harassment of Peloponnesian shipping—one more item of anxiety for the discomfited Corinthians. To the men of Corinth, indeed, it must have seemed that Athens was closing in on all sides.

It was a bit awesome, the number of irons Pericles was able to keep in the fire, giving careful attention to each. He had already accomplished his first objective, beating back Corinth, Epidaurus, and Aegina, the nearest members of that rival League to which Athens had once belonged. The Spartans had yet to be heard from, not being fully recovered from the upheaval in their midst. Pericles did not intend to give them time to recover. While he detailed some Athenians to besiege Aegina, and others to fortify Naupactus, still others were busy cultivating the folk of northern and central Greece, creating a favorable climate for Athens,[30] encouraging the democrats of various localities in their hopes of ousting the oligarchs who generally ruled in the north. For this was the way that Athens in her turn would rule on Greece's mainland, in a manner quite different from the Delian Confederacy: through ties with the local democrats of Phocis, Locris, and Boeotia, who would be dependent on Athens' bounty and thus to a degree subservient to her. Not by direct conquest, which was insulting to the Greek spirit, but by manipulation. Even this was dangerous, requiring the utmost skill, since Athens by an odd trick of fate was also allied with the oligarchs of Thessaly who would not tolerate a vigorous stirring of hoi polloi.

If the Athenians were edging toward a type of empire, it had to be something far removed, far subtler than the blunt Roman *impero,* "I command!" The Greek road to power was a narrow, twisting, stony trail rather than a broad, straight highway. Nevertheless the idea was already more than a germ in the minds of Athenians, and they used the convenient term, arché, which suited their purpose much better than a word like the Latin impero. Arché, rolled on the flexible Hellenic tongue, could mean anything from the innocuous sounding "office" or "responsibility" to an absolutely magisterial "sovereign rule." It was an expression heard increasingly on the streets of Athens, and with good reason. The citizens might not be sure what Pericles was up to, but they could see he was enjoying an amazing success. The year 459, which witnessed most of the foregoing events, has been called an *annus mirabilis* in Athenian history, when Athens' great leader first tried for a dominance on land to match that already achieved on the sea, a drive for primacy in Hellas. The year 458 was almost as good a period. But Pericles and his countrymen had not sufficiently evaluated the tenacious egoism of Greeks with contrary ideas, peoples who were now rousing themselves. The years to follow would be harder.

Most witnesses of Athens' meteoric rise whether well disposed or not, realized almost intuitively that there was one competitor with whom she had not yet measured swords—one, moreover, whose measure *must* be taken if she were to continue on her present course.[31] Lacedaemon. When would Lacedaemon be heard from? An oddity that when so many were fighting, the Spartans should be at peace. Light banter was not the reaction on the banks of the Eurotas, however, where the masters of Peloponnesus were slowly recovering from the devastation of 464, and the round of rebellions consequent upon it. Embarrassment mounted, as defeated members of their League made vain appeals to the famed hegemon. Admittedly, nothing could be done for Aegina, since Lacedaemon had hardly any navy. Aegina was probably lost to the League, as Megara had been shortly before; would Corinth and Epidaurus be next? All the world could see that the Spartans were slipping. Even King Artaxerxes in distant Persia was made aware of the decline in Sparta's prestige, much to his chagrin. After the defeat of his army in Egypt he had sent an envoy with bags of gold trying to induce the Lacedaemonians to invade Attica, in hopes the Athenians would have to call back their expeditionary force from the Nile. Sparta had accepted the gold, but its army did not stir from Laconia.[32] Now dishonesty could be added to other complaints against her.

Needless to say, the Ephors were deeply concerned, and were determined to restore Sparta's former eminence as soon as her reviving strength permitted. In their perplexity, they settled on a strange course. Suddenly a plea for assistance on grounds of consanguinity came from the small state of Doris, in central Greece, one of whose towns had been seized by neighboring Phocians. Since Doris was the area from which all Dorians in Peloponnesus were supposed to have migrated centuries before, the Lacedaemonians could grant the request under an appearance of piety. But their real purpose, plainly, was to counter Athens' thrust into central Greece. In the summer of 457, deciding the time had come for action, the Ephors raised an army of 1500 Spartiates and 10,000 Peloponnesian allies and sent it north under Nicomedes, son of the former regent Cleombrotus. Lacedaemon was in the field at last.

In Athens, Pericles instantly recognized the challenge, boldly took it up. The Peloponnesians would have to pass the Isthmus, which Athens now controlled. Troops along the Megarian border were alerted, and stronger guards placed in the passes of Mount Geraneia. Ordinarily that would have been sufficient, but the clever Nicomedes managed to elude them by surprise tactics that were most un-Spartan. Quietly, he found ships to transport his army across the Corinthian Gulf, and landed his men safely on the far side before the Athenians could do anything about it.[33] Immediately afterward Pericles sent a squadron of fifty galleys to patrol the waters of the Gulf. So Nicomedes could not use that trick again and just as plainly he was going to have a rough time getting back to the southern peninsula. What pretext Pericles had for these moves is a mystery, since the two nations were still formally at peace. The incident is interesting chiefly as a demonstration of the increasingly aggressive imperialism of Athens' radical democrats. Everything north of the Isthmus they now considered their own preserve. Without Athens' permission, strangers must keep out.

Once he was north of the Gulf, Nicomedes easily accomplished his official mission. Cowed by the approach of the renowned Spartans, the Phocians submitted without a struggle, gave back the captured town, and agreed to reparations. Only then did it come out that Nicomedes had secret instructions relating to other regions in central Greece. From Doris he marched east-southeast into Boeotia, and overawing the cities there, compelled them to join a reconstituted Boeotian League under the presidency of conservative Thebes, Athens' traditional enemy. His intent could not be mistaken. The Boeotian League would amount to a northern adjunct of the Peloponnesian, with Athenians hedged in between, cutting off any further expansion on the Greek mainland. Jealous Thebes could be depended upon both to report and resist whenever Athens stirred.

This came close to a direct confrontation, and apparently Athens regarded it as a declaration of war. Her cocky radicals would not let this pass, nor was Pericles inclined to restrain them. How many Boeotian communities that had gone democratic through their manipulation were now lost to them under the new setup? Several, one surmises, though there is no record. That Nicomedes was presently engaged in improving the fortifications of Thebes gave additional provocation.[34] It was time to stop him. Abruptly, the Athenians called up their entire available fighting force of 14,000, and accompanied by 1,000 Argives and a regiment of Thessalian cavalry, they advanced to the Boeotian frontier.

It says something for the stamina and self-assurance of the Athenians that they could contemplate action at such a moment. Their main armament was hundreds of miles away, bogged down in Egypt. Another large expedition was besieging Aegina. Yet Athens was able to field a third army, seemingly not inferior to the other two, since her Assembly was confident enough to send it against the Spartans.

The high morale of those sent forth is revealed also by their decision not to halt at their own frontier, and wait for Nicomedes to cross into Attica on his return march, which he could hardly have avoided doing. This would have been both proper and prudent, but the offense-minded Athenians threw caution to the winds. Eager to test their mettle against those reputed to be Greece's best, they went forward to Tanagra in Boeotia, and there, in June, 457, they drew themselves up in line of battle, in prompt expectation of their opponents, whose camp was nearby.

They were not to be disappointed, but before the battle was joined a surprise awaited them. The exiled Cimon appeared and asked to prove his loyalty by fighting for Athens as a member of his own tribal regiment, at this critical moment. It was a political masterstroke on his part. Cimon could lay to rest the old charges that he was pro-Spartan. This was of signal importance for him and his friends, as rumors were circulating that traitorous aristocrats had invited Nicomedes to invade Attica and demolish the Long Walls, then nearing completion.[35] There was no question that Cimon's help would be valuable, but the open-handed offer was not as innocent as it looked. With it, he presented his opponents with a classic dilemma, beautifully contrived. If they accepted, and he should be instrumental in winning such an important victory, would this not make him more popular then ever? On the other hand, if they refused, and then lost the battle, they would be blamed and Cimon would emerge as a wronged hero, a sentimental favorite. Even if they accepted, but lost, people would say Cimon had done all he could; they were defeated because he was not in command. The perplexed generals, of whom Pericles was one, could not make up their minds. They decided to pass the burden of decision to the Council of Five Hundred and a messenger was sent to Athens with the question. He returned to say that the Council had ruled against Cimon, but there were no stipulations about the actions of his friends. Cimon withdrew to watch from a distance, after exhorting his men to do their utmost for Athens.

The battle of Tanagra can only be described in superlatives. It was one of the longest, bitterest, and bloodiest ever waged between Greeks—between Athenians who, emboldened by many successes, were outraged at the "invasion" of "their" territory; and Lacedaemonians who were grimly resolved to vindicate their military tradition and restore their waning prestige. During the daylong struggle the manhood of Athens proved itself the equal of any, though casualties were heavy on both sides. The fighting was hottest at the middle of the line, where Cimon's Eupatrid relatives and friends had planted his suit of armor as a standard, and fought around it until one hundred (and possibly all of them) were killed.[36] Nevertheless the Athenians gave no ground, and by late afternoon neither side had the advantage. Then through no fault of theirs, the tide began to turn against the Athenians, assertedly, as the Thessalian cavalry suddenly deserted to the enemy. Though unexpected, it was hardly cause for astonishment. The Thessalians were aristocrats who had more in common politically with the Peloponnesians than with their nominal allies. Also, they had a reputation throughout Greece for breaking faith. Getting around behind the Athenians' line, they fell upon the huge supply train coming from Athens and did irreparable damage. The Attic generals finally had to weaken their front by detaching men to deal with the Thessalians, and just as these had stabilized the situation they were hit by a battalion of Peloponnesians, creating more havoc.[37]

Despite their misadventures, the Athenians did not panic. They fell back under cover of darkness, and apparently renewed the conflict the next day. But they no longer had the favorable position originally staked out, and having suffered heavy losses, fought on at a continuing disadvantage. Still, they did not want to give up the struggle; it was remembered that Pericles distinguished himself by his gallantry in combat.[38] The Athenians drew off when it became clear there was no profit in persisting; their morale was unshaken. The Lacedaemonians held the field, and claiming victory, erected a trophy. Then they marched back to Peloponnesus through the Isthmus, their passage unopposed, and ravaged the lands of the Megarians as they went.[39] Spartan valor had acquitted itself.

Tanagra was shortly to show the world how deceptive the results of warfare can be. The palm had seemed to go to the Spartans and Boeotians, notably the levy of Thebes, who must have joined them. The Spartans had strutted and celebrated on the field, yet afterward there was nothing for them to do but return to their own peninsula. Theban smiles must have quickly faded as they contemplated the still formidable, scarcely chastened foe with whom they were left alone. Athens had possibly made a truce with Lacedaemon,[40]—and if so, it soon broke down—but she granted none to the Boeotians who had risen against her. A bare two months after Tanagra, in August, 457, the experienced Myronides was sent northward with an army which resoundingly defeated the Boeotian oligarchs at the battle of Oinophyta, regaining the lost ground.

From start to finish, Myronides' campaign was a succession of triumphs. Immediately after Oinophyta, he pulled down the walls of Tanagra, which had been raised to bar a new Athenian entry. He then proceeded deeper into Boeotia, receiving the submission or adherence of all major cities except Thebes, which was strong enough to hold out but not to risk another battle. From Boeotia the next stop was Phocis, where most of the communities gave the Athenians a warm welcome, influenced partly by their resentment against Sparta. Then on to Locris, the Opuntian Locris, where the job was not so easy. The Locrians were oligarchs, having no previous ties with Athens, and suspicious of her government and policies. Here Myronides had to get his alliances by force, and to insure that the Locrians would keep the agreements he compelled them to send one hundred young men of their nobility to Athens as hostages.[41]

Boeotia, Phocis, Locris. In one astounding campaign Athens had reestablished her grip on the mainland, extending her sway north nearly to Thermopylae and the Malian Gulf. The best part of the other Locris she already held through the acquisition of Naupactus, on the Corinthian Gulf. All of central Greece, from Gulf to Gulf, was in some way dominated by Athens, and a land empire was obviously in the making. Nor was this all. Beyond the Malian Gulf, Athens retained her alliances with the chief cities of Thessaly, in spite of the defection of the Thessalians at Tanagra.

Seen together, these states brought under the Athenian aegis were an odd assortment. Some hated each other. Athens controlled or exerted influence over them through a system of treaties that varied with each particular case. As previously noted, her general policy was to encourage democracies in the allied states, creating a strong bond of sympathy, also because weak democracies would be more dependent on Athens for support. Often the governments were mixed or downright oligarchic, as those of Thessaly. Then Athens gave them a freer rein, interfering as little as possible.[42] For those within the fold, with Pericles in charge, the goad was used sparingly, the whip rarely if at all.

For those who were not, the whip was brandished. The Lacedaemonians had gone home claiming a victory over their rivals. In Athens the cry was for revenge, and an aspiring young general named Tolmides made himself popular by leading an expedition which burned the chief Spartan naval base at Gytheion, Peloponnesus' southern tip. Proceeding on, he harried the peninsula's shorelands, and off its western coast won over the islands of Zacynthos and Cephallenia to the Athenian alliance, thus securing valuable way stations for Athens' fleets. This was conduct highly provocative to the Peloponnesians, and might bring more grief than joy in the long run.

Yet this was the accepted foreign policy of the radicals, and at this juncture it seemed they would get away with it. Concurrently, the Argolic city of Troezen agreed to an alliance with Athens, opening another door to the Peloponnesus. And early in 456, Aegina at last surrendered, pulled down her walls, gave up the remainder of her fleet to Athens, and consented to enter the Delian Confederacy at the staggering tribute of thirty talents a year.[43] Naturally, she was lost to the other League, and a heavy loss it was. So why worry about Sparta, then? In Pericles' design, all the pieces seemed to be falling into place.

All of the pieces but one, and that, ironically, was the biggest. Several years before, the Athenians had sent an expedition to the Nile to support an Egyptian prince's bid for independence from Persia. For Athens, success would mean a steady source of cheap grain to feed her thetes, also a considerable trade in flax, papyrus, and glassware. And success seemed imminent in the early stages. The Athenians sailed up the great river, and with their Egyptian allies, captured the capital city of Memphis except for its inner citadel, the White Fortress. Since nothing but siege warfare was now in prospect, at this point a part of the expedition may have been withdrawn.[44]

After this, King Artaxerxes, who had all but given the province up for lost, finally sent a relief force under his general, Megabyxus. The insurgents were beaten off, and the Athenians retreated down the Nile, barricading themselves between two of its branch streams. Here they remained for eighteen months, until their supplies were gone and their ships burned. Then about 454, accepting the best terms they could get, those still alive marched out of Egypt under the blazing summer sun to the Greek community of Cyrene, 500 miles west. How many survived this second ordeal is unknown, but in the stark words of Thucydides, "Most of them perished; very few ever came back."[45]

To make matters worse, a relief expedition of fifty ships sent from Athens blundered into the wrong channel of the Nile, and was utterly wiped out by the Persians. The Egyptian fiasco was a multidisaster, the worst in Athenian history to date, and after such staggering losses in men, money, and material, the democrats in control at Athens would have to retrench both at home and abroad, to "conserve," however distasteful that notion might be to radicals. It was now a matter of safety first.

Echoes from the Nile disaster produced the most startling event in the history of the Delian Confederacy. In 454, the Confederacy's headquarters and treasury were moved to Athens, with the excuse that Delos was no longer safe after the defeats in Egypt: it was liable to be raided by the victorious Phoenician fleet.[46] This was a flimsy alibi, transparent to all the Hellenes. No aggressive moves by the Phoenicians had been reported. The real reason was that democratic foreign policy demanded it; nearly all democrats would be happy over it. Channeling everything through Athens would be a source of satisfaction to the Middle, accentuating the trade advantages they already had. The Low would benefit from the increase in judicial business, and more frequent jury duty. The politicians, including Pericles, would have readier access to the Delian treasury, which would become more easily confused with the city's treasury. Probably this acted to accelerate a trend already established. It has been previously noticed that the *Hellenotamiai,* the Confederacy's treasurers, were always Athenians.[47] The action of 454 may not have been a sweeping change, but it was difficult to pretend henceforth that the Confederacy was not an Athenian empire. Arché had little leeway in meaning now.

The cry of "danger to Delos" was nothing but a blind, as evidenced by the nonappearance of the Phoenician fleet at Delos or any of the islands. Much worse, it was clearly contrary to the foundation treaty of 478.[48] Stirrings of discontent among the member states over the Egyptian venture were certainly aggravated by the removal, but both before and after, the perimeters of the Confederacy remained intact.[49] Neither Greek Phaselis nor the non-Greek cities of Caria and Lycia in sourthern Asia Minor made any move to leave, proof that Cimon's skillful tempering of "firmness with mercy" when forcing them to join the Confederacy had paid off. Athenians could find comfort in this, but it left them no ethical or even pragmatic ground for the evacuation of Delos. Eyebrows would be raised in some quarters, fists in others.

For the action and its predictable reaction, Pericles cannot escape responsibility. He knew that criticism would come from aristocrats at home, from aristocrats and some democrats abroad, and that Athens' arché would be questioned and tested by those within the Confederacy as never before. The situation called for a fast chase and vigorous activity to make an impressive display of Athens' strength. In 454 and 453, penetration of the north was stepped up. Contracts with the Phocian cities were negotiated, or renegotiated. Before this, Pericles had sent Myronides forth on a repetition of his triumphal progress through Boeotia, Phocis, and Locris, on the pretext of restoring Orestes, a Thessalian ally, to his control of the city of Pharsalus. This object, unimportant in itself, was not accomplished. In the vicinity of Pharsalus, Myronides' hoplite infantry could not catch the speedy Thessalian horsemen, nor did they want to linger as an army of occupation. None dared to face Myronides in open battle; Athens' real purpose was already achieved.

Later in 453, Pericles himself led an expedition to the Corinthian Gulf, repeating in reverse the feats of Tolmides three years before. Marching down the Isthmus, they embarked at Pagai and cruised westward along the Gulf's southern shore. Unrecuperated Corinth did not oppose him, but the people of Sicyon came out to show their hostility. Landing his hoplites, Pericles overwhelmed the Sicyonians at a battle on the banks of the Nemea river, driving them within the walls of their city. He then invested Sicyon itself for the propaganda effect, since Athens could not hold such a place beyond the Isthmus indefinitely. Breaking off when a Peloponnesian army approached, Pericles next visited the towns of Achaea and persuaded them to come into the Athenian alliance. These would serve his purpose better than Sicyon.

From Achaea he crossed to the northern side of the Gulf, and proceeding to its far western corner, sailed up the Achelous river, where he intimidated the people of Acarnania who would not submit. That Acarnanians afterward were among Athens' firmest allies shows that Pericles made friends with most, and that they received good treatment. Whether Pericles duplicated Tolmides' feat by circumnavigating Peloponnesus on his way home, or whether he returned the way he came, is in dispute.[50]

The prostates' Gulf campaign had several motives. The most obvious was to demonstrate Athenian strength and impress wavering Confederates, as well as the rest of Greece; to show, as had Myronides, that Athens was not crippled by the Egyptian loss. Another was strictly political, and perhaps personal. Expansion westward had long been a goal of Athens' democrats, which Pericles as their leader could not ignore. Their loyalty would go to the generals able to achieve it. Pericles had no worries with veterans like Myronides and Leocrates, whose day was passing. But the fire-breathing young Tolmides was close at hand; bids from that quarter had to be matched, and quickly. Tying in closely was economic motivation. Great quantities of Athenian pottery discovered by archeologists in the coastal areas of southern Italy, Sicily,[51] and northwest Greece reveal the determination of Athens' ceramicists to carry their superior product into competition with that of Corinth's potters. In this western sphere, Corinth had maintained a virtual monopoly. To do so, Athenians required protection on both sides of Corinth's Gulf, the main passage west. Pericles was expected to provide it.[52]

Satisfactory as his moves were to some, they did little to solve Athens' prime external problem of ferment within the Confederacy. Many, if not most, of the members had to be dissatisfied with the Egyptian decision, since Athens alone stood to gain. Two Ionian members, Miletus and Erythrae, made their resentment known, and sent very small contingents to Egypt or none at all. As the tragedy in Egypt deepened, oligarchic revolts flared in both cities, adding to Pericles' anxieties. Both were put down, and the states shortly readmitted to the Confederacy, Erythrae as early as 452,[53] Miletus by mid-century, or shortly thereafter.[54] By Pericles' direction, Athens was wisely lenient in both cases, stipulating merely that their constitutions be revised to insure democratic government in the future. By the clever tactic of assuming that a majority of citizens had not favored the revolts, the majority was kept on Athens' side.

Of course, a "democratic form of government" meant one that must be approved by Athens, since only Athens could decide what was and what was not democratic. Slowly, inch by inch, the metropolis encroached on the internal affairs of the Delians, not on principle, but whenever rebellion or some misstep called for intervention. And it turned out later that constitutional restraints were not the only ones; Athens' democrats insisted on safeguarding the Delian relationship by supplementary arrangements that were bound to be resented. So, although their leader had done well, the prospect was for continuing trouble within and without the Confederacy, including unresolved wars with the Persians and the Peloponnesians, plus uncertainties over support by lukewarm allies.

Pericles, contemplating this, steeled himself to an action altruistic but distasteful and even dangerous to him. Going before the Assembly, he recommended the recall of Cimon from exile ahead of time, though just when he did so has not been established. Plutarch says it was immediately after the battle of Tanagra,[55] where Cimon had vindicated his patriotism and so many of his friends had died for their country. Others place it later, pointing out that Cimon is not recorded as being in Athens for two or three more years. The motion passed easily. Again according to Plutarch, Cimon's sister Elpinice acted as go-between in arranging his return with Pericles,[56] and on this basis some have maintained that he gave a pledge to confine himself to military affairs and to abstain from politics if allowed to come back. Whether true or not, it was his military genius that Athens sorely needed.

The theory has its holes, for when Cimon came back he did not keep out of politics. He was highly popular in the Assembly and his voice was decisive. The Great Democrat must have had some anxious moments. Soon after his return Cimon persuaded the Ekklesia to conclude a Five Years' Truce with Sparta, going himself to Lacedaemon in 451 to obtain the ratification. Of all the Athenians he was still the one most welcome there, and probably the Spartans regretted the offense offered him. Probably he tried for a more definite, lasting peace, with which his hosts could not agree in view of Athens' enlarged role in Hellenic affairs and her implied challenge. Concurrently, Sparta made peace with Argos for thirty years, and in consequence the alliance between Argos and Athens was renounced. Cimon returned home with a new diplomatic triumph.

It was a gain for Athens' aristocrats, their first in many years, but not necessarily a loss for the democrats. An understanding with Lacedaemon may not have been unpleasant to Pericles in this period of troubles, although he must have objected to the rupture with Argos.[57] Cimon's reappearance was a trial to him, no question. It has been pointed out that 451 was the year of the citizenship law, possibly also the year when a bill was passed providing payment for jurors, and that both measures may have been products of a renewed struggle with Cimon, attempts by Pericles to counter the popularity of the returning hero.[58] Perhaps. Cimon's main interest, however, was in foreign policy, and Pericles could have few mental reservations about Cimon's central thesis that peace should be maintained with the Peloponnesians so as to concentrate on the all-absorbing crusade against Persia.[59]

So there is no reason to think that Pericles was dissatisfied when, in the spring of 450, the Athenians authorized a new fleet of 200 triremes to resume the war against Persia and gave Cimon the supreme command. His presence would cheer and rally the disaffected Confederates, who trusted in his military prowess and could remember the kindliness with which he had always treated them. Military action was at last necessary. The Persians had remained quiet for several years, consolidating their recovery of Egypt, but now they were on the move, testing the Delian outposts in Cyprus and along the southern coast of Asia Minor. Megabyxus, the conqueror of Egypt, was reported advancing through Syria in preparation for a land and sea offensive in the eastern Mediterranean. To all Greeks thus endangered, the news that Cimon was coming to their rescue provided an image as reassuring to them, as conversely, it would be disturbing to the Persians. Elected general once more, it became obvious to Ekklesia and Strategion that Cimon was the man for the situation. And from a personal point of view, Pericles was glad of an excuse to have him out of Athens.

When all was ready in the summer of 450, Cimon led the Delian fleet out of Piraeus and steered directly for Cyprus, the large frontier island that was a constant bone of contention, being populated partly by Greeks and partly by

Phoenicians. Here the last expedition had been engaged ten years before, when suddenly diverted to Egypt. While nearing his goal, Cimon was opposed by a Phoenician naval patrol, which he promptly destroyed. The main Phoenician fleet (of 300 vessels, Diodorus says) was away, hovering between Cyprus and the Cilician mainland, where Megabyxus' army was now located. Landing on the island, Cimon systematically retook cities that had fallen to Persia, until he reached Kition, Cyprus' largest city, on the southeast coast. Since this place was garrisoned and stoutly walled, a siege became necessary. Cimon disposed his troops around the city, but the Persian garrison held out stubbornly—how long, we are not told. At last the Greeks' provisions began to run low; also they may have become subject to a local epidemic. Cimon himself fell ill and had to stay in his tent. Just then he received word of a huge Persian-Phoenician relief expedition approaching down the coast by sea, obviously sent by Megabyxus, though whether conducted by him personally is not stated.

The newcomers dropped anchor at a Cyprian port town named, oddly, Salamis, which they intended to use as a base of operations against the Greeks at Kition. Cimon determined to anticipate them. Breaking off the siege of Kition, he ordered both his army and navy forward for a double attack on Salamis, and actually planned the maneuvers himself although too sick to leave his quarters. The battle of "second Salamis" resulted in an Athenian victory on land and sea alike, but one that the overextended victors were unable to follow up or turn to advantage. Eventually they went back to the camp at Kition, and either there or on the return voyage to Athens they learned their great commander had died. Vigorous to the end, Cimon had requested his officers to conceal his death, if possible, to keep up morale until the campaign were over and the men safely away.[60]

In their grief, they could find comfort in a task well done. If their enterprise had not been an unqualified success, it was successful enough to convince King Artaxerxes, watching from Susa. Assuming that the events in Egypt had lifted him temporarily, those in Cyprus acted to cancel his joy. The Despot of Asia was ready to call a halt. So was Pericles. Scanning the reports, he could satisfy himself that the Athenians had had the best of the fighting, but he also knew the possibilities in Cyprus were strictly limited.[61] Supply at that distance was difficult; with their food giving out, even Cimon's invincibles could not have gone much farther. Athens' honor had been retrieved, her position secured.

The actual negotiations are as little known as most arrangements between nations in this dimly-illumined span of years. Some sort of embassy was commissioned by Athens and sent to Susa. Tradition indicates that it was headed by Callias, reputedly the richest man in Athens, and husband to Cimon's sister Elpinice. His interests were wide and he was probably not unknown at the Persian court. Guarded and indefinite as were the commitments he gave and got, the results have always been known as the "Peace of Callias." The King of Kings' notions of dignity would not permit recognition of the Greek states, or formal treaties with them. But informal discussions were held and an understanding reached, probably in 448, that Persia would not sail its navy in the Aegean, or station its armies "within three days' march of the coast of Ionia." Athens, on her side, undertook not to attack the ships or lands of the Persian Empire; by conceding that these included Egypt and Cyprus, she abandoned allies still holding out in those areas.[62]

That portion of the agreement, though not very creditable to Athens, was realistic, and her citizens could rest in the knowledge that there had been a settlement with prodigious Persia. For the first time in half a century the Attic commonwealth was at peace with everyone, at home and abroad.

The euphoria of eighteen years before flickered back like a cooling breeze toward the close of hot summer, as the citizens reflected yet again on Cimon's services to the state—as now, at his funeral, they honored him for the last time. Noting that Athens' enthusiasm for Cimon was still alive in his own day, centuries later, Plutarch wonders and asks himself the question "Why were the Athenians so greatly taken with Cimon?" And he finds his answer in the man's genuine, all-around worth; in his wearing of honors with modesty; in the victories to which he had led the Athenians on many a foreign field; in the stone inscriptions he had left on each, always praising his men, never mentioning himself.[63] To the world at large, Cimon had advertised Athenian virtue in a way that no other ever would.

Truly, to Athenians of the mid-century the memory of Cimon was an enlivening breath of air, akin to the Etesian winds of August that in Hellenic lands relieve summer's heat. And if the metaphor occurred to them, they might also have remembered that after the Etesians come searing blasts.

11

Iron Hand and Silken Glove

448–440 B.C.

THE Athenian citizen, four decades after Marathon, was manifestly not the same. Within that remarkable frame of years, mishaps and devastations, problems and decisions, responsibilities and their fulfillments, had transformed the eager, dextrous, but as yet untempered provincial of two generations ago into the experienced, smugly self-assured cosmopolite of the mid-century. The stair of attainment, leading immediately upward from the first Salamis, had conducted him past pitfalls to level at last on the widened climacteric of a second Salamis far distant from his native place.

Naturally, the Athenian gained in skill and confidence with each ascending step, and his spirits surged in proportion. Early expressions of this exuberance abound in Aeschylus' *Persae,* as when the chorus of Persian elders describes the victorious Athenians to the dowager Queen Atossa, Xerxes' mother:

> Not slaves, to feel a despot's sting,
> Nor will they ever brook a king![1]

How the poet, a few years later, saluted Aristides and probably Cimon, recently triumphant at Eurymedon, as masterly helmsmen of Athens' smoothly sailing ship of state, in his *Seven against Thebes,* has already been noticed. Still later, in his magnum opus, the *Oresteia,* he praised the superior political traditions of Athens, and while not deprecating the rising democracy, seemed to advise an amalgam of proven and practical elements. Then, in what was probably his last play, *Prometheus Bound* (ca. 457–456),

Aeschylus pressed farther along the same path, in his powerful drama of the heroically defiant Titan. Chained at the command of a strangely tyrannical Zeus, the Titan registered his approval of the evolving "mixed" democracies of Hellas as clearly surpassing tyrannies which they had replaced.[2] As defender of man's civilization and freedom, Prometheus refuses to break despite fiendish torture. Though the theme is broad and general, its implications for the poet's own city as the home of Greek democracy are plain to see.

The younger Sophocles may also have fanned the flame of Athens' burgeoning self-esteem, in the next several years. In his earliest extant play, *Ajax* (447?), which sets forth the shame, madness, and suicide of the brawny Greek captain after losing in the contest for Achilles' armor, some have seen a parallel between Ajax' fate and that of the fallen Themistocles.[3] However, it has been shown as more likely that Sophocles intended a reference to the disgraceful treatment accorded Cimon at Ithome.[4] This contention is borne out by Teucer's proud statement later in the play that he and his brother Ajax had not gone to Troy as vassals of the Spartan king, Menelaus, but to redeem their contract oaths and to guard their own honor.[5]

Teucer's pronouncement sounds almost like a declaration of independence, more applicable to Athens' position after Cimon's service for the Spartans against their helots than to Ajax's own obligation which, strictly speaking, was to Agamemnon rather than to Menelaus. Finally, it has been pointed out that Teucer's farewell eulogy of his brother may be applied as easily to Cimon, whose Philaid clan claimed descent from Ajax.[6] Sophocles and Aeschylus are but two voices among myriads to represent Athenian opinion, though better ones would be impossible to find. Beyond a doubt Athenians empathized with their heroes as projections of themselves, viewing men and events in the perspective of civic destiny.[7]

Did other Greeks react similarly? For this our best guide is Pindar, no Athenian himself, but normally friendly despite his Boeotian background. His warm feelings for Athens are revealed as early as the first Pythian ode, where he sings Greece's gratitude, equally to the Athenians for Salamis, and to the Spartans for Plataea.[8] Cimon's capture of Eion, four years after Salamis, seems to have been the occasion that called up Pindar's famous dithyramb labeling Athens as the "mainstay of Hellas." He was still laudatory after Eurymedon, when in his Nemean ode for the year 467, he touted "the brave spearmen of the Aiakidai,"[9] another compliment to Cimon's ancestry as well as to that of the athletic victor whom he had been paid to extol. So far, these were matters that all the Greeks could celebrate together.

However, a change was coming. After Athens' aggression against his beloved Aegina, Pindar's heart grew troubled. He continued to speak well of individual Athenians occasionally, but was silent about the city and its policies. After the battle of Oinophyta, when his native Boeotia was coordinated in the Athenian interest, he exploded into a bitter mythological warning: Bellerophon was thrown by the winged horse Pegasus when he presumed to ride to the peak of Olympus.[10] His meaning could not be mistaken. Athens had grown ravenous. A menace to the rest of Hellas, she was courting divine retribution.[11] Many Hellenic bystanders must have felt as Pindar did.

If those dominant in Athens were aware of criticism, they were unruffled by it. So Greeks elsewhere were apprehensive, sensitive to the pinch? Then they should make way, stand back and see what Athenians had done for them. Who had made them safe these past thirty years, when they dispersed to their homes as soon as the Persians were out of the country? An incalculable number of Greeks had never fought, had never lifted a finger to defend their land, intent as they were on their own petty dealings, even fawning on the invader for what they could get out of him. Such could not be said of the Athenians. From the first they had given their blood, their pelf, everything they had so that all might stay free. And from this spirit of self-sacrifice had come the resolution, cohesion, and efficiency that had made them the best in Greece. Athenians had a right to rule. On how many battlefields, far and near, had they not earned that right, unflinchingly giving up their lives when necessary? It was customary in these years, apparently, for the ten Attic tribes to raise stone memorials to their war dead. Among these, one by a single tribe, presumably erected in 459, remains intact. It reads as follows: "Of [our] Erechtheid tribe these are the ones who died in the war, in Cyprus, in Egypt, in Phoenicia, at Halieis, at Aegina, at Megara, in the same year."[12] And beneath it was inscribed a list of 177 names, which also included two generals. Assuming that other tribal regiments labored and suffered in like manner, the Athenian attitude toward nonparticipating Greeks is readily understood.

Even many of those that *had* participated had not done so until after the great events had taken place, and thus in a sense, had their liberty by Athens' leave. This was especially true of the twelve Ionian sister cities across the sea, states that were now bound to her by a double tie. If Athens treated her siblings with condescension that sometimes bordered on the supercilious, such conduct was not altogether indefensible. Throughout the rest of Hellas the Ionians had a reputation for inconstancy, indolence, and easy living, which was quite at odds with their own conception of themselves as high thinkers and doers, the veritable artistic and intellectual leaders of Greece. However popular this idea among the Ionian communities on the Asian side, to European Greeks Athens was the only Ionian city of high esteem, a view that most Athenians seem to have accepted without demur. Sharers of their own continent had noticed that they did not often refer to themselves as Ionians. Whether visitors from Ionia were aware of it is not so certain. With them, Athenians may have made guilty amends through profuse expressions of brotherhood. After all, Athens prided herself on her democracy.

This being so, the question arises whether Athens should not have placed before the Delian Synod the proposition of modifying the Confederacy or dissolving it altogether after the Peace of Callias, presumably made with Persia in 449. And despite a lack of information, perhaps she did. Because seemingly, for some reason, no tribute was collected in 448,[13] yet the next year payments were resumed. Recently, attention has been focused in the intervening period on a series of border incidents between Greeks and Persians in Asia Minor which would justify Athens in resuming her previous policy, and from that time forward an undeclared "cold war" existed with Persia for more than thirty years.[14]

Being Greek, and particularistic, all members did not interpret events in the same fashion. Both before and after the Peace, some dissidents forfeited their rights by nonpayment, and when doing so they had to expect further restrictions prior to readmittance. Erythrae, restored to membership in 452—after an inferred unsuccessful attempt at withdrawal, about which little is known—affords an example of peculiar interest since a portion of the stone inscription containing her new treaty with Athens has been recovered. Under it, Athens soothes Erythrae by assuring her of complete control over her own internal affairs as long as she maintains a democratically chosen council—which, of course, presumes an assembly of all the citizens to choose, or supervise. The council is to have 120 members, proportionately less than Athens' 500, because of Erythrae's smaller population. So far, so good. But then it appears that the councillors are required to take an oath of allegiance to the Athenian People and to the Confederacy as well as to their own city. Political exiles sheltered in Persia will not be allowed to return unless Athenian courts so decide; nor can anyone henceforth be banished from Erythrae without the concurrence of the courts at Athens. Erythrae is further required to send delegations and sacrificial offerings to the Great Panathenaea at Athens every fourth year. Finally, there will be an Athenian commander and garrison in the city to safeguard its constitution and oversee operations under the new treaty, also periodic visitations by Athenian inspectors as a sort of double check.[15]

So much imposition in the name of democracy strikes one as self-defeating. The Erythraeans could do whatever they wanted, so long as they wanted unerringly what Athenians wanted for them. Perhaps this was deemed necessary to protect inexperienced commoners against locally strong oligarchs who had recently demonstrated their ability to overturn the government.[16] But such blatant measures were enough to nudge a good many commoners to the side of oligarchy. In addition, Erythrae's annual assessment of seven talents was for her, a rather stiff sum.[17] One is surprised that Pericles would go so far, or if not responsible himself, that he would permit the more militant among his colleagues to do so. However, he was not all-powerful in these years, and he may have been unable to prevent it. One wonders, too, how many Delians felt such screws. This was not yet an Oriental despotism on the part of their tenderly severe parent, but shortly Ionians might recollect that the King of Persia had not been the worst of masters.

That Pericles' hand may have been forced is shown by other evidence of creeping imperialism, developing concurrently. In the decade of the 450s, Athens sent out several expeditions to establish those unique colonies known as cleruchies, under which Athenian colonists received farm allotments from the Delian lands overseas, working them under a special agreement with the mother city. The cleruchs retained their Athenian citizenship, were liable to military duty, attended the religious festivals in Athens, and paid whatever taxes were imposed. In brief, the cleruchies were small extensions of Athens, and at least some at various stages were governed by officials coming from the metropolis.[18]

The cleruchies are easily recognized as a favorite device of the Athenian radicals, designed to alleviate the distress of their own destitute. The cleruchs were taken mainly from the landless thete class; by acquiring property they raised themselves to the status of zeugites, and hence became more serviceable to Athens as hoplites in her army. Both the individual and the state stood to benefit, but in spite of this the government encountered some difficulty in persuading the thetes to go as colonists. Since the radicals were actively pushing it, Pericles cannot be absolved of all blame, but the principal agent in the affair seems to have been the brash Tolmides, no doubt eager for the prostates' place himself. In 453 Tolmides conducted a body of 500 cleruchs to areas on the island of Naxos, and in subsequent years he led other groups to spots in southern Euboea and in the Chalcidice. Still other companies were conveyed to the islands of Andros, Lemnos, and Imbros. Then finally Pericles himself led a vast expedition of 1,000 cleruchs to the Hellespont for the purpose of repopulating the Thracian Chersonese, Miltiades' old barony. To hold it the more firmly for Athens a wall was now built across the northern neck of the peninsula, to keep out the wild Thracian tribesmen.

Since most of the territory in question belonged to other members of the Delian community, one speculates, by what right did the Athenian Assembly simply expropriate this to its own use? Had it been careful to designate waste lands, or portions unused by the state possessing them, not very much harm would have been done. But the Ekklesia did not follow this course, and there were heated protests from the Confederates. Athens did try appeasement by reducing the tribute on states she had wronged: Andros' annual quota of twelve talents was cut in half, for instance, and Carystus, which had given up ground for the Euboean cleruchy, had been reduced from seven and one-half to five.[19] However, such concessions would hardly compensate for the permanent loss of real property. It's understandable that the Delians continued to feel aggrieved.Of all these sallies into the nooks and crannies of the "empire," Pericles' alone had not offended members who still thought of it as the Confederacy. Contrary to their bland assumptions, Athenians still had much to learn in the art of statecraft.

Pericles could tell them if they were disposed to listen, or he could refer them to his poet friends. Aeschylus had recounted to his countrymen the values of freedom, while Sophocles had cited the sanctity of contract. Athenians would be slaves to none, it had been said; they had best be wary, then, of infringing upon their associates' liberties. And in the case of contracts, it was important to remember that the foundation treaty had guaranteed lasting autonomy to all the Confederates, a clause they would interpret as including territorial integrity.[20] Firmness in rulers is indispensable, but so is forbearance, and one must be adept in finding the right mixture. Luckily, the Athenians had a politician as proficient as their poets, but their voices were not always heeded. If their own sages made no headway, the warnings of Pindar might apply. Prophetically, it was an upheaval close to Pindar's native hearth that gave a much needed jolt to the Athenians' collective ego, leaving them ultimately wiser if somewhat deflated by their experience.

The domination of the mainland to the north constituted a particularly delicate problem for Athens. Here there were no Delian contracts or assessments; a word like arché had to be whispered, if used at all. Athens held on to the states by a number of individual alliances, discreetly supporting control by the democratic faction. Probably key democrats were invited to Athens for an educational tour that amounted to political indoctrination, so they should view matters as Athenians did. To go this far was safe, if done quietly.

Unfortunately, few Athenians were as yet equal to their role of instructors, having considerable distance to cover both in politics and human relations. Rather smug about their worldly wisdom and culture, they tended to regard visitors from the country towns of the north as bumpkins deserving no better than an amused tolerance. Among these, the Boeotians were favorite targets, the butts of many an Athenian joke which characterized them as gross, provincial, or downright stupid.[21] Hardly a way to get on with one's nearest neighbor. Naturally, the Athenians met with stout resistance from these traditional tillers of the soil, whose conservative slant on life was heightened by resentment. Athenian propagandists might dress democracy in a rustic robe for them, but they would not be tempted if they suspected her Athenian origin. Even the occasional Boeotian democrat would feel a slight chill as the connection crossed his mind. With the self-proclaimed egalitarians[22] of Attica laughing at him behind his back, he was not likely to prove an apt pupil.

Such must have been the state of affairs in Boeotia. After the battle of Oinophyta most cities there received democratic governments supported by Athens, a support that must have included, at least temporarily, political advisers and garrisons, though direct evidence is lacking. Because there was little confidence between those involved, the Boeotian democrats bungled badly.[23] A few years after Oinophyta their government in Thebes was overthrown, and Thebes henceforth became a center of oligarchic agitation to "free" the rest of Boeotia. These efforts bore fruit in 447, when the cities of Orchomenus and Chaeronea rebelled and restored their usual oligarchies. Immediately afterward, those exiled a decade before began flooding back across Boeotia's borders toward their native cities. If something were not done quickly, Athens would lose the entire region. While her Ekklesia and Strategion were thrashing out the problem, additional blows fell: Phocis, then Locris had also gone oligarchic and thrown off the Athenian alliance. Could those left, in the distant north, be counted on? It was not encouraging that a large portion of those remaining were Thessalians. Their land empire was crumbling before their eyes.

Athens' superpatriots were unwilling to take this lying down, and behind them, democrats of every shade might well agree that the loss was too serious to ignore. But how to repair it was a tough question. Not to the warlike Tolmides, however, who made light of the whole issue. He declared that if given 1,000 good hoplites to chastise the Boeotians, he would settle them in a single campaign.[24] No need to draft troops from the citizens' lists. He could get enough volunteers from among Athens' bravest and best, if the Ekklesia would give its permission. There should be a minimum of expense and bother.

True to his nature, Pericles was more cautious. As a radical and an imperialist, there can be no doubt that he favored action, but with so grave a problem, a meticulous appraisal should be made first. Just the year before he had led an expedition to help the Phocians recover their claim to Delphi; now the Phocians were deserting Athens. Yet he leashed his temper, and in the Ekklesia sought to dissuade Tolmides, reportedly saying "If you will not listen to me, you would do well to consult that wisest of all counselors, Time."[25] Prudently, Pericles preferred to wait, study the situation, find the most opportune moment for striking. Tolmides had no intention of waiting. He stood by his resolution, demanded a decision, and won. It was Pericles' last significant defeat in city politics until toward the close of his career.

Tolmides easily made good on the first part of his boast. By now his reputation was such that he had no trouble enlisting the thousand hoplites, aristocrats as well as democrats. His march was to be a truly audacious one through hostile country, for Chaeronea and Orchomenus lay on the far side of Boeotia, and though Tolmides was joined by contingents from Plataea and elsewhere, his army was much too small for the job to be done. Yet there was no hesitation on his part. Bypassing the great enemy, Thebes, thus leaving his rear unsecured, he made straight for Chaeronea, stormed the city, and sold the captured inhabitants into slavery. Tolmides would show the world what it meant to trifle with Athens.

Garrisoning Chaeronea from his already undersized army, Tolmides proceeded on to Orchomenus. But the city, located on a steep hillside with its walled citadel on the ridge, presented too many problems. Tolmides could find no means of forcing it, and with the fighting season waning, finally had to end the siege. He started back toward Athens, but with characteristic disdain neglected to send scouts ahead to determine the safety of the road or to sound out the local residents. To the south, the Boeotian oligarchs following him from Thebes lay waiting in ambush with battalions gathered from towns sympathetic to them. As Tolmides emerged from a narrow valley onto the broad plain near the city of Coronea, he was suddenly confronted by the foe in irresistible numbers. Nevertheless the dauntless Tolmides did resist, though his allies fled. The commander and his small band fought until they were overwhelmed and nearly half of them killed, Tolmides among these. Caught so far from the borders of Attica, there had been no hope of rescue or escape. The operation had turned out a total loss.

The battle of Coronea, in the late summer or autumn of 447, changed everything in the north. Those states still in the Athenian alliance, if wavering before, would now drop away. Moreover, the victorious Boeotians were holding several Athenian young men of the best families as hostages, which gave them strong bargaining power in the negotiations sure to follow. Undeniably at a disadvantage, Athens conceded that the Boeotian states should live "only under laws made by themselves,"[26] meaning, in effect, that she must give up all authority over Boeotia, withdraw completely. By implication, this meant also that any attempt to regain Locris or Phocis was now out of the question.

Pericles thus had his hand forced. With so many lives at stake, he had to agree. How he would have played out the hand, had circumstances been different, cannot be known. There are strong indications that he had envisioned Athens as a sort of capital of Hellas, first by land and sea, and that the vision was dear to him.[27] But Pericles was always one to distinguish dreams from reality. Recent events were enough to convince him that the Boeotians would never be admirers or willing subjects of Athens, nor did he have any reason to think those farther north would be more amenable. Already, before Coronea, many in Athens held the opinion that Boeotia could not be retained permanently, at least not all of it; the attempt would weaken Athens and hurt more than help.[28] Pericles may have been veering to the same train of thought. Despite the grandiose dreams he shared with his fellow radicals, empire on the mainland was not actually essential to Athens' power and prosperity, as the empire overseas certainly was. Better to try what was possible by way of conciliation with the mainlanders, especially with those stubborn Boeotians. A bit of what had been lost might be regained through skillful diplomacy, and some part of the radicals' dream yet realized. In the end, Pericles persuaded the Ekklesia to accept the full demands of the Boeotian oligarchs, giving them the assurances they asked and pulling entirely out of their country.[29]

The prostates was wise in so doing. The Five Years' Truce with Lacedaemon would expire in a few months, and he had to consider what effect the Coronea defeat would have on Athens' overall position. His apprehensions were well founded. With what looked like preconcerted oligarchic planning, Megara and the cities of Euboea overthrew their democratic governments the next year, in 446. Then Sparta mobilized its army under the young king, Pleistoanax, to support Megara and invade Attica.

It was too much for Athens to handle at once. Three regiments sent under the general Andocides to help the Megarian democrats had to retreat hastily and return home by a circuitous route. And Pericles, who had started for Euboea with the main force, had to return just as quickly to defend Athens. For a tense period he and Pleistoanax confronted each other in Attica, pondering whether to fight or negotiate. With the Euboean revolt still pending, there was little doubt that Pericles preferred to negotiate, if possible. What followed forms the masterpiece of Periclean diplomacy, so carefully veiled that everybody was left guessing. But suddenly, Pleistoanax broke camp and marched his army back to Lacedaemon.

The Spartans felt sure they knew the reason. Furious at having relinquished such an advantage, they charged that Pericles had bribed not only King Pleistoanax, but also the Ephor, Kleandridas, who had been sent to watch him. Kleandridas saved himself by prompt flight to southern Italy, where he passed his remaining years. Pleistoanax was tried, condemned, dethroned, and banished from Lacedaemon. In Athens, Pericles' treatment of the affair was tantamount to a confirmation. When presenting his financial accounts to the Assembly later, an unexplained deficit of ten talents was discovered. When questioned about it, he replied simply that the money had been spent for "what was needed."[30] And so great was the public's confidence in his integrity that nobody pressed him for a more explicit answer.

The Spartans out of the way, Pericles was free to visit his wrath on the Euboean oligarchs, guilty of breaking their treaties as well as conspiring with the enemy. Crossing to Euboea again, he reduced the island, district by district, and meted out punishment. Chalcis, the island's largest city, saw its entire nobility expelled. And at Hestiaea, where an Athenian ship had been seized and its crew slaughtered, Pericles turned the whole citizenry out of their lands and repopulated this area with one thousand families of cleruchs brought from Attica. Before summer's end in 446, thriving Euboea with its grain and metal was restored to the service of Athens.

At last Pericles was ready to deal for a durable peace. In the winter of 446–45, Athens sent a mission of ten envoys, headed by the general Andocides and the seasoned diplomat Callias, to a comprehensive peace conference scheduled at Lacedaemon. There the details were gradually hammered out. Athens gave up Megara's two ports, also Troezen and the Achaean coastal towns of Peloponnesus, which she could scarcely expect to retain after loss of the Isthmus. It was vital to hang on to Aegina, and here she succeeded despite strong objections. Lacedaemon had pledged its word to restore the island republic's freedom, and sensed a blemish on its honor. But there was no way the Lacedaemonians could reach Aegina to help her. In the end, they had to console themselves with Athens' promise to respect Aegina's "autonomy," though Aegina was to stay in the Confederacy and continue to pay tribute.

If the status of Aegina was the most significant issue at the conference, undoubtedly the hottest was the possession of Naupactus, the shore fortress dominating the Corinthian Gulf. From here Athens had a stranglehold on Corinth, being able at will to reduce her all-important trade with the West to a bare trickle. Of course the Corinthians were vociferous in insisting that Naupactus must be given up, but this was a matter that did not concern the Lacedaemonians directly, and they knew how hard it would be to ferret out the Athenian marines in the rocky fortress, together with those Messenian helots who had resisted so stubbornly at Ithome. The Spartans did not long argue the point, contenting themselves with a promise that Athens would not harass Corinth's ships plying the Gulf.

The Peloponnesian and Delian organizations both received official recognition, a reciprocal action that appears as a gain for Athens, since Lacedaemon had never before deigned to extend acknowledgement. Each side bound itself not to encourage or assist revolting members of the other's alliance, or to shelter fugitives. Argos, free and currently uncommitted, might enter into a new agreement with Athens if she wished, and Greek states as yet nonaligned might join either group.[31] By a general assent, it was resolved that all future disputes between the parties present should be submitted to arbitration. These were the terms of the Thirty Years' Peace, so called because the contracts were intended to be binding during that period and hopefully, might thereafter be renewed. As the conclave dissolved amid perfunctory expressions of goodwill, Athenians could wend their way homeward moderately cheerful in the knowledge that they had defended what was theirs and vindicated Athens' equality with Lacedaemon in the eyes of Greece. Most of the others were less satisfied.

Fittingly, the last word is Pindar's. In the year of the Peace he composed a Pythian ode more gentle and reflective than most, in which, espousing the quiet life as the happiest,[32] he urges an end to civic strife to obtain a united front against the threat of external violence. This danger is personified by the intruding giant Porphyrion, who is "crowding too far" against the rightful occupants, thus certain to provoke their anger and retaliation, to his own eventual sorrow.[33] Pindar goes on to pay his usual compliment to the victor in the games, and to invoke the gods in the victor's behalf, but the poet has already winged his shaft to the visible target. Porphyrion is understood to be Athens, whom Pindar now looks upon as a menace to the liberty of Hellas.[34] It was an opinion that many would come to share.

Needless to say, Pindar's fears met with few sympathetic echoes in Attica. The radicals who framed Athens' policies were not given to soul searching, and even those citizens who criticized them bore down more on their misappropriation of funds than on any infringement of democratic rights.[35] Actually, on the right of others to self-determination, Athens' record was reasonably good, and to justify her frequent interventions she had a stock answer difficult to disprove: the revolts against her were those of aristocrats and oligarchs trying to enslave "the people"; Athens was merely acting for the majority in putting them down; and so far as one can see, the claim was largely true.

This seems to have been Pericles' view,[36] and his conscience was probably the tenderest in the radical party.[37] After the Peace, as he surveyed the overall situation in 445, Athens seemingly had nothing to apologize for and little to regret. Her lost hegemony on the northern mainland had created as many problems as it had solved. Willing or not, she had found herself the arbiter betwixt a flock of quarreling neighbors, with constant calls for military aid that brought her into dubious repute, as in the Delphi incident. She could not satisfy them all. Nor was there money to be made from them, as in the naval empire; rather, it was more likely Athens would have to spend to subsidize democracy in states generally opposed to popular rule of the Athenian type. Finally, the arché on land must have led to an increase in the army, traditionally aristocratic and conservative, at the expense of the navy whence came so much of the radicals' support. Contemplating so many adverse factors, Pericles might well have been glad to find the list reduced a little.

Long since, he had formed a more artful design for dominance, one with infinitely greater possibilities, and by its very nature more difficult for the contrary-minded to oppose. In the century before the Persian Wars, Greeks of the leading states were becoming slowly conscious of the miraculous growth of Hellenic civilization as something peculiarly their own, raising them above foreign breeds—with maybe an exception or two (most notably, the Egyptians; there was also a tendency to regard the Babylonians, and before the invasions, the Persians, as being above the status of barbarians). Here one must tread softly, for Greek thinking on the subject was not crystal clear. What they gradually came to call *oikouménē* had its sources in their alphabet, language, religious symbols, and was ultimately the gift of their gods—the Olympians, the Muses, the Fates. More than anything else it was theology that held the Hellenes together, theology made more impressive by the sublime poetry of Homer and Hesiod. Violent as they might be on other occasions, all grew silent and solemn when approaching a shrine.

Already Pericles had sought to play upon this spirit of reverence when, in 448, he had called a Panhellenic Congress to meet at Athens to restore the temples destroyed by the Persians. In Athens' Ekklesia the prostates himself had moved that 5,000 talents be appropriated from the public treasury (by now merged with the Delian treasury?) for this purpose, and the motion had carried.[38] Here was a project that must touch every Hellenic heart. Twenty commissioners were sent with invitations "to all the Greek cities, large and small" except those of Italy and Sicily, which had not been despoiled by the invaders. This appeal for united action failed when most of Peloponnesus turned a cold shoulder. To the planner, such disappointing response could not have been a total surprise. Attendance would have implied recognition of Athens' leadership of Greece, a leadership transcending the merely political. Despite its rejection, the attempt made clever propaganda, and took deep root throughout the Greek world.

Whether the Hellenic brethren participated or not, Athens could go ahead with the rebuilding of *her* altars. If the rest did not, she would shine by comparison. The Temple of Demeter at Eleusis, so vital to the Mysteries, was already in the process of reconstruction. Cimon had begun the task, sometime in the 460's, probably paying for it out of his private funds, but with only the high priest's room and a part of the initiation chamber completed. The general's exile from Attica must have been the reason that work was intermitted. Now new plans were drawn and labor could be resumed, using the Confederacy's money.

Still, the endeavor at Eleusis limped along a decade or more because the superior brains behind its inception were needed nearer home for a project even more pressing, the creation of a new Temple of Athena Polias on Athens' Acropolis. This edifice, ultimately to be known as the Parthenon, was actually commenced in 447 under charge of Pericles' distinguished artist friends, the architect Ictinus and the sculptor Phidias, and would require fifteen years to finish. Ever since Pisistratus' temple of the same name had been burned by the Persians, the Panathenaic festival held each summer had been constrained to stage its climactic ceremonies on the open hilltop of the Acropolis. No question about it, the Parthenon was a high priority, and until this was well in hand Ictinus' commitment to Eleusis would have to wait. Simultaneously with the Parthenon, and perhaps a bit before, artisans brought from the Aegean islands started rebuilding the Temple of Poseidon, at Sunium, Attica's southeast promontory, making a marble sanctuary fronted by six slender Doric columns, majestically crowning the cape. The revered statue of Poseidon, fortunately preserved from the old temple destroyed by Xerxes, was placed at the altar of the new. Spectacularly situated, the sea-god's temple at Sunium presented striking evidence to all Hellenic mariners and travelers that the Greeks of Attica, at least, had not neglected their common deities.

The Thirty Years' Peace allowed Pericles and his associates time to pause and take stock. What they found must have been to their liking. The Confederacy was intact, and with its treasury and courts both centered in Athens, their city was prosperous. Its people, largely employed on juries, building projects, or overseas service, were presumably as contented as humans ever are. The radicals' original objectives were mostly attained. Was not their best policy, then, to settle down, organize efficiently, protect what they had gained, avoid further turmoil and danger?[39]

Pericles, growing more cautious and perhaps more conservative with age, must have had much to do with this trend, though the degree to which he exercised influence over the other generals is difficult to determine. Whether his probable election as general *ex apanton*—representing all of Athens rather than a single tribe—gave him authority over his colleagues remains in doubt.[40] But it would come to the same thing. Not alone his prestige as prostates, but the seniority acquired from well over a dozen terms as general, together with his knowledge and experience would make him naturally dominant in the Strategion, as in Athens' Assembly.[41]

How well the policies of Pericles satisfied the Confederates is a fair question. There is evidence both pro and con. If the unalloyed enthusiasm of Aristides' day no longer prevailed, it was certainly not the reverse. Even though the Persian menace had faded, there is reason to think that the greater number were relatively content with the bargain. Before the coming of Athens, most islands had been ruled by tyrants or juntos of nobles, with the commons having a very faint voice. Athens had been the first prominent state in Hellas to achieve a lasting democracy; in extending her sway she had given the little people a better life than ever before, more security in which to work and trade, more chances to improve their lot. Formerly the islands had imposed tariff barriers against one another, and while little evidence is available, the probability is that such charges were reduced, perhaps in some instances abolished, between members of the Confederacy.[42] Outlanders couldn't become Athenian citizens—nor would most of them have wished to be—but they could enter more freely into the politics of their own communities. It was no small easement to be delivered from the grip of local nobles and profiteers, to be protected against seizure of power by the affluent. Significantly, all the risings against Athens were oligarchic. While it lasted, the "Athenian Empire" was never faced with anything like a popular revolution. A generation after this, a speaker in the Ekklesia was still able to tell his fellow citizens, "Everywhere out there, the *people* are your friends!"[43]

Yet there were some issues on which even the Confederacy's commoners reacted negatively. They had not been consulted on moving the treasury, and Pericles' "fear of the Phoenicians" was not a very convincing explanation. They must have wondered why the Synod, the only body in which non-Athenians had representation, met so seldom. They could not have been pleased when the assessments were raised, and though these were lowered after the Peace, a certain apprehension would linger. The cleruchies were a sore point too; little replicas of Athens mushrooming around the Aegean, where Athenians competed with natives on their own soil. Finally, it was an increasing irritant to have to take their legal quarrels to the popular courts in Athens, often to wait interminably for a hearing, even though the juries usually found in their favor when disputes pitted them against the rich.[44] Even from the democrats of the Confederacy, some grumbling was to be expected. Their "betters," of course, were implacably alienated.

Inside of Attica or out, scant comfort could be found for the old stalwarts of "the Good and True," but suddenly through the darkness came a solitary ray of light. In 444, for the first time in many years, Pericles was not elected to the Board of Generals. Reasons evade the investigator, since everything had been going well, though possibly some zealots among the radicals may have considered that he gave up too much in the Peace at Lacedaemon, the year before.[45] Pericles had not been among the negotiators, but undoubtedly he had given them their instructions, and the citizens would hold him responsible. His failure at the polls was slight encouragement to oligarchs and aristocrats, but thinking wishfully, they decided on one more try at power.

It had been necessary to hold off as long as the war lasted. Their pro-Spartan leanings were well known, and might get them in trouble. But the Peace had unleashed them as well as the commons, and they were determined to have their say. What had the democratic policy effected? A land empire had been gained, then lost; better to have saved the lives and the expense. Athens had insisted on holding fast to Naupactus—at the price of Corinth's undying enmity. The democrats' Egyptian gamble had been the worst disaster in Hellenic history; it had required their own hero Cimon to redress the balance and save Athens. Imperialism ("enforced contributions") they condemned absolutely, and especially Pericles' recent actions regarding the Confederacy. But persuading their fellow citizens would be a difficult job. The general feeling was that the "Good and True" were angry simply because their side had lost, at home and in the islands; hence they could be expected to damn Pericles and all his works, whatever these might be.

Their group, only now beginning to be called *oligoi* ("the Few")[46]—or oligarchs—had been handicapped for several years by lack of a leader. It was chiefly this that had kept them quiet and rendered them ineffectual. They knew it was impossible to replace the great one lost in the Cyprus campaign, who, though he may have displeased some by his compromising moderation, was sorely missed. After his death they were at a loss, and for a while were hardly noticed. When a new standard bearer at last emerged, he quickly proved his merit by drawing them together again, firing their spirits, devising new tactics. So manifest were his abilities, it is strange he did not rise sooner. For the "fresh face" was one which must have been on the Athenian political scene for at least a decade or two. It was that of Thucydides, son of Melesias, a man honest, direct, and warmhearted, whom Aristotle listed as one of the three best-loved statesmen in Athenian history,[47] and whom Plato said could only be compared with Aristides.[48]

He was probably one of the Philaids, and seems to have been related to Cimon both by blood and marriage.[49] Unlike his illustrious kinsman he did not have an imposing military record, and for a leader of aristocrats this was a serious drawback; without one he could not draw patriotic votes from the other side in Assembly balloting. Thucydides could not do that, but he compensated with remarkable talents along another line. Although relatively inexperienced, he was a forceful speaker in the Assembly and a shrewd organizer able to make the most of his group's small voting strength. Under him, aristocrats and oligarchs attained a cohesion and direction they had not known in over a half century. Thucydides welded their factions into a real party structure for the first time since Cleisthenes swept away the old geographic separatism. In Ekklesia sessions they sat and worked together, shouted their opinions and applauded in unison, making themselves count for more than their actual physical presence, as they acted on the orders of their diligent chief.[50] So much being known, one assumes also that they met in secret to plot political strategy, anticipating many of the practices of the modern party system. A science of politics was in the making.

The sequence of events after the Peace with Persia, and subsequently that with Sparta, points to something of the sort. The oligarch's eventual quarry, of course, was Pericles, but naturally the assailants realized they were not yet ready to take on the Greatest Democrat of All. It would be more expedient to create test cases against some of his intimates, to weaken the prostates little by little, besmirching him with guilt through association. Gradually they would reach the goal.

With this in mind, the conservatives may first have concentrated their attack on the famed philosopher Anaxagoras, who had initiated Athens to the new "science" born in Ionia. Both tutor and friend to Pericles, Anaxagoras was believed to have written some of the prostates' speeches, which often included scientific and philosophical data. And there was no question that the Ionian was vulnerable. Adducing natural causes for even the most awesome mysteries, it seemed to reverent Athenians that he was determined to eliminate the gods, hence they did not hesitate to label him atheist. So there are solid reasons for thinking that the oligarchs' onslaught on Pericles began with their action against Anaxagoras, and that it took place at this time.[51] Thucydides himself followed this with charges that Anaxagoras was an undercover Persian agent. Whether this happened soon after mid-century, or a dozen years later on the eve of the Peloponnesian War, as all the ancient authorities held, Pericles judged it wisest to get his old friend out of town and safely away to the Hellespont before the courts could lay hands on him.

For the oligarchs, this was a victory of sorts. Next they called for an ostracism contest, and selected as their victim a man even closer to Pericles: another former tutor, Damon, who was still useful to the prostates as a political consultant. Rightly or wrongly, Damon was believed to have given Pericles that fateful advice "to bribe the people out of their own pockets" by providing pay for the public juries.[52] Persuading the Ekklesia to hold the contest, the oligarchs also marshaled the required number of 6,000 voters to the polls, and managed well enough that Damon received a plurality of the potsherds. Although not actually a prominent man, he had to go into exile.

This second success must have elated the oligarchs beyond measure. Now they were prepared to go after the top man. Cleverly, they planned to hit him where it had always been assumed he was strongest: the uprightness of his conduct as a statesman, his spotless reputation. At long last he was to be called to an accounting for actions which he and the democratic majority had taken for granted: the moving of the Delian treasury, and the use of its funds for Athens' own purposes as she saw fit. Was not this plain malversation? Moreover, could any good come of this evil? Must not the use of such money result in degradation, a cheapening of Athens itself? Searching questions, all of them, involving issues that could not longer be avoided.

Thucydides and his friends launched the attack, and obviously, with utmost conviction. They reminded their listeners that the money collected from the Confederates was to defend them against Persia; it was morally wrong to turn it to any other purpose. The very worst thing was to use it selfishly to beautify their own city. What had happened to the high Athenian character of earlier days? How will they appear now before the other Greeks?

> Truly, Hellas is outraged and tyrannized when the taxes she pays out of necessity to prevent war, we use to gild and embellish our city, in the manner of shameless, streetwalking women, girding her with sumptuous marbles and statues, and temples costing thousands of talents.[53]

It was direct, powerful speaking, which must have struck home with telling effect.

Thucydides was a worthy challenger, but he was pitted against a champion of champions. In debate before the Ekklesia, Pericles absorbed the blows and gave no ground. With the Parthenon gradually rising in the sight of all, there was no ground to give.[54] When ready, he struck back with masterly precision. Athens owed no accounting to the Confederates for the payments she had from them, he said, as long as she gave adequate protection and fulfilled the contracts. As for the tributary states, "not a horse do they furnish, not a ship, not a hoplite, but money simply."[55] They had commuted their own burdens, thrusting them all on Athens. Thus the metropolis had been forced to undertake the defense of all, and by her own efficiency make up for the laziness of others. If she did her part with honor, managing better than was deemed possible, was it not fitting that she should use what was left over to clothe herself in glory?

Pericles reserved his forensic magic for the greatest occasions, and it was in the nature of his genius that he knew when to display it, and in what measure. Having established his basic position, he turned to economic justifications. Employment of the funds as Athens had done created a condition of abundance, he argued. Nothing would be lost; more wealth was created. The energies and skills of all citizens were being mobilized to produce works that through art and utility would have a far greater worth than their cost. The Delian members had conceded that it was right to pay for military and naval services, for the soldiers and sailors that protected them. But what of those other citizens of Athens who could perform only peaceful labor? Was not this just as important, just as deserving of reward? Pericles thought it right that everyone should have a chance to serve as he was best able; with all the citizens busy at various tasks, Athens would set Greece a healthful example by her industry, while outdistancing the rest in accomplishment, and consequently in power.

The Olympian was soaring like Zeus aloft on a cloud, but his opponents had pursued him too long not to pluck him down. This was all very well, they said, but where had the money gone, what had he actually expended under each heading? Pericles produced his accounts. Had he spent too much? he asked. Yes, it was far too much, the Assembly decided, under prodding of the oligarchs. The prostates asked for specifics, and the argument finally narrowed down to the erection of a single building. Hemmed in for an instant, Pericles quickly glided around them. "Well then," he said, "let it not be charged to you, but to me. And when I have paid, I will make out the inscription of dedication in my own name."[56] Effectively silenced, the Assembly immediately approved this item, then went on to accept the rest. One notes too, that Pericles had already gained his major point by luring the oligarchs to attack his expenditures rather than the economic philosophy, which went unchallenged.

Yet such civility as his adversaries demonstrated was merely the lull in a storm gradually mounting to its expected climax. The next time that the constitution permitted, in the spring of 443, another ostracism meeting was moved, with Thucydides and Pericles himself as the obvious contestants. In spite of their rebuff on the subject of financial administration, the oligarchs thought they had a good issue in the question of the Confederacy, while counting heavily on the impeccability and personal popularity of their new favorite. Unfortunately, they decided to emphasize their hero's character by a simultaneous blackening of Pericles', presenting a dramatic contrast that voters would not be able to ignore.

By now there *was* a smudge or two to expose, if the oligarchs wanted to play that way. Pericles had recently divorced a wife from one of Athens' oldest families, and though he did so with her consent, it broke up a household hitherto considered a model of decorum. Here was matter enough for the oligarchs, but the really tantalizing aspect was the *cause* of the divorce. Lately there had come to Athens from Miletus a girl named Aspasia, beautiful, spirited, and brilliant enough that she was able to win the respect of Athens' most prominent men, including the philosophers, by her apt discourses on intellectual and political developments—perhaps thereby supplementing the courtesan's income by which she was originally forced to make her living. Pericles admired her as the others did, soon fell in love with her, and after arranging his divorce, brought her to his home as a sort of common-law wife. Ironically, he could not marry her because of his own citizenship law, which forbade legal marriage between any but native born Athenians. However, it was a happy union which lasted his lifetime, and Aspasia received every mark of respect, including loving kisses whenever Pericles left or returned home—something his fellow Athenians regarded as monstrous sentimentalism.

All of this gave the oligarchs material to work with, though its value was questionable, since it softened Pericles' image as the cool, aloof, unemotional statesman. Nevertheless on the basis of what they had, the conservatives apparently resolved to unmask the Great Democrat as a lecher, and even worse. The campaign of 443 surpassed all previous ones in Athenian history for mudslinging and outright character assassination. As Plutarch tells it, Pericles was now described as a sexual insatiate who had debauched his son's wife, and who had liaisons with the wives of his colleagues on the Strategion. A rumor was spread that the sculptor Phidias procured women for the prostates under the pretense of taking them to see his own works of art. Another concerned the wealthy Pyrilampes, who, having acquired a number of peacocks in Persia, gave them as presents to Athenian ladies if they would submit to Pericles' advances.[57]

Yet the intriguers had their trouble for nothing. When the ostracons were counted, the public finger came to rest on Thucydides, who consequently had to leave Attica for ten years. He would return and raise his voice again, but he never was to recover the lost ground. For his dismayed friends it was the final gasp. The oligarchic faction in Athens disintegrated for a decade and was not again to be a serious force in the city's politics until a generation had passed.

Pericles could breathe easily once more. The tide that had overtaken Cimon, Themistocles, Aristides, every leading statesman since the century's beginning including his own father, Xanthippus, had not broken upon him. It had to be a tremendous relief, almost dizzying. All his adult political life he must have been dreading that ostracism ordeal, when he in his turn would be pitted against a younger, warmer, more attractive rival. The nerve-wracking moment had come and gone. He had no assurance that it would not come again, but for the present the sea had subsided with barely a ripple. Given the right combination of fortune and skill, the calm might last out his career.

To have surmounted the fearsome obstacle conferred a unique distinction, a sense of elation, a heightened self-confidence. Now, more than ever, he was called the Olympian, and men fell silent while awaiting the authoritative word. In the period ahead his decisions were quicker, surer, more sweeping, yet tacitly admitted to be unexceptional. There were no constitutional changes looking toward such an accommodation; Pericles continued to be elected term after term, one general among ten, but increasingly he dominated the others through experience and prestige. For the next dozen years after 443, and almost until the end of his life, he was virtually the uncrowned king of Athens.[58]

A statesman so prominent had to expect the literary hacks to make the most of their opportunities to satirize his delivery from danger. One such sally has come down to us. In a play lost except for this single comment, the comedian Kratinos observes that "the potsherds have been flying again," and that as a result, "Pericles, our squill-headed Zeus, emerges triumphant, wearing the Odeum for a crown."[59]

However, a more serious reflection on the ostracism and its consequences for Athens may perhaps be found in Sophocles' monumental play *Antigone,* which the poet was busy writing in the following year, and which he finally produced for the Dionysia of 441. Sophocles' vivid drama of Oedipus' proud daughter disobeying the new ruler of Thebes by burying her dead brother contrary to the monarch's order can be called political only in a derivative sense unless one considers that all Greek life, centered in the city state, was inescapably political.[60] Antigone establishes herself, through the author's skill, as one of the vibrant human heroines tinctured with divinity, by her steady insistence on the primacy of moral absolutes, to which all transitory political authority must bow.

Sophocles himself rises to new heights as he builds the Theban princess' character through coordinated speech and action: her love of family, with its attendant sense of duty and responsibility; her unbending defiance of the king; the disdaining of her sister's help; her unshaken devotion to the ideal despite increasing loneliness and eventual despair.[61] Creon's stubborn vanity and shortsightedness, his refusal to yield to either ethical or practical reasoning, then his mistakes in judgment when compelled to do so, set him up as an illuminating contrast to Antigone, while reminding the Athenian audience of the terrors that tyranny may bring. When Haemon, flouting his father's verdict against Antigone, tells him, "It is no proper state that is ruled by one man!"[62] he is speaking not only for Athens of the fifth century, but for all of Hellas.

On the surface, this antithesis between freedom of spirit and an all-devouring authority appears the sum and substance of what is applicable to the contemporary scene in Athens. One of the literary giants of his and every age,

Sophocles is concerned with eternal ideas and values, not parochial ones. But what if the parochial universalizes itself? And is the writer for all ages any less sensitive to the influences of his own?

Sophocles' relationship to the political activity of his day has been as endlessly debated as that of Aeschylus, and with as little agreement. The tendency has been to regard him as interested but detached, or at least as one whose participation shied away from party commitment.[63] However, it may be doubted that Pericles would allow any but a democrat to hold so important an office as that of Delian Treasurer, which Sophocles held in 443–42, or that Sophocles would have wished for that post unless he were one. That does not mean that he had to be a radical; probably he was not. But his tenure as Treasurer, and then as one of the ten generals later in 440–39, indicates not only a vital involvement in politics, but a continuing association with Pericles that must have evolved into a fairly close friendship.

That being so, parallels between the situation in which Sophocles lived and that of which he was writing were bound to occur to the poet, and one looks for them to appear in his literary work, consciously or unconsciously. A curious instance occurs in the *Antigone,* almost immediately. In the opening scene, as Antigone tells her sister of Creon's edict that their brother is not to be buried, she refers to him not as king or regent, but as strategos, a designation not only inappropriate, but as far as we know, an office which did not even exist in Thebes. Neither in this play nor anywhere else does Creon appear to have any military functions.[64] It seems to refer to contemporary Athens, with Pericles as the only strategos on a level comparable with Creon's. Of course, a thoroughgoing comparison between Athens' Olympian and the inept king of Thebes could never have been intended. But throughout the play Creon is depicted as a tyrant, becoming increasingly dictatorial and short-tempered until disaster strikes.

Is this what Sophocles feared for Athens, as a result of Pericles' ego-building triumph at the polls in 443? Was it a gentle covert criticism of his friend, the Great Democrat, whom he had seen becoming less democratic?[65] If so, the blind seer Teiresias' warning to the unrelenting Creon of "sacred birds screaming and tearing each other apart"[66] may also have contained the author's dimly sensed apprehension of the catastrophic Greek Civil War, that with his great friend, he was destined to witness. For Sophocles' words in the mouth of Tiresias might have an application yet wider. Athens, too, had been growing imperceptibly more magisterial in her treatment of the Hellenes drawn into her widening circle. This, the dramatist doubling as Delian Treasurer was in an excellent position to perceive. Poetic prescience has been known to confound the wisdom of politicians.

12

The Glory of Hellas

WHEN Pericles proposed that all of Greece should join Athens in restoring the temples damaged or destroyed by the Persians, he was, as previously intimated, performing more than a normal, pious action. Behind the camouflage was a cleverly calculated move to make his city the undoubted leader of the Hellenic world through an exertion in which she could not be challenged, one in which few if any would think of challenging her. For Athens, the religious appeal was a masterstroke. She could quietly assume the lead because all Greeks knew that none had suffered devastation, particularly religious devastation, more than Athens. Who, indeed, had a better right?

In marked contrast, Lacedaemon, still considered the leading state by countless Greeks, had lost no temples, so had nothing to restore. No one could blame the Spartans, of course, though there was an obvious inference unspoken, that they had not made sacrifices in measure with the other Greeks. A moral disadvantage, some would feel. And it was deplorable that the Spartans, in the light of their own privileged situation, were so unresponsive to the necessity of reestablishing Hellas' beautiful shrines. But who expected a Spartan to be responsive to beauty, anyway?

Here was the wedge that Pericles was determined to widen. The temples, as guardians of Hellas' most sacred traditions, were repositories of her culture hoard, the most conspicuous examples of classic aestheticism as well, dwarfing and demeaning the ordinary structures roundabout. Athens' devotion to this classic ideal should be impressed upon her fellow states whenever their representatives got together, especially whenever these were invited to the metropolis to see for themselves. Thus the word might be disseminated throughout Hellas, from sea to sea. And if the sons of Hellas did not quickly fall in behind the torch-carrying Athenians, give them time. Athens would proceed to rebuild her own temples in peerless beauty, adding to her piety, fame and brilliance till she compelled the Hellenes' admiration and won their nod, regardless. Under Pericles' agile direction, Athens recognized no obstacles and stopped for none.

The Olympian's qualities of judgment are nowhere seen to better advantage than in his planning of the Parthenon, which came to fruition in the summer of 438, the year after his return from Samos. A new Temple of *Athena Polias,* or *Athena Parthenos* ("Athena the Virgin") as it was also called, had been urgently needed ever since 480 when Xerxes' men pulled down the old Pisistratean temple of the same name. How carefully Pericles contrived for, and how doggedly he defended his project, has been observed. For this was the sanctuary most essential to Athens' greatest religious festival, the Panathenaea. Citizens joined in a solemn procession through the streets up to the Acropolis, where the climactic act of reverence to the goddess took place, at the portal of Athena's own palatial mansion. How the Panathenaeas of the last forty years had managed without such a requisite, whether the final ceremonies were held in the open or at some makeshift construction, is not known.

Such an unsatisfactory state of affairs could continue no longer than necessity dictated. A new Temple of Athena had been envisioned as soon as the Athenians returned from Salamis, and one may actually have been started in the days of Aristides' and Cimon's joint leadership.[1] If so, the work was soon halted for lack of funds. Rebuilding slowly on its embers, the city could not support such a lavish outlay. A generation later, Pericles' efficient budgeting had fattened the purse enough that it might safely be opened. The long-awaited Temple of Athena Parthenos, later to be famous as the "Parthenon," was finally begun in 447. Artistic talent was as readily available as money. For chief architect Pericles appointed Ictinus, already widely known for his part in designing Demeter's stately *Telesterion* ("Initiation Hall") at Eleusis, an undertaking currently in progress, and for his Temple of Apollo at Bassae, in Arcadia.[2] As associate architect, the prostates chose Callicrates, who had recently achieved distinction drafting the small but admirably proportioned Ionic temple on the Ilissos, a stream flowing close to Athens' southern edge. Pericles entrusted overall supervision of the project to his close friend Phidias, who was to be master sculptor as well—Phidias, whose many statues of Athena, Apollo, and various immortals, had brought him renown echoing that of his subjects.

The design of the new temple was in many respects predetermined by that of Pisistratus' older shrine, which had possessed two chambers; a nearly square west room, and a larger, oblong east one, surrounded by Doric columns in hexastyle (six each at front and rear), with sixteen down the sides. No explanation of the use of rooms in the Pisistratean version has ever come to light, but presumably the larger contained the cult image of Athena, and was hence the place of worship. Pericles' temple was to be slightly longer than that of Pisistratus (228 feet over 219 feet), but considerably wider (101 feet over 77 feet). The usual rationalization of this is that Phidias' new cult image, his towering ivory-and-gold statue of Athena, would require an altar so huge that the naos would have to be broadened to house it comfortably. On that theory, Phidias must have asked Ictinus to revise his plans and to amplify the entire building.[3] But of this there is no proof.

Evidence does suggest, however, that Ictinus was seriously concerned about preserving the character of the former edifice, while making his own structure bigger and better. The two inner rooms in his temple had the same dimensions in length as those in the previous one, but were of a much greater width. The architect also decided on porticoes of eight Doric columns fore and aft, but retained the hexastyle arrangement in a second row of columns behind the first. The side colonnades were lengthened by a single column, seventeen over sixteen, and the enclosed core—the *cella,* (the interior chamber, containing the cult statue of the deity) with its two rooms—was based on the original layout except that it was slightly longer and wider by about twenty-four feet. The *antae,* those pilastered ends of the side walls, were projected a bit farther also. But despite this, Ictinus never lost sight of his overall plan, and the harmonizing of its parts in a concept truly classical. In Pisistratus' temple, the diameter of the columns had been related to the interaxials (the distance from the axis of one column to the next) in a proportion of four to nine.[4] Ictinus decided to retain this, and, moreover, to make it the basis of all major relationships.[5] The total width (101 feet) of the new structure was related to the length (228 feet) in a measure of four to nine; the height (45 feet) compared to the width by the same ratio. Even the lengths of the two enclosed rooms of the cella were on the same scale.

When construction was ready to begin, a decision was taken against importing the traditional marble of Paros, in favor of that of Mount Pentelicus (a dozen miles from Athens), whose gleaming white stone contained enough iron to turn it a deep cream when oxidized by the open air. While still at the quarry, the stone for the column shafts was cut into cylindrical drums about six and one-quarter feet thick, weighing about three tons each. Individually, they had to be carted by teams of oxen to the Acropolis, where, after their cores had been drilled to permit connecting plugs of olivewood, each drum was carefully fitted upon the one below it, and ground down so tightly that the edges were almost invisible to the naked eye. In this manner drum was piled on drum until the columns rose to a height of over thirty-four feet, giving the shaft a proportion of more than five to one over its widest diameter, a greater margin than is found in any other Doric temple.[6] This accent on verticality through columns commandingly tall and robust gave the Parthenon a majestic grandeur beyond that of any ancient building. In architecture, it was the supreme expression of imperial Athens, also of Hellenic civilization.

Above their Doric abacus capitals, the soaring columns were met at right angles by the long horizontal line of the architrave, which carried the whole superstructure and spread its weight on the colonnades below. However, the striking vitality of the Parthenon depends on more than a simple balancing of erect forceful verticals with equally restful horizontals. Though at first glance its structure seems based on a juxtaposition of straight lines, actually there is not a straight line to be found anywhere. According to the principle which the Greeks called *entasis* ("distension"), the edges of the columns rose in imperceptibly rounded curves, swelling at the center (less than an inch, on shafts six feet thick!), then narrowing again at the top. Nor is this all. The columns lean inward, ever so slightly; over them, the supposedly flat architrave and entablature arch delicately upward; the doorheads do the same. Even the interior walls rise toward the center, though only by an inch or two, to promote a tighter cohesion.[7] Everywhere the curved line is employed, yet so unobtrusively that it takes a practiced eye to see it. But the "unpracticed" spectator feels its force, even without knowing why. The subtle employment and interrelating of curvilinear surfaces give the Parthenon an animation and an organic unity so satisfying that one responds intuitively rather than by rational comprehension.

Everywhere the eye is led higher, higher. Atop the columns, the triple-banded architrave, lowest section of the entablature, sits with a demure grace eclipsed by the more dramatic members above and below. Above, particularly. For here is the entablature's very spectacular middle part, the frieze, actually another series of beams lying perpendicularly upon those of the architrave. In a Doric frieze all that one sees, however, is the beam's end shaped into three vertical bars (*triglyphs*). Between the beam ends were vacant spaces filled in with squares of marble (*metopes*), to which were fastened sculpted figures that related the mythological history of the Hellenes. There were ninety-two of these metopes in the complete frieze, encircling the building. On the east wall the primeval struggle between the Gods and Giants was depicted; the north one took its subject from the *Iliad,* Greeks fighting Trojans; that on the west had Greeks contending with Amazons.[8] But the south frieze was probably the most relevant to the civilizing intentions of Pericles: on this side the "cultivated" Greek Lapiths appear as defenders of humanity and righteousness, staving off the drunken, half-animal Centaurs who tried to seize their women at the wedding feast of the Lapith king, Peirithous. The theme was particularly appropriate, in that the Lapiths were led by the Athenian hero of heroes, Theseus, who had come to the feast especially to honor Peirithous, his bosom friend of many adventures. The panorama was heightened by a lavish laying-on of color. The metopes were painted a bright red, as a dazzling backdrop for the white figures, while the triglyphs were daubed a contrasting blue. Thin lines of gold above and below completed the decorative pattern.[9]

Over the frieze, a projecting cornice capped the entablature, serving also as the hypotenuse base of the pediment, the triangle formed between ceiling and roof. And here was more myth, more art. At each end of the building, the pediments enclosed triangles of sublime sculpture, spanning the entire width. Though these no longer exist, miniature reproductions in Athens' Acropolis Museum show us what they were like. Over the east portal was presented the miraculous birth of Athena. At the group's center, Zeus sits on a high-backed throne, while behind him stands his son Hephaestus wielding the cleaver which has just split open the Father's head, so that Athena—

already emerged, full-grown and full-panoplied—may take her place in the focus opposite her parent. The locale is obviously Mount Olympus, and clustered around, other gods and goddesses are witnesses to the event. Not all can now be identified, but the dignified feminine figure behind Zeus and Hephaestus is probably Hera, a little less prominently enthroned. Balancing her on the other side is a seated male who appears to be Poseidon. Farther out on the left is Iris, the messenger of the gods, hastening to spread the news to Demeter and Persephone, seated together, and to Dionysos, who reclines behind them. On the right hand, beyond Poseidon one can recognize Apollo by his lyre, and his sister Artemis, the divine huntress, by her bow. Farther on are Hestia, protectress of the hearth, and on a couch together, Dione (originally Zeus' wife until, with the syncretizing of religious forces, the Pelasgian Hera displaced her) with her daughter, Aphrodite. At one extremity, the chariot of the sun-god Helios and the upturned heads of his horses can barely be seen, ushering in the day; at the other, Selene, the moon-goddess, with the noses of her steeds down-turned, herald the approaching night.[10]

The sculptures of the west pediment set forth the famed contest between Athena and Poseidon for the sponsorship of the city. In the middle stand the two contestants. The sea-god strikes the ground with his trident, and a salt spring opens—the same spring that purportedly lay beneath the Erechtheum temple, only a few score yards away, on the opposite slope of the Acropolis. Athena, however, outbids him as she plunges her spear into the earth and conjures up the olive tree, symbolic of the civilizing arts. As she does so, the goddess turns triumphantly away, secure in the knowledge of her victory. The two principals are flanked on each side by a chariot and pairs of magnificent, rearing horses; but moving past these, the human figures are less easily identified. They appear to be men and women rather than deities, though in Greek thinking an extraordinary person could readily pass from one class to another, mounting by various intermediate steps—hero, superhuman, lesser divinity, etc. There were no hard and fast distinctions in Greek theology. Perhaps the shapes of the west pediment were intended to be the royalty of early Athens. Certainly they should be royalty, judging by the natural grace of their varied postures, whether standing, sitting, kneeling, or—in the narrow, extreme angles of the pediments—lying down. One can easily believe that the sculptural groups in both pediments were fashioned by the master Phidias, but again, proof is lacking. If all are not by his hand, it is at least certain that he had apt pupils!

So much the spectator could see from the outside, but he would not yet be ready to penetrate the interior. Beyond its first row of eight columns, the Parthenon discloses a second row of six, adjoining the side walls of the cella. High over this inner row, and continuing around the cella's walls, was another frieze, an Ionic one, 594 feet in total length and about 3¼ feet in width, which told the complete story of the Panathenaea, the great festival for which the temple was built. More than half of this Ionic frieze is still in existence, though little of it remains on the Parthenon. The larger part was purchased and shipped to the British Museum by Lord Elgin, early in the nineteenth century (when the entire building was in a state of neglect and disrepair). Other sections are in the Louvre and the Athens Museum.

To read the Ionic frieze properly, visitors had to enter the Parthenon at its west end. Here one saw the Panathenaic procession in the act of forming, men standing while waiting to take their places, some holding their impatient horses, others already mounted and listening for the order to advance. Moving farther along, the north and south walls show what is up ahead, in scenes that are similar to one another though not identical. In these sections the procession is in full swing, with the archons and other city magistrates leading the way, followed by priests folding the sacred peplos for Athena's shoulders, and acolytes bringing sacrificial animals. Then come the maidens of noble families bearing the baskets of holy offerings, and finally the armed citizenry, some in chariots, others restraining their splendidly unruly steeds, with the hoplite infantry bringing up the rear.[11]

The whole concourse moves toward the east end, and here in front we find Pericles with the marshals of the parade. But the glory of the east frieze is the row of seated gods, seated presumably above the very spot where the Athenian people expected them to be invisibly present, at the Parthenon's main entrance where the great procession reached its culminating point. Here Athena sits in regal contemplation of her advancing retainers, while Zeus, to one side, courteously allows her the central place. Down the row of carefully placed stools, Apollo turns with quiet dignity as he looks over his shoulder to talk with Poseidon. Hermes and Dionysus exchange comments while sitting back to back, and Demeter listens in on their conversation. Hera raises an arm by way of greeting. Artemis, solemn-featured, gazes at the spectacle before her. It is plain to all that the family of Olympians has assembled to salute their esteemed relative, Pallas Athena, and to honor the great city that she protects. "Foreign" Greeks from other city states, lucky enough to gaze on this scene, might be impelled to think twice before challenging a polis with such august backing as this.

At last the reverent onlooker is ready to enter the *naos,* the bigger of the two cella rooms. This chamber, called *Hecatompedon* because it measured exactly one hundred Attic feet, had two rows of double-tiered Doric columns, each about one-quarter of the room's width in from the walls. These columns ran nearly the length of the chamber, but stopped abruptly to form a connecting row behind Phidias' creation, the awesome chryselephantine statue of Athena Parthenos. Divinely tall, the Virgin Queen rose to a full forty feet, her thirty-two-foot height enhanced by an eight-foot pedestal. Around a central wooden core Phidias had shaped her face, arms, and other fleshy parts of ivory, while hair and robe were of gold. In one hand, Athena held a six-foot image of Nike, the goddess of Victory; in the other, she gripped a spear and shield, which on its outer side contained scenes of the fight of Greeks against Amazons, and on the inner, that between the Gods and the Giants.[12] A snake, the symbol of immortality, was curled around the shield's edge. If such adornment seems superfluous to celestial majesty, one must seek an explanation in hieratic tradition.[13] Athena's priests presiding in the Acropolis sanctuary must have insisted, and obtained the support of the city's zealots. The ultimate effect was a goddess tailored to everybody's satisfaction. Proudly erect on her pedestal, Phidias' Athena compelled instinctive adulation and obedience.

Sharing a common back wall with the Hecatompedon, but with its doorway at the west end, was the smaller room of the cella. This is the one that originally had the name of *Parthenon*, or "Virgin's Chamber," which afterward came to designate the building as a whole. It alone broke radically with the overall Doric scheme by having four Ionic columns with scroll capitals, so placed that they formed a box or square. Apparently this area was at first intended as a storeroom for the properties of the goddess, but in Pericles' time it came to be used as a treasury for the Delian Confederacy.[14] There might be some question of propriety, since this was assigning to Athena what had customarily belonged to Apollo, but such things were beyond the reckoning of mere mortals. The amends, if necessary, could be made on Olympus.

The Parthenon was officially inaugurated at the Great Panathenaea of 438, even though its sculptural decorations were not completed until 432. But as soon as structural work on the great temple ceased, Pericles diverted the energies of its builders to another project, closely associated. The regular entrance to the Acropolis, at its west end, where it had an overview of the city looking toward the Saronic Gulf several miles away, needed immediate attention if it were to fulfill its function in devotional service to Athena. And beyond a doubt, the entrance area was important. Once the *Enneapylon* had stood here, a succession of nine ornamental gateways that put visitors in a properly chastened frame of mind as they entered this sacred precinct of gods and kings. Later these were replaced by a single gate-building, with four monumental Doric columns in its front wall. Both the columns and the building itself were destroyed by the Persians in 480 – like everything else on the Acropolis. Reconstruction of the *Propylaea* ("before the gates," in other words, entrance to the gates) was long overdue.

This enterprise Pericles placed under the supervision of an architect named Mnesicles, of whom there is no previous mention. Some have speculated that he was a pupil of Ictinus,[15] because of the similarity of his methods to those of the Parthenon's builder. Perhaps Ictinus himself was unavailable because of a commitment to the still unfinished Telesterion at Eleusis. It was apparent from the outset that Pericles intended the new edifice to be much more than a mere entranceway, although just what came from his orders and what from Mnesicles' planning is impossible to determine. Besides the central passage for the Panathenaic procession, there were to be four rooms, two to a side – small ones in front, larger behind; and though the Propylaea was not itself a temple, it was to have the appearance of one, so as to correspond with the Parthenon and the high religious purpose of the Acropolis.

For that reason, the front portico was set out with six majestic Doric columns (in due deference to the Parthenon's eight). Of necessity, a single irregularity disturbed their proportioning to one another. To accommodate the procession, the space between the two inmost columns had to be widened to nearly eighteen feet, while that between the others was somewhat under twelve. Beyond the two central Doric columns, completing the passageway, were five pairs of slender Ionic ones which led to the back porch and its colonnade similar to that in front, then on to the citadel with its Parthenon.

But the Propylaea was to be more than a vestibule. Adjoining the front porch, and projecting forward from it at right angles, were side rooms prefaced by three sentinel-like Ionic columns. That on the south was no more than an anteroom. Indeed, the whole south wing had to be curtailed because it impinged upon the approaches to Athena's Temple of Wingless Victory, on the Acropolis' southwest spur (not the present Temple of Wingless Victory, but a predecessor about which little is known), also upon the precincts of a shrine to Artemis, whose priests put in a vociferous objection.[16]

However, on the north side, the anteroom led to an enclosed chamber known as the *Pinakotheka,* a sort of art gallery whose walls were filled with votive paintings by Athens' leading artists. The ceiling of this area was Mnesicles' special pride: divided neatly into coffers which displayed a gold floral pattern against a blue background. Inside and outside, the emphasis was on lightness, openness of space. To secure this the architect slimmed down the members wherever possible, and in fact made the architraves so shallow that hidden iron beams had to be inserted to strengthen them enough to carry the weight overhead.[17]

Behind the Pinakotheka and its uncompleted opposite number, Mnesicles had originally planned for larger, adjoining rooms with three columns on the axis line of each. These rooms were never built, and their function, if any, is unknown. Apparently the priests of Artemis objected to the south room on the same grounds as before, and without this, a north one would have left the Propylaea distinctly assymmetrical—something unthinkable from a classical, Hellenic point of view. Mnesicles was reluctant to give up this feature of his plan, as his dispositions for the two rooms prove, but eventually the sudden outbreak of the Peloponnesian War and the tremendous military expenditures necessitated thereby put an end to further construction.

Even so, the Propylaea as it stood was imposing enough. Climbing the hill from the town below, approaching Athenians gradually found themselves enveloped by the columns of both wings, as though in the presence of an assembled army. Mnesicles purposely made the columns of the front portico eleven inches taller than the corresponding ones at the rear, so as to counteract the foreshortened aspect when seen from below, and heighten the sense of drama appropriate to the occasion. If procession marchers felt a certain awe on beholding the lofty Doric of the gateway, this was blended with an impression of grace and spaciousness while threading the Ionic of the central passage. What he had been allowed to do, Mnesicles had done well. Nothing more could be expected of a gateway. Too much attention here might detract from the greater glories beyond.

One of these masterpieces was closer than all others. From the back porch of the Propylaea, the processional path led directly to the *Athena Promachos* ("Athena the Champion"), a thirty-foot open-air bronze statue which Phidias had molded from the spoils won from the Persians at Marathon. Here the goddess was shown fully armed, with her traditional attributes, the aegis and Gorgon's head, adorning her breastplate.[18] On bright days the gleam of sun on her helmet and spear blade could be seen as far as Cape Sunium, and farther out at sea, where mariners were said to use it as a direction finder to guide them into Athens' ports. Athena's huge shield was incised with scenes of the struggle between the Lapiths and Centaurs, a theme which seemed to delight Athenian audiences eternally—but the work on the shield may be by artists later than Phidias. Immediately behind the Promachos statue were the ruins of the old Temple of Athena Polias—the site which Pericles was reserving for the Erechtheum Temple, one which would not be built until after his death. Beyond this, the processional path jutted off to the right, toward the Parthenon's entrance, at the Acropolis' southeast corner, and found its journey's end.

The artistic triumphs of Periclean Athens were not all connected with the Panathenaea, or with the numerous other state festivals. They were not all on the Acropolis; some were not even in the city. Nor were all of them sponsored by Pericles, though there is no denying that his leadership, interest, and money provided a mighty impetus to cultural accomplishment. But this would have come to little had there not been a vast array of talent to set at work. That so much of this was Athenian-born excused the prostates and his fellow citizens their touch of pride. With them cooperative effort had achieved much, politically and artistically; at this, Athenians were probably better than most other Hellenes. Even so, Athenians, like their Greek brethren everywhere, were essentially individualists, and it was this surprising diversity of individual talent that created a wealth of beauty for Athens and its environs—creators and their creations which must be viewed separately, to comprehend the whole.

Phidias, son of Charmides, had already distinguished himself as the greatest of Athenian sculptors—some would say as the greatest of classical artists—before Pericles appointed him master sculptor for the Parthenon. He was also a painter and jeweler of considerable reputation. Having demonstrated such breadth and depth of ability, he was made general supervisor over all of Pericles' projects for the beautification of Athens, a sort of minister of fine arts or of cultural affairs.[19] His jurisdiction was not confined to the stately temples of the Acropolis. The theaters for music, drama, and dancing in the area just below; the stoas and monuments of the Agora and Ceramicus; and seemingly, state building throughout Attica, came under his purview. Whether this extended to primarily utilitarian structures; such as those of Piraeus, is less certain. But however the work was organized, Pericles was constructing at a great rate, in his not-so-subtle effort to establish Athens' cultural primacy. As long as he could skimp and scrounge from the Delian funds and those of the city, his ambitious program would continue. Naturally, he wanted the best possible, both in direction and execution. Who could do it better than his time-tested friend?

So much was thrust upon Phidias, one puzzles as to how he reserved leisure for his own work. Perhaps his secret was that he began early, developing habits of industry and concentration that stayed with him through a long life. Wasted motion or moments are, with him, inconceivable. Deciding quickly for an artistic career, he was apprenticed first to the Athenian, Hegesias, a practitioner of the "Severe" Style. But very soon the aspiring tyro departed for Argos to study under Ageladas, who had a wide reputation as master and teacher. Myron, already well established in Athens, had been trained in the same studio. Perhaps it was he who recommended Ageladas to Phidias. The dextrous Argive's own productions are known today only through literary descriptions, but he must have been one of the world's most gifted instructors, judging by the quality of his pupils, among whom Polycleitus is also included.

Phidias learned his lessons well. That he won his way rapidly after returning to Athens, may be inferred from his first spectacular success, the *Athena Promachos,* in the decade between 460 and 450. At that time, the young sculptor was still in his thirties, and though his previous credits are lost, undoubtedly he would not have drawn such an important assignment without repeated distinctions before this. Perhaps the Athena that Pausanias saw at Pallene, in Achaea, was one of these.[20] Or the prototype of the Kassel Apollo (a marble copy of the bronze original, now in a museum in Kassel, West Germany), which shows the archer-god with bow in hand, his graceful yet powerful body taut with the expectancy of conflict, as with sharp eyes he sights his target.

It was for his many renderings of Athena, however, that Phidias was most famous. Throughout Greece, half a dozen temples of the Virgin Goddess proudly displayed one of his compositions as their cult image. And strange to say, the most esteemed of these was not the mighty Athena Parthenos in the Parthenon. Rather, by an admiration almost universal, it was the *Athena Lemnia,* so called because it was commissioned and dedicated by Athenian cleruchs on the island of Lemnos, sometime between 451 and 448.[21] The bronze original, which once stood on the Acropolis, is lost, like nearly all the works of the great Greek artists. But a particularly fine marble replica has been assembled from a head discovered in Bologna, Italy, and a body in Dresden, East Germany. In this, the copyists have preserved remarkably Phidias' intentions. One can readily imagine the effect on the Lemnian worshipers. The goddess stands before them slender, erect, vibrant with graceful dignity, as she leans slightly on the left hand which grasps the spear. Her right one is extended comfortingly toward the devotees, as in it she holds her crested helmet, at once the symbol of protection and victory.

But the most arresting aspect of the Athena Lemnia is the face. The goddess looks down on her subjects with an expression that is bold, resolute, full of intelligence and confidence. The visage is perfection itself, surely one of the great masterworks of human art, a human's conception of the divine. From deep-set, charismatic eyes the goddess gazes with a concentration that is intense, yet somehow easy, effortless. The effect is enhanced by the long, firm line of the forehead continuing down the straight, well-proportioned nose, suggestive of a strong will. The delicately rounded cheeks slope toward a quietly aggressive chin under full, sensuous lips that are firmly compressed. The overall impression is of a being truly superhuman, one filled with primal emotion and energy, yet a monumental calm, revealing the spirit under control of an intellect and a will that are in complete harmony.

Small wonder that immediately after fulfilling his contract with the Lemnians, Phidias was commandeered to make the Athena Parthenos. With this, however, the wishes of the Ekklesia and prostates contravened his own intentions. The Parthenon deity in ivory and gold achieved an awesome splendor, but the sculptor would have preferred less showy materials, and probably would have avoided the ritual snakes on robe and shield, also the curiously ostentatious headdress. To overdecorate Athena in this manner did indeed give some substance to Thucydides' well-known accusation of Pericles and the democratic imperialists. But whatever its truth, the fault did not lie with the artist.

Incredibly, Phidias' greatest work was yet to come. With his two chief pupils, Paionios and Alkamenes, he had been employed sometime previously by the people of Elis to carve the pediments for the Temple of Zeus, which a local architect named Libon had built earlier at Olympia, between 472 and 460. The eastern pediment had dealt with preparations for the epoch-making chariot race between Pelops and Oenomaus, so important to Elis and the whole peninsula; the western one had portrayed yet again the fight between Lapiths and Centaurs, between civilization and barbarism. Now Elis called Phidias back, about 435, to execute the cult statue of Zeus for the same temple, presumably postponed until now from want of funds—it was to be of ivory and gold, like the Parthenon Athena. Glad of a "vacation" away from the metropolis, Phidias accepted with alacrity, and took his two assistants, also his brother, the painter Panaenus. During the next three years they produced the Zeus Enthroned, to be acclaimed by the whole Greek race as the culmination of Hellenic art, and by the Latin author, Pliny, as one of the Seven Wonders of the World.

Unfortunately, we can appraise it only through literary descriptions, and certain coins of Elis which preserve the image in miniature. The statue itself was carted off to Constantinople seven centuries later by the Emperor Theodosius, and destroyed there by a fire in 475 A.D. But the testimony of ancient writers and visitors to Olympia was unanimous. All speak in superlatives. Dio Chrysostom professed himself overwhelmed at the sight, called it an "assuager of sorrow," and pronounced that nobody who had seen Phidias' Zeus could ever be unhappy again.[22] The Roman general Aemilius

Paullus said that, having heard of its utter sublimity, he was prepared to be impressed, but that even so, the reality far exceeded his expectations.[23] The geographer Strabo was struck by its ideal combination of power, beauty, and size, and looking up at it, thought that if the seated god should rise, he would go through the roof![24]

Indeed, there was some likelihood. The chryselephantine Zeus sat more than forty feet tall, and the ceiling of the temple was about sixty. The richness of the scene was almost beyond belief. His snow-white features encased in golden hair and beard, clad in a golden robe, the Father and King of the Gods occupied a throne of cedarwood inlaid with ivory, ebony, and gold, with settings of precious stones. On his head Zeus wore a crown of olive leaves, also of hammered gold (the symbolic prize of victors in the Olympic Games), and his left hand grasped a sceptre surmounted by a gold eagle (Zeus' bird), while his right one held a statuette of Nike, goddess of Victory.[25] But as in the case of the Athena Lemnia, what particularly subdued the onlookers was the piercing eye and the intelligence it conveyed, which together with the majestic demeanor and colossal size, overpowered all who entered the sanctuary. Phidias endowed his forms with such convincing vitality that even normally cool philosophers felt themselves in the actual presence of the god, with no choice but to believe.[26] Of course, magnitude played a part. Actually the cult image took up one-third of the entire naos,[27] so that one was bound to feel dwarfed from the moment of entrance. Altogether, it was simply too much. Cicero declared that nothing could excel Phidias' Zeus,[28] though he thought the artist's other works were all close to the same high standard. The flat surfaces of the throne, also the walls of the sanctuary itself, were painted by Phidias' brother Panaenus with scenes from the labors of Heracles, the Trojan War, the fights between Greeks and Amazons, the slaying of Niobe's children by Apollo and Artemis, the birth of Aphrodite, and so ad infinitum. Like the Parthenon itself, the Temple of Zeus at Olympia presented to the beholder a pagan Greek Bible of mythology and legend, in its many forms of art.

Phidias' last years were troubled, although the truth about him has been obscured. He returned to Athens about 432, and as the friend of Pericles, became involved in the prostates' latest political difficulties. Belated charges were hurled against him in connection with his Athena Parthenos: that he had secreted some of the gold for the statue, also that he had depicted himself and Pericles on Athena's shield. One account has it that he was sent to prison; another, that he was acquitted. Whichever is true, these were unfitting vexations for so deserving a citizen.

Myron, Phidias' older contemporary, also his predecessor as a student in the workshop of Ageladas, was actually a native of Eleutherae, a village in the northwest corner of Attica. Though examples from his formative years are lacking, ancient authorities credited him with first making the transition from the Severe to the mature Classical Style, rendering animals, men, and even gods (!) as they actually lived in nature, whether in motion or at rest.[29]

He worked entirely in bronze, and the many bronze figures of athletes attributed to him by the ancients suggest that on returning to Athens from his schooldays in Argos, he laid a basis for his career by gathering a clientele among those well-favored aristocrats who competed and won in the sacred games held in so many of the Hellenic cities. Young nobles of good physique and sufficient income could devote hours every day to rigorous training in the *palaestra,* they could follow the games from place to place, and—though these were not so numerous or frequent as in our day—lay up a mounting stack of crowns in olive, bay, or laurel. Usually such persons could pay to have themselves memorialized in bronze, marble, or paint, which was more satisfactory, since crowns withered away. Myron and his fellow artists were glad to oblige.

Outstanding among his athletic statues was the *Discobolos,* whose fame may be gauged by the multitude of marble copies made, many still in existence, of the lost bronze original. There is no inscription or literary account to tell who the Discus Thrower was, or whether he won the discus event at Olympia, Nemea, Corinth, or elsewhere. Of the many extant copies, the Lancelotti version, now in the Museo delle Terme, Rome, is considered the best and closest to the archetype.[30] It presents a splendidly muscled athlete balanced on his right foot, as the arm with the discus reaches the top of the backswing, before starting to whirl and throw. The body is organized in a sweeping S-curve that proceeds upward through the right leg, thigh, hip, and torso, to the upflung arm—indicative of harmonious, integrated, flowing motion.[31] The head looks back to check the sequence, showing that the complexities of movement, though entirely physical in themselves, are all ordered by the mind and under its control. Herein lies the fundamental nature of Classicism or Idealism; that in all actions or representation of events, idea should clearly dominate. Appearing first in Myron, this was also the essence of Phidias' various Athenas and his Zeus, to recur later in the works of Polycleitus, Praxiteles, and Lysippus. The same may be found in the dramas of Aeschylus and Sophocles. Later it would achieve full philosophic status with Socrates and Plato.

One other example of Myron's virtuosity survives in a Roman copy, the Athena with the Satyr Marsyas—the same Marsyas who was so proud of his flute-playing that he challenged Apollo to a contest, lost, and was flayed to death for his presumption. However, it was Athena who supposedly invented the flute, then decided not to play it because the puffing out of her cheeks would mar her beauty. As in his Discobolos, Myron chose to depict the climactic moment, when Athena cast the flute on the ground, and Marsyas looks at it longingly, wishing to pick it up. Again, it is idea that rules, and there is a striking realism in the interaction between the two figures. Marsyas is all eagerness as he fixes his eye on the fallen instrument and lifts his arm to sweep it up. However, his zestful body tenses and draws back as Athena, with her divine prescience, raises a hand in warning. The scene is instinct with life. The feisty satyr can scarcely contain himself, is about to succumb to temptation. Myron created the original for one of the Acropolis temples.

Probably the city commissioned him to do so because the legend exalted Athena as patroness of music, and in the aftermath called attention to the victory of their other chief sponsor, Apollo, over a barbarous Asiatic satyr. At Athens and elsewhere in Ionian Greece, this was one of the most popular subjects of art.

The rest of Myron's work is conjectural, through lack of evidence. His "Cow in the Agora of Athens" was highly praised in its day, and more than a score of epigrams were written about it, but the extraordinary bovine has disappeared. The prototype for the several extant copies of the "Old Drunken Woman" is thought to be his, but the attribution is uncertain. Much speculation has arisen about his influence on the rising, young Phidias (which seems obvious on the basis of artistic resemblances), and of the maturing Phidias' counterinfluence on him. Of course, Myron was living in Athens during the great days of the Parthenon project, and it is unlikely that Pericles would waste such a talent. His name is never mentioned in connection with it, though scholars have fancied they detected his hand in some of the Parthenon metopes, particularly in those dramatic ones of the south wall, where Centaurs and Lapiths are shown in desperate, hand-to-hand combat. Tradition has it that Myron lived to a ripe old age in Athens, finally dying rich and honored. He had better luck than Phidias.

Painting until this time had been one of the minor arts of the Athenians, if the term "minor" is appropriate to an industry as important to them as pottery. After such a marked development in the ceramics medium, it was inevitable that the technique should expand to the larger surfaces of walls. Probably the first wall painters were men who had received their instruction in the ceramic field and were vase painters first. Micon of Athens was one such, and we know of nobody earlier than he. Wall painting, with him and others, seems to have started slightly before the middle of the century. But the local practitioners were soon outdone by a newcomer from abroad, the much heralded Polygnotus.

They had good reason to be apprehensive. Polygnotus was a citizen of Thasos, who had his first lessons from his father Aglaophon, either a sculptor or a pottery painter there—Thasos had no occasion for wall painting, that we know of. Evidently though, Polygnotus had already done something in this medium—perhaps some of his murals at Delphi—for it was Cimon who heard of him and sought his acquaintance, when the general was sent to subdue Thasos to the Confederacy in 465. And it was Cimon who persuaded Polygnotus to come to Athens, shortly thereafter, to beautify the city with his painting. Manifestly, the idea of making Athens a cultural center had occurred to others before Pericles. Cimon's notions were on a more modest scale, without political intent, other than a modicum of good will. And in his honest, forthright way, he intended to use his own money, not that of the Confederacy.

Polygnotus came, possibly out of friendship for Cimon, or more understandably, from an attraction to Cimon's sister, Elpinice, with whom he was to have a notorious love affair. It was not purely for business, we know, because he would accept no pay for his work, at least not for work done in Athens.[32] This may mean that he was a Thasian aristocrat, painting out of sheer talent and enthusiasm rather than necessity—his close connection with the Philaids suggest this. Perhaps he refused the money out of gratitude for the Athenian citizenship that was conferred upon him. Another possibility is that he was receiving private remuneration from Cimon, who did not want his benevolence publicized. Such behavior was in keeping with Cimon's performance on other occasions.[33]

Polygnotus' task was to decorate the Agora with its *stoas*, the public buildings, and in particular one that was intended as a showplace, the *Stoa Poikile*, or Painted Porch. Here his most important picture was "The Capture of Troy," in which he presented not the final assault itself, but the morning after, the dead Trojans lying about, and the despairing ladies at the walls, as the victorious Greeks come to claim the spoil.[34] In these earliest mural paintings Polygnotus did not depict the entire subject, complete with background scenery. Nor did he make use of perspective or shading. Probably he did not fresco the walls directly, either, though there is no proof, since the works and the building itself were destroyed.

Rather, he imposed the figures on a neutral, dark background after preparing them in his workshop, then somehow attaching these to the wall surface. His method of indicating depth was simply to place some figures above the others.[35] His coloring is said to have been light and even without much variety. But above all, he was renowned for the boldness and vividness of his forms, their clear, concise outlining, the alive faces and open mouths suggestive of human emotion.[36] The contrast between the dejected Trojan women above—did Euripides get his inspiration from this scene?—and the jubilant Greeks below, was enough to convince all fifth-century viewers. By a general agreement too, his figures were "ideal," "better than ourselves,"[37] and he demonstrated in his medium what the greatest sculptors and architects did in theirs, that nobility of character and idea which is the inner spirit of Classicism.

Apparently, the embellishment of the Stoa Poikile was Cimon's project, at least in the beginning. Polygnotus' "Capture of Troy" took up an entire wall, or nearly so. On an adjoining wall was Micon's "Battle of the Amazons," and on still another Phidias' brother Panaenus painted the "Battle of Marathon." Cimon had an especially strong personal interest in the last of these, since it depicted the exploit upon which his father Miltiades' reputation rested. Panaenus' work has been cited as a basis for faulting Herodotus' account of Marathon,[38] since it showed the Persian army drawn up in front of the Great Marsh,[39] and its shattered remnants fleeing into the marsh rather than toward the sea, as the historian told it. Plenty of glory for Miltiades either way, and an event of which his dutiful son would wish to remind the people of Athens, eternally.

The Stoa Poikile was only a first step. Near the Agora was a Temple of the *Dioscuri*—Castor and Pollux, the brothers of Helen of Troy. The associations of these twin sons of Zeus and Leda were with Sparta rather than Athens (Leda had been a queen of Sparta); perhaps their temple in the Agora goes back to that earlier period of Spartan friendship, to Pisistratus or before. Obviously, the philo-Laconian Cimon would have an interest in decorating it, if anybody would, and because the same artists were chosen points again to him. For the Temple of the Dioscuri, Polygnotus painted the "Abduction of the Daughters of Leucippus," surely not the most respectable incident in the lives of Leda's turbulent twins, but certainly the most colorful, and one that establishes a behavioral parallel with their famous sister. As a subject of art, it was to attract the attention of Renaissance masters such as Titian and Rubens. Polygnotus would have some trouble with "idealism" here, but doubtless he made the brothers bold and resourceful. Among the more primitive Greeks, rape was not such a serious matter anyway, as Homer makes clear in the opening passages of the *Iliad*. For the same temple, Micon limned the "Return of the Argonauts," which although an equally familiar story, does not come much closer to Victorian respectability. Pausanias was impressed with the work, and complimented the painter's "intensity of effort."[40] Micon was no Polygnotus, but a skilled craftsman, all the same.

Failure to use Polygnotus did not prevent those who came after Cimon from obtaining some of his most prized compositions. When the Propylaea was completed in 432, its northern wing was a large enclosed chamber called the Pinakotheka, because its purpose was to receive and display votive wooden tablets (*pinakes*), dedicated to the gods in thanksgiving for an answer to prayer. Because these tablets were often in the form of pictures, and professional artists frequently hired to paint them, the items stored took on more and more the attribution of high quality art. At last the Pinakotheka turned into a sort of state art gallery for Athens,[41] the first such building exclusively devoted to the purpose. How long the process took, we do not know, but from the arrangement of windows and mouldings it would appear that Pericles intended this from the start. It had long possessed this character when Pausanias visited it, and he noted his pleasure on seeing Polygnotus' magnificent "Achilles on Scyros" there,[42] in the midst of several more paintings by Polygnotus, and those of other leading painters, Athenian and non-Athenian.

Did Pericles somehow acquire this artistic gem, one among many, with or without paying for it? Of all Athens' statesmen, he was the one with the best opportunities and the most ready cash, if he wanted to dip into the two treasuries, Athenian and Delian. In his program to center Greek culture in Athens, he had already in a sense universalized her festivals, her celebrations of the Homeric epics, her religious mysteries, by advertising them, even occasionally inviting participation. Architecture and sculpture, temples and statues, had followed the same pattern. Hellenes everywhere were made aware of them, that they were located at Athens, that directly or indirectly the great treasures were all in some sense Athenian. To see and experience, one must come to Athens. This being so, he would also want an Art Museum on the Acropolis, filled with the best paintings. Would he then be willing to buy, bargain, even wheedle, to get what he wanted? Knowing the man and his objectives, the answer seems obvious.

In the amazing circle of genius that constituted Pericles' circle of friends, nearly all have been treated except those "pure" idea-men, the philosophers who had brought to Athens the new "science" first developed at Miletus in Ionia a century before. Pericles, with all cultivated Athenians, had been interested in attempts to find a reasonable principle at work behind the forces of nature, whether in the unsuspected wonder-working properties of water, as Thales maintained, or of Anaximenes' air, or of Heraclitus' fire, as the agent of change. A good case could be made for any one of these as the ultimate reality, the basic world-substance from which all diverse matter came. Such noble concepts were thought-provoking, but it was regrettable how little agreement existed among these high thinkers, also how involved their explanations tended progressively to become. Anaximander's uniform "endless," separating into opposites that conflict, to destroy or unite, then separate again, endlessly repeating, was an ingenious way to set cause and effect going—but rather tiresome all the same—and besides, what was this "endless"? In the same vein, Heraclitus might tell them that everything moved and changed, while Parmenides and others denied that any real change took place. Many exciting discoveries were made in physics, in astronomy, in geometry. Yet interested Athenians might wish these learned ones could get their views together; also that a savant or two would come to their city and try to straighten them out.

Rather soon, one did come. Anaxagoras, son of Hegesibulus, was originally from Clazomenae in Ionia, and reportedly had studied under Anaximenes at Miletus,[43] before coming to Athens about 480, apparently an Ionian forced to serve in Xerxes' army. Having some of the answers that Athenians wanted, he stayed behind to expound the new "science" when the Persians left. And coming to him for instruction were many of the most noted Athenians of the day, including Pericles himself.

What they received from Anaxagoras were the doctrines of Miletus seen through his own eyes and pushed farther by his own thinking. He could agree with the Milesians that the universe was infinite, that its materials constantly interacted through a steady, causal process,[44] while denying that any real change took place, or that anything could be created, added, or subtracted from what was already in existence. No problem there, certainly, since what already existed was an "absolute" infinity! Change was only a transformation of basic matter, which did not lose its identity. Anaxagoras was too cautious to say what this was, that is, to designate a basic substance, since the Milesians had come to grief over it.

One important aspect of the problem neither the Milesians nor anyone else had attempted to deal with in a satisfactory way, concerned *how* these apparent changes took place. How did food and drink when ingested, for instance, turn itself into flesh, skin, hair, etc.? Anaxagoras sensed the opportunity to make a real contribution, and on this problem he concentrated his faculties. Changes in nature, he claimed, take place so gradually, unobtrusively, minutely as not to be detected in normal observation. All substance is infinitely divisible; there is no end to smallness, just as there is no end to vastness—Anaxagoras was still in step with the Milesians here, with them and their precious infinity. But for the moment he would let the big go, concentrate on the little. Every "smallest" particle in the universe, he went on, is homogeneous to every other particle in the sense that each has within it absolutely all the qualities to be found in the universe as a whole[45] (with one exception, to be noted presently). These particles he simply called *moirai* ("portions"), but Aristotle would later refer to them as *homoeomera,* which in translation has been rendered as "molecules."[46] These terms recede into the background, however, before another which Anaxagoras also used. Because each particle had within it a creative power to change and reproduce, if combined with others in the right way,[47] he referred to them also as *spermata* ("seeds"), and the term quickly became standard.

But back to the central problem. With this as a basis, how can food become hair? Because all food contains hair factors, as Anaxagoras sees it. But how can this be so, when there is no visible evidence of hair in food? The Clazomenaean's solution here is remarkable in its ingenuity. Each "moira" of "sperma" has all qualities, but it need not have them in equal proportions. Molecules of bread will appear as bread, and make up a loaf, because each one contains more bread factors or wheat factors than it has of any other individual qualities. But when digested, new molecular combinations are formed, and in some of these hair factors will have a majority.[48] Not in very many, of course, but the amount of hair grown, and its rate of growth, is manifestly small when compared with the amount of food eaten.

Now Anaxagoras is ready to proceed from the little to the big. And, in the main, he is content to travel with his revered preceptors. Accepting Eternity as well as Infinity, however, he cannot agree to a "beginning" or "becoming," but insists that Being has always existed, as a homogeneous world-stuff. After that, he assents to the world-process starting just about as the Milesians said it did—in a whirling mass with the cold, damp, and dark falling toward a center, while the hot, light, and dry rose away from it. In this manner the sun, moon, and stars were created; as the whirling motion accelerated, masses of burning rock flung violently away from the center.

What particularly dissatisfied him with all philosophic systems thus far was their failure to account for directed mobility, the dual agent that set all matter to revolving, which allowed it both to act and to be acted upon, with the chain of attendant consequences. This was a fundamental, inescapable puzzler affecting the little with the big, the creative power of the individual seed equally with the primordial whirling gases. The answer to it all Anaxagoras found in Mind (*Nous*); the principle of Intelligence itself, which he clothed with an all-pervasive motive power.[49] Mind he saw at work everywhere without and within, an intrinsic factor in every molecule that moved; energizing wind, water, and fire equally with the bursting bud and the regeneration of animal life. Mind was both an entity in itself and a quality in other entities.[50]

However, Mind—Nous—is simply intelligence at work in Nature.[51] It may seem to be personalized at times because bits of it are bound up with personality in the minds of individuals. But even in humans, Nous is really something apart. The element of Nous enters into other elements, other molecules, but does not mix with them; it affects them without being itself affected; the molecules of Nous remain pure Mind; they infiltrate and dominate, but are themselves uncontaminated. And, infuriatingly, they slip away from attempts to analyze or pin them down. Even the term "quality" is hard to use because Anaxagoras did not conceive of them as qualitative. All molecules of Nous were the same. Man simply had more of them than the horse, the dog, the insect; and these in turn had more than trees, bushes, and plants. Obviously, there was more Nous in the animate than in the inanimate. And when objects could not be moved at all, presumably, Nous had vanished from them—although the fragments of Anaxagoras' treatise do not explicitly cover this situation.

Athenians as a whole looked on Anaxagoras with an admiration that amounted to awe. They had never known a person before who knew so many things, or could explain them so well. The universe he unfolded to them was positively dazzling. The heavenly bodies in reality were fiery stones of enormous size, flung off from the earth—the sun being "larger even than the Peloponnesus"! From his explanation of meteorites, a rumor gained credence that he had actually predicted the time and place of a meteor falling near Aegospotami, in the Hellespont, around the year 467 or 468.[52]

His intellectual feats, real or fancied, caused Athenians to nickname him with his own term, Nous, "The Brain."[53] And from this, some formed the opinion that his brain served the democratic party; that he continued to help Pericles with his speeches, as formerly he had advanced the prostates' education. It had been noticed early that these orations were very thoughtful, logically ordered, and studded with examples from the natural sciences rather than the usual references to the gods—something Athenians were not entirely happy about.

In fact, many Athenians were distinctly unhappy with Anaxagoras on this subject. His burning stones in the sky made an interesting speculation, if it ended there. Athenians prided themselves on their broadmindedness and freedom of thought. But all Greeks had been taught that the sun and moon, at least, were gods. Differences of opinion existed here, and some difference was permissible. The more traditional among them regarded *Helios* ("sun") as a god in his own right. Recently, as concepts about the deities had enlarged, many of the more liberal-minded had come to think of the sun as a manifestation of Apollo, and the moon as perhaps being one of his sisters, Artemis, instead of the more ancient Selene. The most daring might attempt a synthesis. But to reduce these to fiery rock was irreverent and sacrilegious. They all knew from the *Iliad* how Apollo could punish blasphemy. Suppose Athena became offended also? Anaxagoras was carrying matters too far. Old-line Athenians, remembering that the city had done well enough without him, began to wish he had never come to town.

But for the moment, there was no getting rid of him. Currently, in Athens, none could match his mental powers and encyclopedic knowledge. His life was circumspect and he had powerful friends to protect him. As long as Athens' navy ruled the Aegean, assuring control of the state to the democrats and their great leader, Anaxagoras would have fair sailing. And certainly he deserved it, as the philosopher who had first focused the attention of educated Athenians on the paramount significance of Mind.

If this was not quite enough for the burgeoning Idealists of generations to come, who admitted their indebtedness to him,[54] however reluctantly, it is paradoxical that the most immediate opposition came from exponents of a stricter materialism. In that rim of Greece beyond the Aegean, a trend of thought was developing which would mount a challenge to him in the years ahead and give him the test of strength which his contemporaries in Athens could not give. The seas would roughen for Anaxagoras, eventually.

Leucippus, the inventor of the atomic theory that was to break up Anaxagoras' molecules, is a man of considerable mystery. Nothing is known of his parentage, and even his place of birth is disputed. Because of his many associations, several spots have been named. Among these, Miletus is regarded as his most likely point of origin.[55] Thus he may have studied under the same teachers as Anaxagoras. The possibility exists that the two may have known each other when young, but of this there is not the faintest evidence. Leucippus' ideas about the universe were suggestive of the Infinity that stemmed from Anaximander and Anaximenes; also, he agreed with them as to the primal whirl of gases. Of Leucippus' writings, unfortunately, only a fragment or two remain.

It was on his conception of basic substance that he parted company. Unlike Anaxagoras, he thought that matter was not infinitely divisible. There had to be a stopping point. Hence his system rested on a multiplicity of tiny, indivisible units called "atoms" ("noncuttables"), which were identical internally, without individual qualities—their only important difference being in shape.[56] They entered into combinations by hitting during the whirling process, and all qualities or characteristics assumed were due to these temporary spatial relationships (positions in space), which were also dissolved by more whirling and hitting, to be followed by new combinations. Beyond this it is impossible to distinguish the individual views of Leucippus, which were taken up and more fully developed by his distinguished pupil, Democritus of Abdera.

Where the two met, and Democritus had his tutelage is another mystery. Ancient tradition connected Leucippus with Abdera—an Ionian colony on the coast of Thrace—and he may have passed a period of his life there; perhaps he was the real founder of the Abderan school, usually associated with Democritus. Since both were reputed to be extensive travelers, they could also have met in Miletus or a dozen other places and still have collaborated at Abdera. For it was here, in his native city, that Democritus at last settled down to teach and write voluminously on nearly every philosophic subject for over four decades, all the while propagating Leucippus' atomic theory.

On the subject of atoms, he made certain additional observations which may or may not trace to Leucippus. Besides various shapes, Democritus allowed them difference in size and weight.[57] Motion had been elucidated by the Milesians. Democritus needed only to add that their own nature would cause atoms to spin endlessly through the infinity of space provided, without any element of Mind having to be included. Anaxagoras' help was not needed; in fact, he was positively excluded. In Democritus' cosmic whirl, the larger bodies would sink inward hitting the smaller ones that were rising, either to recoil or to stick and combine with them, or else to start off on different trajectories to encounter other bodies. This became his explanation of all change in the universe, a mechanistic principle of cause and effect through the combining, dissociating, and recombining of atoms, acting according to natural law.[58]

Furthermore this constituted the only true knowledge one could have of the world in which he lived. All personal experiences are but the result of combinations of atoms striking our sense organs so as to create certain impressions, to make an apple taste sweet or sour, to make a sky look white, blue, or pink. All such impressions were "dark knowledge," subjective, transitory, and remote from the reality of the true knowledge, the movement of atoms, which, as separate entities, were so small that they escaped the senses altogether. Nevertheless their combinations and the spatial relationships established in these compounds strike the eye, ear, or nose in distinctive ways, giving humans the only impressions they can have. On this rigorous materialism Democritus founded his system, and on its "dark knowledge," surprisingly, he was able to build a very practical ethic that advocated moderation, responsible conduct, and a serene cheerfulness as the best guides to life.[59] In Abdera his fellow townsmen honored him highly, referred respectfully to him by the name of *Sophia* ("wisdom"), and came to him for shrewd bits of advice on their private affairs. The man was not nearly as remote as his philosophy.

Democritus is supposed to have said that he came only once to Athens, and then nobody recognized him. Possibly it was just as well; he could hardly hope for the degree of praise there that he had at home. But another native of the same soil would bring the thought of Abdera to Athens and gain credit thereby.

Protagoras, son of Artemon—though some gave the father's name as Maeandrius—was obviously of uncertain parentage, and is said to have begun his adult life as a common porter. By the same account, it was Democritus who noticed something superior in the brisk, cheerful way Protagoras went about his humble business, his neat packaging of bundles, and the cushion he had thoughtfully invented for the easing of loads. So Democritus, impressed, had offered to educate him in philosophy.[60] Democritus' tutelage has often been questioned, since Protagoras appears to be the older of the two, but in both cases the date of birth is extremely uncertain.[61] One remembers too, that Protagoras' education began late, and that he might never have had one except for an act of generosity. Other possibilities exist: that his instruction at Abdera came directly from Leucippus, or someone of the previous generation, because the marks of his home city were still upon him when he began to make his own career in the world.

Reportedly, he served as Democritus' secretary for a time[62] — a reasonable way for him to repay the master's kindness — then began to teach the rudiments himself in the country villages roundabout, for whatever he could get. His warm, pleasing disposition, no less than his knack at teaching quickly won him friends and a good reputation. Before long he was able to leave Abdera for greener fields in that Greater Greece where he was destined to become the most celebrated expositor of his time.The course of his early travels is unknown, but presumably these included Ionia, the original home of philosophy, as well as Greek Italy and Sicily, where it had been born anew with the Eleatics, for by the time he emerges in Athens[63] he has a well-rounded formulation to which something distinctively his own has been added.

The Abderan atoms are still recognizable at its base, also Heraclitus' doctrine of continuous change, and the doctrine of Parmenides the Eleatic that all sense phenomena were illusory and unreal. Protagoras could find room for them all. Doubtless the atoms were in a state of flux. No two individuals' sense organs would be exactly alike, or register in the same way; indeed, each individual's organs would differ somewhat within themselves, constantly changing as time passed. By applying them to external phenomena, it was the unreal interpreting the unreal, with each individual apprehending things differently, according to his own peculiar circumstances.[64] Here was a degree of changefulness to outrun Heraclitus, and hard to account for except as Abderan doctrine — Democritus' (and also Leucippus'?) "dark knowledge" pushed to its logical extreme — a darkness almost pitch black. Ultimate reality is lost behind the gloom. Protagoras had to be a hardy individual to preach such skepticism in buoyant Athens, where Anaxagoras' Nous was shining brightly by contrast. Besides, he was close to demonstrating the futility of all knowledge, and hence of his own profession. It was time for him to turn the corner.

Doing so, he picked up the light. In this maze of uncertainty, each person must determine for himself what the world means and what he is to do about it. His most famous saying, "Man is the measure of all things, of existing things that they exist, and of non-existing things that they exist not"[65] (the latter two-thirds of which seems to refer to the Abderan atoms and space, or "void"), quickly caught on with the self-assured humanists of prospering Athens. In a certain sense then, Man himself is Basic Reality and everything else is relative to him and his experience. Knowledge is meaningful and has value only insofar as it helps man — a healthy position in philosophy, a field that tends almost irresistibly toward abstractions.

Protagoras never lost sight of this, aiming always to make his knowledge useful. The first known to apply to himself the term "Sophist," or "wise man"—though all he may originally have meant by this was that he taught the wisdom (Sophia) of Democritus—his course of instruction was tailored to the needs of the individual and to the problems of life one would have to face. Certainly, he *could* teach physics and astronomy, the science of Ionia as it was handled at Abdera, but he provided only as much of this as his students needed or wanted to know. And for most, their interests and their problems lay elsewhere.[66]

Of vital concern to all was the recognition that in Athens a good half of the citizen's life was taken up with duties, political and legal, for which there was no real preparation. Yet one's fortune, one's very life, might hang by them. It was necessary to know how to speak effectively in one's own interest in the Assembly and in the courts—all the more so as ancient Greece had no lawyers to represent plaintiff or defendant. Protagoras addressed himself particularly to this problem, one which he insisted was tied up with the building of character,[67] since obviously none would believe any speaker unless they thought he could be trusted. Hence Protagoras called this study "virtue" or "manliness," since it involved an improving of the whole man. (This was the issue he debated so warmly with Socrates, who believed or defended the position that virtue could not be taught.) To Protagoras, a perfected character implied the ability to express oneself perfectly through logical thinking and organized discourse.

He made an early use of all the methods that the Platonists were later to claim as their own: dialectic, analogy, and the attack by questioning, which, strange to say, finally became known as "socratic." He especially called his students' attention to a correct understanding and use of words and how entire arguments could hang on their meaning and manipulation. Such knowledge and skill were indispensable to defending themselves and their families before the community. There were two sides to every question—his pupils must learn that in disputation their business was to present their cases as forcefully and effectively as possible. Lives, property, reputations might hang in the balance.

Protagoras has often been blamed, mostly by the Idealist successors,[68] for an attitude that is similar to the lawyers' creed of today. One forgets that he made virtue and sound character the basis of his teaching, and therefore assumed that his followers would normally be in the right; their conduct and any necessary oral defense of it would be shaped and limited by conscience. Was not this the whole purpose of philosophy, to inculcate noble living? The Platonic tradition accused Protagoras of using tricks and playing with words; then Plato goes on to show us his hero, Socrates, winning an argument against the renowned Sophist—by using these identical methods. In spite of this, it is Socrates, in the same dialogue, who calls Protagoras "the wisest of all living men."[69] Such praise from the contrary-minded should settle all doubts.

From the above it can be seen that Protagoras had no trouble gaining admittance to the highest circles of Athenian society. People at the top could hardly fail to be involved in politics, and were always in need of his services or advice. And in his doctrine of *euboulia,* that those who are best in virtue and wisdom through education have a right to rule,[70] they found a reasoned justification for their dominance. Rather pointedly, it reinforced Pericles' own position, that as the best man in the state, affairs were safest in his hands.[71] Pericles himself could not but be pleased with this, and there are some grounds for believing that Protagoras' influence with the prostates increased, while Anaxagoras' decreased as time wore on.[72] This suggests an intellectual rivalry of sorts, but Protagoras really had no quarrel with Anaxagoras. True, his educational background placed him in the opposite camp, but he had long since added modifications of his own, admitting also the views of others. Since there were two sides to everything, and the truth so hard to come by, Anaxagoras might well be right on many points. The two men were temperamentally unlike: the Clazomenaean positive and enthusiastic, though with a tempering calm; the Abderan more skeptical, but in a genial, good-natured way. Both were tolerant; each must have appreciated the other's ability and outlook. Were there real, insurmountable obstacles to a modus vivendi? It is hard to think of any.

Athens needed them both. The one emphasized the constructive activity of Mind, the other its realistic application to the problems of life, and the harnessing of the ideal to the practical. It was a method already popular in the city. Solon and Cleisthenes had thus arranged her government; Phidias and Ictinus were doing the same with her art and architecture. Now Anaxagoras and Protagoras had established some elements of a theoretical base. In so acting, they were contributors to the procedure for which, of all others, Athens is best remembered. If she were to take her place as the intellectual and cultural center of the Mediterranean world—as "the school of Hellas," to quote her greatest citizen—synthesizing of the eternal opposites became a necessary final step.

The period just passed was by all odds the happiest chapter in Pericles' life. He had recouped Athens' previous losses and strengthened the maritime empire without overmuch protest from the allies, or animosity from the other Greeks. Avoiding war when possible, he yet had mastered Athens' enemies when forced to it. His cultivation of the arts had diverted attention from the infrequent military reverses of other commanders; moreover this was earning Athens a prestige in Hellas that none could challenge or deny. The Great Panathenaea of 438 and the dedication of the Parthenon had established the point in spectacular, incomparable fashion, acting powerfully to draw around Athens all who were Ionians, and to compel the admiration of all who were not. Much wealth had been lavished on these and similar projects, but in spite of the money spent Pericles had been a careful manager, able to announce a few years later that the city owned a treasury reserve of 6,000 talents.[73] It was hardly possible to fault such a paragon; on his record, Pericles was not only invincible, but invulnerable.

Even his home life was serene. His union with Aspasia had given him both emotional and intellectual satisfaction. Most Athenians now accepted the relationship placidly. Passing through their doors was a steady stream of friends that included the most brilliant and devoted companions a statesman ever had. Behind them followed an adulating public, to applaud whenever the prostates appeared in Assembly or Agora. His dignified aloofness that people were inclined a little to resent formerly, was now regarded universally as the mark of majesty, and the identification of a soul at once great and simple. Those who pressed close with respectful gaze were grateful for a half-smile or a few words from the lips of their distinguished leader.

Was his head turned by all of this? There is no sign that it was, and the general stability of his character belies such an intimation. In any case, one as steeped in the lore of the Muses as Pericles would take care to avoid the pitfalls of pride. At the same time, he did not rest altogether easy. Ceaselessly, Greece's poets and prophets had proclaimed that the gods begrudged unmeasured success.

13

A World without End

"IT is *we* who are Hamlet." Thus succinctly, a distinguished dramatic critic, William Hazlitt, convinces us of the accessibility and universality of Shakespeare's powerful drama, so Greek in its tapping of intellect and emotions, yet so curiously un-Greek in its shifts of mood and sudden, unrestrained violences. That Shakespeare was indebted to the classic tradition reaching back to Aeschylus and Sophocles, few will deny, and if any should, the prince's own "tragic hero" speech in Act I stands as ready refutation. There is much more in Shakespeare than this, needless to say, and the former Stratford schoolboy with his "small Latin and less Greek" is hardly the ideal exemplar of classicism in the postclassical world. But if a Stratford nongraduate could not escape the all-pervasive influence, who could? The ancient Greeks are gone, but their Greece endures, as universal and accessible as Shakespeare.

To find what is genuinely Hellenic, one turns naturally to Athens, for Athens' experience was that of the rest of Hellas "read large," as Jowett's Plato would say. Athens *was* Hellas, only more so. The whole land was, and continues to be poor, much of it with soil so thin as to be barely productive; in a country of reluctant vegetation, Attica's is possibly the worst. Given such an area as Greece, the limits of cultivation and hence of population are quickly reached, and Attica was overpopulated sooner than most. It follows that all but a few Hellenes had to struggle merely to live above the level of subsistence, as Hesiod tells us. However, the common run of sixth-century Athenians seem at one time to have lived almost below subsistence level, setting a standard of frugality hard even for Hellenes to match—and in consequence generated a degree of ill will toward those better off which must also have been extreme.[1] The seeds of social upheaval and tyranny were sown here early as elsewhere, with the succeeding metamorphoses that led through oligarchy to democratic, and eventually, to demagogic rule.

The exigencies faced by Athens are those that have recurred endlessly in the western world. We remember Athens as a democracy, and of course she had the first system that might fairly be called such. Actually however, at one time or another the Attic metropolis had almost every type of government conceivable, responding and adapting to nearly every kind of situation. That her responses fell short of perfection was to be expected. Considering all the circumstances, remembering there was little in the way of historical precedent to guide her as her own experiments have enlightened those coming after, it is amazing how good were the answers she found.

In devising their solutions, the Athenians could only have recourse to trial and error, especially in the initial stages. They were never absolutely without precedent, but the earliest examples were so unsatisfactory that, as witnessed by the laws of Draco, much had to be discarded. Even so, there was always *respect* for precedent. Solon had to soften Draco's table of punishments, but he did not sweep them entirely away. And though his own arrangements could not please everybody, recognition of their intrinsic merit was so widespread that the statesmen coming afterward retained and enforced most of his legislation by occasional judicious pruning, wisely preferring to supplement and strengthen rather than to uproot. Herein one perceives the unfolding of a process that Athenians and their Greek brethren would gradually apply to virtually all fields of endeavor, a process distinctive of their civilization: by a ceaseless, well-directed activity discovering the most workable outcomes, then abstracting from these their principles as pointers to improve future enterprise.

Thus the maturing of the Greek genius produced the method known as classicism, which in general can be described simply as "a right way of doing things," a conviction that the best results will flow from an application of time-tested principles. Quality, to be approved, must meet certain standards. The wisdom of the gods may proceed from a source within you, as Socrates held, but the effluence must still be sifted and judged in the final assay. By this concept, classicism is seen as the elixir of an intellectualism distilled from experience. Though the ultimate, quintessential distillation was the work of philosophers surveying an operation largely completed, that should not obscure the truth of a process operational from the beginning. In Solon's dictum of "nothing too much" appears the modicum of intelligence that will be reproduced and elaborated countless times in Greece's subsequent attainments, an insistence on justice, logic, proportion, discipline. Someone once called the long procession of western philosophy essentially a series of commentaries on Plato. Theology aside, Plato might almost be called an amplification of Solon. Thus did the Greek mentality magnify itself.

And as Socrates asserted, this increment is best observed in the development of the state, which for him, as for us, must mean Athens. In the organic growth of Athens as a polis, one sees government becoming a science, whose very name, politics, derives from this Greek word for the city-state. That

Athens' growth *was* organic is easily recognized in her union with Attica in legendary history, in the differentiation between metropolis and hinterland, between city and country dweller. This was not in itself remarkable; the same must have been true of most Greek states. But unlike the others, Athens extended her citizenship to the outlying communities she had absorbed, to Eleusis, Brauron, Marathon, and the rest. The importance of this step for Athens, and for the world, cannot be overemphasized. An idea had burst from its bud, outgrown its physical base. Citizenship leapt beyond the bounds of a particular city and was on its way to universality, in the geographic sense, at least. A beginning had been made.

The synoecismus of Attica held intellectual implications even more far-reaching. By voluntarily sharing their political privileges with equals in the surrounding communities, Athenians were tacitly conceding that domination and rule, the rule of law, however that term was currently understood, still admitted certain rights to the governed; that where prohibitive law stopped, freedom began. The synoecismus in itself must have been strictly a pragmatic affair to obtain friends, and to insure that Athens would not quickly lose what she had gained.[2] A doctrine of natural rights could not have been imagined by the framers of the synoecismus, but all such doctrines were ultimate outgrowths of this all-but-forgotten event. Athens' allowance that government under law implied a degree of liberty, and a proper balance between the two, was almost prehistoric in origin.[3]

Subsequent political progress was marked by a similar application of reason rooted in practice. At first Athens' laws had been traditional and unwritten (like those of Sparta), and it was obviously in the interest of Athens' aristocratic judges and administrators to keep them that way, despite increasing pressure from below. Gradually becoming convinced that the only alternative to a known, authoritative code, universally applicable, was a nation of heavily militarized masters, a tense police state like Sparta's, they quite sensibly agreed that the laws had to be placed in writing. The first code did not concede much, but the balance had shifted imperceptibly toward liberty.

The oft-applauded seisachtheia is another such instance. The world's first noteworthy act of emancipation, it eased the pressure on the Athenian lower classes. By assuring them personal freedom *with* their lands (some of them, at least), it encouraged this ailing segment of the population to work in harmony with others, to promote the overall health of the state. In the same spirit, and distinctively classical in its ideology, was Solon's reordering of the citizens into four collaborating groups for political purposes. By giving all a stake in government in proportion to their abilities demonstrated in terms of income, he hit upon a method of securing administration by the more intelligent while providing an incentive to self-improvement. With this impetus came another huge gain for liberty, as law was tempered by reason and measure, and rewarded those who had deserved well of the state.

It was characteristic of Athens too, that when difficult and dangerous problems loomed—with her hard-run proletarians, for instance—she proceeded cautiously, temperately, toward solutions both practical and just.

When the issue of expropriation was raised to help the landless peasants, only the lands of disloyal magnates were confiscated. Much later, when the state had to care for its unemployed, it made sure that work was performed for the money received. And when the classes got to quarreling seriously, Cleisthenes put them together into artificial units, obliging them to settle their disputes safely and sanely by reasoned discussion at the local level before these created a national crisis.

Meanwhile an important concept had been slowly developing out of circumstances peculiar to the politics of Athens, one that would follow a tortuous trail to distant magnificence. This was the odd, because unofficial, role of the prostates, or first man of the state. When, and to whom the term was earliest applied, is not definitely known. It is a good guess that the word was first used in the years following the tyranny when the Athenian populace, habituated to one-man rule and a single source of authority, groped for an expression to apply to the new man at the top who had replaced the exiled Pisistratids. Such an idea was rendered easy and natural because the tyranny itself had been unofficial. Pisistratus and his sons had permitted the time-honored elective offices to remain, had directed that archons be chosen regularly, as before. The catch was that the tyrants had power and wealth enough to coerce the archons, if necessary. So now the tyranny was gone, and the very word "tyrant" fell into disfavor. No discreet statesman would admit to such again. Well, somebody still had the power; and at this juncture, the "somebody" would be Cleisthenes. So he insists he is not a tyrant? All right, let's just call him our outstanding man, our prostates.

Another factor contributing to the prostates concept was the fragmentation of power among so many offices, and the single-year limitation on tenure of many offices, barring immediate reelection. Under such a system the officers of the state were so numerous, and so rapidly changing, that the average citizen was bound to be confused. To whom could he turn, if his need were desperate? Since officials were so hesitant, constrained, and transitory, his best bet would be the man most respected in the Assembly, the Ekklesia, where the essential public business was done—the person whose measures were most likely to pass.

The first man discernible on these nebulous heights was undoubtedly Cleisthenes, and after his death, Xanthippus.[4] At one time Aristides seemed to be replacing Xanthippus, until Themistocles snatched the prize by arranging so that both were ostracized. Thus far, all these statesmen, as prostatai, had also held the archonship at one time or another. But in 487, this foundation was knocked out when the archons were deprived of nearly all power. Furthermore, Themistocles' continuance as leader for several years without holding any subsequent office after his term as strategos autocrator in 480, shows that the prostates did not actually need such a power base. And Aristides, when he regained the topmost spot, seemed to draw more support from his universally admired character than from the generalships to which he was annually elected. In this there was much that coincided with the classic ideal of leadership: the patriotic, great-spirited man naturally dominant through superior intellectual and moral force, able almost effortlessly to motivate his nation even without any official post. Very possibly, it was contemplation of this ideal that inspired the Emperor Augustus to mold his position to the same lineaments, perpetuating in Rome and its western descendants a brainchild of the Agora in Athens. Of that, more presently.

Scant need to wait for Roman examples, however. It is indeed ironical that Aristides, who did so much to ennoble the image of the prostates, should have paved the way for Athens' own brand of imperialism. And ironically again, he was successful because he had intended nothing of the sort. The Delian Confederacy was principally his creation, certainly more his than anyone else's. Many, if not most, members had come in because they trusted him to make assessments and administer them fairly, because they had confidence in Aristides when they had none in Themistocles, whose imperialistic aims were obvious to all. Aristides had dealt honestly, irreproachably, with them during the years of his leadership. When he left the scene without having coerced any, the Confederacy was so well established that Athens was able to restrain all who showed signs of leaving. Moreover, she had a legal right to do so.

Without the Delian foundation, the full tide of Athenian democracy under Pericles and Ephialtes would not have been possible. Their era is memorable for the first welfare system known to history; the first time any nation ever undertook on a comprehensive scale to pay its citizens for services rendered to the state. This was financed at least in part from Delian funds. But there is more, on the political side. It was under the radical democrats that all the offices were opened to the entire citizenry, to the zeugites and probably also the thetes, the two lowest classes. One would like to know the arguments advanced in support of a move that overstepped the principles of Solon and Cleisthenes. If government should be considered a science, as their actions implied, this would be difficult to justify. Did the radicals contend that the lowest classes were now better equipped by education and/or experience to hold the highest offices, or simply that to deny them would be "undemocratic"? Yet without emolument few zeugites and no thetes could have afforded to run for office. Probably not many were elected, in view of the ancillary expenses of campaigning and entertaining. Still, the radicals had finished by taking the longest step possible toward bringing liberty into balance with law. In terms of opportunity, at least, all Athenians now had an even chance at the offices.

Was the young Pericles conscious of these problems when, as a political fledgling, he stood at Ephialtes' side to endorse the radical reforms? Almost certainly he was, because earlier than most, he understood that politics was at its base a matter of economics. He may even have used the latter word in a literal sense, for it too is Greek in origin, coming from *oecus,* or more properly *oikos* ("house") and *nomikos* ("ordering"). Conceiving of the state as a vast aggregate of households, or one gigantic household, figuratively, to order or arrange for the prosperity of all, was an equally colossal task. Solon had taken note of the problem when setting up his four classes. He had taught his fellow

Athenians too that they must compensate for their underproductive soil by greater productivity of brains and body—one of Athens' most important legacies to mankind. He expected that with the blessings of freedom the classes could work out their own salvation on a laissez-faire basis. Solon had made one slight miscalculation. Athens' economy, though slowly strengthening, was not yet hardy enough to stand freely on its feet.

Help for the weaker elements was a necessity, and Pisistratus made this his springboard to power. Once in control, he addressed himself to economics as soundly and scientifically as a modern efficiency expert. Justifiably, his prime attention went to the small peasants, who received from him land, tools, loans, and sometimes even exemption from taxes to spur their lagging production. But very soon Pisistratus was delighting the merchants by building ships, establishing trade depots overseas, cultivating his brother tyrants in the hope of favorable markets, and one suspects, providing bounties for struggling industries—as evidenced by the mushrooming of family workshops throughout Attica. The Eupatrid landowners did not need his assistance, but even they were assured there would be no confiscations and no interference with their estates as long as they attended to their affairs and did not leave Attica. Under the steady, skilled hand of the gentle tyrant, all received an incentive to produce to the maximum, and possibly—almost unbelievably in barren Attica—one saw for the first time the miracle of supply balancing demand.

This was the general pattern which persisted into Pericles' day, nearly a century later. Attica had become a mosaic of small farms amid the remaining large estates, with an economy in which urban-dwelling citizens could be part-time agriculturists, growing much of their own food, supplementing normal income. Productivity thus remained high, especially if the citizen also had a shop in town where members of the family pooled their skills in making a particular article. Many citizens and many more metics were so employed, getting the most out of slender resources at home, and when they could, trading abroad for the raw materials they lacked. Athens provided a shining example for the world, of a state that could make both ends meet without abundant means.

The chief economic perplexity of Pericles' epoch revolved around the tremendous increase in population, which by the middle of the fifth century had reached an estimated total of 315,000.[5] What it had been a hundred years previously no authority has ventured to surmise, but before Pisistratus Athens had been a relatively small place. The celebrated tyrant, who induced so many back to the farm, also created economic opportunities that drew even more to the city, so that for the first time it deserved the name of metropolis (in the modern sense; in the Greek sense, of course, any city that had colonies could be called a metropolis). This was so true that Pisistratus had been accused of subordinating the country to the city, of holding that "whatever was good for Athens was good for Attica."[6]

A swelling population was the predictable result. Success usually means a rising standard of living, a high birth rate, also a wider flow of immigration.

As the center of the Confederacy, Athens came to have a good many Ionians from Asia and the islands as rather steady residents. The influx created additional jobs, particularly in the jury courts, and it was only right that the Confederates should pay the costs of their judicial business. To that extent, everyone concedes, Pericles was entirely justified in tapping their funds. But an expanding population pressured him onward; with Athens performing so many services for the outlanders, it was difficult to draw a fast line, or to hew to a line when drawn.

Toward the metics and transients Pericles had few obligations, but with more citizens than ever living in depleted Attica, it was a staggering proposition to keep all able bodies and minds productive, bringing supply to the level of an accelerated demand. Somehow it had to be done. Other states might ignore the poor, the landless, the unemployed, and leave them to make shift or die, but Athens could not do so. Her thetes had enough votes in the Assembly to make themselves felt and had proved their value as rowers in Athens' all-important navy. Since they lacked the wherewithal to support themselves on campaigns, pay for military and naval duty became a necessity. But Pericles could not stop there. These were also the people who, possessing neither shops nor lands, were employed irregularly if at all. In any economic abnormality they were the first to suffer, curiously, in good times as well as bad. If all were quiet in the Confederacy, not as many men would be needed on expeditions. Without lands to cultivate or trades to ply, Athens' thetes would be lolling in the Agora or wandering about the dockyards of Piraeus, getting hungrier and angrier. Radicals to a man, if something were not done for them they were sure to blame the leadership.

So it was up to Pericles to provide payment for other services, for juries and public works, if military service were not forthcoming. Actually, he had little choice, and since the revenues of the city were not sufficient, his only recourse was to use the Confederacy's funds.[7] On this ground there was an obvious pragmatic justification. Whether Pericles can be justified absolutely, morally, for applying Delian funds to purposes not specified in the foundation treaty is a more complicated question. Many, though not all of those purposes would benefit the allies, directly or indirectly. They used the jury courts, they attended the Panathenaea, and they might worship in the beautiful new temples. Some might even obtain theater tickets and hear the majestic periods of Aeschylus chanted to the skies. But it is useless to pretend that the Confederates would have voted all of this of their own free will, to embellish a city which comparatively few of them would ever visit. Disapproval would have been almost universal.

If there is to be moral justification, then it must rest on another basis. Probably the best excuse is the case that Pericles pled for full employment. Surprisingly, he reveals himself as something of an economic theorist, if one pursues the implications of his argument in favor of utilizing all the human resources of Attica in the manner best suited to individual abilities.[8] The positively certain result would have been a wider distribution of wealth to accompany the increased production, and a renewed stimulus to demand—the creation of wants largely to be satisfied through increased trade with the Delian allies, since Attica itself could supply so little. We are not told specifically that Pericles carried the argument to its logical conclusion, but since it is so elementary and obvious, is not one safe in assuming that he did? The silent acquiescence of the Delian community is at least presumptive evidence. Significantly, the only ones to denounce Pericles' policy as immoral were those belonging to the distinct minority of oligarchs and aristocrats who needed no aid, those who had little to gain economically and who stood to lose politically by his actions. From the democratic majority among the Delians, we do not hear of any protests.

If this were the case, the aspect of supply is easier to explain. The Ionians overseas had vigorous industries and agriculture, with no lack of vessels to transport their products. Athens also had plenty of ships, merchant as well as naval, and an economy complementing that of Ionia. The metropolis constituted the greatest single source of demand, and her coins were the most sought after in the Hellenic world. Hence she furnished a ready market for the high-quality goods of Ionians abroad: the fine cloth of Miletus, the marble of Paros, the select wines of Samos, Lesbos, and Chios. And of course, wheat (little grown in Attica) came from many of the outlying Greek areas: from Lesbos and Naxos, but principally from Cyprus and the Hellespont, as well as lands beyond the rim of Hellas.

On the other hand, Athens' exports, except for her pottery and objets d'art, were not quality products.[9] Attica's wines and olive oil varied in worth; likewise, her woollens were coarse and heavy. But after home demand had been saturated—by the lowest classes, naturally—there was enough left for considerable shipment overseas. These cheaply priced items could be conveyed in bulk at small expense by shippers who expected to make their main profit from carrying quality goods on the return journey, and it speaks well for Athenian ingenuity that Athens' sea captains found ports where they could dump their cargoes advantageously, securing their margin from the quantities sold. Through a felicitous exchange, always arranged in terms of Athens' currency, supply was brought into near balance with the city's enormous demand—no mean feat for her democratic administrators and their great chieftain.

In maintaining the cordial relations necessary for such an interchange, Pericles' skills as a diplomat—not the least of his aptitudes—were undeniably valuable. Like most of his predecessors, he took care that Athens lost no friendships which were essential, and that she kept her lines of communication open with all. In this Athens could claim to be ahead of most Hellenic states, though not too far ahead. All Greeks prided themselves on their arts of persuasion, their ability to outtalk an opponent, even to conciliate him while gaining the essential point. Yet Athenian diplomacy too had the classic touch. There was a general recognition that, whatever one's secret objectives, successful negotiations could rest only on a basis of common courtesy and respect for human dignity (the dignity of fellow Hellenes, that is!), on the assumption of a reasonable quid pro quo for the contracting parties, and that all engagements would be honorably kept.

The Greeks did not invent diplomacy, but here too is a word that is Greek in origin, deriving from the double-folded sheets of papyrus or parchment that were first used as ambassadors' passports. The Hellenic states were in the habit of sending *presbeis* ("envoys") or *kerukes* ("heralds") to one another from an early period, though their use was by custom confined to special occasions. For diplomatic relations of a permanent nature they preferred to employ some trustworthy citizen of the responding state, usually a man of wide prestige in his home community, to whom the title of "friend" was given. Thus Athens' representative at Corinth or Argos, for instance, would be a locally prominent Corinthian or Argive who held the honorary title of "official friend of the Athenian people." This was not a salaried position, but was commonly occupied by persons whose commercial interests were served through a continuing friendship. We do know that the posts were highly prized, conferring a signal honor on the holder. And there were many occasions when the fortuitous intervention of the official "friend" *(proxenos)* was able to prevent an outbreak of war between contending nations.[10] In straightening out the jealous and quarrelsome Greeks, the arts of diplomacy were a healing of peace.

The value of these friends to Athens had been attested before the fifth century. One reason she had found it so hard to get rid of her tyrants was that Pisistratus had cultivated good relations with everybody, including states like Sparta that were not normally friendly to tyrants. As a result, the Spartans had been unusually reluctant to intervene against Hippias, and it had required constant prodding from the Delphi oracle to secure his expulsion. Furthermore, the oracle's friendly assistance was doubtless based on influence exercised there by the Alcmaeonids, who on this occasion maneuvered with greater finesse than the Pisistratids. Ingenious Athenians were among the first to demonstrate that even gods were not immune to flattery—and money.

Afterward Cleisthenes had gone beyond the bounds of Hellas, and negotiated with the Great King—who was the closest thing to a god on earth at the time—only to discover how dangerous it was to play with heavenly fire. He needed Persian help to counter the wrath of Sparta, but the King's price was too high, and his ire worse than Lacedaemon's. In the events that followed, the Athenians acted with less than customary discretion, and their narrow escape reminded them of the value of polite behavior. So when setting up their own Delian organization, Athenians were gratified that Aristides was the very soul of tact and kindly consideration toward the allies, though one feels he would have acted nobly without any lessons.

In this area none was more expert than Pericles himself. In his attitude toward the Samian War he was a model of decorum, allowing participants a wide freedom to work out their quarrel, avoiding Athenian involvement until one disputant grew unreasonable. None would say the Athenians were harsh masters if he could help it, or speak of masters at all. In such matters he preferred to insinuate, move in obscurity, and attain his ends while outsiders were still guessing what these were.

It was the same in his relationships with Athens' equals. Some might suspect that his proposal to restore the temples was more than an act of disinterested piety, but they could not prove it, nor even predict with any assurance just what his aims were. Even had they known, the knowledge would not have done them much good; there was scarcely any way to forestall this impassive masker of moves. Urbane and confident, he invited delegates from the sister states to Athens to discuss the shrines. Without any appearance of pressure or ulterior motive, but simply through civility and force of reason, he sent them home favorably impressed with Athenian democracy and convinced of Athens' destiny.

Pericles seemed as inexorable as the turning of the seasons, and as unobtrusive. His handling of Lacedaemon is a case in point. Whether it was undercover bribery of a vulnerable Spartan king to withdraw his army from Attica, or his unaffected goodwill toward a stronger member of royalty, by which he subtly influenced that monarch in Athens' behalf, Pericles achieved his goals.[11] It was alleged that he regularly suborned officials at Sparta; indisputably, by one method or another, he used economic pressure to influence policy among Athens' neighbors. By tactful but ceaseless probing, he always found a way.

But Pericles was also wise enough to realize that the best diplomacy was one founded on principles which were intrinsic to Greek civilization: that of an Athens made strong by the devotion, discipline, and sacrifice of her citizens, of a city so exalted by political, military, and cultural attainments that Greeks elsewhere envied, admired, and were consciously or unconsciously eager to serve her. Hellenes loyal to other states, even adversary states, would be hesitant and half-hearted in their opposition to Athens, willing to fight her only when they had overwhelming odds (as at Coronea), and conversely, ready to cave in whenever events developed in Athens' favor. Under such circumstances it would be easy for Pericles to find sympathizers in every important city, partisans who would espouse his cause and report to him even without pay or prompting.

For diplomacy was, and is, the art of human relations on a grand scale. Pericles understood perfectly that the small states and many of the small people would defer to Athens simply because she was great, strong, and admired. The Greeks' vaunted individualism might brake the trend somewhat, but could not entirely stop it. Basic human nature, at the last, asserts itself. Places, no less than persons, have their charisma, and when the two coincide, creating unmistakable omens for success, the compulsion to follow becomes almost irresistible. Everyone adores a winner, particularly a magnanimous one.

Among Athens' many gifts to posterity, none stands out more vividly in the minds of latter day devotees than the legacy of democracy. Traditionally, its development has been ascribed to the indigenous self-reliance and multifarious experience of a people toughened by the constant struggle to overcome their harsh environment. Although the Athenians became proudly conscious of such distinction in due course, their "democracy" was at first a natural, undeliberate growth, dictated by circumstance. In common with other primitive Indo-Europeans, all the Greeks had possessed their tribal assemblies, where every free male had some right of expression while he remained an able-bodied fighter. But the tribal assemblies had faded badly when the Greeks passed from wandering herdsmen to settled, agricultural life, and the unspecialized warrior afoot gave way to the noble on horseback, or fighting in chariot. The equity of the primitives was lost.

What brought the assemblies back, at Athens and elsewhere, was the emergence of a middle class making enough money from commerce to purchase weapons and armor, whereby its members became components of a massed infantry formation able to overcome aristocratic cavalry that was not as well coordinated. The process was not unlike that which developed on a more complex scale in seventeenth century Europe, and in both cases the result was a widened participation in governments that could not yet be called democratic, but with oligarchies tending steadily in that direction. At Athens, these forces found satisfactory outlet in the reforms of Solon.

In the march of Athenian democracy, some elements may have been fortuitous. Cleisthenes is said to have extended the franchise in an effort to outbid a rival for public affection,[12] and Pisistratus' redistribution of land to the destitute was obviously in a line with his own political ambitions. However, such actions were but catalyzers to a movement already under way. In the expanding state that was Athens, the dissatisfied would have found a means to their ends in some fashion. The statesmen who accommodated them did so because they well understood that such a reservoir of discontent, if long dammed up, might overwhelm them.

Other features were unique to the Greek historical experience. The miracle of Marathon, and the even greater one at Salamis ten years later, gave Athenians an increased awareness of their own worth; a conviction that having come through such trials, they, as a people, must be in some degree superior, possessing a competence well nigh universal.[13] This sentiment is reflected in the opening of all civic offices except the very highest to the entire citizenry through the device of sortition (lot), which the Greeks considered a more democratic process than election. The rest of the Hellenes, those who had resisted the invader, must have felt and acted in like manner. The crucible of the Persian Wars may thus have been the most important force shaping democracy among the Greeks as a whole. Liberty meant more to them than it ever had, since such exertion had been needed to defend it. Beyond this, the memory that they had been part of a glowing victory against formidable opponents, and even more formidable odds, gave them a fellow feeling which was a strong, if subconscious, impetus to democracy. It did not make the Hellenes a single nation, but it brought them closer together than ever before.

In Athens, this spirit is instantly recognized in the euphoric era that prevailed after her arms had liberated Ionia, to everyone's benefit. This was the period of the "mixed constitution," of the joint leadership of the aristocrat Cimon with the democrat Aristides, when nobles of the Areopagus were able to regain a portion of their past power through a judicious wooing of the commons. The friendship that everyone perceived in their leaders was echoed over the state. The gain to Athens' civic health was immediately manifest, and in large measure the gain was permanent. Despite political antagonisms that arose with Ephialtes a generation later, social distinctions were finally minimized. That is not to say that these were extinguished, nor was a classless society in prospect. But henceforth Athenians of the highest class would associate with those of the lowest, or even with noncitizens and slaves, whenever they found them to be congenial spirits.

Formerly, before the fifth century, relationships between freeman and slave must have been confined to the individual household, while those between citizen and metic would have been no stronger than the necessities of business dictated. But by the mid-fifth century we see Pericles, the aristocratic democrat, picking men from the lowest class as his lieutenants, while still later Socrates and his socialite friends are discovered hobnobbing with the metic Cephalos, who throws open his home for their philosophical discussions. Ability and understanding, rather than birth or wealth, are recognized as the true tests of acceptance.

Herein lies the lasting significance of Athens' democracy for the modern world. To gain approval, one had to prove himself. Athens might look past this principle, in the flood tide of her Delian imperialism, envisioning a more complete equality to please the rowers of her preponderant navy, but in the end she came back to it. Pericles held sway by dint of a personal capacity acknowledged by his countrymen.[14] Athens would have leaders who might be considered more democratic than he, but if their acumen were not equal to the occasion they did not stay long at the top. However, the right to try, and the opportunity to demonstrate one's worth should be open to all.

Here the surge of democracy broke against a rather firm shore. Some problems were too imposing, some matters too grave and consequential to be turned over to the untested potentialities of the average Athenian. It is noteworthy that not a person among them, not even the most ardent democrat, is on record as suggesting that the generalships should be determined by lot. They did not carry democracy as far as did Andrew Jackson, who is reported to have said that there was no public office beyond the capabilities of the ordinary citizen. It is true that some of their elected strategoi did not perform well, and some would be utter disasters, but when affairs of great moment were at hand, responsibility was entrusted to a Themistocles, a Cimon, a Pericles, if such were available. To militant leftists, recurrent choice of the same men might seem a backward step, a step away from *isonomia,* political equality. But much as they shouted equality, they never lost sight of its limitations. As evidenced by their practice, Athenians knew where the line had to be drawn.

In exploring this area, it was easier to decide "where" than to penetrate the depths of "why." Actually, most Athenian democrats would not care to sound such depths, to explain why they preferred a Pericles to a Tolmides, apart from saying that one was obviously more reliable than the other. To dig deeper into the topic of Pericles' excellence must uncover subjects they were loath to analyze: heredity, character, education. For to admit that these had a bearing on the situation was to take unwitting steps toward that other camp so close to them, and to admit that there was a case for aristocracy after all. To Greeks growing more assured of an innate superiority, to cross over was always a temptation and a danger. Only economic status, fellow feeling, and their love of freedom confirmed them as egalitarians.

To dyed-in-the-wool democrats, it must have been extremely distasteful to contemplate how many of their leaders had been nobles, and how many of these had been members of a single dominant family. What had qualified them so highly? Ancient Athenians knew nothing about genes, of course, but the same argument was present in a different form. Was the success of the Alcmaeonids and their ilk owing to their boasted descent from the gods?—something which ordinary demos could not claim. The poets, and particularly Pindar, had told them ceaselessly that it was so. To hardheaded radicals this might be a good reason for agnosticism, but not to the credulous public. Religion's hold was strong, and its force was clearly on the side of the old order. Just as clearly, the issue of heredity was a bad one for the democrats.

Nor could they gain much comfort from a consideration of character and education. That the one was largely formed by the other had been asserted by Greek teachers long before Protagoras. Here was an explanation more acceptable to the man in the street, though on closer inspection it did not really allow him much. Since tuition was private, each person received only what his parents could afford. Unless the family were fairly well-off, most citizens would not get beyond the rudiments of reading and writing. If they did go farther, much of what they learned would be either unsuitable or repugnant to their class interest.

There was no getting around it; Greek education proceeded from an aristocratic base that presupposed money and breeding along with brains. It had been founded primarily upon Homer, who had made plain that it was the special preserve of princes like Achilles, carefully tutored by Chiron and Phoinix. Actually, since its original purpose was to inculcate areté, manly excellence in war, plowmen and craftsmen had little to gain. Their cause brightened a bit after the lore of Homer had been supplemented by that of Hesiod; virtue, to him, was labor rather than fighting, but his outlook on life was fundamentally as conservative as Homer's.[15] No basic quarrel existed between them.

Nor did the younger versifiers noticeably alter the perspective when their opinions seeped into the instruction offered by various private schoolmasters. Tyrtaeus and Theognis, Alcaeus and Sappho, sang powerfully, beautifully, memorably, but all were upper class by birth or adoption. The only one out of step was Archilochus of Paros, the son of a slave mother, who sometimes inveighed against the master class, but his basic philosophy was simply to accept ill-fortune with good, and resolve to ride out the storm. There was scant consolation for democrats here.

Consequently, of all the poets whose works had crept into the schools since that practically deified original pair, there was only one whom Athenians below the Eupatrid level would find completely satisfactory, both because of the breadth of his views and because he happened to be their fellow countryman: the man already famous as their great emancipator. Feeling the urge for self-expression, Solon never hesitated to array his thoughts in verse since the days when, as a comparative unknown, he exhorted his compatriots not to give up the struggle with Megara over Salamis. Having acquired the poetic habit, he registered his opinions on every topic concerning life at Athens, on patriotism, politics, economics, or the wisdom that brings happiness. Whatever Solon said was so appropriate, so reasonable and helpful that Athenians down the centuries were forever repeating the maxims attributed to him, such as "Nothing too much," "Know thyself," "Virtue cannot be stolen," "Justice is slow but sure." In the instruction at Athens, Solon's influence must finally have outweighed that of every other poet save Homer alone. He was the first Athenian to contribute notably to the forming of the Greek intellect.[16] Athens always remembered the fact with pride and gratitude.

Not for several decades would native Athenian talent be able to advance the cause again. In the generations after Solon, distinguished visitors like Anacreon and Simonides would linger awhile in the city, leaving praiseworthy verse, and in these same years tragic drama was receiving its first impetus from the glittering Pisistratean court. But such creativity was only a promise, in part because of the slow development of the still low level of education, barely above the primary. Athens was fortunate in that Anaxagoras chose to settle there, and itinerant Sophists like Protagoras were often in town. Eventually, Athens would become the great university city of the ancient world, with regular schools of rhetoric, philosophy, and law for those who wanted advanced or professional training, but as yet nothing existed except infrequent classes offered by visiting savants, or even less formal discussions and conversations when adulators flocked around.

If Athens were to make a distinctive contribution to the field of letters, that most fitting was the tragic drama, her own indigenous art form embracing the entire life of the city. After obscure beginnings it leapt to first magnitude in the hands of Aeschylus, whose grandiose, power-packed diction was equally effective in relating the acts of gods or heroic men. The classic author most often compared with Milton, and sometimes with Shakespeare, his language became a model of the schools of rhetoric.

Actually, there were good reasons why the philosophers as well as the rhetoricians should pay respectful heed to Aeschylus. He had dared, before anyone else, to make a critical reappraisal of the old religious myths and legends on the basis of natural cause and effect.[17] Not that he doubted the gods. His faith was as strong as Hesiod's, but more consistently than Hesiod he viewed the gods as civilized, rational beings who must use their supernatural powers in a just, humane way. His Athena of the *Eumenides* is always judicious and conscientious in the citizens' behalf, a far cry from Homer's virago warrior who exulted over Odysseus' deceits and savagery. Similarly, Aeschylus' Apollo is protective and compassionate (except to the murderess Clytemnestra), unhesitantingly responsible, professing to do the will of Zeus the All-Wise.

Sophocles is said to have caused Aeschylus' withdrawal from Athens by defeating him in a dramatic competition. If so, he won through a close study and eventual improvement on the elder master's strongest points. Aeschylus pulled his plots together through clever manipulation of his dialogues, raised to equal importance with the choruses; Sophocles made these longer yet, and provided tighter interrelation of chorus and episode. The older playwright had introduced a second actor on the stage to give his colloquies increased interest and animation; the younger one added a third actor, supplying "more of the same." Aeschylus had made his actors plausible counterparts of the persons represented, more than mere spokesmen of lines; Sophocles aimed to make his even more realistic, so that each would stand forth with traits individual and believable, establishing contact with the experience of the spectators. To this end, he abandoned the magniloquent speech of his predecessor, and strove for a simple, conversational style adapted to the person speaking.

Desiring to make his plots and persons as accessible as he could, Sophocles gave deeper attention to character than any before had done. In so doing, he developed the idea of the tragic hero, of a person whose qualities should be great and good so as to command the admiration of the audience, but rendered credibly human by a single flaw which under extraordinary conditions outweighs the virtues and creates tragedy, exciting the spectators' sympathy. His Antigone is such a person—a girl fearless, proud, determined, noble, but tactless and uncompromising in her quest of decent burial for her brother, conduct which leads to catastrophe. Yet throughout, she is true to the exalted idea that motivates her, the ideal imposed by conscience.

The primacy of ideas and the ideal is at all times visible in Sophocles, and quite significantly so. It is not only that he packs his plays with powerful truths, such as the superiority of universal moral law to the merely political, or that collective wisdom is safer than one man's outlook. In his supremely organized dramas, the central ideas are reflected in the personal attributes of the chief characters. They are heroes and heroines precisely because of this ideal side to their natures, conveying a nobility which compels admiration, but which also connects with the tragic flaw in each of them, simply by turning virtue into its opposite through an excess of the quality, so that the strong and weak aspects of character are convincingly united in a realistic, organic whole.[18] It is a simple but effective technique, often used, showing how well aware Sophocles was of Solon's "Nothing too much!" An Athenian saying that Athenians had good reason to remember.

But it must not be thought that Sophocles, among the poets, had a corner on the ideal. The same process can be discerned in Aeschylus' dramas, if somewhat less clearly. Agamemnon, for all his faults, returns to Argos as a benevolent father to his family and people, trying to appear modest in victory, intending a kind and moderate rule for his subjects. Pindar's odes repeatedly embodied the ideal. Among the artists, Phidias, Myron, Polygnotus, and many another exemplified it.

In reality, Greece of the fifth century was alive with ideas, and Athens was its very center. A man of able and open mind positioned there would find himself literally bombarded. Historically, the upsurge of idealism received its strongest impetus from the triumph over Persia; from the joy, the sense of dignity and self-esteem that accrued to the victors. It was the inferential base of Herodotus' explanation for the Greek success: the Hellenes knew what they were doing, they acted on the principles of reason and self-control, they were willing to sacrifice for the ideal of freedom—all in remarkable contrast (he thought) to the Persians. Idealism was certainly the principle upon which the Delian structure was founded; it explains why both the Athenians and their Delian comrades preferred Aristides to Themistocles in the long run. And, one is tempted to add, why they liked Cimon better than his father, Miltiades. Also perhaps, why they never failed to rally around Pericles, in any extremity, though many men in Athens were personally more popular than he. At the end, one remembers that Pericles had had the climactic phase of his education under the proto-Idealist, Anaxagoras.[19]

It would be generations before the most meaningful elements of Greece's, and more particularly Athens', experience would be distilled into a systematic philosophy of Idealism, to form the heart of the classical tradition, the distinctive civilization which antiquity bequeathed to the western world. The notion that ideas themselves are basic reality, *the* basic reality, has a long ancestry reaching back through Plato and Socrates to Anaxagoras, almost to Anaximander and his "Endless." Indeed, it lurks silently behind most of the materialists' explanations of the universe. Given the Greeks' view of nature as a harmonious whole, how could thinking men make a positive denial? Hard-headed materialists would want to stop there, but for those mystically or poetically inclined, the Platonic thesis that ideas have an existence of their own in an ideal, perfect world transcending the physical, where they attract and lift man by the beauty of their perfection, was a natural culmination.

This is at once recognized as an optimistic creed, and a triumphant climax to the educated Greek's ruminations about his universe. All who accepted it, consciously or unconsciously, had to assume that essential wisdom came to them from above. This became very significant in the development of the classical tradition, confirming its aristocratic orientation. In their willingness and their capability to realize the ideal within themselves, or to identify with the ideas above, people were manifestly unequal, implying a selectivity of the best. "Aboveness" had to lead to an aristocracy of some sort. For if idealism lay at the base of Herodotus' theory of success, it was also the foundation of Pindar's. Not everyone might agree with the celebrated lyricist in his conviction that the well-born were the strongest and most intelligent, but none could deny that the strong and the intelligent were well born. Some emendation was overdue in Pindar's view of mankind, but he could smile as he counted the many highborn Athenians, some of them his friends, who had made Athens' democracy a qualified success. On that ground the twain could meet. Considerations of class paled and disappeared in the presence of proven ability. Government by the people cannot be faulted when the right people are elected to govern.

The effects of such thinking on those coming after are easy to trace. In their Italian peninsula, the Romans had always been impressed by Hellenic neighbors whose social graces and acquaintance with the arts so vastly exceeded their own. As the Romans rose to power and wealth, those who were appreciative hired Greek tutors for their children, and in time sent them directly to Hellas, usually to Athens, to finish their education at one of the famed schools of philosophy. Those sent were in almost all cases patrician youths from Rome's best families, and what they heard in Athens was mostly congenial to their point of view. Aristocracy was firmly entrenched at Plato's Academy and Aristotle's Lyceum, only a little less so among the Epicureans. It is true that the Cynics, and later, the Stoics, opined that fundamentally men were pretty much alike, but neither group was deeply interested in politics or inclined to draw out the social implications of their beliefs.

Though the Romans inherited the Greek aristocratic tradition in education and the arts, much of what they knew about democratic theory and practice is also traceable to Greece. Sometimes the two currents became mixed. A good example is the highest Roman office of all, that of emperor, or *princeps* ("first citizen") as Augustus preferred to call himself. In creating the post he seems to have borrowed a concept of his mentor, Cicero, who advocated strengthening Rome's sagging republic through military backing of an unofficial strong man able to hold the balance between the Senate and the people. Cicero does not tell us how he came by the idea, but he studied in Athens at the Academy, and was a lifelong admirer of Greek civilization. Was he remembering the prostates' role in fifth-century Athens? Augustus did not act much like Pericles—but he appears to have made use of the idea. After the power-hoarding egoism of Julius Caesar, Augustus seems to be reassuring the nervous, apprehensive senators by saying, "That's not my notion, I see myself as more of a Pericles." Reading his "official" autobiography, the *Res Gestae,* one gets this feeling from phrases such as "I had no more power than my colleagues, I excelled them only in prestige." Then Augustus recounts his many acts of generosity, the great building projects such as the Temple of Mars and the Theater of Marcellus, while the reader visualizes images of the Parthenon and the Odeum, and glimpses an Augustus striving to make Rome's Golden Age a grander vision of Athens'.

Augustus and succeeding emperors became generally more autocratic, but there is little doubt that the founder of the Roman Empire wished for an image like that of the great Athenian, and that he considered himself both the representative and protector of the common people. The best of the later emperors, such as Hadrian and Marcus Aurelius (both of whom were ardent Hellenophiles) thought and acted similarly.

Since the Romans, the aristocratic side of Hellenism has several times reasserted itself in western civilization. During the early and central Middle Ages, the chief influence on Christian theology and education was that of the very genteel Plato, whose magisterial views were a boon to the authority of the church. Even when the rediscovery of Aristotle in the thirteenth century and the deepening effects of Aristotelianism subjected church authority to searching examination and logical analysis, the fundamental emphasis was not changed. The selective discipline of the ancient Athenian schools obtained new laurels when the works of Athens' two great Idealist philosophers stimulated the rising universities of medieval Europe to their crowning intellectual accomplishments.

The Renaissance of the fifteenth and sixteenth centuries saw a return of classicism that was much more thoroughgoing, so complete that in some parts of western Europe Christianity was eclipsed or ignored. Not merely the ancient philosophers, but ancient literature and art came once again to the fore, inculcating a humanism that was frankly secular and pagan, one which recalled attention to the beauties and truths of the present world rather than to the misty values of the hereafter. Such sentiments were widespread even within the church. Popes and cardinals vied with dukes and kings as connoisseurs of the antique, priding themselves also on their openmindedness in matters religious. For the "well-rounded men of the Renaissance," an education in the Greek poets and historians was as important as knowledge of the philosophers, and they were more inclined to pattern their conduct on that of a Caesar or an Alexander than on any of the familiar Christian types. The "cult of the great man" replaced that of the saint and anchorite.

The eighteenth century witnessed yet another renewal of the classic impulse, though proceeding from different motives. This was the period when the buildup of inductive science since Bacon's day reached an early apex and synthesis in the laws of Newton. In this "Age of Reason," those who cherished the new science looked back with reverence to the Greeks, who had first seen and proclaimed a rational order in the universe. Though the thinking of those ancients had been mainly deductive, nevertheless they had pointed the way, made the later achievements possible, and in doing so had given dignity to man. In keeping with this reverence, eighteenth century literature, art, and music reflected the clarity, balance, logical construction, and intellectualism of classical models. Alexander Pope's *Essay on Man,* a philosophical treatise in the guise of a poem, which attempts to demonstrate that man and the world have developed in the most rational, and the only possible way, is typical of the ebullient classicism of the age.

Naturally, such a state of affairs presumes an aristocratic continuance. Only the educated elite would be interested in pronouncements such as Pope's, or capable of understanding them. Education, which had been increasingly classical since the Middle Ages became, if anything, more intensely so. Young English gentlemen, and those wealthy enough elsewhere, formed the habit of topping off their university learning with a grand tour of the cultural centers of the continent, which took them to France, Germany, then eventually to Italy and the remains of ancient Rome—though few of them got as far as Greece, which was still subject to the hostile Turk. The scientific as well as the humanistic spirit now insisted that they should check their knowledge by going directly to the sources. This trend of thought and practice, only lightly shaken by the Age of Revolutions, has persisted until our day.

This is all very well, a restless reader may respond, but what about the other side? Are we not forgetting that Greece and Athens stand first of all for democracy? Cannot as good a case be made in this direction? And of course, the answer is yes. Always bearing in mind that Greek democracy was different from the modern form, yet the Athenian experience was deeply meaningful, and its impact was immediate.

Whether or not one accepts the tradition according to Livy, that Rome in the earliest days of her republic sent a commission to Athens to study the Athenian laws as a model for her own Twelve Tables (the tradition is highly dubious; Rome's Twelve Tables are more akin to the laws of Draco than to Athens' later, democratic legislation), it is obvious that educated Roman statesmen, on the left as well as the right, knew about the Athenian accomplishment, and utilized the ideas. While not a carbon copy, Rome's Servian constitution bears too close a resemblance to the legislation of Solon, especially to his four classes, for it to be entirely coincidental. Measures taken a little later by the Romans are curiously reminiscent of Cleisthenes' democratization of the Assembly and his mixing of High and Low. Certainly the reforms of Caesar and the Gracchi betray familiarity with the welfare schemes of Pericles. And as already observed, the institution of the emperor probably owed something to Athenian democracy.

During the Middle Ages, elements of Greek democracy went into the making of Christianity—a factor often overlooked because Christianity was democratic before it was Greek, and only afterward did it take on aristocratic and authoritarian characteristics. From its earliest period in Judea, Christianity had been open to all upon profession of belief and moral rebirth, but it was left to Christianized Greeks to complement this principle in church government. Because of them, decisions were made, doctrines were adopted, and officers elected by majority vote of ecumenical councils and ecclesiastical assemblies—significantly, both adjectives are of Greek origin—the latter one appropriating a word which can be traced to that original Ekklesia in Athens. The will of the majority was for a long period a vital force in the medieval church, dwindling only when the conciliar movement itself retreated before the onrush of papal sovereignty in the late Middle Ages.

Then, for a spell, the Hellenic influence on government was lost to view. Political democracy rose again in western Europe, indeed, was already rising, but at first it had very little to do with classical antecedents. Rather, it sprang directly from the problems of the medieval towns, the struggles of the burghers to escape control by the nobles, and finally, from their ability to wring constitutional rights from the kings through the money they might give or withhold. In this story of gradual success Calvinism had a larger role than Hellenism. Knowledgeable leaders of the people were unquestionably aware of the classical experience, but in their speeches they usually preferred to cite legal precedents from their own nations' past, or to quote scripture instead of Aristotle, Plutarch, or Thucydides. In education and the arts these authors might serve very well, but in politics their resurrection was not yet discernible.

Oddly, it was the Age of Revolutions, and more specifically, the French Revolution, which brought back the democratic side of Hellenism. Odd, because the revolutions ushered in the great era of nineteenth-century romanticism, which with its emphasis on the individual and his emotions, its hailing of private inspiration as superior to standards and rules, and above all, its negation of authority, was considered to be the very antithesis of classicism. But it was only now that the amazing diversity of Greek achievement could be fully appreciated, with a dawning understanding that Greece could mean different things to different men (or to the same man, for that matter), with some of those concepts almost diametrically opposed.

As it happened, nearly everything the romanticists stood for called up illuminating examples from ancient Greece. Romanticism exalted the individual and his right to self-expression. Where could one discover better exponents in all phases of life and art than the Greeks, whose individualism had been both their glory and their destruction? Professing to despise formal education, many romantics gave primacy to nature, and the wisdom to be gained directly from it. Again, the Greeks had sung of earthly beauty and truth, in ode and idyll, before anyone and better than most. Then, if personal inspiration were placed at a premium, who had been inspired to loftier heights than Homer and Aeschylus? Even pagan gods were seen in a mellow light, in an age when Christianity was regarded as corrupt and decadent, a symbol of the old, repressive order.

Naturally, in an Age of Revolutions to overthrow absolute monarchy, what appealed most was that Greece, and especially Athens, had been the home of liberty, producing the first and "purest" democracy the world had known. Also, it was remote enough in time to awaken a certain nostalgia in romantic breasts. By coincidence, a patriotic rising of modern Greeks to gain independence from their Turkish oppressors fired liberal sympathies throughout the West. The combination of circumstances created a fervor for all things Hellenic, one which was unparalleled in modern history. For the first time, ancient Greek became almost as familiar to the literati of Europe as the old standby, Latin.[20]

Romanticists saw nothing inconsistent in this bow to the classics. Shelley was moved by his love of Greece and his love of freedom to compose a play on the subject of Aeschylus' lost *Prometheus Unbound,* and his later drama, *Hellas,* tells a story of Greece's liberation from the Turks which had for its model Aeschylus' *Persae.* Goethe tried his hand at a Greek-style drama that was based on Euripides' treatment of the Iphigenia theme. Keats' greatest delight came from the contemplation of Greek statues and vases. Lord Byron's devotion to both ancient and modern Greece, even led him to raise and equip a regiment at his own expense, and to join the Greek War of Independence, where, at Missolonghi, he finally laid down his life for the cause. So well did the romanticists and their liberal friends popularize the idea of democracy that by the century's end the franchise had been greatly extended in many nations of Europe and America, and a few had granted complete manhood suffrage.

In our own day, literary reliance on the classics has not faded. Twentieth-century authors have made ceaseless use of myth, epic, and drama, even of incidents and characters as aids to strengthen and clarify their own efforts. Repeatedly, in their writing, some instance of classic form or sequence has given needed unity to literary works that might otherwise become a welter of mental images, semiconscious drives, and unrelated impressions. In a world of increasing complexity and confusion, one finds some comfort in hearkening back to the poet who mused

> Many marvels come to be,
> But man is far the best,
> Who lightly masters land and sea,
> Earth from her gods to wrest.[21]

NOTES

1 *Antecedents: Myth and Reality* 1000-600 B.C.

1. J. H. Breasted, *History of Egypt* (New York, 1909), p. 467, who calls them "Ekwesh"; *Cambridge Ancient History,* 3rd ed. (Cambridge, 1975), 2:366.
2. O. Gurney, *The Hittites* (London, 1975), pp. 46-55; *CAH*[3], 2(2):261-4.
3. Herodotus, *History,* Loeb Classical Library (London, 1946), 1. 56-7; for probable identity of the Pelasgians, see J. A. R. Munro, "Pelasgians and Ionians," *Journal of Hellenic Studies* 54 (1934):109-28.
4. C. G. Starr, *The Origins of Greek Civilization* (New York, 1961), p. 121; J. Chadwick, "The Greek Dialects and Greek Pre-History," *Greece and Rome* 3(1955):38-46; *CAH*[2], 3:607.
5. J. L. Myres, *Who Were the Greeks?* (New York, 1967), p. 117; N. G. L. Hammond, *Studies in Greek History* (Oxford, 1973), p. 33.
6. G. Murray, *Rise of the Greek Epic* (Oxford, 1960), pp. 233 ff.; C. Whitman, *Homer and the Heroic Tradition* (Cambridge, Mass., 1948), p. 9, agrees in part.
7. *CAH*[3], 2(2):688; a hint supplied by H. D. F. Kitto, *The Greeks* (Baltimore, 1965), p. 29, is also a possible explanation.
8. F. H. Stubbings, *CAH*[3], 2(1):629.
9. M. Ventris and J. Chadwick, *Documents in Mycenaean Greek* (Cambridge, 1975), pp. 37-48; J. Chadwick, *The Mycenaean World* (Cambridge, 1976), pp. ix-xv, 15-33, 84-99.
10. Homer, *Iliad,* (Chicago, 1951), 6. 234-6.
11. Thucydides, *History of the Peloponnesian War,* Loeb Classical Library (London, 1951), 1. 2; M. I. Finley, *The World of Odysseus* (New York, 1965), p. 88; Murray, *Greek Epic,* pp. 57-8.
12. A. W. H. Adkins, *Merit and Responsibility: A Study in Greek Values* (Oxford, 1960), pp. 34-6, 70-3.
13. G. S. Kirk, *CAH*[3], 2(2):821, now places the Trojan War late in the thirteenth century, rather than early in the twelfth, as heretofore accepted.
14. N. G. L. Hammond, *Epirus* (Oxford, 1967), pp. 378-9; *CAH*[3], 2(2):682 ff; Starr, *Origins,* p. 72, was apparently unconvinced at the time of his writing (previous to Hammond's).
15. Myres, *Who Were the Greeks?* pp. 148 ff., discusses the derivation and movements of the Dorians, and their linguistic relationships with other Hellenic peoples; *CAH*[3], 2(2):694-9; Starr, *Origins,* pp. 62-3, 70-4; K. J. Beloch, *Griechische Geschichte* (Strassburg, 1912), 1:2.

76ff.; and G. De Sanctis, *Storia dei Greci delle Origini alla Fine del Secolo V* (Florence, 1939), 1:152 ff., are so sceptical as to deny there ever was a Dorian invasion.

16. Hdt. 1. 146; Thuc. 1. 12; Strabo, *Geography,* Loeb Classical Library 14. 633-4; *CAH*[3], 2:783-6; *CAH*[3], 2:812-3.
17. Hdt. 1. 56; W. W. How and J. Wells, *A Commentary on Herodotus* (Oxford, 1975), 1:444-5, explore the theory of Pelasgic origins in Attica.
18. J. A. R. Munro, "Pelasgians and Ionians," *JHS* 54(1934):124.
19. Pausanias, *Description of Greece,* Loeb Classical Series (London, 1949), 7. 2-4; Strabo 14. 633-4; Hdt. 1. 146; How and Wells, *Commentary,* 1:122, remark that Athens is asserting her claims while castigating Ionian pride; Thuc. 1. 12; A. W. Gomme, *A Historical Commentary on Thucydides* (Oxford, 1959), 1:120, does not accept the Athenian claims; J. M. Cook in *CAH*[3], 2(2):784, tends to believe them.
20. Hdt. 1. 143; How and Wells, *Commentary,* 1:120, see evidences of anti-Ionian bias in Herodotus' treatment of this subject.
21. Hdt. 1. 57; How and Wells, *Commentary,* 1:80, make it clear that the distinction between Pelasgian and Hellene cannot be made so simply on the basis of linguistic differences.
22. H. J. Rose, *Handbook of Greek Mythology* (London, 1965) p. 109; *Oxford Classical Dictionary,* 2nd ed., (Oxford, 1970), pp. 138-9; M. P. Nilsson, *Minoan-Mycenaean Religion* (Lund, 1950), p. 417; W. K. C. Guthrie in *CAH*[3], 2(2):879, grants that Athens had antecedents at Mycenae, but doubts that these can be traced as far as Crete; L. R. Farnell, *Cults of the Greek States* (Oxford, 1896), 1:260.
23. G. Murray, "Daimon and Hero," in J. Harrison, *Epilegomena to the Study of Greek Religion, and Themis* (New York, 1962), p. 267; Eitrem, "Kekrops," Pauly, Wissowa, Kroll, *Real Encyclopädie der Classischen Altertumswissenschaft* (Stuttgart, 1921), 11:119-25; J. B. Bury, *A History of Greece to the Death of Alexander the Great* (London, 1931), p. 164.
24. F. Jacoby, *Atthis, the Local Chronicles of Attica* (New York, 1973), p. 105.
25. Rose, *Handbook,* pp. 261-2.
26. R. Graves, *The Greek Myths,* (New York, 1959), 1:327, points out that the drawing of a sword from a rock was an ancient test of royalty (likewise undergone by Odin, Arthur, and Galahad), and that it probably formed a part of the Bronze Age coronation ritual.
27. *CAH*[3], 2(2):884.
28. Plutarch, *Theseus,* Loeb Classical Library (London, 1948), p. 25; Jacoby, *Atthis,* p. 121-3, emphasizes that Plutarch's sources had little agreement as to the main elements of the Theseus legend.
29. Plut., *Thes.* 30; Rose, *Handbook,* pp. 256-7, thinks this legend may have a basis in fact, that the Lapiths were inhabitants of northern Thessaly, and that the Centaurs were actually wild hill-men nearby.
30. Jacoby, *Atthis,* p. 126, regards the union of Attica under Theseus, at least, as certain.
31. K. Scherling, "Kodros," *PW* 11:984-94; Jacoby, *Atthis,* p. 145, cites this incident as a pretext for abolishing monarchy; A. R. Burn, *The Lyric Age of Greece* (London, 1960), p. 22, agrees.
32. H. T. Wade-Gery, "Eupatridai, Archons, and Areopagus," *Classical Quarterly,* 25 (1931):2-4, thinks that a lost section of Aristotle's *Athenaion Politeia* was Plutarch's source; Jacoby, *Atthis,* pp. 247-8, prefers Theophrastus.
33. *OCD,* pp. 461-2, 828-9.
34. Plut., *Thes.* 25, says "geomoroi" instead of "georgoi" for the second of Theseus' three classes; Wade-Gery, "Eupatridai, etc.," *CQ,* 25(1931):5, thinks Plutarch meant to say "georgoi." My view is that Plutarch made no mistake, that he deliberately said "geomoroi" to distinguish "landowners" as a separate class, since "georgoi," as "landworkers," was a vaguer, wider term that could pertain to both upper and lower classes.
35. *OCD,* p. 829.
36. H. Francotte, *La Polis Grecque* (Paderborn, 1907), pp. 10-13, was the first to rank the georgoi with the lower classes; for a criticism of his position, see C. Hignett, *A History of the Athenian Constitution* (Oxford, 1958), pp. 48-50.
37. Against the majority opinion, I have become convinced by the reasoning of W. J. Woodhouse, *Solon the Liberator* (New York, 1965), pp. 42-47; in brief, he argues that in Greek usage, *hektemoroi* can only mean those living off a sixth share, that no other interpretation is possible.
38. Thuc. 1. 17; Gomme, *Commentary,* 1:127, considers Thucydides' view of the tyrants a bit too negative.

39. A. French, "Solon and the Megarian Question," *JHS* 77(1957):241; R. J. Hopper, "The Solonian Crisis," *Ancient Society and Institutions: Studies Presented to Victor Ehrenberg* (New York, 1967), p. 141, puts it in another way, showing that the conditions favorable to tyranny did not yet exist in Athens; P. N. Ure, *The Origin of Tyranny* (New York, 1962), is in essential agreement.
40. R. Sealey, *A History of the Greek City States ca. 700–338 B.C.* (Berkeley and Los Angeles, 1976), p. 99, thinks Cylon's coup failed possibly because it was "regional" in character; L. H. Jeffery, *Archaic Greece ca 700–500 B.C.* (London, 1976), p. 88, suggests that it may have been because the aristocracy was divided against itself; A. Andrewes, *The Greek Tyrants* (London, 1956), p. 84, stresses that Athenians were not yet exasperated enough to look for an alternative to aristocratic rule; Burn, *Lyric Age,* p. 286, makes the same point, limiting his discussion to the farmers.
41. Aristotle, *Athenaion Politeia,* text of Kenyon (London, 1912), 1; Jacoby, *Atthis,* p. 186, accepts the traditional account, with reservations; J. Day and M. Chambers, *Aristotle's History of Athenian Democracy* (Berkeley and Los Angeles, 1962), pp. 162-3, likewise accept it, but note it contains "journalistic embellishments."
42. Jeffery, *Archaic Greece,* p. 88, calls particular attention to this.
43. I. M. Linforth, *Solon the Athenian* (Berkeley, 1919), pp. 275-6, doubted that Draco's decrees were a regular code; Beloch, *Gr. Gesch.* 1:2, 258 ff., even doubted Draco's existence; for a discussion of the "Draco problem" and its scholarship, see Hignett, *Hist. Ath. Const.,* pp. 305-11; K. von Fritz and E. Kapp, *Aristotle's Constitution of Athens* (New York, 1961), p. 11, think Aristotle did not mean to say Draco made any changes in the existing constitution.
44. Plut., *Solon* (London, 1948), 17.
45. Day and Chambers, *Aristotle's History,* p. 163; Fritz and Kapp, *Aristotle's Constitution,* p. 19, agree that Draco was primarily concerned with criminal law.
46. H. T. Wade-Gery, "Eupatridai, Archons, and Areopagus," *CQ* 25(1931):10, makes it clear that all such actions, because of their religious connection, were at this time reserved to the Areopagus.
47. J. Harrison, *Prolegomena to the Study of Greek Religion* (Cleveland, 1959), pp. 120-50, especially at 136-7.
48. F. E. Adcock, *CAH,* 2nd ed. (New York, 1926): 4:31; E. Barker, *The Political Thought of Plato and Aristotle* (New York, 1947), p. 450; Aristotle, in *Ath. Pol.,* 4, seems to be talking more about the enactments of Solon than those of Draco, but his account shows that in spite of a possible mistake, Draco's reputation was high among writers of the fourth century.

2 *The Tempering Wind* 600-590 B.C.

1. H. T. Wade-Gery, *Cambridge Ancient History,* 2nd ed. (Cambridge, 1925), 3:527-69 develops this theme in a general way.
2. L. R. Farnell, *Cults of the Greek States* (Oxford, 1896), 1:34-41.
3. H. W. Parke and D. E. W. Wormell, *The Delphic Oracle* (Oxford, 1956), 1:17-41, explain the ancient process of query and response in the light of modern science, disposing of many of the "myths" created by hostile writers.
4. Pausanias, *Description of Greece,* Loeb Classical Library (London, 1954), 1:28.
5. Paus. 1.22; A. N. Oikonomides, *The Two Agoras of Ancient Athens* (Chicago, 1964), pp. 3-14; the present remains have not been identified as earlier than the fourth century B.C.
6. W. J. Woodhouse, *Solon the Liberator* (New York, 1965), p. 75; N. G. L. Hammond, *Studies in Greek History* (Oxford, 1973), p. 120; CAH^2, 4:34.
7. Woodhouse, *Solon,* pp. 157-8, thus explains *Ath. Pol.* 2, as a natural mistake on Aristotle's part which has been responsible for much confusion about the facts; Aristotle was really referring to life tenants in the earliest stages of debt as paying one-sixth of his produce to the creditor; afterward he would remit more sixths until he fell to hektomor status; even A. Andrewes, *The Greeks* (London, 1967), pp. 106-7, while defending the traditional view, admits that "Payment of one-sixth does not seem mountainously oppressive . . . and might have been paid for generations without hardship."
8. Regarding the *horoi* there is a variance of opinion among scholars. That they were monument stones of some sort on landed property, none doubt. F. E. Adcock, CAH^2, 4:36,

calls them boundary markers but doubts that they recorded mortgages; K. Freeman, *Work and Life of Solon* (New York, 1976), pp. 62-3, thinks they were mortgage records but admits there is no proof; A. Andrewes, *The Greek Tyrants* (London, 1956), p. 86, calls attention that Solon does not seem to be referring to them as boundary stones; Woodhouse, *Solon,* pp. 101 ff., shows that the etymology of *horoi* is diverse; he prefers to call them "ward-stones"; R. J. Hopper, "The Solonian Crisis," *Ehrenberg Studies,* p. 140, says they were "marker-stones" but not necessarily boundary stones.

9. Solon, *Elegies,* Loeb Classical Library (London, 1954), 1.13.
10. Herodotus, *History,* Loeb Classical Library (London, 1946), 5: 82-9; R. Sealey, *A History of the Greek City-States,* pp. 83-4; F. E. Adcock, *CAH*^{2}, 4:26.
11. Woodhouse, *Solon,* p. 120.
12. Solon, *Elegies,* 1. 4, 6; I. M. Linforth, *Solon the Athenian* (Berkeley, 1919), pp. 49-51.
13. Aristotle, *Athenaion Politeia,* Loeb Classical Library (London, 1971), p. 13; Plutarch, *Solon,* Loeb Classical Library (London, 1948), p. 13; a problem occurs in interpreting the passage from Plutarch, since oligarchy has usually been regarded as a milder form than aristocracy; however, use of the superlative, "oligarchikotaton," seems to indicate an extreme reactionary course, and the similar use of "demokratikotaton" a contrasting extremity in the other direction; A. French, "The Party of Peisistratos," *Greece and Rome,* 2nd series 6(1959):46-57, does not think the groups can be separated so neatly on geographic lines, but concedes that it was a fluid situation.
14. The term "party" is not used here in any modern sense but rather to identify groups with continuing common interests. On the nature of early Athenian political alignments, see V. Ehrenberg, "The Origins of Democracy," *Historia* 1(1950):530 ff.; also, his *From Solon to Socrates* (London, 1968), pp. 74-7; for another view, see F. Jacoby, *Atthis: the Local Chronicles of Ancient Athens* (New York, 1973), pp. 152 ff.
15. C. Hignett, *History of the Athenian Constitution* (Oxford, 1958), pp. 109-10; P. N. Ure, *The Origin of Tyranny* (New York, 1962), pp. 47 ff., and G. Busolt, *Griechische Geschichte* (Gotha, 1904), 2: 46 ff., present analyses that differ with this one in certain respects, tending to align the demiourgoi with the Hill faction; but see J. Holladay, "Followers of Peisistratus," *Greece and Rome* 24(1977):42, for exceptions to Ure's analysis.
16. Woodhouse, *Solon,* p. 117.
17. Plut. *Sol.* 2.
18. K. Hönn, *Solon, Staatsmann und Weiser* (Vienna, 1948), p. 57; Freeman, *Work and Life,* pp. 157-8, says "the evidence for pre-legislation travels is not strong . . . However, the probability that he gained from travels the knowledge of constitutions and of foreign commerce exhibited in his laws is very great."
19. Solon *Elegies* 1. 7; Arist. *Ath. Pol.* 5.
20. Plut. *Sol.* 12; Freeman, *Work and Life,* p. 163, says there is no good reason for doubting Plutarch's account at this point.
21. Freeman, *Work and Life,* p. 165.
22. L. H. Jeffery, *Archaic Greece* (London, 1976), pp. 94-5; Jacoby, *Atthis,* p. 40, builds a case for Solon's connection with the Alcmaeonids, who were the backbone of the Shore party.
23. Freeman's arguments are very convincing as to this; *Work and Life,* pp. 169-72.
24. Freeman, *Work and Life,* pp. 171-4; Linforth, *Solon,* p. 54; A. R. Burn, *The Lyric Age of Greece* (London, 1960), p. 220, states a cautious acceptance; so does Adcock, *CAH*^{2}, 4:61, though he places it after the reforms. Ehrenberg, *From Solon to Socrates,* pp. 60-1, does not accept it.
25. Plut. *Sol.* 14.
26. Linforth, *Solon,* pp. 52-5; G. Ferrara, *La Politica di Solone* (Naples, 1964), pp. 38-9, essentially agrees, but sees Solon as a savior of the old order, renovating and reconstituting it.
27. Arist. *Ath. Pol.* 5; H. T. Wade-Gery, *Essays in Greek History* (Oxford, 1958), p. 145; in note 1, Professor Wade-Gery asks, "In what other way could the Seisachtheia have been executed?"
28. Solon *Iambi* 3. 36; Ehrenberg, *From Solon to Socrates,* p. 62, calls this "a kind of habeas corpus act, rare if not unique in the Greek world." Solon does not say how he was able to recover those who had been sold abroad, a point on which much speculation and doubt have centered. It seems virtually impossible that he could have had any way of doing this, and his assertion that he had done so naturally creates suspicion that he may be claiming to have done too much generally.

29. Arist. *Ath. Pol.* 9; J. Day and M. Chambers, *Aristotle's History of Athenian Democracy* (Berkeley and Los Angeles, 1962), pp. 168-9, warn against Aristotle's simplistic interpretation, pointing out that he does not explore the implications of "plucking up the *horoi*."
30. R. J. Hopper, "The Solonian Crisis," *Ehrenberg Studies,* pp. 139-40, is one of the most recent to make this point; in agreement are A. French, "Land Tenure and the Solon Problem," *Historia* 12(1963):244; A. Masaracchia, *Solone* (Florence, 1958), pp. 137-44.
31. W. G. Forrest, *The Emergence of Greek Democracy* (New York, 1966), pp. 160-1 particularly; also Linforth, *Solon,* p. 86; Woodhouse, *Solon,* leans this way in Chs. 13 and 14, but more mildly.
32. For this, see Hignett, *Hist. Ath. Const.,* pp. 17-27; also, for an earlier treatment, C. Gilliard, *Quelques Réformes de Solon* (Lausanne, 1907), pp. 16-28.
33. Androtion, cited by Plut. *Solon* 15; Androtion's view has been generally described by modern scholars as proceeding from his own conservatism; see Day and Chambers, *Aristotle's History,* p. 17; also, Jacoby, *Atthis,* pp. 44-8; Masaracchia, *Solone,* leans toward a modern conservative interpretation, as does Ferrara, *La Politica di Solone,* which emphasizes that Solon's ideal was the same as Hesiod's; Hignett, *Hist. Ath. Const.,* is moderately conservative.
34. Solon *Iambi* 3. 37; Gilliard, *Quelques Réformes,* especially, sees Solon as a moderate; also, F. E. Adcock, in *CAH*[2], 4:57 who says that Solon's ordering of the state had "an oligarchical air," but was "a stage on the road to democracy."
35. Woodhouse, *Solon,* p. 100; A. French, "Land Tenure," *Historia* 12(1963):242-7, emphasizes how little is known about the land system in seventh century Attica, also how confused the situation remains as seen today. K. von Fritz and E. Kapp, *Aristotle's Constitution of Athens* (New York, 1961), p. 154, agree that it is hardly possible that all debts were remitted.
36. Woodhouse, *Solon,* p. 158; for a comparable view on the inalienability of land, see J. V. A. Fine, "Horoi," *Hesperia* (1951), Supplement IX, pp. 177-90.
37. R. J. Bonner and G. Smith, *The Administration of Justice from Homer to Aristotle* (Chicago, 1930), 2:21 ff., stress the great disadvantage under which the poor labored in litigation against rich, even as late as the fourth century (Dem. 21. 112); both in and out of court in the seventh and sixth centuries the situation was obviously much worse.
38. A. French, "The Economic Background to Solon's Reforms," *Classical Quarterly* 50(1956):18.
39. Arist. *Ath. Pol.* 6.
40. M. I. Finley, *Studies in Land and Credit in Ancient Athens: 500–200* B.C. (New Brunswick, 1951), pp. 91, 94; N. G. L. Hammond, "Land Tenure in Attica and Solon's Seisachtheia," *Journal of Hellenic Studies* 81(1961):90; Hönn, *Solon,* pp. 106-10, thinks Solon determined each case according to the "worth" of the individual.
41. Freeman, *Work and Life,* p. 63; G. Glotz, *The Greek City and its Institutions* (New York, 1965), p. 120, insists that all debts were canceled and lands freed; Masaracchia, *Solone,* pp. 137-44, is convinced that land was inalienable generally, and thus minimizes the results.
42. French, "Economic Background," *CQ* 50(1956):22.
43. Solon *Iambi* 3. 37; G. De Sanctis, *Atthis*: *Storia della Repubblica Ateniese* (Turin, 1912), pp. 206 ff., emphasizes that Solon could not have canceled all debts; Forrest, *Greek Democracy,* p. 160, disagrees strongly with the notion that Solon was a compromiser.
44. French, "Economic Background," *CQ* 50(1956):24-5, calls particular attention to this.
45. Ibid., pp. 19-20; Ferrara, *La Politica di Solone,* pp. 65-75, cites the elegies as the best evidence of this work of reconciliation; Gilliard, *Quelques Réformes,* p. 207, discusses the effect on the Eupatrids.
46. Woodhouse, *Solon,* pp. 176-8; French, "Economic Background," *CQ* 50(1956):19-20; Jacoby, *Atthis,* p. 40, thinks the support of the Alcmaeonids helped Solon with the nobles throughout.
47. Plut. *Sol.* 16; N. G. L. Hammond, "The Seisachtheia and the Nomothesia of Solon," *JHS* 60 (1940): 82-3; Linforth, *Solon,* p. 271, doubts that a festival called Seisachtheia ever existed. The point is well taken; Plut. *Sol.* 16. 3 says "sympherontos aisthomenoi"—"they all perceived together" the advantages of the seisachtheia. One wonders who "all of them" were, since there had to be losers as well as gainers, and only the latter would favor a festival.
48. C. M. Kraay, *Archaic and Classical Greek Coins* (Berkeley and Los Angeles, 1976), p. 56; C. T. Seltman, *Athens: Its History and Coinage before the Persian Invasion* (Cambridge, 1924), p. 17; Day and Chambers, *Aristotle's History,* p. 77; but Solon's coinage is defended by H. A.

Cahn, *Kleine Schriften zur Münzkunde und Archäologie* (Basel, 1975), pp. 81 ff.; also, more doubtfully, by E. S. G. Robinson, "The Coins from the Ephesian Artemision Reconsidered," *JHS* 71(1951):156-66.

49. K. H. Waters, "Solon's Price Equalisation," *JHS* 80(1960):154; J. Johnston, "Solon's Reform of Weights and Measures," *JHS* 54(1934):180-4, who estimates a 27-30% reduction in the volume of the measure (medimnos) previously in use in Athens; Gilliard, *Quelques Réformes*, p. 249; Freeman, *Work and Life*, p. 107.
50. Plut. *Sol.* 22
51. G. De Sanctis, *Storia dei Greci*, 1:484.
52. T. J. Cadoux, "The Athenian Archons from Kreon to Hypsichides," *JHS* 68(1948):97.
53. Hammond, "Seisachtheia and Nomothesia," *JHS* 60(1940):78, whose view was first advanced by Beloch, *Griech Gesch.*, 1. 2. 165.
54. Hignett, *Hist. Ath. Const.*, p. 317, says that Cadoux's argument "seems to me unanswerable."
55. E. M. T. Chrimes, "On Solon's Property Classes," *Classical Review* 46(1932):2-4, was one of the first to call attention to Solon's staggering problems as to this, simply ignored by Plutarch and Aristotle. A main difficulty was that of equating "wet" and "dry" measures, grain land with that planted to olives and grapes; a man might find himself in top or bottom class, depending on what he planted. Chrimes thinks there must have been some kind of primitive survey or census, unmentioned, as a basis. U. Wilcken, "Zu Solons Schatzungklassen," *Hermes* 68(1928):236-8, suggests an emendation of Plutarch which would include the Attic sheep owners; J. H. Thiel, "On Solon's System of Property Classes," *Mnemosyne* 3(1950):1-11, agrees with Wilcken's emendation, but not his interpretation, holding that Athenians must have had the option of equating their products to the market price; C. M. A. Van den Oudenrijn, "Solon's System of Property Classes Once More," *Mnemosyne* 5(1952):19-27, rejecting the emendation and both interpretations, casts new light on Plutarch's disputed passage, but admittedly does not resolve Solon's problem. K. H. Waters, "Solon's Price Equalisation," *JHS* 80(1960):162 holds that all products must have been equated to the market price.
56. Hignett, *Hist. Ath. Const.*, p. 98; F. E. Adcock, *CAH*², 4:48-9, accepts the traditional view, as does R. J. Bonner, *Aspects of Athenian Democracy* (New York, 1933), p. 3. Fritz and Kapp, *Aristotle's Constitution*, p. 155, point out that Aristotle is not quite clear regarding the offices reserved to the various classes.
57. Freeman, *Work and Life*, p. 52; Jeffery, *Archaic Greece*, p. 94. Solon's sponsorship has been questioned without any satisfactory conclusion; Day and Chambers, *Aristotle's History*, p. 79, say of this, "It . . . appears impossible to confirm or to refute the tradition that Solon established the census classes."
58. A. W. Gomme and T. J. Cadoux, "Ekklesia," *OCD*, p. 376.
59. G. T. Griffith, "Isegoria in the Assembly at Athens," *Ehrenberg Studies* (New York, 1967), p. 120.
60. J. J. Keaney and A. E. Raubitschek, "A Late Byzantine Account of Ostracism," *American Journal of Philology* 93(1972):87-91, are able to supply proof that Solon's Council of Four Hundred, long challenged by modern scholars, actually did exist; Andrewes, *Greek Tyrants*, p. 88, remarks that the new council was necessary to give Solon's reforms a fair trial, since the Areopagus could not be trusted to do this.
61. Solon *Iambi* 3. 37A; Ferrara, *La Politica di Solone*, p. 140, without citing the councils, makes it his main thesis that through such evenhanded measures Solon guided the state toward moderate democracy, avoiding the extremes of factionalism, tyranny, and mob rule.
62. Linforth, *Solon*, p. 84, commenting upon Arist. *Ath. Pol.* 8; Wade-Gery, *Essays in Greek History*, p. 145; Forrest, *Greek Democracy*, p. 166; Masaracchia, *Solone*, pp. 158-60.
63. Plut. *Sol.* 19; V. Ehrenberg, *The Greek State* (London, 1960), p. 64; Masaracchia, *Solone*, pp. 173-4.
64. Arist. *Ath. Pol.* 9; Freeman, *Work and Life*, p. 81, qualifies Aristotle's judgment, stating that such was not Solon's intention; R. J. Bonner, *Aspects of Athenian Democracy* (New York, 1933), p. 3, concurs.
65. Hignett, *Hist. Ath. Const.*, p. 97-8; Bonner and Smith, *Administration*, 1:159; Day and Chambers, *Aristotle's History*, p. 80; Wade-Gery, *Essays in Greek History*, pp. 173-4: De Sanctis, *Storia dei Greci*, 1:479; Ehrenberg, *The Greek State*, p. 72: U. von Wilamowitz-Moellendorff, *Aristoteles und Athen* (Berlin, 1966), 1:60; Hönn, *Solon*, pp. 97-8, sees the Heliaea as playing a somewhat larger role.

66. Bonner and Smith, *Administration,* 1:161; Glotz, *The Greek City,* p. 232, considers that Solon gave the Heliaea appellate jurisdiction only, without any check on the Areopagus.
67. Arist. *Ath. Pol.* 8; De Sanctis, *Atthis,* p. 356, claims on the basis of this that the Areopagus was given the right to act as a Supreme Court over the Athenian judicial system.
68. Linforth, *Solon,* p. 83, accepts this, as does Freeman, *Work and Life,* pp. 76-7, and F. E. Adcock, *CAH*², 4:52; Day and Chambers, *Aristotle's History,* p. 84, do not; neither does Wilamowitz, *Arist. und Athen,* 2:186-8; Gilliard, *Quelques Réformes,* p. 281, expresses grave doubts, judging it an error on Aristotle's part; Hignett, *Hist. Ath. Const.*, p. 91, takes a middle position; Wilamowitz, *Arist. und Athen,* 2:189, and De Sanctis, *Atthis,* p. 150, claim the Areopagus had the right to conduct the examination of magistrates; Day and Chambers, *Aristotle's History,* pp. 82-4, disagree.
69. Bonner and Smith, *Administration,* 2:305; Linforth, *Solon,* p. 83; Hignett, *Hist. Ath. Const.*, p. 82; Busolt, *Gr. Gesch.*, 2:138-40; De Sanctis, *Storia dei Greci,* 1:481.
70. Sealey, *Greek City States,* p. 122; Freeman, *Work and Life,* p. 180; Forrest, *Greek Democracy,* p. 158; Hammond, *Studies,* p. 161, however, is of the opinion that the Alcmaeonids were excluded from the amnesty; also, Adcock, *CAH*², 4:45; but see Jacoby, *Atthis,* p. 232, note 225, who thinks the Alcmaeonids had been allowed to return before this.
71. Ehrenberg, *From Solon to Socrates,* p. 69; Freeman, *Work and Life,* pp. 114-22.
72. As to Solon's family legislation, there is a wide range of opinion, from Glotz, *The Greek City,* and Hönn, *Solon,* who accept a good deal of it, to Gilliard, *Quelques Réformes,* and Hignett, *Hist. Ath. Const.*, who accept comparatively little; other writers exhibit varying degrees of scepticism.
73. Solon *Iambi* 3. 36, 37; Arist. *Ath. Pol.* 12; Hönn, *Solon,* pp. 75-6, takes this as an indication of Solon's sincerity, grounded in his deep religious faith; Ferrara, *La Politica di Solone,* pp. 135-41, agrees, stressing Solon's sense of responsibility to the gods; De Sanctis, *Storia dei Greci,* 1:484; is particularly impressed with Solon's championing of the individual, and his rewarding of honest labor.
74. Arist. *Ath. Pol.* 11.
75. Hdt. 1. 30; Plut. *Sol.* 25, declares the laws were to be in force for a hundred years; How and Wells, *Commentary on Herodotus,* 1:67, call this "an exaggeration . . . characteristic of later Greek historians."
76. Plut. *Sol.* 25.
77. Freeman, *Work and Life,* pp. 184-7, 197-8.

3 *Tyranny and Constitutionalism* 590-500 B.C.

1. R. J. Bonner and G. Smith, *The Administration of Justice from Homer to Aristotle* (Chicago, 1930), 1:157-67, analyze the probabilities.
2. *OCD*², p. 38.
3. Hdt. 6. 130; N. G. L. Hammond, "The Family of Orthagoras," *Classical Quarterly* 50 (1956):45-53.
4. A. Andrewes, *The Greek Tyrants* (London, 1956), pp. 21-2, shows that the word "tyrant" did not at first have a derogatory meaning. But it could never have sounded good to deep-dyed aristocrats.
5. Arist. *Ath. Pol.* 13.1; K. von Fritz and E. Kapp, *Aristotle's Constitution of Athens* (New York, 1961), pp. 80, 158, support the chronology used here.
6. The possibility that he may have been elected by popular vote (Arist. *Ath. Pol.* 13. 2; C. Hignett, *History of the Athenian Constitution* (Oxford, 1958), p. 322, lends credence to this. And of course he knew that all except discontented demos would resist illegal prolongation. Von Schoeffer, "Damasias," A. Pauly, G. Wissowa, and W. Kroll, *Real Encyclopädie der Classischen Attertumswissenschaft* 4(1901):2035-7, also inclines to this interpretation, while emphasizing that cooperation from some nobles was necessary.
7. The entire subject of the many wars between Athens and Megara in this period is obscure and confused. See K. Freeman, *The Work and Life of Solon* (New York, 1976), pp. 169-70; also, A French, "Solon and the Megarian Question," *Journal of Hellenic Studies* 77 (1957):238-46.
8. Plut. *Solon* 29; I. M. Linforth, *Solon the Athenian* (Berkeley, 1919), p. 303, and Freeman, *Work and Life,* p. 199, agree in branding the stories of Solon's involvement with Pisistratus as fiction.

9. K. H. Waters, "Solon's Price Equalisation," *JHS* 80(1960):189, points out that Pisistratus actually pursued the same economic policies that Solon had laid down.
10. A. French, "The Party of Peisistratus," *Greece and Rome* 6(1959):50.
11. P. N. Ure, *The Origin of Tyranny* (Cambridge, 1922) declared that Pisistratus' following was originally founded on the depressed and aroused silver miners of the Laurium area. It appears now that this idea should not be pushed overmuch. In criticism of Ure, J. Holliday, "The Followers of Peisistratus," *Greece and Rome* 24(1977):42, points out that the Laurium mines did not become really important until about 525. C. J. K. Cunningham, "The Silver of Laurium," *Greece and Rome* 14(1967):145-56, reports that the mines produced other valuables besides silver.
12. French, "The Party," pp. 52-3; Holliday, "The Followers," pp. 50-3; in support of this position, R. Sealey, *A History of the Greek City-States* (Berkeley and Los Angeles, 1976), p. 123, points out that Herodotus' term, *hyperakrioi* ("men beyond the hills") is preferable to Aristotle's term, *diakrioi* ("men of the hills").
13. It is hardly credible that Pisistratus was able to seize and hold the Acropolis with fifty men. These must have been merely the vanguard of a larger body in the city and the surrounding country who soon joined him. For the general situation, see K. J. Beloch, *Griechische Geschichte* (Strassburg, 1912) I:1, pp. 367-9, who asserts that Pisistratus took advantage of a split between the Shore and the Plain.
14. The chronology of Pisistratus' exiles and returns has been the subject of much scholarship and speculation, because of the difficulty of reconciling Herodotus' and Aristotle's accounts. The most recent study is that of J. G. F. Hind, "The 'Tyrannis' and the Exiles of Peisistratus," *CQ* n.s. 24(1974):1-18; but see also J. S. Ruebel, "The Tyrannies of Peisistratus," *Greek, Roman, and Byzantine Studies* 14(1973):125-36, as well as the older, classical solution of F. E. Adcock, "The Exiles of Peisistratus," *CQ* 18(1924):174-81.
15. Hdt. 1. 60; Arist. *Ath. Pol.* 14. Many have doubted or rejected the story, most notably P. N. Ure, *Origin of Tyranny,* pp. 51-9, who thought it a retrojection from a similar story about Darius; however, J. Boardman, "Herakles, Peisistratos, and Eleusis," *JHS* 95(1975):1-13, shows that it was a popular subject for ceramic art in the Pisistratean period.
16. Hind's chronology; Ruebel places the second expulsion a year earlier, Adcock a year later; G. Sanders, "La Chronologie de Pisistrate," *Nouvelle Clio*(1955-7):161-79, presents an interesting and completely different arrangement.
17. J. W. Cole, "Peisistratus on the Strymon," *Greece and Rome* 22(1975):43, says that his founding of a settlement in the north indicates joint action with a city of Euboea, and "the strongest candidate is Eretria."
18. Ibid., 43-4; Cole thinks he flattered the Edonian Thracians with attentions to their local god, Dionysus, also, perhaps, by promising to advance the worship of Dionysus at Athens.
19. C. T. Seltman, *Athens: Its History and Coinage before the Persian Invasion* (Cambridge, 1924), pp. 55-7.
20. Hdt. 1. 61.
21. Ure, *Origin of Tyranny,* makes it his main thesis that the Greek tyrants of the seventh and sixth centuries won their positions by being quickest to take advantage of the rise of commerce, and the possibilities of the new coinage.
22. Seltman, *Athens,* p. 57, estimates Pisistratus was nearly nine years on the Strymon, on the evidence of twenty-six anvil-dies on record to represent his coinage there.
23. Hdt. 1. 63: Fritz and Kapp, *Aristotle's Constitution,* p. 159, estimate the total duration of Pisistratus' rule at seventeen years instead of nineteen.
24. A. French, *The Growth of the Athenian Economy* (New York, 1964), pp. 21-2.
25. Arist. *Ath. Pol.* 16; J. Day and M. Chambers, *Aristotle's History of Athenian Democracy* (Berkeley and Los Angeles, 1962), p. 95, show that the anecdote was in keeping with Aristotle's general thesis, but they do not seem to reject it.
26. Ibid. Day and Chambers, *Aristotle's History,* p. 99, doubt that the traveling judges go back to Pisistratus' time; Hignett, *Hist. Ath. Const.*, p. 115, thinks they do.
27. Andrewes, *Greek Tyrants,* p. 111.
28. French, *Athenian Economy,* p. 43; *CAH*², 4:66
29. Hdt. 6. 34-5.
30. Opinions differ as to this. They were neighbors in the Brauron area. Andrewes, *Greek Tyrants,* p. 105, thinks the Philaids supported Pisistratus, originally. How and Wells, *A Commentary on Herodotus,* 2:76, observe that it was part of the usual policy of despots to

remove dangerous citizens. Hignett, *Hist. Ath. Const.*, pp. 110, 326, and Wilamowitz, *Aristoteles und Athen*, 2:66, seem to hold a different opinion, seeing the Philaids as rather more friendly to Pisistratus.

31. Hdt. 6. 39; *CAH*², 4:69. T. J. Cadoux, "The Athenian Archons from Kreon to Hypsichides," *JHS* 68(1948):110, finds presumptive evidence that Miltiades had already been archon in 524/3 B.C.
32. Plut. *Solon* 31. 1; Linforth, *Solon*, p. 303, remarks that stories of Pisistratus' kindness toward Solon are probably based on nothing more than the tyrant's well-known mildness.
33. J. Harrison, *Prolegomena to the Study of Greek Religion* (Cleveland, 1959), p. 446-53; H. J. Rose, *Handbook of Greek Mythology* (London, 1965), pp. 149-57.
34. R. Graves, *The Greek Myths* (New York, 1959), 1: 106; M. P. Nilsson, *Greek Folk Religion* (New York, 1940), pp. 35-6, discusses the various Dionysian festivals in Attica.
35. J. W. Cole, "Peisistratus on the Strymon," *Greece and Rome* 22(1975):44, thinks Pisistratus may earlier have promised the Thracians to expand Dionysus' worship at Athens; see above, note 18.
36. J. A. Davison, "Notes on the Panathenaea," *JHS* 78(1958):23; L. Deubner, *Attische Feste* (Berlin, 1932), presents the most extended discussion of this subject.
37. L. R. Farnell, *The Cults of the Greek States* (Oxford, 1896), 1:296.
38. G. Murray, *The Rise of the Greek Epic* (New York, 1960), p. 192; C. Whitman, *Homer and the Heroic Tradition* (Cambridge, Mass., 1958), pp. 76, 81.
39. Thuc. 3. 104.
40. Andrewes, *Greek Tyrants*, p. 106, finds indications that the Great Panathenaea was actually started in 566, several years before Pisistratus' accession.
41. Murray, *Greek Epic*, p. 307; Andrewes, *Greek Tyrants*, p. 114.
42. I. T. Hill, *The Ancient City of Athens* (London, 1953), pp. 137-9.
43. M. Lang, "The Murder of Hipparchus," *Historia* 3(1955):395-407, explores this problem, in all its complexities; see also T. R. Fitzgerald, "The Murder of Hipparchus: A Reply," *Historia* 6(1957):275-86, and C. W. Fornara, "The Tradition about the Murder of Hipparchus," *Historia* 17(1968):400-24, who traces and assesses the ancient viewpoints on the subject.
44. A. W. Gomme, "Athenian Notes: Athenian Politics, 510-483 B.C.," *American Journal of Philology* 65(1944):324; Hignett, *Hist. Ath. Const.*, pp. 124-6; Sealey, *Greek City States*, pp. 149-51.
45. Day and Chambers, *Aristotle's History*, pp. 117-8, discuss the various theories as to this; H. T. Wade-Gery, *Essays in Greek History* (Oxford, 1958), p. 149, doubts that very many were enfranchised; Fritz and Kapp, *Aristotle's Constitution*, p. 163, agree.
46. G. De Sanctis, *Storia dei Greci* (Florence, 1939), 1:542.
47. T. J. Cadoux, "Athenian Archons. . . ," *JHS* 68(1948):109-10, finds presumptive evidence that Cleisthenes had been archon as early as 525/4 B.C.; J. Keaney, "The Structure of Aristotle's *Athenaion Politeia*," *Harvard Studies in Classical Philology* 67(1963):127; Hignett, *Hist. Ath. Const.*, p. 127; Wade-Gery, *Essays*, p. 136.
48. C. A. Robinson, Jr., "The Struggle for Power at Athens in the Early Fifth Century," *AJP* 60(1939):232.
49. Arist. *Ath. Pol.* 21; Day and Chambers, *Aristotle's History*, p. 112, call Aristotle's use of information here "questionable;" *CAH*², 4:143-7, also considers it highly dubious; Fritz and Kapp, *Aristotle's Constitution*, p. 164, call attention that in Aristotle's time there was no reliable tradition to give him information of Cleisthenes' tribal reform.
50. This is essentially the view of V. Ehrenberg, "Origins of Democracy," *Historia* 1(1950), especially pp. 542 ff.
51. Day and Chambers, *Aristotle's History*, p. 119.
52. W. R. Connor, "The Athenian Council: Method and Focus in Some Recent Scholarship," *Classical Journal* 70(1974):32-40. P. J. Rhodes, *The Athenian Boule* (Oxford, 1972), p. 200, thinks, however, that Cleisthenes took no powers away from the Areopagus.
53. Hignett, *Hist. Ath. Const.*, pp. 201 ff.
54. G. T. Griffith, "Isegoria in the Assembly at Athens," *Ehrenberg Studies* (New York, 1967), p. 117.
55. N. G. L. Hammond, "Strategia and Hegemonia in Fifth Century Athens," *CQ* n.s. 19(1969):111-44.
56. A. R. Hands, "Ostraka and the Law of Ostracism—Some Possibilities and Assumptions,"

JHS 79(1959):69-79; J. Keaney and A. Raubitschek, "A Late Byzantine Account of Ostracism," *AJP* 93(1973):87-91; D. McCargar, "New Evidence for the Kleisthenic Boule," *Classical Philology* 71(1976):248-52; D. Kagan, "The Origin and Purposes of Ostracism," *Hesperia* 30(1961):396-7; Bonner and Smith, *Administration,* 1:194-5.

57. P. Leveque and P. Vidal-Naquet, *Clisthène l'Athénien* (Paris, 1964), pp. 77-107.
58. Ure, *Origin of Tyranny,* p. 45, who attributes the discovery to Milchhoefer, *Abhandlungen Berliner Akademie* (1892), p. 47; Leveque and Vidal-Naquet, *Clisthène,* pp. 73-5, minimize this evidence.
59. L. H. Jeffery, *Archaic Greece* (London, 1976), pp. 101-2; W. G. Forrest, *The Emergence of Greek Democracy* (New York, 1966), p. 187.
60. R. Sealey, "Regionalism in Archaic Athens," *Historia* 9(1960):173-4.
61. Sealey, "Regionalism," *Historia* 9(1960):173; D. W. Bradeen, "The Trittyes in Cleisthenes' Reform," *Transactions of the American Philological Association* 86(1955):22-30, presents a parallel view; likewise, D. Kienast, "Die Innenpolitische Entwicklung Athens im 6. Jahrhundert und die Reformen von 508," *Historische Zeitschrift* 200(1965):265-83; D. M. Lewis, "Cleisthenes and Attica," *Historia* 12(1963):22-40, differs to a degree.
62. Hdt. 5. 67; How and Wells, *Commentary,* 2:34, remark that the resemblance is "less clear than the contrast," showing how little Herodotus understood the true nature of Cleisthenes' reforms; Day and Chambers, *Aristotle's History,* p. 104, likewise scout the idea.
63. Hignett, *Hist. Ath. Const.,* p. 157.
64. V. Ehrenberg, "The Origins of Democracy," *Historia* 1(1950):515-47; Wade-Gery, *Essays in Greek History,* pp. 138-9, also testifies to the fact; also see R. Sealey, "Demokratia," *California Studies in Classical Antiquity* 6(1974):253-95; L. Whibley, *Greek Oligarchies, Their Character and Organisation* (London, 1896), p. 99.
65. Hdt. 5. 66; J. A. O. Larsen, "Cleisthenes and the Development of the Theory of Democracy at Athens," *Essays in Political Theory Presented to George H. Sabine,* pp. 1-16, treats the development of Cleisthenes' ideas; see also Larsen, "Demokratia," *Classical Philology* 68(1973):45-6.
66. E. Ruschenbusch, "Patrios Politeia," *Historia* 7(1958):398-424; J. A. R. Munro, "The Ancestral Laws of Cleisthenes," *CQ* 33(1939):84-97.

4 *The First Blast from Asia* 500-490 B.C.

1. A. N. Oikonomides, *The Two Agoras of Ancient Athens* (Chicago, 1964), pp. xii-xiii.
2. T. L. Shear, Jr., "The Athenian Agora, Excavations of 1970," *Hesperia* 40(1971):243-8, 265-7.
3. This subject is treated at length by T. L. Shear and H. A. Thompson, their associates and successors, in periodic reports on excavations in the Athenian Agora, published in *Hesperia,* vol. 1 (1931) to present.
4. A. Procopiou, *Athens: City of the Gods* (New York, 1964), p. 104.
5. A. W. H. Adkins, *Merit and Responsibility: a Study in Greek Values* (Oxford, 1960), pp. 195-8, makes it plain that the Greek view of areté had changed considerably between Homer and the fifth century; otherwise, a man of "quiet virtue," such as Aristides, could hardly have been regarded as a model.
6. Plut. *Aristides* 2; G. De Sanctis, *Atthis: Storia della Repubblica Ateniese* (Turin, 1912), p. 368, agrees, considering that he helped Cleisthenes with the reforms of 508, and was thus an Alcmaeonid ally; U. von Wilamowitz-Moellendorff, *Aristoteles und Athen* (Berlin, 1966) 2:87, sees him taking a more independent line.
7. Pl. *Grg.* 526 E; R. Meiggs, *The Athenian Empire* (Oxford, 1972), p. 42, warns against too much faith in the "later moralizing stories" about Aristides; C. W. Fornara, "The Hoplite Achievement at Psyttaleia," *Journal of Hellenic Studies* 86(1966):53, points out that the aristocracy built up Aristides' reputation as a "counterpoise" to that of Themistocles.
8. H. T. Wade-Gery, *Essays in Greek History* (Oxford, 1958), p. 150.
9. Since there was no formal party structure, and no officers to be elected, it was comparatively easy for Cleisthenes simply to designate his successor as leader. See R. J. Bonner, *Aspects of Athenian Democracy* (New York, 1933), p. 50.
10. G. Glotz, *The Greek City* (New York, 1965), pp. 176-7.
11. Arist. *Ath. Pol.* 28.2.

12. Wilamowitz, *Aristoteles und Athen,* 2:87, insists on this.
13. De Sanctis, *Atthis,* pp. 230-1; R. Sealey, "Regionalism in Archaic Athens," *Historia* 9(1960):162.
14. W. Donlan, "The Origins of Kalos Kagathos," *American Journal of Philology* 94(1971):367.
15. The "Homeric" Hymn to Delian Apollo expands upon this theme; see the translations by C. Boer, *The Homeric Hymns* (Chicago, 1970); T. Sargent, *The Homeric Hymns* (New York, 1973); and A. N. Athanassakis, *The Homeric Hymns* (Baltimore, 1976).
16. Hdt. 1. 142; W. W. How and J. Wells, *A Commentary on Herodotus,* 1:119-20, cite Arist. *Pol.* 1327 B as evidence the Greeks believed that the equable climate had a beneficial effect on human character.
17. Hdt. 5. 34; How and Wells, *Commentary,* 2:13, remark that Herodotus' story of Persian treachery is very improbable. A. de Selincourt, *The World of Herodotus* (London, 1962), p. 248, thinks it was a jurisdictional quarrel; G. Busolt, *Griechische Geschichte* (Gotha, 1893), 2:540, deals with Aristagoras and his background.
18. Hdt. 5. 50.
19. Hdt. 5. 97; R. W. Macan, *Herodotus: The Fourth, Fifth, and Sixth Books* (New York, 1973), 1:248, suggests that Melanthios may have been chosen as commander because he had family ties with Miletus.
20. See G. Grote, *History of Greece* (New York, 1881), 2:165-6; E. Curtius, *Geschichte Griechenlands* (New York, 1886), 2:204; G. Grundy, *The Great Persian War* (London, 1901), p. 96; K. J. Beloch, *Griechische Geschichte* (Strassburg, 1912), II, 1:10; Busolt, *Griech. Gesch.,* 2:543. The majority opinion is that the insurgents attacked Sardis in the hope that such a spectacular accomplishment would encourage others still hesitating, and touch off a general revolt against Persia.
21. Hdt. 6. 12; Macan, *Her.,* 1:277, thinks that, on the contrary, Herodotus reflects the prevailing Athenian prejudice against Ionian seamanship as being inferior to their own; J. B. Bury, *The Ancient Greek Historians* (New York, 1908), agrees.
22. Hdt. 5. 105; Macan, *Her.,* 1:255, observes that this was merely the usual formula.
23. Ibid. Herodotus says Darius invoked Zeus, but Macan, *Her.,* 1:255, observes that of course the Persian king would invoke his own god.
24. Hdt. 4. 83-98; A. T. Olmstead, *History of the Persian Empire* (Chicago, 1948), pp. 147-50.
25. A. R. Burn, *Persia and the Greeks* (New York, 1962), pp. 127-8; R. Sealey, "The Pit and the Well: the Persian Heralds of 491 B.C." *Classical Journal* 72(1976):15; How and Wells, *Commentary,* 2:57, point out that Hdt. 3:134 reveals that Darius had planned the conquest of Greece long before this.
26. Hdt. 7. 133; Macan, *Her.* 1:174, thinks no heralds went to Athens. Sealey, "Pit and Well," *CJ* 72(1976):18-20, thinks heralds were sent, but that Athens' treatment of them was an impulsive, emotional reaction motivated by her hostility to Aegina, which had sent Persia the desired symbols.
27. Arist. *Ath. Pol.* 28; W. Donlan, "The Origins of Kalos Kagathos," *AJP* 94(1973):365-75, shows that most of the terms applied to both parties were not in general use until later in the century.
28. A. Pauly, G. Wiscowa, and W. Kroll, *Real Encyclopädie der Classischen Altertumswissenschaft* 9(1967):1343-7; W. G. Forrest, "Themistocles and Argos," *CQ* 54(1960):233, claims that Xanthippus was never an Alcmaeonid, despite his marriage.
29. Plut. *Them.* 1. 1.
30. Hdt. 7. 143; Macan, *Her.,* 1:193, calls this a "literary flourish."
31. C. Hignett, *History of the Athenian Constitution* (Oxford, 1958), p. 183, seems to think it was unconnected with schemes for self aggrandisement; Wade-Gery, *Essays,* p. 177, also tends to exculpate Themistocles; F. J. Frost, "Themistocles' Place in Athenian Politics," *California Studies in Classical Antiquity* 1(1968):107, warns that the evidence for regarding him as a democrat is slight. I agree, tending to view him as mainly an opportunist; and it is obvious from my wording of the text that I think he was not unaware that his Piraeus policy would win him favor with the demos.
32. H. T. Wade-Gery, "Miltiades," *JHS* 71(1951):212; T. J. Cadoux, "Athenian Archons . . . ," *JHS* 68(1948):110; N. G. L. Hammond, "The Philaids and the Chersonese," *CQ* 50(1956):118.
33. Diod. Sic. 10. 19; Hdt. 6. 140, appears to believe Miltiades' story; How and Wells, *Commentary,* 2:124, are likewise inclined to credit it; Macan, *Her.,* 2:396, remarks that it

allows Herodotus to finish his sixth book on a constructive note, complimentary both to Miltiades and Athens.

34. Burn, *Persia and the Greeks,* p. 133.
35. C. A. Robinson, Jr., "Athenian Politics, 510-486 B.C.," *AJP* 66(1945):260; see also M. F. McGregor, "The Pro-Persian Party at Athens from 510-480 B.C.," *Harvard Studies in Classical Philology,* suppl. 1(1940):71-95, for another view of the political spectrum.
36. C. Hignett, *History of the Athenian Constitution,* p. 326.
37. A. W. Gomme, "Athenian Notes: Athenian Politics, 510-483 B.C.," *AJP* 65(1944):321-2.
38. P. Treves, "Xanthippus," *OCD*[2], 1140; V. Ehrenberg, *From Solon to Socrates* (London, 1962), p. 128, calls the accusation "ridiculous;" also, see H. Berve, *Miltiades, Studien zur Geschichte des Mannes und Seiner Zeit* (Berlin, 1937), pp. 66-7.
39. Wade-Gery, *Essays,* p. 178, thinks Themistocles used his position as judge to help acquit Miltiades.
40. Hdt. 6. 99-100.
41. J. A. R. Munro, in *CAH*[2], 4:234; R. Sealey, *A History of the Greek City States* (Berkeley and Los Angeles, 1976), p. 188, makes an even lower estimate for the Persians, placing their entire force at around 20,000.
42. T. S. Brown, *The Greek Historians* (Lexington, Mass., 1973), p. 40.
43. Plut. *Quaest. Conv.* 1. 10; Dem. *Orationes* 19:303; M. Chambers, "The Authenticity of the Themistocles Decree," *American Historical Review* 67(1962):313, finds good grounds for also doubting the Miltiades decree as it existed in the fourth century, but does not deny that it may derive from an authentic tradition.
44. *CAH*[2], 4:244; F. Maurice, "The Campaign and Battle of Marathon," *JHS* 52(1932):13-24; see also N. Whatley, "Reconstructing Marathon," *JHS* 84(1964):119-39.
45. Maurice, "Marathon," *JHS* 52(1932):21.
46. N. G. L. Hammond, "The Campaign of Marathon," *JHS* 88(1968):18; W. K. Pritchett, "Marathon Revisited," *Studies in Ancient Greek Topography, University of California Publications in Classical Studies,* 1(1965):1:91-2.
47. The so-called "Suidas," more properly "Souda."
48. Hammond, "Campaign of Marathon," *JHS* 88(1968):36-7.
49. *CAH*[2], 4:237.
50. *PW* 6(1907):1281-2; W. Smith, *Dictionary of Greek and Roman Geography* (London, 1873), 1:599.
51. Robinson, "Athenian Politics," *AJP* 66(1945):251; Hignett, *Hist. Ath. Const.*, pp. 179-81, points out, however, that Cleisthenes had followed a pro-Persian policy, at least temporarily.
52. Robinson (above, n. 51); McGregor, "Pro-Persian Party," *Harvard Studies,* suppl. 1 (1940):74, points out that much of the former Pisistratid support had been attached by Cleisthenes.
53. Gomme, "Athenian Notes," *AJP* 65(1944):321-4; E. Gruen, "Stesimbrotus on Miltiades and Themistocles," *California Studies in Classical Antiquity* 3(1970):92; Wade-Gery, *Essays,* pp. 171-9; Berve, *Miltiades,* p. 70.
54. Hdt. 6. 109; A. W. Gomme, "Herodotus and Marathon," *Phoenix* 6(1952):78, says flatly that this is a speech that Miltiades must have made to the Ekklesia, not to the polemarch; Macan, *Her.*, 2:366, remarks that the speech "appears to be coloured by later ideas."
55. Arist. *Rhet.* 3. 1411 A; some scholars, such as Munro, in *CAH*[2], 4:237-8, and Maurice, "Marathon," *JHS* 52(1932):16-8, seem by implication, at least, to have regarded the expedition to Eretria as feasible; Ehrenberg, *From Solon to Socrates,* p. 131, dismisses it, saying it would have meant the "complete loss" of the Athenian force.
56. Hdt. 6. 103; Macan, *Her.*, 1:358, doubts that a decree of the Assembly was necessary to set the troops in motion in 490 B.C.; he sees a clear inference however, that Callimachus led the march; Berve, *Miltiades,* pp. 78-83, analyzes in detail.
57. Arist. *Ath. Pol.* 22.5; K. von Fritz and E. Kapp, *Aristotle's Constitution of Athens* (New York, 1961), p. 165, remark that Herodotus is clearly in error as to this.
58. Hdt. 6. 109; Macan, *Her.*, 1:365, thinks the polemarch voted equally with the generals; N. G. L. Hammond, "Strategia and Hegemonia in Fifth Century Athens," *CQ* n.s. 19(1969):119-23, agrees entirely with Herodotus; A. W. Gomme, "Herodotus and Marathon," *Phoenix* 6(1952):78, says these words were a part of Miltiades' earlier speech to the Assembly, thus not addressed to Callimachus; How and Wells, *Commentary,* 2:111, point out that Miltiades' confident prophecy of Athens' future greatness was an anachronism which Herodotus must have gotten from his Philaid sources.

59. Hdt. 6. 111; Macan, *Her.*, 1:368-9, finds several possible interpretations of the phrase "as they were numbered," hence he thinks it impossible exactly to determine the order of the tribal regiments at Marathon.
60. Gomme, "Herodotus and Marathon," *Phoenix* 6(1952):82-3.
61. Maurice, "Marathon," *JHS* 52(1932):22; W. Donlan and J. Thompson, "The Charge at Marathon; Herodotus 6. 112," *CJ* 71(1976):339-43.
62. Many attempts have been made to fix the exact date of the battle of Marathon, with no general agreement. A few historians think the year was 491, instead of 490. It is now conceded that the problem is impossible of solution, partly because of insufficiencies in Herodotus' account, partly because of those inherent in the Athenian moon calendar. See B. D. Meritt, *The Athenian Year,* p. 239. A date in late August has found the most general acceptance.
63. There is some difference of viewpoint among the standard modern authorities. See Grote, *History of Greece,* 2:201; Beloch, *Griech. Gesch.* II, 1:20; Busolt, *Griech. Gesch.*, 2:589-92; In the more recent scholarship, C. Hignett, *Xerxes' Invasion of Greece* (Oxford, 1963), pp. 70-3, goes along with much of Herodotus' account, without trying to rationalize the Persians' strange, vulnerable position south of the stream; A. R. Burn, *Persia and the Greeks,* p. 248, thinks they were placed there as a decoy.
64. Hignett, *Hist. Ath. Const.*, p. 172.
65. P. K. Baillie Reynolds, "The Shield Signal at the Battle of Marathon," *JHS* 49(1929):101-2; Burn, *Persia and the Greeks,* p. 251, thinks it was a signal from Hippias' friends in the city advising the Perisans to come around to Athens immediately.
66. H. G. Hudson, "The Shield Signal at Marathon," *American Historical Review* 42 (1931):443-59; Maurice, "Marathon," *JHS* 52(1932):18.
67. Hdt. 6. 121; Macan, *Her.*, 1:376, faults Herodotus' logic in defending the Alcmaeonids, and suspects that the whole passage may be spurious; How and Wells, *Commentary,* 2:115, agree; T. S. Brown, *The Greek Historians,* p. 40, stresses that Herodotus' defense of the Alcmaeonids is colored by his friendship for Pericles.
68. Pl. *Leg.* 3. 698 E.
69. Plut. *Aristides,* 5; Hdt. 6. 116, implies it was the same day; How and Wells, *Commentary,* 2:113, remark that the march back could hardly have been accomplished on the same day; Macan, *Her.*, 2:372, agrees.
70. Plut. *Them.* 5; A. J. Podlecki, *The Life of Themistocles* (Montreal, 1975), p. 8-9, believes that, whether true or not, the story is indicative of Themistocles' real attitude toward Miltiades.
71. Hdt. 6. 135; How and Wells, *Commentary,* 2:121, remark that Herodotus' account is here affected by the idea of nemesis, divine retribution following Miltiades' overweening success.
72. Hdt. 6. 136; How and Wells, *Commentary,* 2:121, affirm that the charge against Miltiades was clearly one of treason; Hignett, *Hist. Ath. Const.*, p. 154, calls it merely a charge of "deceiving the people;" Berve, *Miltiades,* pp. 99-100, agrees.
73. J. A. R. Munro, in *CAH*², 4:252-3; de Selincourt, *The World of Herodotus,* pp. 100-1, at the other extreme (and with some justification), calls Miltiades' Paros expedition "an example of piracy."

5 *The Main Storm Approaches* 490-480 B.C.

1. Plut. *Aristides* 5. 3: I. Limentani, *Plutarchi Vita Aristidis* (Florence, 1964), p. 22, however, doubts that there was much glory for either Aristides or Themistocles at the center of the battle; B. Perrin, *Plutarch's Themistocles and Aristides* (New York, 1901), pp. 273-4, calls attention, however, that Themistocles' and Aristides' tribes were far away from each other in the order of battle.
2. T. J. Cadoux, "The Athenian Archons from Kreon to Hypsichides," *Journal of Hellenic Studies* 68(1948):116-7.
3. Plut. *Aristides* 22. 1; However, Plutarch places the reforms a decade later, after the second Persian invasion; Limentani, *Aristidis,* p. 92, agrees that this activity properly belongs to the earlier period, after Marathon; see K. J. Beloch, *Griechische Geschichte* (Strassburg, 1912), II, 2:139, for the correct placing.
4. Arist. *Ath. Pol.* 22. 5; R. J. Buck, "The Reforms of 487 B.C. in the Selection of Archons," *Classical Philology* 60(1965):96-101, sees Aristides not as the prime mover, but as an impor-

tant collaborator (along with Themistocles and Megacles) in helping the archon Telesinus to secure the reform, aimed mainly at Pisistratid influence in the Areopagus. It seems to me that a more prestigious sponsor than the inconspicuous Telesinus was needed for so important a reform, thus that the tradition Plutarch had found about Aristides must have been the right one.

5. J. Day and M. Chambers, *Aristotle's History of Athenian Democracy* (Berkeley and Los Angeles, 1962), p. 113.
6. C. Hignett, *History of the Athenian Constitution* (Oxford, 1958), p. 175; on the method of selecting the generals, see E. S. Staveley, "Voting Procedure at the Election of Strategoi," *Ehrenberg Studies* (New York, 1967), pp. 275-288.
7. G. De Sanctis, *Atthis: Storia della Repubblica Ateniese* (Turin, 1912), p. 374, sees evidence here of a revulsion against an Alcmaeonid stranglehold on the chief offices, which would be very natural; however, Aristides seems for the most part, to have been on friendly terms with them. For the general esteem in which Aristides was held, see Wilamowitz, *Aristoteles und Athen* (Berlin, 1966), 1:159-61.
8. Hignett, *Hist. Ath. Const.*, p. 185; De Sanctis, *Atthis*, pp. 367-8; E. M. Walker, in *CAH²*, 4:266.
9. C. A. Robinson, Jr., "Athenian Politics, 510-486 B.C.," *American Journal of Philology* 66(1945):251-4; E. M. Walker, *CAH²*, 4:266.
10. C. W. Fornara, "Themistocles' Archonship," *Historia* 20(1971):534-40, thinks Themistocles' program of naval building was undertaken through a special commission, not when he held the archonship; D. M. Lewis, "Themistocles' Archonship," *Historia* 22(1973):757-8, and W. W. Dickie, "Thucydides 1. 93. 3," *Historia* 22(1973):758-9, dispute this.
11. Plut. *Aristides* 5. 3; but see Limentani (above, n. 1).
12. Arist. *Ath. Pol.* 22. 4.
13. F. J. Frost, "Themistocles' Place in Athenian Politics," *California Studies in Classical Antiquity* 1(1968):124. However, Mr. Frost relates these ostraca to the contest with Megacles in the following year; my feeling is, that with Themistocles' name found on so many ostraca, and in so many places, he was probably involved both times, and later as well.
14. A. W. Gomme, "Athenian Notes: Athenian Politics, 510-483 B.C.," *AJP* 65(1941):324.
15. R. Meiggs and D. Lewis, *A Selection of Greek Historical Inscriptions to the End of the Fifth Century* B.C. (Oxford, 1969), p. 46; this information may now be outdated by new discoveries in Athens' Ceramicus, such as a recent find of more than 2,000 votes for Megacles; but Themistocles has also gained 1,000 more; see F. J. Frost, "Themistocles and Mnesiphilus," *Historia* 20(1971):23.
16. Plut. *Them.* 2. 4; for the relations between Themistocles and the sophist Mnesiphilus, see Frost, "Themistocles and Mnesiphilus," *Historia* 20(1971): 20-25.
17. Arist. *Ath. Pol.* 22. 6.
18. E. Vanderpool, "The Ostracism of the Elder Alkibiades," *Hesperia* 21(1952):1-8.
19. Arist. *Ath. Pol.* 22. 6.
20. This is, of course, a hypothetical judgment; for a differing opinion, see W. G. Forrest, "Themistocles and Argos," *Classical Quarterly* n.s. 10(1960):233-4, who thinks Xanthippus was not an Alcmaeonid partisan, despite his marriage.
21. Plut. *Them.* 4; Hignett, *Hist. Ath. Const.*, p. 183, disagrees, maintaining that the Persian threat was a sufficient motivation, as does K. J. Beloch, *Griechische Geschichte* (Strassburg, 1912), II, 2:134-5.
22. A. R. Burn, *Persia and the Greeks* (New York, 1962), p. 291.
23. Hignett, *Hist. Ath. Const.*, p. 183; De Sanctis, *Atthis*, pp. 367-8; Beloch, *Griech. Gesch.*, II, 2:134-5.
24. P. A. Brunt, "The Hellenic League Against Persia," *Historia* 2(1953):156, citing Paus. 3. 12.
25. Hdt. 7. 5.
26. Hdt. 7. 5-6; R. W. Macan, *Herodotus: The Seventh, Eighth, and Ninth Books* (New York, 1973), 1:6, observes that this would seem more important to a Greek than to a Persian.
27. Hdt. 7. 20; Macan, *Her.*, 1:29, states that this is a "mere formula for a heightened superlative;" but W. W. How and J. Wells, *A Commentary on Herodotus* (Oxford, 1928), 2:133, note that Thucydides has agreed with the statement. (Thuc. 1. 123).
28. Hdt. 7. 35; Macan, *Her.*, 1:49, calls this narration "unfortunate for the authority of Herodotus;" How and Wells, *Commentary*, 2:141, however, remark that Herodotus may have misunderstood what was actually a religious ceremony "to attempt by magical rites to compel the Hellespont to submit."

29. J. B. Bury, *History of Greece* (London, 1931), p. 268.
30. Burn, *Persia and the Greeks*, p. 327; How and Wells, *Commentary*, 2:367-8; F. Maurice, "The Size of Xerxes' Army in the Invasion of Greece," *JHS* 50(1930):227, agrees with J. A. R. Munro, *CAH*[2], 4:273, in placing the total at around 180,000; C. Hignett, *Xerxes' Invasion of Greece* (Oxford, 1963), p. 94, makes an even smaller estimate of about 80,000.
31. Maurice, "The Size of Xerxes' Army," *JHS* 50(1930):228-32.
32. Hdt. 7. 89; Hignett, *Xerxes' Invasion of Greece*, p. 93, estimates that there were perhaps 600 triremes in the Persian fleet; Macan, *Her.*, 1:112, notes a discrepancy between Herodotus' figures and those of Aeschylus.
33. Brunt, "The Hellenic League against Persia," *Historia* 2(1953): 135-63, and H. D. Westlake, "The Medism of Thessaly," *JHS* 56(1936):12-24, have differences of opinion on the representation of the northern Greeks at the congresses, but they agree that the Thessalians were represented at some stage, despite Hdt. 7. 138.
34. Brunt, "Hellenic League," *Historia* 2(1953):142-3.
35. Hdt. 7. 162; Macan, *Her.*, 1:225, calls this "possibly authentic;" How and Wells, *Commentary*, 2:198, appear to accept it.
36. Westlake, "The Medism of Thessaly," *JHS* 56(1936); 19, remarks that this reveals how little the Congress Greeks knew of the north, that the pass in question was a precipitous one which they could easily have guarded; however, there were more distant ones which the Persians could have used, eventually; Macan, *Her.*, 1:253, says that Herodotus' account here (at 7. 173) is "lamentably inadequate and incorrect."
37. G. B. Grundy, *The Great Persian War and its Preliminaries* (London, 1901), p. 231.
38. Hignett, *Xerxes' Invasion*, p. 115; J. A. S. Evans, "Notes on Thermopylae and Artemisium," *Historia* 18(1969):393; Grundy, *Great Persian War*, p. 270 ff., disagrees; see also Beloch, *Griech. Gesch.*, II, 1:42.
39. *CAH*[2], 4:281; Grundy, *Great Persian War*, p. 543.
40. Hdt. 8. 15; Macan, *Her.*, 1:378, calls Herodotus' explanation a "misconception;" How and Wells, *Commentary*, 2:239, say that Herodotus "insufficiently recognizes" the interdependence of Thermopylae and Artemisium.
41. A. Ferrill, "Herodotus and the Strategy and Tactics of the Invasion of Xerxes," *American Historical Review* 72(1966):111; J. A. S. Evans, "Notes on Thermopylae and Artemisium," *Historia* 18(1969):389-405, has similar views, but credits the Congress with a more definite plan.
42. Hignett, *Xerxes' Invasion*, p. 114.
43. Ibid., p. 149.
44. Burn, *Persia and the Greeks*, p. 350.
45. Diod. Sic. 11. 12, insists that though Eurybiades was admiral, Themistocles determined the strategy.
46. R. Sealey, *A History of the Greek City States* (Berkeley and Los Angeles, 1976), p. 210.
47. Brunt, "Hellenic League," *Historia* 2(1953):140-1, points out that the great number of Athenian ships in the Greek fleet enabled Themistocles to put pressure on the admiral.
48. Hdt. 8. 5; This story has of course often been doubted, partly because of the tremendous sums involved, and the difficulty of keeping such a secret. But Themistocles' spending of money to erect statues and even a temple glorifying himself to the Athenians of later days points to at least a modicum of truth in the tale. Macan, *Her.*, 1:364, in disbelief, objects that this reflects discredit on Themistocles. It certainly does! Furthermore, it is difficult to explain the sudden aggression of Eurybiades and the Peloponnesian units otherwise; if it was hard to force them to risk a naval battle later at Salamis, nearer to their homes, how much harder must it have been to get them to launch an unprovoked attack in open waters well north of the Euripus, designated by Herodotus as their first defense commitment. Perrin, *Themistocles and Aristides*, p. 196, thinks the money was pay for the ships' crews, and that most of it really came from Athens.
49. J. A. S. Evans, "Notes on Thermopylae and Artemisium," *Historia* 18(1969):389, calls attention that whatever strategy the Greeks may have intended to use at Artemisium, it did not work; K. Sacks, "Herodotus and the Dating of the Battle of Thermopylae," *CQ* n.s. 26(1976):232-48, places the ending of the battles of Thermopylae and Artemisium on September 19, 480 B.C.
50. Some are of the contrary opinion. J. F. Lazenby, "The Strategy of the Greeks in the Opening Campaign of the Persian War," *Hermes* 92(1964):271, sees no reason why Thermopylae could not have been held indefinitely, except for Ephialtes' treachery; Hignett, *Xerxes' Inva-*

sion, pp. 127-41, thinks Leonidas could have held it if promptly and properly reenforced. But that is just the point; he wasn't.

51. Hdt. 8. 19; Macan, *Her.,* 1:381, finds many difficulties here also, especially because it makes Themistocles assume Eurybiades' function as commander in chief.
52. Evans, "Notes on Thermopylae and Artemisium," *Historia* 18(1969):395-400.

6 *Cloudburst over Hellas* 480-479 B.C.

1. A. R. Burn, *Persia and the Greeks* (New York, 1962), p. 349.
2. M. H. Jameson, "A Decree of Themistocles from Troezen," *Hesperia* 14(1960):198-223, was an early advocate of authenticity; C. W. Fornara, "The Value of the Themistocles Decree," *American Historical Review* 78(1967):425-33, shows it is consistent with Herodotus; C. Habicht, "Falsche Urkunden zur Geschichte Athens im Zeitalter der Perserkriege," *Hermes* 89(1961):1-35, is a leading opponent; so is M. Chambers, "The Authenticity of the Themistocles Decree," *AHR* 67(1962):306-16. A review of the scholarship on the subject has been made by S. Burstein, "The Recall of the Ostracized and the Themistocles Decree," *California Studies in Classical Antiquity* 4(1971):93-110.
3. The "Themistocles Decree" is a stone tablet found at Troezen on the Peloponnesian coast, and made public about 1960. It was inscribed in the third century B.C., supposedly a copy of a decree by Themistocles at Athens in 480, before he left for Artemisium. In its main provision he orders the able-bodied men up for military duty on Athens' 200 ships, 100 of which are to proceed northward with him, while the rest stay to guard Salamis, where the women, children, and unfit men are to be evacuated, some going also to Troezen. R. Meiggs and D. Lewis, *A Selection of Greek Historical Inscriptions to the End of the Fifth Century B.C.* (Oxford, 1969, pp. 48-52). It tends to show Themistocles as masterminding the entire Greek defense, with a plan different from that of the Greek High Command, which he intends to bring around to his thinking. The authenticity of the "Decree" has been attacked on many grounds; linguistic, as anachronistic, and as a slick, after-the-fact invention. By one view, it may have been intended as a compliment by the people of Troezen to Athens. M. Chambers, "The Authenticity of the Themistocles Decree," *American Historical Review* 67(1962):316. Even so, the "Themistocles Decree" may have preserved much that is true.
4. Hdt. 7. 140; R. W. Macan, *Herodotus: The Seventh, Eighth, and Ninth Books* (New York, 1973), 1:189, and W. W. How and J. Wells, *A Commentary on Herodotus* (Oxford, 1928), 2:181, agree that Herodotus was wrong on the time relationships concerning the two oracles, that the first one must have been after the Tempe expedition, not before; also, that there was a considerable time interval between the two oracular consultations.
5. H. W. Parke and D. E. W. Wormell, *The Delphic Oracle* (Oxford, 1956), 1:170.
6. Ibid., 1:171.
7. Arist. *Ath. Pol.* 23. 1.
8. Hdt. 8. 51; Macan, *Her.,* 1:437, doubts the story, suspecting that those who chose to stay and defend the Acropolis were neither so few, so poor, so abject, or so superstitious as the story asserts; How and Wells, *Commentary,* 2:251, observe that the wooden barricades must have been at the western end of the Acropolis, where the Propylaea was later built, the other sides being so rocky and precipitous that no barricades were needed.
9. R. Sealey, "Again the Siege of the Acropolis, 480 B.C.," *Calif. Studies* 5(1972):183-94; J. B. Bury, "Aristides at Salamis," *Classical Review* 10(1896):414-18.
10. Hdt., 8. 52, merely says "a long time"; Macan, *Her.,* 1:434, calls this "lamentably vague" but says it indicates the relative success of the resistance; G. Busolt, *Griechische Geschichte* (Gotha, 1893), 2:695, estimated the period at two weeks; C. Hignett, *Xerxes' Invasion of Greece* (Oxford, 1963), p. 200, cautiously avoids a commitment.
11. P. A. Brunt, "The Hellenic League against Persia," *Historia* 2(1953):140-1, explains that the rights of the commanders were not precisely defined under the League. Eurybiades, the admiral, apparently had a right of final decision which included overruling, but often decisions were taken by vote of all the captains. And commanders of the larger squadrons, such as the Athenian, had a wider authority than others.
12. G. Grote, *History of Greece* (New York, 1881), 2:302, was one of the first to make this point.
13. Hdt. 8. 59; Plut. *Them.* 11. 2; Macan, *Her.,* 1:446, observes that the statement seems

designed to reflect discredit on Themistocles; How and Wells, *Commentary,* 2:254, appear to accept it; also B. Perrin, *Plutarch's Themistocles and Aristides* (New York, 1901), p. 202.

14. Hdt. 8. 62; Macan, *Her.,* 1:451-2, admits this, but calls attention that Athenians had had westward colonization on their minds for a long time; How and Wells, *Commentary,* 2:256, point out that Themistocles had named his daughters Italia and Sybaris, indicating his real interest in the area; Hignett, *Xerxes' Invasion,* p. 204, thinks the story may be a fabrication; Perrin, *Themistocles and Aristides,* p. 202, points out that Themistocles' speech is much like the one Miltiades made to Callimachus at Marathon.
15. Hdt. 8. 90; Macan, *Her.,* 1:494, observes that Xerxes' throne would have had to have been placed high up on Mt. Aigaleos for a proper viewing of the whole battle; How and Wells, *Commentary,* 2:266, add that it must have been opposite the town of Salamis.
16. N. G. L. Hammond, "The Battle of Salamis," *Journal of Hellenic Studies* 76(1956):39-45, sifts these and other accounts, with the modern interpretations, though without particularly pursuing the matter of the secret messenger; see also A. R. Burn, *Persia and the Greeks* (New York, 1962), pp. 451-3; J. L. Myres, *Herodotus: Father of History* (Oxford, 1953), pp. 271-3, is helpful in a general way.
17. None as to sites at the bay's mouth. There is considerable dispute about its interior, especially over the identification and position of the islands. See W. K. Pritchett, "Salamis Revisited," *Studies in Ancient Greek Topography,* Part I, *University of California Publications: Classical Studies* 1(1965):94-102.
18. Hignett, *Xerxes' Invasion,* pp. 213-5.
19. Hdt. 8. 75; Macan, *Her.,* 1:476, comments on the differences between Herodotus' account and that of Aeschylus, which does not taint the sender, as Herodotus' does; How and Wells, *Commentary,* 2:261, remark that Aeschylus has rightly attributed Xerxes' decision to advance on his receipt of Themistocles' message.
20. Aesch. *Pers.* 353-7.
21. See A. W. H. Adkins, *Merit and Responsibility, a Study in Greek Values* (Oxford, 1960), pp. 153-71, and especially pp. 156-63.
22. The attitude of the oracle at Delphi is the best evidence of the way realistic Greeks assessed the situation. See Parke and Wormell, *The Delphic Oracle,* Ch. 7.
23. Hignett, *Xerxes' Invasion,* pp. 408-11. But the story of the Tenian trireme is almost as difficult to accept; why would any ship, even a Greek one, have deserted the Persians at this moment?
24. Burn, *Persia and the Greeks,* p. 443; Hignett, *Xerxes' Invasion,* p. 232, places the Greek total at 310.
25. Hdt. 8. 48, ftn. 5. (G. Rawlinson tr., F. Godolphin, ed.); B. Perrin, *Plutarch's Themistocles and Aristides* (New York, 1901), pp. 206-7, thinks no ships, either Persian or Greek, were sent to the western outlet, which, if true, would have left the Corinthians in the main battle line.
26. Burn, *Persia and the Greeks,* p. 474, here corrects Plutarch, who had assumed the Persian admiral's name was "Ariamenes."
27. Hammond, "The Battle of Salamis," *JHS* 76(1956):52, considers the Persian strategy was excellent; E. Potter and C. Nimitz, *Sea Power: A Naval History* (Englewood Cliffs, 1960), pp. 7-9, believe it was the only sensible course, dictated largely by weather considerations and seasonal change.
28. Burn, *Persia and the Greeks,* p. 324.
29. Plut. *Them.* 14.2. W. W. Tarn, "The Fleet of Xerxes," *JHS* 28(1908):208, however, takes exception to some of Plutarch's statements. R. Flacelière, *Plutarque, Vie de Thémistocle* (Paris, 1972), p. 66, remarks that Themistocles could speak with certainty of the 200 Athenian triremes, 20 of which had been lent to the Chalcidians.
30. Aesch. *Pers.* 341-3.
31. Hignett, *Xerxes' Invasion,* p. 235.
32. Plut. *Them.* 14.3. Flacelière, *Thémistocle,* p. 66, calls attention to the discrepancy in names for the King's brother, whom Plutarch had called "Ariamenes," but Herodotus "Ariabignes."
33. Diod. Sic. 11. 18; G. Grundy, *The Great Persian War and its Preliminaries* (London, 1901), p. 399; K. J. Beloch, *Griechische Geschichte* (Strassburg, 1912), II, 1, p. 42.
34. C. W. Fornara, "The Hoplite Achievement at Psyttaleia," *JHS* 86(1966):51-4, doubts that Aristides and the hoplites really landed on Psyttaleia, this version being the invention of a later, conservative tradition.

35. K. Sacks, "Herodotus and the Dating of the Battle of Thermopylae," *Classical Quarterly* n.s. 26(1976):232, dates the battle of Salamis on Sept. 28 or 29, 480 B.C., by relating it to the solar eclipse known to have taken place a few days later, on Oct. 2.
36. Hdt. 8. 90; Diod. Sic. 11. 18.
37. P. Green, *The Year of Salamis* (London, 1970), pp. 202-3, notices this particularly.
38. Hammond, "The Battle of Salamis," *JHS* 76(1956):52-3.
39. Hdt. 8. 108; Macan, *Her.*, 1:525, agrees to the implication here.
40. Hdt. 8:110; Macan, *Her.*, 1:530, rejects Sicinnus' second mission as an example of Herodotus' hostility to Themistocles; Hignett, *Xerxes' Invasion*, p. 242, likewise rejects it; A. J. Podlecki, *The Life of Themistocles* (Montreal, 1975), pp. 22-6, accepts the first mission, but not the second; How and Wells, *Commentary*, 2:272, however, point out that this second mission can be construed from a proper reading of Thuc. 1:137.
41. Hdt. 8. 123; Macan, *Her.*, 1:550, mistrusts this, since the war was not yet over; has the incident been antedated, he asks, or is it entirely apocryphal?; Podlecki, *Life*, p. 28, opts for the latter, calling attention that the same story has been told about others, in another context. Being so typical of the ancient Greeks, (and of the ancient world generally) it could have happened many times—in my opinion.
42. Grundy, *Great Persian War*, p. 360.
43. Plut. *Them.* 17; H. Martin, Jr., "The Character of Plutarch's Themistocles," *Transactions of the American Philological Association* 92(1961):337, says that Plutarch's conception of Themistocles' character is mainly along this line, in terms of his love of glory (*philotimos*), joined with native intelligence (*synesis*); Flacelière, *Thémistocle*, p. 71, remarks that the bodyguard which accompanied Themistocles in Sparta were the elite of their young warrior class.
44. Ibid.; Podlecki, *Life*, pp. 135-42, emphasizes the need for caution in accepting the anecdotes about Themistocles, since we don't know Plutarch's unnamed sources. This one is consistent both with the course of events and with what is known of Themistocles' character.
45. Since no complete lists exist, one cannot be absolutely sure. But Themistocles is not mentioned as having any command this year, and it would not be like him to linger inactive in the background, if he were, indeed, one of the generals. Podlecki, *Life*, p. 30, thinks, however, that Themistocles was one of the generals for the year 479.
46. Diod. Sic. 11. 27.
47. Grundy, *Great Persian War*, p. 437.
48. *CAH*², 4:317-8.
49. Hdt. 8. 143; Plut. *Aristides* 10.5; Macan, *Her.*, 1:588, considers this speech is pre-Periclean; How and Wells, *Commentary*, 2:286, think that Plutarch's attribution of the Athenian speech to Aristides is conjectural; I. Limentani, *Plutarchi Vita Aristidis* (Florence, 1964), p. 47, apparently accepts it, and considers that Aristides' speech to the ambassadors must have been made in the Council, before taking the issue to the Assembly.
50. Plut. *Aristides* 10.5; this speech seems to reflect Aristides' personality in the same way that the Funeral Oration (Thuc. 2:35 ff.) did Pericles'. One must remember, however, that Aristides was highly regarded by Athenian writers.
51. Hdt. 8. 144; Macan, *Her.*, 1:589, sees later accretions here. It sounds not so much like an apology, he says, as a "bid for the hegemony of a free Hellas." How and Wells, *Commentary*, 2:286, however, see it as "in harmony with the struggle against the Mede."
52. Hdt. 9. 5.
53. Hignett, *Xerxes' Invasion*, pp. 280-3.
54. Hdt. 9. 11.
55. J. A. R. Munro, in *CAH*², 4:321.
56. Burn, *Persia and the Greeks*, p. 505.
57. Hdt. 9. 9; Macan, *Her.*, 1:607, remarks that the warning was overdue; How and Wells, *Commentary*, 2:289-90, are inclined to credit the Argive threat.
58. Hignett, *Xerxes' Invasion*, pp. 286-7, discusses Pausanias' background; see also, M. White, "Some Agiad Dates: Pausanias and his Sons," *JHS* 84(1964):150-1.
59. Munro's estimate, *CAH*², 4:324.
60. This is the most obvious, central route, preferred by a majority of modern writers. Other roads, one farther east, one farther west, have some support. Neither Herodotus nor Plutarch sheds any light on the problem.
61. Grundy, *Great Persian War*, p. 462.

62. Hdt. 9. 51.
63. W. K. Pritchett, "Plataia Revisited," *Studies in Ancient Greek Topography,* Part I, *University of California Publications*: *Classical Studies* 1(1965):115, says that the site of "the island" cannot now be identified.
64. Grundy, *Great Persian War,* p. 473, believes that Herodotus has misinterpreted Pausanias' strategy at this point. He maintains that Pausanias' shift of position was not for a better water supply, but to place his men for a surprise flanking attack, which the Persians promptly frustrated by an alert movement of their own.
65. Hdt. 9. 53; Macan, *Her.,* 1:709-14, doubts the whole story.
66. J. F. C. Fuller, *A Military History of the Western World* (New York, 1954), 1:48.
67. Grundy, *Great Persian War,* p. 500; Busolt, *Griech. Gesch.,* 2:735-6.
68. Hdt. 7. 211; How and Wells, *Commentary,* 2:224, cite Diod. Sic. 11. 7, as attaching greater importance to the larger shields of the Greeks.
69. Hdt. 9. 41; Macan, *Her.,* 680-1, thinks Artabazus' advice was bad; How and Wells, *Commentary,* 2:306, on the contrary, speak of Artabazus' "prudent counsel."
70. Paus. 9. 2; Diod. Sic. 11. 33.
71. Grundy, *Great Persian War,* p. 515.
72. Hdt. 9. 106; Macan, *Her.,* 1:807, cautions that, obviously, the Greeks at Mycale did not really encounter the main Persian army guarding Ionia.
73. Hignett, *Xerxes' Invasion,* pp. 249, 455, holds simply that both were fought in August, 479, and that because of the complex problems in regard to both, that it is difficult to fix them more precisely than this.

7 *The Leadership of Themistocles* 479-473 B.C.

1. Diod. Sic. 11. 44.
2. R. Meiggs and D. Lewis, *Greek Historical Inscriptions to the End of the Fifth Century* B.C. (Oxford, 1969), p. 60.
3. Thuc. 1. 130; Plut. *Aristides* 23. 3; A. W. Gomme, *A Historical Commentary on Thucydides* (Oxford, 1959), 1:433, remarks that royalty in Sparta did not customarily act this way.
4. C. W. Fornara, "Some Aspects of the Career of Pausanias of Sparta," *Historia* 15(1966):257-71.
5. M. Lang, "Scapegoat Pausanias," *Classical Journal* 63(1967):182.
6. Fornara, "Aspects of Pausanias," *Historia* 15(1966):266.
7. Plut. *Aristides* 23. 4; Arist. *Ath. Pol.* 23. 4 is not so certain as to this; however, J. Day and M. Chambers, *Aristotle's History of Athenian Democracy* (Berkeley and Los Angeles, 1962), p. 181, blame Pausanias' arrogance for the change; I. Limentani, *Plutarchi Vita Aristidis* (Florence, 1964), p. 95, points out that the captains petitioning Aristides were precisely those islanders who were convinced the Spartans would do nothing more for them.
8. Arist. *Ath. Pol.* 23. 4; R. Meiggs, *The Athenian Empire* (Oxford, 1972), p. 42, is not inclined to credit the story of the ramming of Pausanias' vessel; L. I. Highby, *The Erythrae Decree, Klio,* Beiheft 36 (Leipzig, 1936), pp. 39-57, while discounting the traditional accounts blaming Pausanias, tends to justify Athens' assumption of power; see H. Meyer, "Vorgeschichte und Begründung des Delisch-Attischen Seebundes," *Historia* 12(1963):405-46, for a less favorable view of Athens' role. Limentani, *Aristidis,* p. 96, thinks it has the earmarks of an anecdote.
9. Thuc. 1. 95; Gomme, *Commentary,* 1:272, comments ironically on the "politeness" of the Athenians in this episode.
10. P. J. Rhodes, "Thucydides on Pausanias and Themistocles," *Historia* 19(1970):390.
11. Arist. *Ath. Pol.* 23. 2.
12. Diod. Sic. 11. 50.
13. W. W. How and J. Wells, *A Commentary on Herodotus* (Oxford, 1928) 2:286, call Plutarch's attribution to Aristides of the anonymous Athenian speech given by Hdt. 8. 143, "a mere conjecture;" however, the fact that the Athenians soon afterward elected Aristides their strategos autocrator points to strong, responsible leadership by him at this point.
14. Thuc. 1. 93; Gomme, *Commentary,* 1:263-5, in general substantiates Thucydides' account; E. Cavaignac, *Études sur l'Histoire Financière d'Athènes au Ve Siècle* (Paris, 1908), p. 20,

adds that some parts of this construction had to be by professional workmen, paid by the state.

15. Plut. *Them.* 18.
16. The Andros and Carystus incidents (Hdt. 8. 111, 112) are leading instances of Themistocles' growing imperialism; the second Carystus incident can probably be charged to him too, though Thucydides does not name him.
17. W. S. Ferguson, *Greek Imperialism* (Boston, 1913), pp. 39-40, 61-2; A. French, *The Growth of the Athenian Economy* (New York, 1964), pp. 96-7.
18. Thuc. 1. 91; Gomme, *Commentary,* 1:260, emphasizes that Themistocles had in mind his pre-Salamis experiences in this conversation with the Spartans; K. J. Beloch, *Griechische Geschichte* (Strassburg, 1912), II, 2, 146-54, rejected Themistocles' visit to Sparta as unhistorical; likewise, G. De Sanctis, *Atthis: Storia della Repubblica Ateniese* (Turin, 1912), p. 392; Gomme, *Commentary,* 1:267-70, analyzes and disposes of their objections.
19. G. Busolt, *Griechische Geschichte* (Gotha, 1901), 111, 1:43-6.
20. J. B. Bury, *A History of Greece to the Death of Alexander the Great* (London, 1931), p. 330.
21. Ar. *Eq.* 815.
22. Plut. *Them.* 19.
23. Plut. *Them.* 20; A. J. Podlecki, *Life of Themistocles* (Montreal, 1975), p. 29, calls this episode "not . . . implausible;" F. J. Frost, "Themistocles' Place in Athenian Politics," *California Studies in Classical Antiquity* 1(1968):120, credits the story; so does Flacelière, *Plutarque, Vie de Thémistocle* (Paris, 1972), p. 78.
24. *The Greek Historians* (New York, 1941), 1:504, n. 13 (F. Godolphin, ed.)
25. Hdt. 8. 111; R. W. Macan, *Herodotus: The Seventh, Eighth, and Ninth Books* (New York, 1973), 1:535, thinks this prejudicial to Themistocles; How and Wells, *Commentary,* 2:272, concede that some money may have stuck to Themistocles' fingers, but contend that his exactions were mainly in the public interest; this is the position taken earlier by Cavaignac, *Histoire Financière,* p. 47; also, by E. Meyer, *Geschichte des Altertums* (Stuttgart, 1936), 3:396.
26. Frost, "Themistocles' Place in Athenian Politics," *Calif. Studies* 1(1968):122, remarks that a "democrat" during this period was one who lacked influence in the councils of the great families, and was forced to take his proposals directly to the People; as to this, see also Frost, "Themistocles and Mnesiphilus," *Historia* 20(1971):20-5, who finds indications that Themistocles may have been out of favor with his noble relatives, and perhaps even with his own father.
27. Gomme, *Commentary,* 1:259, adds his voice to others in warning against Plutarch's picture of Aristides as entirely good, and Themistocles as rather the reverse; it is well to keep this in mind; Aristides had the favor of the Alcmaeonids, Themistocles was their enemy. Nevertheless the weight of the testimony makes the traditional picture seem fairly true. One is left with the impression that the reason the Alcmaeonids were successful in foisting their view on the historians is that the circumstances tended to bear them out. See Pl. *Grg.* 526 B.
28. Meiggs, *Athenian Empire,* p. 43, makes it plain that fear was a leading motive for Athens' acceptance of the leadership, knowing that Persia's enmity was directed chiefly against her.
29. R. Sealey, "The Origins of the Delian League," *Ehrenberg Studies* (New York, 1967), pp. 233-55, especially emphasizes this; but see also the criticism by A. H. Jackson, "The Original Purpose of the Delian League," *Historia* 18(1969):12-16.
30. Diod. Sic. 11. 47.
31. Arist. *Ath. Pol.* 23. 5; B. Perrin, *Plutarch's Themistocles and Aristides* (New York, 1901), p. 322, remarks that the Greek historical tradition "tended to exalt more and more the individual services of Aristides," also, that Thuc. 1. 96, the earliest treatment, does not even mention Aristides.
32. Plut. *Aristides* 25. 1; Limentani, *Aristidis,* p. 102, sees this as proof of a bilateral agreement.
33. Thuc. 1. 96.
34. See the discussion in Meiggs, *Athenian Empire,* pp. 62-7.
35. B. D. Meritt, H. T. Wade-Gery, M. F. McGregor, *The Athenian Tribute Lists* (Princeton, 1950), 3:342.
36. M. Chambers, "Four Hundred Sixty Talents," *Classical Philology* 53(1958):26-32, thinks it would have been difficult, if not impossible, for Aristides to have translated ships' services into cash, that these were probably not included in his total; S. K. Eddy, "Four Hundred Sixty Talents Once More," *CP* 63(1968):184-95, in partial disagreement, suggests a method by which these may have been equated.

37. Gomme, *Commentary,* 1:271, in criticism of Arist. *Ath. Pol.* 23. The point is well taken; Themistocles' domination of the Ekklesia seems to have been rather like that of the elder Pitt over the British House of Commons, prevailing by sheer will and ability, without much of an organized or personal following.
38. N. G. L. Hammond, "Origin and Nature of the Athenian Alliance," *Journal of Hellenic Studies* 87(1967):58.
39. Meiggs, *Athenian Empire,* p. 47, n.1.
40. Differences between the views of Meiggs and Hammond are largely reconciled, I think, as being merely the differences between theory and practice. A remaining point in dispute, whether or not Athens was also represented in the Synod, is not easily determined.
41. Meritt, Wade-Gery, and McGregor, *Athenian Tribute Lists,* 3:237. Plut. *Aristides* 25. 2 indicates that Aristides was probably aware of the views of Athens' imperialists, and may even have bowed to the "realities" of the situation; however, Plutarch cites his authority as Theophrastus, who probably followed the much challenged account in Arist. *Ath. Pol.* 24; as to the latter, see Day and Chambers, *Aristotle's History,* p. 124.
42. Hammond, "Origin and Nature," *JHS* 87(1967):53.
43. Thuc. 1. 96. 2; Gomme, *Commentary,* 1:272-3; *Inscriptiones Graecae* (Berlin, 1877-), I. 2:191 ff.
44. Fornara, "Aspects of Pausanias," *Historia* 15(1966):262-6, points out chronological difficulties which make Thucydides' account of Pausanias unreliable, holding, however, that Pausanias may have been guilty of Medism during his second visit to Byzantium, but not his first; Lang, "Scapegoat Pausanias," *CJ* 63(1967):81, thinks Pausanias' second visit to Byzantium represented a covert Spartan attempt to regain hegemony by coming to terms with Persia; D. J. Stewart, "Thucydides, Pausanias, and Alcibiades," *CJ* 61(1966):145-52, interprets Pausanias as a self-seeker, aiming at personal empire.
45. Bury, *History of Greece,* p. 325.
46. E. Gruen, "Stesimbrotus on Miltiades and Themistocles," *Calif. Studies* 3(1970):91-8, calls attention, however, that the two had cooperated before Marathon, when both had advocated a hard line toward Persia.
47. Plut. *Cim.* 9. 4; see G. Lombardo, *Cimone, Ricostruzione della Biografia e Discussioni Storiografiche* (Rome, 1934), pp. 51-2, for an evaluation of the incident.
48. Plut. *Aristides* 23; Podlecki, *Life of Themistocles,* p. 35, sees the friendship between Aristides and Cimon as ominous for Themistocles; Limentani, *Aristidis,* p. 94, doubts that Cimon was old enough to be a general as yet (the minimum age being 30).
49. Plut. *Cim* 5; this, from Plutarch, is high praise indeed; however, G. De Sanctis, *Storia dei Greci* (Florence, 1939), 2:56, has a similarly high opinion of Cimon.
50. *CAH*^{2}, 5:49.
51. Hdt. 7. 107; Thuc. 1. 98; Macan, *Her.,* 1:138, remarks that the inscription at Athens "kept the story green" (and doubtless advanced Cimon's popularity). J. D. Smart, "Note on Kimon's Capture of Eion," *JHS* 87(1967):136-8, holds that Eion was taken in 469/70, but admits there is still a strong case for the traditional date of 476/5; Lombardo, *Cimone,* p. 71, is certain that the beginnings of Cimon's popularity date from this incident.
52. H. W. Parke and D. E. W. Wormell, *The Delphic Oracle* (Oxford, 1956), 1:181.
53. Plut. *Cim.* 8. 4; A. J. Podlecki, "Note on Cimon, Skyros, and Theseus' Bones," *JHS* 91(1971):141-3, notices the difficulty of dating the event, then asks: What proof is there, beyond the bare assertion, that the Dolopians were pirates? He points out that Cimon greatly magnified the whole exploit for his own political purposes; Lombardo, *Cimone,* pp. 72-3, accepting the allegation of piracy, thinks it was increased commercial use of the Aegean sea lanes which compelled the Athenians to act.
54. *CAH*^{2}, 5:52.
55. Plut. *Cim.* 8. 6. Lombardo, *Cimone,* pp. 73-4, remarks that Cimon took advantage of a wave of religious fervor at Athens, but that his conquest secured concrete political, military, and naval benefits for her.
56. Plut. *Them.* 2; *Cim.* 9; though Cimon is not specifically mentioned as the object of Themistocles' spiteful remark, it is an obvious product of Themistocles' last period in Athens, when his fortunes were deteriorating and Cimon's were rising; since the intent was clearly to compare the traditional aristocratic type of education adversely with his own common sense understanding (*synesis*), he could hardly have had anyone else in mind. See H. Martin, Jr., "Themistocles, 2, and Nicias, 2. 6," *American Journal of Philology* 83(1964):142-5, which, however, does not mention Cimon by name.

57. Gomme, *Commentary*, 1:261, especially notices this, remarking that it illustrates how little we know of the internal politics of Athens in this period.
58. C. Hignett, *History of the Athenian Constitution* (Oxford, 1958), p. 190; Busolt, *Griech. Gesch.*, III, 1:109.
59. Frost, "Themistocles' Place in Athenian Politics," *Calif. Studies* 1(1968):114. remarks upon the fact that the really important people in Athens could make their presence felt without the necessity of holding office; W. R. Connor, *The New Politicians of Fifth Century Athens* (Princeton, 1971), substantially agrees, stressing that personal relationships among the great families were fundamentally more significant than offices.
60. Plut. *Them.* 22.2. The passage does not state that Themistocles placed it there himself, but neither the city government nor any private Athenian was likely to erect, or to leave standing, a statue of one later condemned on a charge of treason. Podlecki, *Life*, p. 144, calls it "a likely inference;" Flacelière, *Thémistocle*, p. 81, thinks it was a "portrait" rather than a "statuette."
61. Another faint possibility exists, that Themistocles held some special office during these years, which escaped the notice of the historians. This was first suggested by Gomme, "Athenian Notes: Athenian Politics, 510-483 B.C.," *AJP* 65(1944):323, n. 13.
62. G. L. Cawkwell. "The Fall of Themistocles," *Auckland Classical Essays Presented to E. M. Blaiklock* (Auckland, N. Z., 1970), p. 39, who says simply that he continued to be important until his ostracism. But who else in the city was of equal importance?
63. Plut. *Aristides* 24. 4. Podlecki, *Life of Themistocles*, p. 34, calls this a foolish story, apparently in reference to Themistocles' disdainful remark; however, great men, and particularly megalomaniacs, often say foolish things; Limentani, *Aristidis*, p. 101, thinks the remark may have been comically intended, and doubts that it contains any real hostility toward Aristides.
64. Thuc. 1:93; see Gomme, *Commentary*, 1:263-6, for a detailed explanation.

8 *An Era of Good Feeling* 473-467 B.C.

1. The term prostates tou demou has such an innocent ring, yet is so completely to the purpose, one wonders whether the Alcmaeonids coined the expression and propagandized it throughout Attica. For more on this remarkable family and its position in Athens, see J. Toeppfer, "Alkmaionidai," A. Pauley, G. Wissowa, W. Kroll, *Real Encyclopädie der Classichen Altertumswissenschaft* (Stuttgart, 1894):1556-62; also, see T. L. Shear, Jr., "Koisyra: Three Women of Athens," *Phoenix* 17(1963):99-112.
2. G. E. M. de Ste. Croix, "The Character of the Athenian Empire," *Historia* 3(1954):152-3, speaks of "the People's Interest" as seen by aristocratic leaders; also, see V. Ehrenberg, "Origins of Democracy," *Historia* 1(1950):518-47.
3. The manner of its emergence is deceptive because partly negative, since the leadership of Themistocles was sustained by consecutive ostracisms of his opponents. For the effects of the ostracisms, see C. Hignett, *A History of the Athenian Constitution* (Oxford, 1958), pp. 184-90; also, see A. E. Raubitschek, "The Ostracism of Xanthippus," *American Journal of Archeology* 51(1947):257-62.
4. F. J. Frost, "Themistocles and Mnesiphilus," *Historia* 20(1971):24-5.
5. W. G. Forrest, *The Emergence of Greek Democracy* (New York, 1966), p. 219; F. J. Frost, "Themistocles' Place in Athenian Politics," *California Studies in Classical Antiquity* 1(1968):121-4.
6. G. L. Cawkwell, "The Fall of Themistocles," *Auckland Classical Essays Presented to E. M. Blaiklock* (Auckland, N.Z., 1970), p. 44; Hignett, *Hist. Ath. Const.*, p. 190; E. Meyer, *Geschichte des Altertums* (Stuttgart, 1928), 3:511.
7. Particularly, W. G. Forrest, "Themistocles and Argos," *Classical Quarterly* n.s. 10(1960):236.
8. Plut. *Them.* 18. 3. B. Perrin, *Plutarch's Themistocles and Aristides* (New York, 1901), p. 227, appears to accept this. It was certainly a natural reaction on Themistocles' part.
9. Statues of Themistocles are known to have been placed in the Prytaneion and in the Orchestra (later, the Theater of Dionysus), as well as the one in the Temple of Artemis Aristoboule. See A. J. Podlecki, *The Life of Themistocles* (Montreal, 1975), p. 144, citing Paus. 1. 18. 3.

10. C. W. Fornara, "Some Aspects of the Career of Pausanias of Sparta," *Historia* 15(1966):258-9, in apparent agreement with K. J. Beloch, *Griechische Geschichte,* (Strassburg, 1912), II, 2:144, n. 2, thinks Timocreon's attacks must have come after 478; U. von Wilamowitz, *Aristoteles und Athen,* (Berlin, 1966) 1:138, n. 27, thought they were written before that date; likewise, G. Busolt, *Griechische Geschichte,* (Gotha, 1901), III, 1:14, n. 1, and E. Meyer, *Geschichte des Altertums,* 3:396.
11. Plut. *Them.* 21. 2; an important fact to be noted here is a contemporary's praise for Aristides, which gives support to Plutarch's often-attacked judgment of him.
12. Plut. *Them.* 21. 5; Podlecki, *Life of Themistocles,* pp. 51-4, 64, cites difficulties in evaluating the evidence of Timocreon's hostility toward Themistocles, and concludes that it is "largely enigmatic."
13. Arist. *Ath. Pol.* 28. 2, identifies him as having been leader of the nobles at one time; K. von Fritz and E. Kapp, *Aristotle's Constitution of Athens* (New York, 1961), p. 169, point out, however, that Aristotle's overall judgment of Aristides places him definitely on the democratic side.
14. Plut. *Aristides* 22. 1.
15. Arist. *Ath. Pol.* 24. 1; R. J. Bonner and G. Smith, *The Administration of Justice from Homer to Aristotle* (Chicago, 1938), 1:217, remark on the value of this in promoting Aristides' democratic image.
16. The incident involving Themistocles with Ephialtes against the Areopagus is not generally accepted, but it does point to a connection between them; and Pericles' participation as *choregos* in *Persae* is certainly significant of his admiration for Themistocles; see G. M. Calhoun, *Athenian Clubs in Politics and Litigation* (New York, 1970), p. 101, n. 2.
17. A. J. Podlecki, *The Political Background of Aeschylean Tragedy,* (Ann Arbor, 1966), p. 14.
18. Cawkwell, "Fall of Themistocles," *Auckland Essays,* pp. 39-58, develops this theme at length; also, see Forrest, "Themistocles and Argos," *CQ* n.s. 10(1960):226.
19. Hignett, *Hist. Ath. Const.,* p. 191, and n. 4.
20. Diod. Sic. 11. 55; Plut. *Them.* 22. 3.
21. Plut. *Them.* 21. 4.
22. *CAH*², 5:63.
23. M. Lang, "Scapegoat Pausanias," *Classical Journal* 63(1967):83-84, thinks the Spartans maneuvered his suicide to cover their own machinations: H. Konishi, "Thucydides' Method in the Episodes of Pausanias and Themistocles," *American Journal of Philology* 91(1970):52-3, agrees with J. H. Finley, *Thucydides* (Cambridge, Mass., 1947), p. 130, in accusing Thucydides of distorting his account to make Pausanias look like the prototype of Spartan stupidity.
24. Thuc. 1. 135; Diod. Sic. 11. 55; A. W. Gomme, *A Historical Commentary on Thucydides* (Oxford, 1959) 1:437, remarks that Themistocles had been living at Argos so as not to be in too close proximity to Athens, where he might be accused of trying still to influence politics.
25. Cawkwell, "Fall of Themistocles," *Auckland Essays,* p. 48.
26. Plut. *Them.* 23. 1; Diod. Sic. 11. 55. 7-8; Podlecki, *Life,* pp. 97-8, is inclined, on the whole, to credit Diodorus' description of the trial as a "coherent account."
27. E. M. Walker, in *CAH*², 5:63, declares it was the Ekklesia which condemned Themistocles; Wilamowitz, *Aristoteles und Athen,* 1:140, is equally certain it was the Areopagus.
28. Thuc. 1. 137; P. N. Ure, "When Was Themistocles Last in Athens?" *Journal of Hellenic Studies* 41(1921):176, thinks Themistocles' arrival in Persia took place several years after Artaxerxes came to the throne in 465; his thesis is that Themistocles was still in Athens as late as 462.
29. Thuc. 1. 138; Gomme, *Commentary.* 1:440, asks very shrewdly, "how was it discovered what Themistocles wrote to the King?"
30. H. Konishi, "Thucydides' Method in the Episodes of Pausanias and Themistocles," *AJP* 91(1970):52-69, in a brilliant analysis, accuses Thucydides of purposely digressing and manipulating his evidence to make Themistocles look good and Pausanias bad, that in adversity the one was a model of Athenian rationality, the other of Spartan irrationality; P. J. Rhodes, "Thucydides on Pausanias and Themistocles," *Historia* 19(1970):389-400, in an equally able treatment, comes to similar conclusions; likewise, E. Schwartz, *Das Geschichtswerk des Thukydides* (Bonn, 1960), p. 161.
31. G. Thomson, *Aeschylus and Athens, a Study in the Social Origins of Drama* (London, 1973), p. 281.
32. G. Murray, *Aeschylus* (Oxford, 1940), p. 127.

33. Ibid., p. 10.
34. Arist. *Ath. Pol.* 23. 2; J. Day and M. Chambers, *Aristotle's History of Athenian Democracy* (Berkeley and Los Angeles, 1962), p. 121, offer a differing explanation. Fritz and Kapp, *Aristotle's Constitution,* p. 95, appear to accept Aristotle's view. E. Cavaignac, *Études sur L'Histoire Financière d'Athènes au Ve Siècle* (Paris, 1908), p. 45, sees the action taken by the Areopagus in the Salamis crisis as merely a ruse of Themistocles to get the action he wanted.
35. Day and Chambers, *Aristotle's History,* pp. 120-1, make a strong case that the dominance of the Areopagus in this period is nonhistorical, an invention of Aristotle to fit his preconceived notions of democracy as advanced in his *Politics.* While conceding that Aristotle may have exaggerated the Areopagite resurgence, it is difficult to believe he had not *some* factual basis for his position.
36. M. Giffler, "The Boule of Five Hundred from Salamis to Ephialtes," *AJP* 62(1941):224-6; P. J. Rhodes, *The Athenian Boule* (Oxford, 1972), in an eminent and more recent study, agrees that the Areopagus remained strong until the reforms of 462/1, and in fact, is of the opinion that the Council of Five Hundred's prytaneis were not created until then.
37. Arist. *Ath. Pol.* 23. 3, mentions Aristides as prostates tou demou, coupling him with Themistocles in this, and implying that they shared a joint authority; while it is hard to imagine Themistocles sharing authority with anyone, Aristides conceivably achieved an equal prestige while he was away administering the Delian organization; however, the *Ath. Pol.* goes on that Aristides as prostates distinguished himself in *politikà* ("city affairs"); to be true, this surely would have had to occur after Themistocles' ostracism (about 472), in the half-dozen years between this and Aristides' probable retirement (or death), around 466.
38. Plut. *Cim.* 5. 4; Gomme, *Commentary,* 1:284-5, remarks that Plutarch has been influenced by a historical tradition going back to Isocrates, representing Cimon as the good, ideal statesman always on the side of freedom, in deliberate contrast with the demagogues of later days. As to the influence of Isocrates on historical writing, see C. H. Wilson, "Thucydides, Isocrates, and the Athenian Empire," *Greece and Rome* 13(1966):54-63.
39. Plut. *Cim.* 5. 4.; G. Lombardo, *Cimone, Ricostruzione della Biografia e Discussioni Storiografiche* (Rome, 1934), pp. 15-25, has a more extensive treatment of Cimon as a person.
40. Despite the judicious cautioning of Gomme (*Commentary,* 1:259), Meiggs (*Athenian Empire,* p. 42), and others, that Plutarch's moralizing tendency may make Aristides look "too good," the worth of his character is attested in Timocreon's poem, already mentioned; Lombardo, *Cimone,* doubts some of the stories as to Cimon's generosity, but admits that such practices made political capital for him.
41. Arist. *Ath. Pol.* 27. 3, is here at variance with Plutarch (*Cim.* 10. 4), saying that usually Cimon did this for the members of his own deme, which does seem more reasonable; even one such as he was hardly rich enough to undertake a public dole for all of Athens.
42. *OCD*^{2}, p. 240.
43. Hdt. 6. 136.
44. Plut. *Cim.* 10. 7-8; Lombardo, *Cimone,* p. 41, mentions, in this connection, his upright, independent attitude in politics, for which some credit is given to the teachings of the Sophist, Gorgias.
45. Plut. *Cim.* 15. 1-2; Hignett, *Hist. Ath. Const.,* p. 193.
46. B. D. Meritt, H. T. Wade-Gery, M. F. McGregor, *Athenian Tribute Lists* (Princeton, 1950), 3:241.
47. N. G. L. Hammond, "Origins and Nature of the Athenian Alliance," *JHS* 87(1967):54, is insistent as to this; Meiggs, *Athenian Empire.* pp. 70-1, is more cautious, calling attention that little is known of the background of the Naxian revolt.
48. *CAH*^{2}, 5:51; Lombardo, *Cimone,* p. 78.
49. R. Sealey, "The Origin of the Delian League," *Ehrenberg Studies* (New York, 1967), p. 241.
50. There is a problem of chronology in these years, with no general agreement among authorities. Some place this campaign in 470/69 (Gomme, *Commentary,* 1:286), some later, in 467 (Burn, *Persia and the Greeks,* p. 560); Meiggs, *Athenian Empire,* p. 81, places it in 466. In my account, I have accepted Bury's chronology (*History of Greece,* p. 84).
51. Plut. *Cim.* 12. 2; Meiggs, *Athenian Empire,* p. 76, observes that Cimon's innovations in naval building disclose that land operations in Asia had been contemplated before the beginning of the campaign; he thinks the victory at the Eurymedon would have been followed by a

large scale land-and-sea offensive in the eastern Mediterranean the next year, calculations which were upset by the sudden revolt of Thasos.

52. Gomme, *Commentary,* 1:237.
53. Plut. *Cim.* 13. 1-2.
54. Plut. *Cim.* 13. 3; W. Peek, "Die Kämpfe am Eurymedon," *Athenian Studies Presented to William Scott Ferguson* (New York, 1973), pp. 93-116, sifts the probable truth from the conflicting accounts of Thucydides, Diodorus, and Plutarch; see Lombardo, *Cimone,* pp. 89-91, for another reconstruction of the battles.

9 *Drift and Rift* 467-460 B.C.

1. Aesch. *Sept.* 592-6.
2. Plut. *Aristides* 3. 4; B. Perrin, *Plutarch's Themistocles and Aristides* (New York, 1901), p. 271, allows it, if somewhat ambivalently; likewise, L. I. Highby, *The Erythrae Decree, Klio,* Beiheft 36(1936):86, who builds his case for the dating of Themistocles' departure from Athens upon it; others (Schoeffer, E. Meyer, De Sanctis) do not, but merely on the supposition that by this time Aristides must have been dead, for which there is no proof. I. Limentani, *Plutarchi Vita Aristidis* (Florence, 1964), p. 17, is noncomittal, but cites Perrin's acceptance, also that of G. Hermann, *Aeschyli Tragoediae* (Berlin, 1859), 2:315 ff., pointing out also that Plutarch's citation is corrupt, that the key word spoken was not *dikaios,* but *aristos.* To me, this promotes authenticity, since it deprives the anecdote of the key word long associated with Aristides, which would have sparked a later storyteller's imagination; ironically, the twisted version points back to an earlier one with a better chance of being true. (The term dikaios is ascribed, however, a little later in the play, at l. 605, l. 610).
3. Perrin, *Themistocles and Aristides,* p. 271.
4. A. J. Podlecki, *The Political Background of Aeschylean Tragedy* (Ann Arbor, 1966), pp. 37-8.
5. Thuc. i. 138 does not report Themistocles as arriving at the Persian court until the time when Artaxerxes replaced Xerxes on the throne (465 B.C.); however, in the previous paragraph, he is reported as crossing to Asia while the Athenians were besieging Naxos (470-69), and barely escaping capture there; in view of Themistocles' previous messages to the King, nobody at Athens could longer have any doubts of his ultimate intentions, as first suggested by L. A. Post, *From Homer to Menander* (Berkeley, 1951), p. 73; later, by F. Stoessl, "Aeschylus as a Political Thinker," *AJP* 73(1953):132-3, who, however, thinks Aeschylus remained friendly to Themistocles.
6. Aesch. *Sept.* 790-6.
7. Aesch. *Sept.* 1178-84.
8. Plut. *Aristides* 27. 1; the tomb constructed for him, assertedly at public cost, as well as the gifts, honors, and pension voted to his son and daughters seem convincing evidence that the Athenians regarded him as their prostates at the time of his death; Perrin, *Themistocles and Aristides,* p. 328, calls this "stock rhetorical material," but his skepticism, however well founded, can hardly discredit statements which must have rested on public records.
9. Arist. *Ath. Pol.* 26. 1; G. Busolt, *Griechische Geschichte,* (Gotha, 1901) III, 1:140; G. De Sanctis, *Storia dei Greci,* (Florence, 1939), 2:56.
10. C. Hignett, *A History of the Athenian Constitution* (Oxford, 1958), p. 256; G. Lombardo, *Cimone, Ricostruzione della Biografia e Discussioni Storiografiche* (Rome, 1934), p. 44, calls him "a moderate".
11. Arist. *Ath. Pol.* 25. 1; H. Swoboda, "Ephialtes," A. Pauley, G. Wissowa, W. Kroll, *Real Encyclopädie der Classichen Altertumswissenschaft* 5(1905):2849-53; B. Perrin, *Plutarch's Cimon and Pericles* (New York, 1910), p. 217, observes that Aristotle, though usually severe on democrats, praises Ephialtes' justice and incorruptibility.
12. R. Sealey, "Ephialtes," *Classical Philology* 59(1964):14-18; *Essays in Greek Politics* (New York, 1967), pp. 46-52, believes this is the proper interpretation of Arist. *Ath. Pol.* 25. 2; J. Day and M. Chambers, *Aristotle's History of Athenian Democracy* (Berkeley and Los Angeles, 1962), p. 128, however, speak of Aristotle's "extreme vagueness" in this passage; elsewhere, they doubt that he had any real knowledge of what Ephialtes did to the Areopagus; K. von Fritz and E. Kapp, *Aristotle's Constitution of Athens* (New York, 1961),

p. 170, points out that much of the Areopagus' jurisdiction had already been transferred to other courts.

13. R. J. Bonner and G. Smith, *The Administration of Justice from Homer to Aristotle* (Chicago, 1938), 1:256.
14. Arist. *Ath. Pol.* 25. 3, which assumes that Themistocles was still in Athens in 462, and that he helped Ephialtes in the attack on the Areopagus. P. N. Ure, "When Was Themistocles Last in Athens?" *Journal of Hellenic Studies* 41(1921):165-78, makes out a plausible case for this. Most scholars have disagreed, preferring to follow Thuc. 1. 137, which has Themistocles leaving Athens about 472; Fritz and Kapp, *Aristotle's Constitution,* p. 170, call the story of Themistocles' participation "very strange, to say the least."
15. Arist. *Ath. Pol.* 26. 1; Day and Chambers, *Aristotle's History,* p. 121, while denying that the Areopagus had regained power, concede the genuineness of Ephialtes' attacks on it; P. J. Rhodes, *The Athenian Boule* (Oxford, 1972), p. 206, from another point of view, calls attention that Ephialtes justified his attack on the ground that the Areopagus "had been improperly extending its powers," a contention he takes pains to disprove.
16. Thuc. 1. 100; A. W. Gomme, *A Historical Commentary on Thucydides* (Oxford, 1959), 1:297, calls it a serious defeat, but doubts that the casualties were as heavy as represented, thinking the casualty lists may have been augmented with those fallen elsewhere.
17. *CAH*², 5:58.
18. Hdt. 6. 46.
19. Ibid.
20. Thuc. 1. 101. 1, says that the Thasians appealed to Sparta only after their own city was under siege; but it seems highly unlikely that they would wait until the last gasp before seeking aid.
21. Thuc. 1. 101. 3; A. H. M. Jones, *Sparta* (Cambridge, Mass., 1967), p. 60, remarks that the Ephors who promised aid to the Thasians apparently belonged to Sparta's war party; he calls it an act of treachery toward Athens, which was still an ally of Sparta.
22. Gomme, *Commentary,* 1:298, points out that Cimon must have won a land battle, unmentioned by Thucydides, before settling down to the siege of the city.
23. Thuc. 1. 101. 3; R. Meiggs, *The Athenian Empire* (Oxford, 1972), p. 85; Gomme, *Commentary,* 1:299, observes that Thasos' previous annual tribute of 3 talents was small for an island of such size; he thinks that the later severe tribute of 30 talents was connected with the restitution of some Thasian property on the mainland.
24. Plut. *Cim.* 14. 3; U. von Wilamowitz-Moellendorff, *Aristoteles und Athen* (Berlin, 1966) 2:245.
25. *CAH*², 5:68.
26. Plut. *Cim.* 14. 3; it is a curious speech that Plutarch reports Cimon as making, castigating the Ionians for their greed in wanting to exploit his victories, on the other hand praising the Spartans for sacrificing personal profit to the good of the state; Meiggs, *Athenian Empire,* p. 88, says that presumably Cimon was known to be friendly to King Alexander.
27. Plut. *Cim.* 14. 3. Lombardo, *Cimone,* p. 94, calls the charges against Cimon "absolutely unfounded."
28. W. G. Forrest, *The Emergence of Greek Democracy* (New York, 1966), p. 146: R. Sealey, "The Entry of Pericles into History," *Essays in Greek Politics,* p. 63, thinks, on the other hand, that Cimon's friends may have persuaded the Assembly to elect Pericles as one of the prosecutors. G. De Sanctis, *Pericle* (Milan, 1944), p. 60, points out that the inquest had at least the good effect of bringing Pericles into public notice as a defender of the demos.
29. Diod. Sic. 11. 63. 1; Plut. *Cim.* 16. 5, says that mortality was especially high among the young men; also see Jones, *Sparta,* pp. 60-1.
30. Ar. *Lys.* 1137 ff.
31. A. E. Zimmern, *The Greek Commonwealth* (Oxford, 1924), Ch. 4, provides a good explanation of the problem in general. Also, see E. Cavaignac, *Études sur l'Histoire Financière d'Athènes au Vᵉ Siècle* (Paris, 1908), pp. 49-69.
32. G. B. Grundy, "The Population and Policy of Sparta in the Fifth Century," *JHS* 28(1908):77-82.
33. Plut. *Cim.* 16. 8; E. Ruschenbusch, "Ephialtes," *Historia* 15(1966):369-76, thinks that the real purpose of Ephialtes' reform was to thwart Cimon's policy of friendship toward Sparta.
34. Gomme, *Commentary,* 1:298.
35. Plut. *Cim.* 17. 1. Lombardo, *Cimone,* p. 101, accepts Cimon's retort to the Corinthians as "historical," but finds certain features of his reponse anachronistic as reported by Plutarch.

36. Thuc. 1. 102. 2; D. M. Lewis, "Ithome Again," *Historia* 2(1953-4):414, believes it was not really any Spartan deficiency in siege warfare, but the fact that the Spartans were so greatly reduced in numbers by the earthquake, which compelled them to call for Athenian help; on the plausibility of Sparta's second appeal, see G. A. Papantoniou, "Once or Twice?" *American Journal of Philology* 72(1951):176-81. Perrin, *Cimon and Pericles*, p. 199, takes the opposite side, and is too hard on Plutarch here, in my opinion.
37. Plut. *Cim.* 15. 2; Day and Chambers, *Aristotle's History*, p. 134, seem to accept Plutarch's assertion as to this; also see Sealey, (above, n. 7), and Ruschenbusch (n. 28); De Sanctis, *Pericle*, p. 64, speaks of Pericles as joint leader with Ephialtes in the assault on the Council of Areopagus.
38. Arist. *Ath. Pol.* 26. 1-2; Fritz and Kapp, *Aristotle's Constitution*, p. 171, agree that the aristocracy must have suffered because of Cimon's expedition to Messenia.
39. *CAH*², 5:71.
40. Thuc. 1. 102. 3; Gomme, *Commentary*, 1:302, notices that Thucydides digresses here to explain the growing differences between Athens and Sparta which finally broke up the friendship going back to Persian War days; Jones, *Sparta*, p. 60, theorizes that the Ephors who promised aid to the Thasians in 465 belonged to the anti-Athenian war party at Sparta; it is a fair guess that the Ephors of 462, who dismissed Cimon, belonged to the same party.
41. Diod. Sic. 11. 64. 3, here differs with Thucydides and Plutarch, holding that the Athenians were not immediately offended, but that the feeling of resentment grew gradually upon them.
42. Plut. *Cim.* 16. 3-4.
43. Plut. *Cim.* 17. 2; De Sanctis, *Storia dei Greci*, 2:60. also, De Sanctis, *Atthis, Storia della Repubblica Ateniese* (Turin, 1912), p. 401 ff., which shows that Cimon's expulsion preceded the final assault on the Areopagus, and made it possible.
44. H. Swoboda, "Ephialtes," *PW* 5(1905):2850, first suggested this, though he does not call Robespierre by name.
45. Arist. *Ath. Pol.* 25. 2.
46. Bonner and Smith, *Administration*, 1:260 ff., present a judicious appraisal of the Ephialtic reforms; also see Wilamowitz, *Arist. und Athen*, 2:8 ff.; Busolt, *Griech. Gesch.*, III, 1:269-70; P. J. Rhodes, *The Athenian Boule*, is the most recent scholarly study; see his "Conclusions" (Ch. 5), especially pp. 210-1.
47. The only comparable event would be the struggle over Themistocles' ostracism, which was not nearly so prolonged. G. Grote, *A History of Greece* (New York, 1881), 2:430-8, particularly develops this theme of factional bitterness.
48. The smallest Athenian coin, one-sixth of a drachma. For further information, see "Coinage, Greek," *OCD*², pp. 258-61.
49. Ar. *Vesp.* 661 ff., cited by Hignett, *Hist. Ath. Const.*, p. 219; for another distinguished scholar's view of the development of Athens' law courts and their relation to the allied cities, see H. T. Wade-Gery, "The Judicial Treaty with Phaselis and the History of the Athenian Courts," *Essays in Greek History* (Oxford, 1958), pp. 180-200; also, Sealey, *Essays*, pp. 42-58.
50. Most authorities choose one of these two dates, if they choose any. A notable dissenter is E. M. Walker, in *CAH*², 5: Ch. 4.
51. The evidence that Ephialtes courted the zeugitai is only circumstantial. But that the zeugites could be manipulated, sometimes contrary to their interests, is pointed out by A. W. Gomme, "Aristophanes and Politics," *Classical Review* 52(1938):99; De Sanctis, *Pericle*, p. 67, sees the zeugite eligibility as one of the most durable of the radical reforms.
52. P. J. Rhodes, *The Athenian Boule*, pp. 97 ff., finds evidence, however, that the archons' residual powers at this time may have been greater than formerly assumed by modern scholarship.
53. Arist. *Ath. Pol.* 25. 1.
54. Plut. *Per.* 10. 7; Arist. *Ath. Pol.* 25. 4.
55. Aesch. *Cho.* 45-53.
56. Aesch. *Cho.* 1075-6.
57. Aesch. *Eum.* 235-45. Rather a free translation, but one which, I believe, retains the spirit and meaning of the original.
58. Aesch. *Eum.* 470-90.
59. A. J. Podlecki, *The Political Background of Aeschylean Tragedy* (Ann Arbor, 1966), p. 83; J. H. Quincey, "Orestes and the Argive Alliance," *Classical Quarterly* N.S. 14(1964):190; M.

Gagarin, "The Vote of Athena," *AJP* 96(1975):121, thinks the vote ended in a tie, even with Athena's ballot, but that the tie freed Orestes anyway.

60. Particularly, J. B. Bury, *A History of Greece* (London, 1931), p. 348; Podlecki, *Political Background,* pp. 94-6; C. M. Bowra, *Periclean Athens* (New York, 1971), p. 150, agrees to an extent.
61. R. W. Livingstone, "The Problem of the *Eumenides* of Aeschylus," *JHS* 45(1925):120 ff.; J. A. Davison, "Aeschylus and Athenian Politics, 472-456 B.C.," *Ehrenberg Studies* (New York, 1967), p. 102; G. Thomson, *Aeschylus and Athens, a Study in the Social Origins of Drama* (London, 1973), p. 271, also calls the poet "a moderate democrat."
62. C. M. Smertenko, "The Political Sympathies of Aeschylus," *JHS* 52(1932):233-5.
63. K. J. Dover, "The Political Aspects of Aeschylus' *Eumenides,*" *JHS* 77(1957):234, most notably; also, see A. Sidgwick, *Aeschylus, Eumenides* (Oxford, 1887), p. 25.
64. Bowra (above, n. 60); Smertenko (n. 62); Podlecki, *Political Background,* pp. 96-100, thinks Aeschylus agreed with Ephialtes' measures concerning the Areopagus, but that he objected to a later assault on the body by Pericles; V. Ehrenberg, *From Solon to Socrates* (London, 1968), pp. 206-7, advances similar views, and thinks Aeschylus warned against admitting the zeugitai to the archonship.
65. W. Jaeger, *Paideia: The Ideals of Greek Culture* (New York, 1965), 1:260.
66. Aesch. *Eum.* 1-20.
67. The date of Aeschylus' Promethean plays has not been absolutely determined, but are considered to have come later than the *Oresteia.* See *OCD*², p. 18.

10 *Moving toward Empire* 460-448 B.C.

1. C. Hignett, *A History of the Athenian Constitution* (Oxford, 1952), p. 190, who thinks, however, that the leadership fell to Cimon even earlier, after the fall of Themistocles.
2. Arist. *Ath. Pol.* 35. 2; G. De Sanctis, *Pericle* (Milan, 1944), p. 65, however, sees Pericles as "without a rival" for Ephialtes' vacated position.
3. Arist. *Pol.* 1274 A.
4. Arist. *Ath. Pol.* 27. 1; R. Sealey, "The Entry of Pericles into History," *Essays in Greek Politics* (New York, 1967), pp. 65-6, points out that since the Assembly normally voted by show of hands, it was easy for a wealthy family like the Alcmaeonids to exert influence on it through economic pressure; L. Homo, *Périclès, Une Expérience de Democratie Dirigée* (Paris, 1954), p. 49, agrees, that in the presumed contest between Archestratus and Pericles, Archestratus' social inferiority was probably decisive.
5. J. Toeppfer, "Alkmaionidai," A. Pauley, G. Wissowa, W. Kroll, *Real Encyclopädie der Classichen Altertumswissenschaft* 1(1894):1561-2.
6. Plut. *Per.* 7. 1.
7. Thuc. 2. 65. 10; Sealey, "Entry of Pericles," *Essays in Greek Politics,* pp. 70-1, thinks that from the first Pericles was more of a harmonizer than a radical, friendly to Cimon and to all of the great families; A. R. Burn, *Pericles and Athens* (London, 1948), Chs. 2-3, makes the case for the more traditional view of Pericles, the young radical follower of Themistocles and Ephialtes.
8. Plut. *Per.* 7. 6.
9. Pl. *Phdr.* 270 A.
10. Ar. *Ach.* 528-31.
11. Pl. *Phdr.* 269 C.
12. Thuc. 2. 65. 9; Plut. *Per.* 16. 1; R. Flacelière and E. Chambry, *Plutarque, Vies* (Paris, 1964), 3:1-5 agree, warning that Plutarch has in general softened the description of Pericles available to him from earlier writers.
13. G. T. Griffith, "Isegoria in the Assembly at Athens," *Ehrenberg Studies* (New York, 1967), pp. 125-9, believes that equal right of speech in the Assembly came only with the reform of 462, and that it was a most important factor in establishing the Assembly's control over the whole government in Periclean Athens; R. J. Bonner, *Aspects of Athenian Democracy* (New York, 1933), pp. 67-9, sees it as developing somewhat earlier.
14. *OCD*², p. 1059; Homo, *Périclès,* p. 110; De Sanctis, *Pericle,* does not accept it.
15. Hignett, *Hist. Ath. Const.,* p. 219.

16. Ibid., p. 225; Arist. *Ath. Pol.* 7. 4.
17. The gist of E. M. Walker's position, *CAH*[2], 5:103-6; also, see Homo, *Périclès*, pp. 112-3, who emphasizes that none but the rich could afford to accept civic responsibilities without recompense.
18. H. T. Wade-Gery, "The Judicial Treaty with Phaselis and the History of the Athenian Courts," *Essays in Greek History* (Oxford, 1958), pp. 195-7.
19. Wade-Gery, *Essays*, p. 196, citing *Hesperia* 26(1954):33-9.
20. R. J. Bonner and G. Smith, *The Administration of Justice from Homer to Aristotle* (Chicago, 1938), 2:7-38.
21. *OCD*[1], p. 276.
22. Pseudo-Xenophon, *Athenaion Politeia* 1. 7; H. Frisch, *Constitution of the Athenians* (New York, 1976), p. 199.
23. Hignett, *Hist. Ath. Const.*, p. 255; W. S. Ferguson, *Greek Imperialism* (New York, 1963), p. 14; A. W. Gomme, "The Law of Citizenship at Athens," *Essays in Greek History and Literature* (Oxford, 1937), pp. 86-8, points out that something had to be done to check the immoderate growth of Attica's population, and the large number of aliens who were taking advantages of faulty civic procedures to get themselves fraudulently enrolled as citizens; the fear of an enlarging population is based on Arist. *Ath. Pol.* 26. 3; V. Ehrenberg, *From Solon to Socrates* (London, 1968), p. 220, sees the citizenship law rather as a response to the rapid growth of cleruchies abroad.
24. Burn, *Pericles and Athens*, pp. 91-3.
25. E. M. Walker, in *CAH*[2], 5:103.
26. Aesch. *Eum.* 762-6; A. J. Podlecki, *The Political Background of Aeschylean Tragedy* (Ann Arbor, 1966), p. 83. Aeschylus was born an aristocrat, the scion of a noble family from Eleusis; his political position is more difficult to determine.
27. Thuc. 1. 105. 2; A. W. Gomme, *A Historical Commentary on Thucydides* (Oxford, 1959), 1:308, points out that the Athenian commander Leocrates had had a distinguished military career, being probably the same Leocrates who was one of the generals at the battle of Plataea.
28. Thuc. 1. 105. 3; Gomme, *Commentary*, 1:304.
29. Thuc. 1. 105. 5-6; Gomme, *Commentary*, 1:308-9, says that Myronides was likewise one of Athens' most famous generals, having participated in several of her great victories, beginning with Plataea, and regrets that so little is known about him; De Sanctis, *Pericle*, p. 105, calls Pericles' policy toward Corinth "audacious and aggressive."
30. Pl. 1 *Alc.* 104 B ("Pericles . . . doing what he pleases not only in our city, but in all of Hellas"); Pl. *Menex.* 242; Arist. *Pol.* 1307 B; Dem. *De Cor.* 66; Isoc. *Paneg.* 80 ff., 106 ff.; Isoc. *Panath.* 54 ff.; Isoc. *Phil.* 146; as well as Plut. *Per.* 17, provide enough indications more or less direct of Pericles' policy of dominating other Greek states from within, culminating with the Congress Decree of ca. 448, to convince me. Use of the infinitive (*ienai*) at *Per.* 17. 3 indicates an understanding that the policy had been developing for some time. I am of course aware of the articles by R. Seager, in *Historia* 18(1969):129-41, and by A. B. Bosworth, in *Historia* 20(1971):600-16, but their reasoning, though ingenious, leaves many aspects untouched, in my opinion. However, their penetrating analyses establish the possibility that fourth century propagandists tampered with the Congress Decree. But it would have been hard to convince Greeks of the reality of a decree of which they had never heard.
31. W. G. Forrest, "Themistocles and Argos," *Classical Quarterly* n.s. 10(1960):239, calls attention that Pericles and his friends had by this time come to the same conclusion that resulted in Themistocles' expulsion a dozen years before.
32. Thuc. 1. 109; A. H. M. Jones, *Sparta* (Cambridge, Mass., 1967), p. 64.
33. Thuc. 1. 107. 2-3; Gomme, *Commentary*, 1:314, asks, what happened to the transports for 11,500 men?
34. D. W. Reece, "Note on the Battle of Tanagra," *Journal of Hellenic Studies* 70(1950):75-6, thinks, however, that the strengthening of Thebes was not a part of Sparta's original plan; that it was Athens' belligerence which caused this, forcing Nicomedes to strengthen Thebes in return for the Theban reinforcements he would need against Athens' formidable challenging army; R. Meiggs, *The Athenian Empire* (Oxford, 1972), pp. 417-8, agrees in general. Pl. *Menex.* 242 B makes it plain that in the aftermath, the Athenians considered they were fighting for the "freedom of Boeotia."

35. Thuc. 1. 107. 4; Gomme, *Commentary,* 1:314, feels sure the plotters could have been only a few "desperate oligarchs," and that the main body of aristocrats were undoubtedly loyal to Athens, like Cimon and his friends.
36. Plut. *Cim.* 17. 4-5; G. Lombardo, *Cimone, Ricostruzione della Biografia e Discussioni Storiografiche* (Rome, 1934), p. 111, seconds Plutarch's judgment that the brave conduct of Cimon's tribesmen at Tanagra brightened his prospects for a speedy return to Athens; B. Perrin, *Plutarch's Cimon and Pericles* (New York, 1910), p. 200, says that Plutarch's account of the conduct of Cimon and his friends at Tanagra has "the air of authenticity" although it is mentioned nowhere else.
37. Diod. Sic. 11. 80. 4-6; Gomme, *Commentary,* 1:316, says of the treacherous Thessalian attack, "some of this may come from a good tradition," but clearly he is doubtful.
38. Plut. *Per.* 10. 2.
39. Thuc. 1. 108. 2; Gomme, *Commentary.* 1:316, observes that the Athenians were probably content to see the Spartans go home "now that all danger of an attack on Attica and of a conspiracy at home was past."
40. Burn, *Pericles and Athens,* p. 72.
41. Diod. Sic. 11. 83. 2-3; *CAH*[2], 5:83; Gomme, *Commentary,* 1:319, observes that the Locrians would naturally be hostile after the Athenians possessed themselves of Naupactus.
42. Ps.-Xen. *Ath. Pol.* 3 insists that this policy did Athens little good; R. Meiggs, "The Growth of Athenian Imperialism," *JHS* 63(1943):21-33, disagrees, pointing to a judicious tightening of Athens' hold; G. E. M. de Ste. Croix, "The Character of the Athenian Empire," *Historia* 3(1954-5):1-40, insists that Athens was adroit enough in this to retain the allies' goodwill.
43. B. D. Meritt, H. T. Wade-Gery, and M. F. McGregor, *The Athenian Tribute Lists* (Princeton, 1950), 3:20.
44. M. O. B. Caspari, "On the Athenian Expedition of 459-4," *CQ* 7(1913): pp. 198-201, first asserted this; followed most recently, by H. D. Westlake, "Thucydides and the Athenian Disaster in Egypt," *Classical Philology* 45(1950):209-16; also by P. Salmon, *La Politique Égyptienne d'Athènes* (Brussels, 1965), pp. 90-192; disagreeing, and defending Thucydides' account, are J. M. Libourel, "The Athenian Disaster in Egypt," *American Journal of Philology* 92(1971): pp. 605-15; also, Meiggs, *Athenian Empire,* pp. 104-8, and Sealey, *A History of the Greek City-States,* p. 272.
45. Thuc. 1. 110. 1; Libourel, (above, n. 44), presents a well-reasoned defense of Thucydides.
46. B. D. Meritt, H. T. Wade-Gery, M. F. McGregor, *The Athenian Tribute Lists,* 3:263; W. K. Pritchett, "The Transfer of the Delian Treasury," *Historia* 18(1969):17-21, sees the transfer as a gradual process, one which had probably been completed earlier, before the battle of the Eurymedon.
47. Hignett, *Hist. Ath. Const.,* p. 244.
48. N. G. L. Hammond, "Origin and Nature of the Athenian Alliance," *JHS* 87(1967):57; A. B. West, "The Tribute and the Non-Tributary Members of the Delian League," *American Historical Review* 35(1929):271-2, takes a somewhat milder view of the situation; H. B. Mattingly, "The Growth of Athenian Imperialism," *Historia* 12(1963):257-73, sees the really important transition as taking place fifteen years later, after the Samian War. E. Cavaignac, *Études sur l'Histoire Financière d'Athènes au Ve Siècle* (Paris, 1908), p. 48, however, credits the report (Plut. *Aristides* 25. 2) that removal of the Delian treasury to Athens had been seriously discussed by the members much earlier.
49. Gomme, *Commentary,* 1:323.
50. Plut. *Per.* 19, treats it as a circumnavigation; Diod. Sic. 11. 85 does not. Perrin, *Cimon and Pericles,* p. 240, is certain that the expedition was not a circumnavigation.
51. J. Boardman, *The Greeks Overseas* (Baltimore, 1964), pp. 175-231.
52. F. M. Cornford, *Thucydides Mythistoricus* (London, 1907), develops the thesis of economic motivation at length, though he does not relate it specifically to the ceramics industry. W. J. Davisson and J. E. Harper, *The Ancient World* vol. 1 of *European Economic History* (New York, 1972), present an up-to-date treatment of the general subject, but without special reference to Pericles.
53. B. D. Meritt, H. T. Wade-Gery, and M. F. McGregor, *Athenian Tribute Lists* (Princeton, 1949), 2:D10.
54. Ibid., 3:257; also, see J. P. Barron, "Milesian Politics and Athenian Propaganda, 460-440 B.C.," *JHS* 82(1962), pp. 1-6, essentially in agreement; C. W. Fornara, "The Date of the'Regulations for Miletus'," *AJP* 92(1971):473-5, places it somewhat later, in the 440's.

55. Plut. *Cim.* 17. 6; R. Meiggs, "The Crisis of Athenian Imperialism," *Harvard Classical Studies* 57(1963), p. 10, supports this view, holding that Cimon was recalled precisely for the purpose of arranging peace with Sparta; Lombardo, *Cimone,* pp. 112-3, says that he returned "after a few years," and "a little before the end of the ostracism."
56. Plut. *Per.* 28. 4; H. T. Wade-Gery, "The Question of Tribute in 449/8 B.C.," *Hesperia* 14(1945):221-2, accepts this; Hignett, *Hist. Ath. Const.*, p. 347, doubts it, but thinks it does point to some sort of understanding between Pericles and Cimon; Burn, *Pericles and Athens,* p. 93, agrees; so does Homo, *Périclès,* p. 56.
57. Gomme, *Commentary,* 1:328, although he rejects the idea that Pericles was badly beaten by Cimon on this issue, advanced by F. Miltner, "Perikles," *PW* 19(1937):761; for Argive policy toward Athens, see T. Kelly, "Argive Foreign Policy in the Fifth Century B.C.," *CP* 69(1974):81-94.
58. *CAH*², 5:103; V. Ehrenberg, *From Solon to Socrates* (London, 1968), pp. 219-20, agrees to an extent, seeing the citizenship law as directed against Athens' aristocracy, if not against Cimon specifically.
59. *CAH*², 5:86-7.
60. Diod. Sic. 12. 3-4. One has to make the best one can out of Diodorus' jumbled narrative. Thucydides' and Plutarch's accounts are too sketchy to be of much value. See G. Busolt, *Griechische Geschichte* (Gotha, 1901), III, 1:322 ff., for a coherent picture; J. Barns, "Cimon and the First Athenian Expedition to Egypt," *Historia* 2(1953-4):163-76, thinks Diodorus has conflated accounts of two expeditions which Cimon led to Cyprus, this one in 450, and an earlier one in 462 (largely diverted to Egypt), thus the resultant confusion; Lombardo, *Cimone,* pp. 118-9, in effect, agrees. B. Perrin, *Plutarch's Themistocles and Aristides* (New York, 1901), p. 255, makes the same point.
61. S. T. Parker, "The Objectives and Strategy of Cimon's Expedition to Cyprus," *AJP* 97(1976):30-8, stresses this; Cimon could have had no grandiose plans of conquest in the eastern Mediterranean, and even his moderate objectives were only partially achieved, the military ones being the most successful. Perrin, *Cimon and Pericles,* p. 203, goes even farther, calling the Cyprus campaign a failure.
62. Diod. Sic. 12. 4-5; Gomme, *Commentary,* 1:331; K. J. Beloch, *Griechische Geschichte* (Strassburg, 1912), II, 1:177; also, see Gomme, "The Peace of Kallias," *AJP* 65(1944):334; H. T. Wade-Gery, "The Peace of Kallias," *Essays in Greek History,* pp. 201-32, who is very critical of Diodorus' account, and calls it "bowdlerized;" S. K. Eddy, "On the Peace of Callias," *CP* 65(1970):8-14, in agreement with Wade-Gery, also calling attention to a veritable copy of the treaty, once known to exist; Meritt, et al., *Athenian Tribute Lists,* 3:257, also accept it; D. Stockton, "The Peace of Callias," *Historia* 8(1959):61-79, does not.
63. Plut. *Cim.* 7-8.

11 *Iron Hand and Silken Glove* 448-440 B.C.

1. Aesch. *Pers.* 243.
2. A. J. Podlecki, *The Political Background of Aeschylean Tragedy* (Ann Arbor, 1966), pp. 121-2; C. M. Bowra, *Periclean Athens* (New York, 1971), pp. 152-3, however, sees in the predicament of Zeus a clear warning to Athens to be wise and vigilant in her use of power, which otherwise might some day be turned against her.
3. C. M. Bowra, *Sophoclean Tragedy* (Oxford, 1944), pp. 49-50.
4. C. H. Whitman, *Sophocles: A Study of Heroic Humanism* (Cambridge, Mass., 1951), p. 45.
5. Soph. *Aj.* 1102-12.
6. Whitman, *Sophocles,* p. 46.
7. V. Ehrenberg, *Sophocles and Pericles* (Oxford, 1954), pp. 13-4.
8. Pind. *Pyth.* 1. 76-7.
9. Pind. *Nem.* 7. 84-5.
10. Pind. *Isthm.* 7.
11. C. M. Bowra, *Pindar* (Oxford, 1964), p. 154.
12. R. Meiggs and D. Lewis, *A Selection of Greek Historical Inscriptions to the End of the Fifth Century B.C.* (Oxford, 1969), p. 73.
13. H. T. Wade-Gery, "The Question of Tribute in 449/8," *Hesperia* 14(1945):212-29, and later in B. D. Meritt, H. T. Wade-Gery, and M. F. McGregor, *Athenian Tribute Lists*

(Princeton, 1950), 3:44–52; however, doubts started early among interested scholars, including Wade-Gery's co-worker, B. D. Meritt, "Athens and the Delian League," *The Greek Political Experience: Studies in Honor of William Kelly Prentice* (New York, 1941), pp. 50–60, esp. p. 53. The matter is still unresolved.

14. S. K. Eddy, "The Cold War Between Athens and Persia, 448–412 B.C.," *Classical Philology* 68(1973):241–58.
15. *Inscriptiones Graecae* (Berlin, 1877--), I, 2:10–13; see L. I. Highby, *The Erythrae Decree, Klio,* Beiheft 36(Leipzig, 1936), especially pp. 10–38, for an interpretation of the decree in full, one which sees Athens as protecting Erythrae's democracy; for contrary views, see W. Kolbe, "Die Anfänge der Attischen Arché," *Hermes* 73(1938):249–68; also, H. Nesselhauf, *Untersuchungen zur Geschichte der Delisch-Attischen Symmachie, Klio,* Beiheft 30 (Leipzig, 1933):1–35.
16. G. E. M. de Ste. Croix, "The Character of the Athenian Empire," *Historia* 3(1954–5):9.
17. *OCD*², p. 408.
18. For an extended treatment of this subject, see P. A. Brunt, "Athenian Settlements Abroad in the Fifth Century B.C.," *Ehrenberg Studies* (New York, 1967), pp. 71–92.
19. Meritt, et al., *The Athenian Tribute Lists,* 3:57.
20. Thuc. 1. 97. 1; N. G. L. Hammond, "Origins and Nature of the Athenian Alliance," *Journal of Hellenic Studies* 87(1967):52, interprets this to mean a positive guarantee; R. Meiggs, *The Athenian Empire* (Oxford, 1972), pp. 45–6, does not think it was included in the oath.
21. Ar. *Ach.* 860 ff., is a good example; M. Croiset, *Aristophanes and the Political Parties at Athens* (New York, 1973), pp. 56–7, indicates that city Athenians laughed also at their own rustics.
22. A. H. M. Jones, *Athenian Democracy* (Oxford, 1966), p. 45, sees Athenian democrats as in general approving the egalitarian principle; his main citation is from Demosthenes, a century later, but he also quotes Pericles to that effect.
23. A. W. Gomme, *A Historical Commentary on Thucydides* 1:318; Arist. *Pol.* 1302 B, says they failed badly, particularly in Thebes.
24. Plut. *Per.* 18. 2; L. Homo, *Périclès, Une Expérience de Democratie Dirigée* (Paris, 1954), p. 161, surprisingly defends Tolmides' venture into Boeotia, and implies that Pericles agreed to it, objecting only to the small number of troops sent.
25. Plut. *Per.* 18. 3; Meiggs, *Athenian Empire,* p. 122, remarks that the moral flavor of Pericles' advice (as reported by Plutarch) does not commend it to historians, but that Tolmides does seem to have misjudged the situation; G. De Sanctis, *Pericle* (Milan, 1944), p. 134, remarks that if Pericles advised restraint, this time he was mistaken. B. Perrin, *Plutarch's Cimon and Pericles* (New York, 1910), p. 238, also suspects that Plutarch has gone out of his way to contrast the characters of Pericles and Tolmides, but accepts Pericles' reported remarks as authentic.
26. Diod. Sic. 12. 6. 2; Thuc. 1. 113. 3–4; Xen. *Mem.* 3. 5. 4, says the battle was fought closer to Libadeia than to Coronea.
27. G. De Sanctis, *Storia dei Greci* (Florence, 1939), 2:139–40, hints at this, saying that Athens' own interests and her greatness became paramount with him; A. E. Raubitschek, "The Peace Policy of Pericles," *American Journal of Archeology* 70(1966):137–41, develops his subject similarly.
28. Gomme, *Commentary,* 1:339.
29. Thuc. 1. 113. 3–4, who, however, does not say it was Pericles who persuaded them; but on the basis of his policy and his responsibilities, it had to be either himself or speakers selected by him; nobody else could have headed off the radicals, who, naturally, were opposed to the concessions.
30. Plut. *Per.* 23. 1; Ar. *Nub.* 859, has been generally accepted as a reference to this event; De Sanctis, *Pericle,* p. 139, is noncommittal as to the bribery, but thinks that if money was given, it was spent needlessly, since the Spartans would have been compelled to return home soon anyway; also see R. Flacelière and E. Chambry, *Plutarque, Vies* (Paris, 1964), 3:40.
31. Paus. 5. 23. 4–5, contains a partial description of the Peace, from an inscription seen in Elis; for a complete discussion, see Gomme, *Commentary,* 1:347–9.
32. Pind. *Pyth.* 8. 1–5.
33. Pind. *Pyth.* 8. 10–4.
34. Bowra, *Pindar,* p. 157.

35. Plut. *Per.* 12. 1-2.
36. Thuc. 2. 40. 4; De Sanctis, *Pericle,* p. 143, emphasizes this.
37. Thuc. 2. 63. 2; none of the other radicals were likely to admit that Athens' rule might be wrong; Gomme, *Commentary,* 2:175, says Pericles was the first Athenian to refer to Athens' rule as a tyranny.
38. Meritt, et al., *Athenian Tribute Lists,* 1:572; Gomme, *Commentary,* 2:28 ff.; Flacelière and Chambry, *Vies,* 3:36.
39. W. G. Forrest, *The Emergence of Greek Democracy* (New York, 1966), p. 221, emphasizes the growing conservatism of Athens' democrats in these years.
40. K. J. Dover, "Dekatos Autos," *JHS* 80(1960):61-77, thinks it did not; D. M. Lewis, "Double Representation in the Strategia," *JHS* 81(1961):118-23, disagrees; C. Hignett, *A History of the Athenian Constitution* (Oxford, 1958), pp. 347-55, leans toward Dover's position.
41. Xen. *Mem.* 3. 6. 1-18, develops this point, especially at 6. 17; Socrates here does not call Pericles by name, but clearly has him in mind.
42. J. Hasebroek, *Trade and Politics in Ancient Greece* (London, 1932), pp. 112-22.
43. Thuc. 3. 47. 2; Ste. Croix, "Character," *Historia* 3(1954-5):16, calls attention that the mass of the citizens in the subject states remained loyal to Athens until her final collapse at the end of the Ionian War; in criticism, see D. W. Bradeen, "The Popularity of the Athenian Empire," *Historia* 9(1960):257-69.
44. Ps.-Xen *Ath. Pol.* 1. 16; Ste. Croix, "Notes on Jurisdiction in the Athenian Empire," *Classical Quarterly* n.s. 11(1961):95, points out that in the Athenian courts "political cases" could not be properly defined, that any case might become "political;" R. J. Hopper, "Interstate Agreements in the Athenian Empire," *JHS* 63(1943): 35-51, stresses Athens' attempts to secure fair, impartial judgments in suits involving the allies.
45. A. R. Burn, *Pericles and Athens* (London, 1948), p. 118; H. T. Wade-Gery, "Thucydides, Son of Melesias," *JHS* 52(1932):217.
46. Plut. *Per.* 11. 3; W. Donlan, "The Origins of Kalos Kagathos," *American Journal of Philology* 94(1973):365-75, says that these and related terms came into political usage about the middle of the fifth century.
47. Arist. *Ath. Pol.* 28. 5.
48. Pl. *Lach.* 178, cited by Wade-Gery, "Thucydides," *JHS* 52(1932):205, who calls Thucydides "Kimon's political heir."
49. Arist. *Ath. Pol.* 28. 2; for his background, see A. E. Raubitschek, "Theopompos on Thucydides, the Son of Melesias," *Phoenix* 14 (1960):81-95; Wade-Gery, (above, n. 45):211; also, a new perspective, based on the *philia* of the great families, is presented by W. R. Connor, *The New Politicians of Fifth Century Athens* (Princeton, 1971), p. 67 ff.
50. Plut. *Per.* 11.2; F. J. Frost, "Pericles, Thucydides, Son of Melesias, and Athenian Politics Before the War," *Historia* 13(1964):398-9, attributes these methods to Cleon, not Thucydides; also, see G. M. Calhoun, *Athenian Clubs in Politics and Litigation* (New York, 1970), p. 120.
51. A. E. Taylor, "On the Date of the Trial of Anaxagoras," *CQ* 11(1917):81-7; H. T. Wade-Gery, *Essays in Greek History* (Oxford, 1958), p. 259, however, concludes that Professor Taylor has not "decided the point absolutely."
52. Arist. *Ath. Pol.* 27. 4 (called "Damonides" by Aristotle); Bowra, *Periclean Athens,* p. 69; Flacelière and Chambry, *Vies,* 3:17, remark that Damon was more than ordinarily useful as a tutor to Pericles, being skilled not only in "music," that is, in the general curriculum, but also in sophist reasoning, which included the art of politics.
53. Plut. *Per.* 12. 2; Perrin, *Cimon and Pericles,* p. 228, considers this "an authentic report" of a great debate in Athens' Assembly, recorded by a contemporary.
54. G. H. Stevenson, "The Financial Administration of Pericles," *JHS* 49(1929):1-10, maintains there is a strong possibility that the Parthenon and the other Acropolis buildings were financed from the "reserve of Athena" rather then from Delian funds, hence that Pericles was much more careful and circumspect than he is usually considered to have been. For the traditional view, that mainly Delian funds were used, see the discussion by E. Cavaignac, *Études sur l'Histoire Financière d'Athènes au Ve Siècle* (Paris, 1908), pp. 80-5.
55. Plut. *Per.* 12. 3; Homo, *Périclès,* pp. 207-12, considers that the prostates was entirely justified in these expenditures; Cavaignac, *Histoire Financière,* p. 83, cites this as an example of the reasoning Pericles had learned from the Sophists.
56. Plut. *Per.* 14. 1.

57. Plut. *Per.* 13. 9. These stories seem credible in that they fit the oligarchs' general pattern of attack on Pericles, emphasizing the theme of prostitution: that he was living with a courtesan, that with the Delian funds he was bedecking Athens "like a shameless street-walker," that now he was prostituting the wives of his relatives and friends.
58. Hignett, *Hist. Ath. Const.*, p. 253; De Sanctis, *Pericle,* p. 181.
59. From *The Thracian Women;* Plut. *Per.* 13. 6.
60. W. S. Ferguson, "Polis and Idia in Periclean Athens," *American Historical Review* 45(1940):271 ff., maintains this thesis; also, Bowra, *Periclean Athens,* p. 139.
61. T. B. L. Webster, *An Introduction to Sophocles* (London, 1969), pp. 56-7.
62. Soph. *Ant.* 737.
63. Ehrenberg, *Sophocles and Pericles,* p. 140, is particularly insistent upon this; Bowra, *Sophoclean Tragedy,* p. 63, agrees; G. H. Macurdy, "References to Thucydides, Son of Melesias, and to Pericles in OT 863-910," *Classical Philology* 37(1942):307-10, sees Sophocles as nonactive politically, and rather more favorable to Thucydides than to Pericles in the duel of wits between them. Whitman, *Sophocles,* pp. 87-8, agrees that the *Antigone* has no direct current reference to Athens, but sees the heroine as expressing Athenian *areté,* in general.
64. Ehrenberg, *Sophocles and Pericles,* p. 109.
65. J. S. Morrison, "The Place of Protagoras in Athenian Public Life," *CQ* 35(1941):14, so interprets it; at the same time, he thinks Sophocles is reassuring the Athenian people that since Pericles has been Protagoras' pupil, as all know, everything should come right in the end.
66. Soph. *Ant.* 1003-4.

12 *The Glory of Hellas*

1. R. Carpenter, *The Architects of the Parthenon* (Baltimore, 1964), pp. 21-81, who finds evidence that Callicrates, not Ictinus, was originally intended to be architect-in-chief.
2. W. B. Dinsmoor, *The Architecture of Ancient Greece* (New York, 1950), p. 148; L. Homo, *Périclès, Une Expérience de Democratie Dirigée* (Paris, 1954), p. 229.
3. H. Berve and G. Gruben, *Greek Temples, Theaters, and Shrines* (New York, 1963), p. 374; B. Perrin, *Plutarch's Cimon and Pericles* (New York, 1910), p. 230, believes that the friendship between Pericles and Phidias cannot have been as intimate as some have claimed, since they belonged to different social classes.
4. A. W. Lawrence, *Greek Architecture* (Baltimore, 1957), p. 158.
5. Berve and Gruben, *Greek Temples,* p. 376; Carpenter, *Architects of the Parthenon,* p. 128, points out that Ictinus varies slightly from the exactitude of these proportions in order to preserve the "organic body" of the temple, that is, to avoid the lifelessness of a geometric or mathematical rigidity.
6. Berve and Gruben, *Greek Temples,* p. 374.
7. Carpenter, *Architects of the Parthenon,* pp. 116-9; J. D. Beazley, in *CAH*², 5:449-50.
8. I. T. Hill, *The Ancient City of Athens* (Chicago, 1969), p. 155; N. Yalouris, *Classical Greece: The Elgin Marbles of the Parthenon* (Greenwich, Conn., 1950), p. x; P. E. Corbett, *The Sculpture of the Parthenon* (Baltimore, 1959), p. 12.
9. Berve and Gruben, *Greek Temples,* p. 378.
10. Corbett, *Sculpture of the Parthenon,* pp. 26-9; Yalouris, *Elgin Marbles,* p. xii.
11. R. Lullies, *Greek Sculpture* (New York, 1957), p. 57; Corbett, *Sculpture of the Parthenon,* pp. 15-23, who, however, thought Athens' infantry had been slighted in the total arrangement.
12. Paus. 1. 24; G. Richter, *The Sculpture and Sculptors of the Greeks* (New Haven, 1950), p. 159 ff.; R. Flacelière and E. Chambry, *Plutarque, Vies* (Paris, 1964), 3:28, assert that the Athena Parthenos had a wooden core, with thin slabs of ivory and gold as an exterior coating.
13. E. A. Gardner, *Handbook of Greek Sculpture* (London, 1915), p. 284 ff.; R. S. Stites, *The Arts and Man* (New York, 1940), p. 240.
14. R. S. Stanier, "The Cost of the Parthenon," *Journal of Hellenic Studies* 73(1953):68-76, who estimates the total cost of the Parthenon probably approached 500 talents, and may have exceeded it.

15. Berve and Gruben, *Greek Temples,* p. 382; Carpenter, *Architects of the Parthenon,* p. 136, thinks Mnesicles was given charge of the Propylaea because Ictinus had a more important assignment waiting for him in the Temple of Demeter at Eleusis; Homo, *Périclès,* p. 229, calls Mnesicles "the rival of Ictinus in audacity and grandeur."
16. Dinsmoor, *Architecture of Ancient Greece,* pp. 199-201; G. De Sanctis, *Pericle* (Milan, 1944), p. 215.
17. Lawrence, *Greek Architecture,* p. 161.
18. Paus. 1. 28; Homo, *Périclès,* p. 242.
19. Plut. *Per.* 13. 4; Corbett, *Sculpture of the Parthenon,* pp. 30-1, takes exception to this, and thinks that Phidias' whole time must have been taken up with his creation of the Athena Parthenos, for several years, at least.
20. Paus. 7. 27.
21. Paus. 1. 28; J. Dorig, *Greek Art and Architecture* (New York, 1968), p. 356; De Sanctis, *Pericle,* p. 212, who, however, does not mention dates for the work.
22. Dio Chrys. *Or.* 12. 50-2.
23. Polyb. 30. 10.
24. Strab. 8. 353-4.
25. Paus. 5. 11.
26. Plotinus, *Enn.* 5. 8.
27. Berve and Gruben, *Greek Temples,* p. 323.
28. Cic. *Orat.* 8-9.
29. Pliny *HN* 34. 57-8; Homo, *Périclès,* p. 230, sees Myron as a rival of Phidias, and thinks the latter's jealousy may have prevented Myron from obtaining employment on the Parthenon, or that Pericles may have been less admiring of his style than that of Phidias.
30. Dorig, *Greek Art,* p. 363.
31. Richter, *Sculpture and Sculptors of the Greeks,* p. 161.
32. Pliny *HN* 35. 58; Perrin, *Cimon and Pericles,* p. 182, believes that the oft-asserted love of Polygnotus for Elpinice rests on nothing more than the fact that the painter included her likeness among those of the Trojan women depicted in his "Capture of Troy" in the Stoa Poikile.
33. Plut. *Cim.* 10. 5-6.
34. Paus. 10. 25.
35. M. Robertson, *Greek Painting,* (Geneva, 1959), p. 122.
36. Pliny *HN* 35. 58.
37. *OCD*², p. 855.
38. F. Maurice, "The Campaign of Marathon," *JHS* 52(1932):22-3.
39. Paus. 1. 15.
40. Paus. 1. 18.
41. Dinsmoor, *Architecture of Ancient Greece,* p. 103.
42. Paus. 1. 22.
43. Diog. Laert. 2. 6.
44. Anaxagoras, frgs. B4, B9, H. Diels, *Die Fragmente der Vorsokratiker* (Berlin, 1972), 2:33-4, 36; see D. Lanza, *Anassagora, Testimonianze e Frammente* (Florence, 1966), p. 206 ff., for scholarly opinion on Anaxagoras' concept of the cosmic process.
45. Anaxagoras, frg. B3, Diels, *Vorsokr.,* 2:33; F. M. Cleve, *The Philosophy of Anaxagoras* (New York, 1949), pp. 13-6, explains in detail.
46. Arist. *Meta.* 1. 3. 984A; L. Robin, *Greek Thought and the Origins of the Scientific Spirit* (New York, 1967), p. 124, translates it as "things of like parts;" D. E. Gershenson and D. A. Greenberg, *Anaxagoras and the Birth of Physics* (New York, 1964), p. 12, remark as to this, that Anaxagoras' concept was basically a molecular theory of physics.
47. Gershenson and Greenberg, *Anaxagoras and the Birth of Physics,* pp. 15-6.
48. Anaxagoras, frg. B10, Diels, *Vorsokr.,* 2:36-7; Robin, *Greek Thought,* p. 123; Cleve, *Philosophy of Anaxagoras,* pp. 88-9, questions the authenticity of frg. B10.
49. Anaxagoras, frg. B6, Diels, *Vorsokr.,* 2:35; see Cleve, *Philosophy of Anaxagoras,* pp. 19-27, for a full discussion of the Nous concept; for scholarly comment on it, see Lanza, *Anassagora,* p. 233 ff.
50. Gershenson and Greenberg, *Anaxagoras and the Birth of Physics,* pp. 25-6.
51. Robin, *Greek Thought,* p. 126.
52. Diog. Laert. 2. 10.

53. B. A. G. Fuller, *History of Greek Philosophy* (New York, 1928), 1:212, translates it thus—quite felicitously, in my opinion.
54. Robin, *Greek Thought*, p. 128.
55. *OCD*², p. 600.
56. C. Bailey, *The Greek Atomists and Epicurus* (New York, 1964), pp. 79-80.
57. Implicit in Democritus, since he allows solidity to the atoms as well as size, although weight is not specifically mentioned until Epicurus. See Bailey, *Greek Atomists*, pp. 300-9.
58. Bailey, *Greek Atomists*, 138-9.
59. Democritus, frg. B91, Diels, *Vorsokr.*, 2:184.
60. Diog. Laert. 9. 50.
61. Cleve, *The Philosophy of Anaxagoras*, pp. ix-x, discusses concisely but adequately the difficult problem of Anaxagoras' birthdate, and shows that any attempt to establish Democritus' birthdate by the usual method of accepting his purported statement that he was forty years younger than Anaxagoras, is both difficult and tenuous; for the other, more traditional view, see J. A. Davison, "Protagoras, Democritus, and Anaxagoras," *Classical Quarterly* n.s. 3(1953):38-9.
62. Ath. 8. 354 C.
63. J. A. Davison, "The Date of the *Prometheia*," *Transactions of the American Philological Association* 80(1949):78-82, sees indications that Protagoras, immediately successful in Athens, first was associated with Cimon and his friends until, disgusted by the non-progressive attitude of most aristocrats, he transferred his friendship to Pericles, about the time of the assault on the Areopagus.
64. Sext. Emp. *Pyr.* 1. 217-8; M. Untersteiner, *Sofisti, Testimonianze e Frammenti* (Florence, 1949), pp. xv-xxii, comments on the wide range of individual views among the Sophists—which may proceed from this attitude toward sense phenomena.
65. Pl. *Tht.* 152 A.
66. It occurs to me that Protagoras was following the line already taken by Anaxagoras, the practical one that any shrewd philosopher coming to Athens would take. Anaxagoras, too, had come prepared to teach (and did teach) Ionian science. But we are told (Plut. *Per.* 4-6) that he also taught Pericles (and doubtless others as well) how to organize his discourses so as to speak effectively, and to maintain a calm, confident, self-composure before the public, who were also impressed by the scientific data learned from Anaxagoras. There are close similarities in their courses of action, the main difference being that the one taught incidentally what the other would make the center of his instruction.
67. Pl. *Prt.* 321-9.
68. A. D. Winspear, *The Genesis of Plato's Thought* (New York, 1940), pp. 138-42, makes a strong case that the Idealists' opposition to Protagoras was owing to the fact that he was progressive, materialistic, and relativistic, while they were conservatives in politics, and just as obviously, neither materialists nor relativists.
69. Pl. *Prt.* 309 C.
70. Pl. *Prt.* 319-23; M. Untersteiner, *Sofisti*, p. 31, remarks that the term *euboulía* was probably advanced by Protagoras himself.
71. J. S. Morrison, "The Place of Protagoras in Athenian Public Life," *Classical Quarterly* 35(1944):9.
72. Plut. *Per.* 36. 3; 16. 7.
73. Thuc. 2. 13.

13 *A World without End*

1. Arist. *Ath. Pol.* 2; *CAH*², 4:32-6.
2. C. Hignett, *A History of the Athenian Constitution* (Oxford, 1958), p. 37.
3. Thuc. 2. 16.
4. Arist. *Ath. Pol.* 20 ff. Both Solon and Pisistratus are also referred to as "prostates," (*Ath. Pol.* 28. 2) but it is unlikely that the word was in common use as early as their day.
5. A. W. Gomme, *The Population of Athens in the Fifth and Fourth Centuries* (Oxford, 1933), p. 26.
6. A. French, *The Growth of the Athenian Economy* (New York, 1964), p. 58.
7. *CAH*², 5:166.

8. Plut. *Per.* 12. 4.
9. French, *Athenian Economy,* p. 123.
10. Thuc. 5. 59, is a good example; F. E. Adcock and D. J. Mosley, *Diplomacy in Ancient Greece* (London, 1975), pp. 152-82, has the best recent treatment of the subject.
11. Plut. *Per.* 22, 29.
12. Arist. *Ath. Pol.* 20. 2.
13. Aesch. *Pers.* 584-96; V. Ehrenberg, *From Solon to Socrates* (London, 1968), pp. 176-80.
14. Pl. *Phdr.* 269 D; Xen. *Mem.* 2. 6.
15. W. Jaeger, *Paideia* (New York, 1965), 1:60.
16. Ibid., 1:137-9, 149.
17. G. Murray, *Aeschylus* (Oxford, 1940), pp. 18-9, 32-6.
18. C. M. Bowra, *Sophoclean Tragedy* (Oxford, 1944), pp. 371-4.
19. Pl. *Phdr.* 270 A; A. D. Winspear, *The Genesis of Plato's Thought* (New York, 1940), pp. 130-7.
20. G. Highet, *The Classical Tradition* (New York, 1949), p. 360.
21. Soph. *Ant.* 332-40. A considerable liberty has been taken here, and much left out, but the essential meaning remains intact.

SELECTED BIBLIOGRAPHY

THE scope of this book necessitates restricting the references to citations in the chapter notes, and to certain others cited below to which my indebtedness is so great that acknowledgement must be made.

GENERAL

Andrewes, A. *The Greeks.* London: 1967.
______. *The Greek Tyrants.* London: 1956.
Beloch, K. J. *Griechische Geschichte.* Vols. 1, 2. Strassburg: 1912, 1916.
Boardman, J. *The Greeks Overseas.* Baltimore: 1964.
Bowra, C. M. *Periclean Athens.* New York: 1971.
Brown, T. S. *The Greek Historians.* Lexington, Mass.: 1973.
Brunt, P. A. "Athenian Settlements Abroad in the Fifth Century B.C." *Ancient Society and Institutions: Studies Presented to Victor Ehrenberg,* pp. 71-92. New York: 1967.
Burn, A. R. *Pericles and Athens.* London: 1948.
______. *The Lyric Age of Greece.* London: 1960.
Bury, J. B. *A History of Greece to the Death of Alexander the Great.* Rev. by R. Meiggs. London: 1951.
______. *The Ancient Greek Historians.* New York: 1958.
Bury, J. B., Cook, S. A., Adcock, F. E., eds., *The Cambridge Ancient History.* Vols. 4, 5. New York: 1926, 1927.
Busolt, G. *Griechische Geschichte.* Vols. 2, 3. Gotha: 1895-1904.
Chadwick, J. "The Greek Dialects and Greek Pre-History." *Greece and Rome* 3(1955):38-46.
Cornford, F. M. *Thucydides Mythistoricus.* New York: 1969.
Curtius, E. *Geschichte Griechenlands.* Vols. 1, 2. New York: 1886.
De Sanctis, G. *Pericle.* Milan: 1944.

______. *Storia dei Greci delle Origine alla Fine del Secolo V*. Vols. 1, 2. Florence: 1939.

De Selincourt, A. *The World of Herodotus*. London: 1967.

Ehrenberg, V. *From Solon to Socrates: Greek History and Civilization during the Sixth and Fifth Centuries* B.C. London: 1966.

______. *The Greek State*. London: 1969.

Ferguson, W. S. "Polis and Idia in Periclean Athens." *American Historical Review* 45(1940):269-78.

Finley, J. H. *Thucydides*. Cambridge, Mass.: 1947.

Flacelière, R. *Plutarque: Vie de Thémistocle*. Paris: 1972.

Flacelière, R., and Chambry, E. *Plutarque: Vies*. Vol. 3. Paris: 1964.

Freeman, K. *The Work and Life of Solon*. New York: 1976.

Gilliard, C. *Quelques Réformes de Solon*. Lausanne: 1907.

Gomme, A. W. *A Historical Commentary on Thucydides*. Vol. 1. Oxford: 1959.

______. *Essays in Greek History and Literature*. Oxford: 1937.

Grote, G. *A History of Greece from the Earliest Period to the Close of the Generation Contemporary with Alexander the Great*. Vol. 2. New York: 1881.

Habicht, C. "Falsche Urkunden zur Geschichte Athens im Zeitalter der Perserkriege." *Hermes* 89(1961):1-35.

Hammond, N. G. L. *Studies in Greek History*. Oxford: 1973.

Hill, I. T. *The Ancient City of Athens*. Chicago: 1969.

Hönn, K. *Solon: Staatsmann und Weiser*. Vienna: 1948.

How, W. W., and Wells, J. *A Commentary on Herodotus*. Oxford: 1975.

Hunter, V. "Athens Tyrannis: A New Approach to Thucydides." *Classical Journal* 69(1973-4):120-6.

Jeffery. L. H. *Archaic Greece: ca. 700–500* B.C. London: 1976.

Keaney, J. J. "The Structure of Aristotle's *Athenaion Politeia*." *Harvard Studies in Classical Philology* 67(1963):115-46.

Kolbe, W. "Die Anfänge der Attischen Arché." *Hermes* 7(1938):249-68.

Konishi, H. "Thucydides' Method in the Episodes of Pausanias and Themistocles." *American Journal of Philology* 91(1970):52-69.

Leveque, P., and Vidal-Naquet, P. *Clisthène l'Athénien*. Paris: 1967.

Lewis, D. M. "Cleisthenes and Attica." *Historia* 12(1963):22-40.

Limentani, I. C. *Plutarchi Vita Aristidis: Introduzione, Testo, Commento, Traduzione, ed Appendice*. Florence: 1964.

Linforth, I. M. *Solon the Athenian*. Berkeley: 1919.

Lombardo, G. *Cimone: Ricostruzione della Biografia e Discussioni Storiografiche*. Rome: 1934.

Macan, R. W. *Herodotus: The Fourth, Fifth, and Sixth Books*. New York: 1973.

______. *Herodotus: The Seventh, Eighth, and Ninth Books*. New York: 1973.

Martin, Hubert, Jr. "The Character of Plutarch's Themistocles." *Transactions of the American Philological Association* 92(1961): 326-39.

Meiggs, R. *The Athenian Empire*. Oxford: 1972.

______, and Lewis, D. M. *A Selection of Greek Historical Inscriptions to the End of the Fifth Century* B.C. Oxford: 1969.

Meritt, B. D. "Athens and the Delian League." *The Greek Political Experience: Studies in Honor of William Kelly Prentice*. New York: 1941.

Meyer, E. *Geschichte des Altertums*. Vol. 3. Stuttgart: 1939.

Munro, J. A. R. "Pelasgians and Ionians." *Journal of Hellenic Studies* 54(1934): 109-25.

Oikonomides, A. N. *The Two Agoras of Ancient Athens*. Chicago: 1964.

Percival, J. "Thucydides and the Uses of History." *Greece and Rome* 18(1971): 199-212.

Perrin, B. *Plutarch's Themistocles and Aristides.* New York: 1901.
______. *Plutarch's Cimon and Pericles.* New York: 1910.
Podlecki, A. J. *The Life of Themistocles: A Critical Survey of the Literary and Archeological Evidence.* Montreal: 1975.
Rhodes, P. J. "Thucydides on Pausanias and Themistocles." *Historia* 19(1970): 389-400.
Sealey, R. *A History of the Greek City States ca. 700–338 B.C.* Berkeley and Los Angeles: 1976.
______. *Essays in Greek Politics.* New York: 1967.
Wade-Gery, H. T. *Essays in Greek History.* Oxford: 1958.
White, M. "Some Agiad Dates: Pausanias and his Sons." *Journal of Hellenic Studies* 84(1964):140-52.
Zimmern, A. *The Greek Commonwealth: Politics and Economics in Fifth Century Athens.* New York: 1956.

INTERNAL POLITICAL

Adcock, F. E. "The Exiles of Peisistratus." *Classical Quarterly* 18(1924):174-81.
Barker, Ernest. *Greek Political Theory: Plato and His Predecessors.* New York: 1960.
Berve, H. *Miltiades: Studien zur Geschichte des Mannes und Seiner Zeit. Hermes,* Heft 2. Berlin: 1937.
Bonner, R. J. *Aspects of Athenian Democracy.* New York: 1967.
Bonner, R. J., and Smith, G. *The Administration of Justice from Homer to Aristotle.* Vols. 1, 2. Chicago: 1938.
Bradeen, D. W. "The Trittyes in Cleisthenes' Reform." *Transactions of the American Philological Association* 81(1955):22-30.
Buck, R. J. "The Reforms of 487 B.C. in the Selection of Archons." *Classical Philology* 60(1965):96-101.
Burstein, S. M. "The Recall of the Ostracized and the Themistocles Decree." *California Studies in Classical Antiquity* 4(1971):96-101.
Cadoux, T. J. "The Athenian Archons from Kreon to Hypsichides." *Journal of Hellenic Studies* 68(1948):70-123.
Calhoun. G. M. *Athenian Clubs in Politics and Litigation.* New York: 1970.
Cawkwell, G. L. "The Fall of Themistocles." *Auckland Classical Essays Presented to E. M. Blaiklock.* Auckland, N.Z.: 1968.
Chambers, M. "The Authenticity of the Themistocles Decree." *American Historical Review* 67(1962):306-16.
Connor, W. R. "The Athenian Council: Method and Focus in Some Recent Scholarship." *Classical Journal* 70(1974):32-40.
______. *The New Politicians of Fifth Century Athens.* Princeton: 1971.
Davison, J. A. "Aeschylus and Athenian Politics, 472-456 B.C." *Ancient Society and Institutions: Studies Presented to Victor Ehrenberg,* pp. 93-107. New York: 1967.
Day, J., and Chambers, M. *Aristotle's History of Athenian Democracy.* Berkeley and Los Angeles: 1962.
De Sanctis, G. *Atthis: Storia della Repubblica Ateniese dalle Origini alla Eta di Pericle.* Turin: 1912.
Dover, K. J. "Dekatos Autos." *Journal of Hellenic Studies* 80(1960):61-77.
______. "The Political Aspects of Aeschylus' *Eumenides.*" *Journal of Hellenic Studies* 77(1957):230-7.
Ehrenberg, V. "The Origins of Democracy." *Historia* 1(1950):518-48.

Eliot, C. W. J., and McGregor, M. F. "Kleisthenes: Eponymous Archon, 525/4 B.C." *Phoenix* 14(1960):27-35.
Ferrara, G. *La Politica di Solone.* Naples: 1964.
Fornara, C. W. "Themistocles' Archonship." *Historia* 20(1971):534-9.
______. "The 'Tradition' about the Murder of Hipparchus." *Historia* 17(1968): 400-24.
Forrest, W. G. *The Emergence of Greek Democracy, 800–400 B.C.* New York: 1966.
French, A. "The Party of Peisistratos." *Greece and Rome* 2nd Series 6(1959):46-57.
Fritz, K. von, and Kapp, E., *Aristotle's Constitution of Athens and Related Texts.* New York: 1950.
Frost, F. J. "Pericles, Thucydides, Son of Melesias, and Athenian Politics Before the War." *Historia* 13(1964):385-99.
______. "Themistocles and Mnesiphilus." *Historia* 20(1971):20-5.
______. "Themistocles' Place in Athenian Politics." *California Studies in Classical Antiquity* 1(1968):105-24.
Gagarin, M. "The Vote of Athena." *American Journal of Philology* 96(1975):121-7.
Giffler, M. "The Boulé of Five Hundred from Salamis to Ephialtes." *American Journal of Philology* 62(1941):224-6.
Glotz, G. *The Greek City and Its Institutions.* New York: 1965.
Gomme, A. W. "Aristophanes and Politics." *Classical Review* 52(1938):99-109.
______. "Athenian Notes: Athenian Politics, 510-483 B.C." *American Journal of Philology* 65(1944):321-34.
Griffith, G. T. "Isegoria in the Assembly at Athens." *Ancient Society and Institutions: Studies Presented to Victor Ehrenberg,* pp. 115-38.
Gruen, E. "Stesimbrotus on Miltiades and Themistocles." *California Studies in Classical Antiquity* 3(1970):91-8.
Hammond, N. G. L. "Strategia and Hegemonia in Fifth Century Athens." *Classical Quarterly* n.s. 19(1969):111-44.
Hands, A. R. "Ostraka and the Law of Ostracism—Some Possibilities and Assumptions." *Journal of Hellenic Studies* 79(1959):69-79.
Hignett, C. *A History of the Athenian Constitution to the End of the Fifth Century B.C.* Oxford: 1958.
Hind, J. F. G. "The 'Tyrannis' and the Exiles of Peisistratus." *Classical Quarterly* n.s. 24(1974):1-18.
Holliday, J. "The Followers of Peisistratus." *Greece and Rome* 2nd Series 24(1977): 40-56.
Homo, L. *Périclès: une Expérience de Democratie Dirigée.* Paris: 1954.
Jacoby, F. *Atthis: The Local Chronicles of Attica.* New York: 1973.
Jones, A. H. M. *Athenian Democracy.* Oxford: 1966.
Kagan, D. "The Origin and Purposes of Ostracism." *Hesperia* 30(1961):396-7.
Keaney, J. J. "The Text of Androtion F6 and the Origin of Ostracism." *Historia* 19(1970):1-11.
Keaney, J. J., and Raubitschek, A. E. "A Late Byzantine Account of Ostracism." *American Journal of Philology* 93(1972):87-91.
Kienast, D. "Die Innenpolitische Entwicklung Athens in 6. Jahrhundert und die Reformen von 508." *Historische Zeitschrift* 200(1965):265-83.
Lang, Mabel. "The Murder of Hipparchus." *Historia* 3(1955):395-407.
Larsen, J. A. O. "Cleisthenes and the Development of the Theory of Democracy at Athens." *Essays in Political Theory Presented to George H. Sabine.* Ithaca: 1948.
______. "Demokratia." *Classical Philology* 68(1973):45-6.
______. *Representative Government in Greek and Roman History.* Berkeley and Los Angeles: 1955.
Lewis, D. M. "Double Representation in the Strategia." *Journal of Hellenic Studies* 81(1961):118-23.

Masaracchia, A. *Solone.* Florence: 1958.
McCarger, D. "New Evidence for the Kleisthenic Boule." *Classical Philology* 71(1976):248-52.
McGregor, M. F. "The Pro-Persian Party at Athens from 510-480 B.C." *Harvard Studies in Classical Philology,* suppl. 1(1940):71-95.
Munro, J. A. R. "The Ancestral Laws of Cleisthenes." *Classical Quarterly* 33(1939):84-97.
Podlecki, A. J. *The Political Background of Aeschylean Tragedy.* Ann Arbor: 1966.
Raubitschek, A. E. "The Ostracism of Xanthippus." *American Journal of Archeology* 51(1947):257-62.
______. "Theopompos on Thucydides, the Son of Melesias." *Phoenix* 14(1961): 81-95.
Rhodes, P. J. *The Athenian Boule.* Oxford: 1972.
Robinson, C. A., Jr., "Athenian Politics, 510-486 B.C." *American Journal of Philology* 66(1945):243-54.
______. "The Struggle for Power at Athens in the Early Fifth Century." *American Journal of Philology* 60(1939):232-7.
Ruebel, J. S. "The Tyrannies of Peisistratus." *Greek, Roman, and Byzantine Studies* 14(1973):125-36.
Ruschenbusch, E. "Patrios Politeia." *Historia* 8(1958):398-424.
______. "Ephialtes." *Historia* 15(1966):369-76.
Sealey, Raphael. "Regionalism in Archaic Athens." *Historia* 9(1960):155-80.
______. "The Origins of Demokratia." *California Studies in Classical Antiquity* 6(1974):253-95.
Smertenko, C. M. "The Political Sympathies of Aeschylus." *Journal of Hellenic Studies* 52(1932):233-5.
Staveley, E. S. "Voting Procedure at the Election of Strategoi." *Ancient Society and Institutions: Studies Presented to Victor Ehrenberg,* pp. 275-88.
Taylor, A. E. "On the Date of the Trial of Anaxagoras." *Classical Quarterly* 11(1917):81-7.
Ure, P. N. *The Origin of Tyranny.* Cambridge: 1922.
______. "When Was Themistocles Last in Athens?" *Journal of Hellenic Studies* 41(1921):165-78.
Vanderpool, E. "The Ostracism of the Elder Alcibiades." *Hesperia* 21(1952):1-8.
Wade-Gery, H. T. "Eupatridai, Archons, and Areopagus." *Classical Quarterly* 25(1931):2-4.
______. "Miltiades." *Journal of Hellenic Studies* 71(1951):212-21.
______. "Thucydides: Son of Melesias." *Journal of Hellenic Studies* 52(1932):205-27.
Waters, K. H. "Herodotos and Politics." *Greece and Rome* 2nd Series 19(1972): 136-50.
White, M. "Greek Tyranny." *Phoenix* 9(1955):1-18.
Wilamowitz-Moellendorff, U. von. *Aristoteles und Athen.* Vols. 1, 2. Berlin: 1966.
Wilson, C. H. "Thucydides, Isocrates, and the Athenian Empire." *Greece and Rome* 13(1966):54-63.

DIPLOMATIC AND MILITARY

Adcock, F. E., and Mosley, D. J. *Diplomacy in Ancient Greece.* London: 1975.
Barns, J. "Cimon and the First Athenian Expedition to Egypt." *Historia* 2(1953-4):163-76.
Barron, J. P. "Milesian Politics and Athenian Propaganda, ca. 460-440 B.C." *Journal of Hellenic Studies* 82(1962):1-8.
Bradeen, D. W. "The Popularity of the Athenian Empire." *Historia* 9(1960):257-69.

Brunt, P. A. "The Hellenic League against Persia." *Historia* 2(1953-4):135-63.
Burn, A. R. *Persia and the Greeks: The Defence of the West ca. 546-478 B.C.* New York: 1962.
Bury, J. B. "Aristides at Salamis." *Classical Review* 10(1896):414-8.
Caspari, M. O. B. "On the Athenian Expedition of 459-4." *Classical Quarterly* 7(1913):198-201.
De Ste. Croix, G. E. M. "Notes on the Jurisdiction of the Athenian Empire." *Classical Quarterly* n.s. 11(1961):94-112.
______. "The Character of the Athenian Empire." *Historia* 3(1954):1-40.
Eddy, S. K. "Athens and the Peacetime Navy in the Age of Perikles." *Greek, Roman, Byzantine Studies* 9(1968):141-56.
______. "The Cold War between Athens and Persia, 448-412 B.C." *Classical Philology* 68(1973):241-58.
______. "On the Peace of Callias." *Classical Philology* 65(1970):8-14.
Evans, J. A. S. "Notes on Thermopylae and Artemision." *Historia* 18(1969):389-405.
Ferguson, W. S. *Greek Imperialism.* New York: 1963.
Ferrill, A. "Herodotus and the Strategy and Tactics of the Invasion of Xerxes." *American Historical Review* 72(1961):102-15.
Fornara, C. W. "Some Aspects of the Career of Pausanias of Sparta." *Historia* 15(1966):257-71.
______. "The Hoplite Achievement at Psyttaleia." *Journal of Hellenic Studies* 86(1966):53-4.
______. "The Value of the Themistocles Decree." *American Historical Review* 73(1967):425-33.
Forrest, W. G. "Themistocles and Argos." *Classical Quarterly* n.s. 10(1960):221-41.
French, A. "Solon and the Megarian Question." *Journal of Hellenic Studies* 77(1957):238-46.
Fuller, J. F. C. *A Military History of the Western World.* Vol. 1. New York: 1954.
Gomme, A. W. "Herodotus and Marathon." *Phoenix* 6(1952):77-83.
Green, P. *The Year of Salamis.* London: 1970.
Grundy, G. B. *The Great Persian War and Its Preliminaries.* London: 1901.
Hammond, N. G. L. "The Battle of Salamis." *Journal of Hellenic Studies* 76(1956):32-54.
Highby, L. I. *The Erythrae Decree: Contributions to the Early History of the Delian League and the Peloponnesian Confederacy. Klio,* Beiheft 36. Leipzig: 1936.
Hignett, C. *Xerxes' Invasion of Greece.* Oxford: 1963.
Hopper, R. J. "Interstate Agreements in the Athenian Empire." *Journal of Hellenic Studies* 63(1943):35-57.
Hudson, H. G. "The Shield Signal at Marathon." *American Historical Review* 42(1931):443-59.
Jackson, A. H. "The Original Purpose of the Delian League." *Historia* 18(1969): 12-16.
Jameson, M. H. "A Decree of Themistocles from Troezen." *Hesperia* 14(1960): 198-223.
Lang, M. "Scapegoat Pausanias." *Classical Journal* 63(1967):79-85.
Lazenby, J. F. "The Strategy of the Greeks in the Opening Campaign of the Persian War." *Hermes* 92(1964):264-84.
Lewis, D. M. "Ithome Again." *Historia* 2(1953-4):412-18.
Libourel, J. M. "The Athenian Disaster in Egypt." *American Journal of Philology* 92(1971):605-15.
Maurice, F. "The Campaign and Battle of Marathon." *Journal of Hellenic Studies* 52(1932):13-24.
______. "The Size of Xerxes' Army in the Invasion of Greece." *Journal of Hellenic Studies* 50(1930):210-35.

Meiggs, R. "The Crisis of Athenian Imperialism." *Harvard Studies in Classical Philology* 67(1963):1-36.

———. "The Growth of Athenian Imperialism." *Journal of Hellenic Studies* 63(1943):21-34.

Meyer, H. D. "Vorgeschichte und Begründung des Delisch-Attischen Seebundes." *Historia* 12(1963):405-46.

Papantoniou, G. A. "Once or Twice?" *American Journal of Philology* 72(1951): 176-81.

Parker, S. T. "The Objectives and Strategy of Cimon's First Expedition to Cyprus." *American Journal of Philology* 97(1976):30-8.

Peek, W. "Die Kämpfe am Eurymedon." *Athenian Studies Presented to William Scott Ferguson. Harvard Studies in Classical Philology,* suppl. 1(1940):93-116. Reprint. New York: 1973.

Potter, E., and Nimitz, C., *Sea Power: A Naval History.* Englewood Cliffs: 1960.

Pritchett, W. K. *Studies in Ancient Greek Topography,* Part 1. *University of California Publications in Classical Studies* 1(1965):83-93, 94-102, 103-21.

Quincey, J. H. "Orestes and the Argive Alliance." *Classical Quarterly* n.s. 14(1961):190-206.

Raubitschek, A. E. "The Peace Policy of Pericles." *American Journal of Archeology* 70(1966):137-41.

Reece, D. W. "Note on the Battle of Tanagra." *Journal of Hellenic Studies* 70(1950):75-6.

Reynolds, K. F. B. "The Shield Signal at the Battle of Marathon." *Journal of Hellenic Studies* 49(1929):100-5.

Sacks, K. S. "Herodotus and the Dating of the Battle of Thermopylae." *Classical Quarterly* n.s. 26(1976):232-48.

Salmon, P. *La Politique Égyptienne d'Athènes.* Brussels: 1966.

Sealey, R. "Again the Siege of the Acropolis, 480 B.C." *California Studies in Classical Antiquity* 5(1972):183-94.

———. "The Origin of the Delian League." *Ancient Society and Institutions: Studies Presented to Victor Ehrenberg,* pp. 233-55. New York: 1967.

———. "The Pit and the Well: The Persian Heralds of 491 B.C." *Classical Journal* 72(1976):13-20.

Stewart, D. J. "Thucydides, Pausanias, and Alcibiades." *Classical Journal* 61(1966): 145-52.

Stockton, D. "The Peace of Callias." *Historia* 8(1959):61-79.

Tarn, W. W. "The Fleet of Xerxes." *Journal of Hellenic Studies* 28(1908):202-9.

Westlake, H. D. "The Medism of Thessaly." *Journal of Hellenic Studies* 56(1936): 12-24.

———. "Thucydides and the Athenian Disaster in Egypt." *Classical Philology* 45(1950):209-16.

Whatley, N. "Reconstructing Marathon." *Journal of Hellenic Studies* 84(1964): 119-39.

ECONOMIC AND SOCIAL

Boardman, J. *The Greeks Overseas.* Baltimore: 1964.

Boeckh, A. *The Public Economy of Athens.* New York: 1976.

Cavaignac, E. *Études sur l'Histoire Financière d'Athènes au Ve Siècle.* Paris: 1908.

Chambers, M. "Four Hundred Sixty Talents." *Classical Philology* 53(1958):26-32.

Chrimes, K. M. T. "On Solon's Property Classes." *Classical Review* 46(1932):2-4.

Cole, J. W. "Peisistratus on the Strymon." *Greece and Rome* 2nd Series 22(1975): 42-4.

Cunningham, C. J. K. "The Silver of Laurium." *Greece and Rome* 2nd Series 14(1967):145-56.

Davisson, W. J., and Harper, J. E. *The Ancient World.* European Economic History, vol. 1. New York: 1972.

Donlan, W. "The Origins of Kalos Kagathos." *American Journal of Philology* 94(1973):365-75.

Eddy, S. K. "Four Hundred Sixty Talents Once More." *Classical Philology* 63(1968): 184-95.

Finley, M. I. *Studies in Land and Credit in Ancient Athens, ca. 500–200 B.C.* New Brunswick: 1951.

French, A. "Land Tenure and the Solon Problem." *Historia* 12(1963):242-7.

______. "The Economic Background to Solon's Reforms." *Classical Quarterly* n.s. 6(1956):11-25.

______. *The Growth of the Athenian Economy.* New York: 1964.

Frost, F. J. *Greek Society.* Lexington, Mass.: 1971.

Glotz, G. *Ancient Greece at Work: An Economic History of Greece from the Homeric Period to the Roman Conquest.* New York: 1967.

Gomme, A. W. *The Population of Athens in the Fifth and Fourth Centuries B.C.* Oxford: 1933.

Hammond, N. G. L. "Land Tenure in Attica and Solon's Seisachtheia." *Journal of Hellenic Studies* 81(1961):76-98.

______. "The Philaids and the Chersonese." *Classical Quarterly* n.s. 6(1956):113-29.

______. "The Seisachtheia and Nomothesia of Solon." *Journal of Hellenic Studies* 60(1940):71-83.

Hasebroek, J. *Trade and Politics in Ancient Greece.* London: 1932.

Hopper, R. J. "The Solonian Crisis." *Ancient Society and Institutions: Studies Presented to Victor Ehrenberg,* pp. 139-46. New York: 1967.

Kraay, C. M. *Archaic and Classical Greek Coins.* Berkeley and Los Angeles, 1976.

Mattingly, H. B. "The Growth of Athenian Imperialism." *Historia* 12(1963):257-73.

Meritt, B. D., Wade-Gery, H. T., McGregor, M. F. *The Athenian Tribute Lists.* Vols. 1, 2, 3. Princeton: 1939-50.

Nesselhauf, H. *Untersuchungen zur Geschichte der Delisch-Attischen Symmachie. Klio,* Beiheft 30. Leipzig: 1933.

Noonan, T. S. "The Grain Trade of the Northern Black Sea in Antiquity." *American Journal of Philology* 94(1973):231-42.

Pritchett, W. K. "The Transfer of the Delian Treasury." *Historia* 18(1969):17-21.

Robinson, E. S. G. "The Coins from the Ephesian Artemision Reconsidered." *Journal of Hellenic Studies* 71(1951):156-66.

Seltman, C. T. *Athens: Its History and Coinage before the Persian Invasion.* Cambridge: 1924.

Shear, T. L., Jr., "Koisyra: Three Women of Athens." *Phoenix* 12(1963):99-111.

Stanier, R. S. "The Cost of the Parthenon." *Journal of Hellenic Studies* 73(1953):68-76.

Starr, C. G. *Athenian Coinage, 480–449 B.C.* Oxford: 1970.

Stevenson, G. H. "The Financial Administration of Pericles." *Journal of Hellenic Studies* 49(1929):1-10.

Thiel, J. M. "On Solon's System of Property Classes." *Mnemosyne* 3(1950):1-11.

Van den Oudenrijn, C. M. A. "Solon's System of Property Classes Once More." *Mnemosyne* 5(1952):19-27.

Wade-Gery, H. T. "The Question of Tribute in 449/8 B.C." *Hesperia* 14(1945): 212-29.

Waters, K. H. "Solon's Price Equalisation." *Journal of Hellenic Studies* 80(1960): 181-90.

Webster, T. B. L. *Athenian Culture and Society.* Berkeley and Los Angeles: 1973.
———. *Everyday Life in Classical Athens.* New York: 1969.
West, A. B. "The Tribute Lists and the Non-Tributary Members of the Delian League." *American Historical Review* 35(1929-30):267-75.
Wilcken, U. "Zu Solons Schatzungklassen." *Hermes* 58(1928):236-8.
Woodhouse, W. J. *Solon the Liberator.* New York: 1965.

CULTURAL

Adkins, A. W. H. *Merit and Responsibility: A Study in Greek Values.* Oxford: 1960.
Bailey, C. *The Greek Atomists and Epicurus: A Study.* New York: 1964.
Berve, H., and Gruben, G., *Greek Temples, Theaters, and Shrines.* New York: 1963.
Boardman, J. "Herakles, Peisistratus, and Eleusis." *Journal of Hellenic Studies* 95(1975):1-13.
Boardman, J., Dorig, J., Fuchs, W., Hirmer, M. *Greek Art and Architecture.* New York: 1968.
Bowra, C. M. *Pindar.* Oxford: 1964.
———. *Sophoclean Tragedy.* Oxford: 1944.
Carpenter, R. *The Architects of the Parthenon.* Baltimore: 1970.
Cleve, F. M. *The Philosophy of Anaxagoras: An Attempt at Reconstruction.* New York: 1949.
Corbett, P. E. *The Sculpture of the Parthenon.* Baltimore: 1959.
Creed, J. L. "Moral Values in the Age of Thucydides." *Classical Quarterly* n.s. 23(1973):213-31.
Croiset, M. *Aristophanes and the Political Parties at Athens.* New York: 1973.
Davison, J. A. "Notes on the Panathenaea." *Journal of Hellenic Studies* 78(1958):23-41.
———. "Protagoras, Democritus, and Anaxagoras." *Classical Quarterly* n.s. 3(1953): 33-45.
———. "The Date of the *Prometheia.*" *Transactions of the American Philological Association* 80(1949):78-82.
Diels, H., and Kranz, W. *Die Fragmente der Vorsokratiker.* Vol. 2. Berlin: 1972.
Dinsmoor, W. B. *The Architecture of Ancient Greece.* New York: 1950.
Ehrenberg, V. *Sophocles and Pericles.* Oxford: 1954.
Farnell, L. R. *The Cults of the Greek States.* Vols. 1, 2. Oxford: 1896.
Gardner, E. A. *A Handbook of Greek Sculpture.* London: 1915.
Gershenson, D. E., and Greenberg, D. A., *Anaxagoras and the Birth of Physics.* New York: 1964.
Graves, R. *The Greek Myths.* Vols. 1, 2. New York: 1959.
Harrison, J. E. *Mythology and Monuments of Ancient Athens.* London: 1894.
———. *Prolegomena to the Study of Greek Religion.* Cleveland: 1959.
Jaeger, W. *Paideia: The Ideals of Greek Culture.* Vol. 1. New York: 1965.
Lanza, D. *Anassagora: Testimonianze e Frammenti.* Florence: 1966.
Lawrence, A. W. *Greek Architecture.* Baltimore: 1957.
Livingstone, R. W. "The Problem of the *Eumenides* of Aeschylus." *Journal of Hellenic Studies* 45(1925):120-31.
Lullies, R. *Greek Sculpture.* New York: 1957.
Morrison, J. S. "The Place of Protagoras in Athenian Public Life." *Classical Quarterly* 35(1941):1-16.
Murray, G. *Aeschylus: The Creator of Tragedy.* Oxford: 1940.
———. *The Rise of the Greek Epic.* New York: 1960.
Mylonas, G. E. *Eleusis and the Eleusinian Mysteries.* Princeton: 1961.

Nilsson, M. P. *Greek Folk Religion.* New York: 1961.
______. *Minoan-Mycenaean Religion.* Lund: 1953.
Parke, H. W. and Wormell, D. E. W. *The Delphic Oracle.* Vols. 1, 2. Oxford: 1956.
Pollitt, J. J. *The Art of Greece, 1400–31 B.C.: Sources and Documents.* Englewood Cliffs: 1965.
Richter, G. M. A. *The Sculpture and Sculptors of the Greeks.* New Haven: 1950.
Robertson, M. *Greek Painting.* Geneva: 1959.
Robin, L. *Greek Thought and the Origins of the Scientific Spirit.* New York: 1967.
Rose, H. J. *Handbook of Greek Mythology.* London: 1965.
Sidgwick, A. *Aeschylus: Eumenides.* Oxford: 1887.
Thomson, G. *Aeschylus and Athens: A Study in the Social Origins of Drama.* London: 1973.
Untersteiner, M. *Sofisti: Testimonianze e Frammenti.* Florence: 1949.
Webster, T. B. L. *An Introduction to Sophocles.* London: 1973.
Whitman, C. H. *Homer and the Heroic Tradition.* Cambridge, Mass.: 1948.
______. *Sophocles: A Study of Heroic Humanism.* Cambridge, Mass.: 1951.
Winspear, A. D. *The Genesis of Plato's Thought.* New York: 1940.
Yalouris, N. *Classical Greece: The Elgin Marbles of the Parthenon.* Greenwich, Conn.: 1950.

INDEX